D1441332

MARRIAGE

MARRIAGE

An Examination of the Man-Woman Relationship

HERMAN R. LANTZ

Department of Sociology, Southern Illinois University

and

ELOISE C. SNYDER

Department of Sociology, Columbia College, Columbia, South Carolina

SECOND EDITION

John Wiley & Sons, Inc.

NEW YORK • LONDON • SYDNEY • TORONTO

CAPTION FOR TITLE PAGE ILLUSTRATION
Exterior of the Fanny Hayes Doll House. Courtesy
of The Rutherford B. Hayes Library, Fremont, Ohio.

10 9 8 7 6 5 4 3

Library of Congress Catalog Card Number: 69-16038
SBN 471 51730 5
Printed in the United States of America

The authors dedicate this book to

Sarah Coburn Lantz

daughter, friend, and shrewd observer of the social scene.

Preface

THIS REVISION represents our effort to update our work. We have assessed the pertinent literature that has appeared since the publication of the first edition of this book and have incorporated pertinent new data and new insights. We have used also the comments and observations that the users of the book, both faculty and students, were kind enough to communicate to us.

We carefully screened the material in each chapter as to its relevance to understanding the man-woman relationship today, deleting some parts and adding others. Major additions include sections on the history of the American family, marriage and the family in cross-cultural perspective, and role conflict for women, as well as its implications for men. The basic orientation of the book remains unchanged; it is an orientation to which we are committed and which seems to have an interested readership.

There are many ways in which marriage and the family can be described, as shown by the use of different frames of reference in the many published works on the subject. We have chosen as our task a behavioral analysis of the middle-class man-woman relationship as it is found in dating, courtship, and marriage in the United States today.

We have tried to identify the kinds of relationships that middle-class persons increasingly seek, the nature of their involvements with one another, and the types of problems that come about. In such an analysis it becomes clear the social controls that formerly governed and dictated the goals of the man-woman relationship are no longer so effective. Indeed, these goals are the results of a search for personal satisfactions, such as companionship, love, and self-realization. Such goals are largely a result of changes from a rural, religious society to an urbanized, secular society. Although social change inevitably brings with it dislocation, the current difficulties in marriage and the family are deeply rooted in the fact that many of the goals that men and women seek in such relationships are not easily realized. Thus although many seek the personally fulfilling goals, they are lacking in the intellectual and emotional maturity that is needed to realize these goals. Whereas in the past marriage and the family derived their stability from social, economic, and religious expectations, today the willingness of persons to remain married depends to a great extent on whether or not they, in effect, find marriage and the family meaningful and personally satisfying. There is, to be sure, no single path to follow in the search for love, companionship, and self-realization, but there are patterns that are fraught with difficulty and in the end prove to be self-defeating. We have tried, in this book, to identify these negative patterns, as well as those more positive patterns that may facilitate the search for the personally fulfilling goals. We have attempted to relate both types of patterns to what is currently accepted in behavioral science and have employed modified versions of case histories to illustrate our points. The histories used here, although disguised, are taken from actual cases, but in each instance only that part of the case is used that pertains to the material being illustrated. In this manner we have tried to show relationships between points being made in the discussions and life histories, without complicating the history to the extent that the point being illustrated is lost. As such, our histories are more representative of categories of behavior than they are of actual complete case histories.

In analyzing the man-woman relationship we repeatedly refer to such terms as "constructive" and "meaningful." In our use of these words, they refer to relationships in which the individuals are intrinsically interested in each other as people, not as commodities, and in which each person has the opportunity to grow intellectually and emotionally.

These terms have value connotations, to be sure, but we should like to suggest that these values are derivatives from much that is evident in behavioral science. Moreover, the concepts have analytic significance in understanding the man-woman relationship.

The revision is in every sense a collaboration. The book, however, is inevitably a result of the contributions of many persons, especially individuals at Ohio State University, Pennsylvania State University, and Southern Illinois University, who have contributed so much to our thinking and orientation toward family sociology.

Herman Lantz is deeply grateful to Ralph N. Harris, M.D. Dr. Harris contributed to the development of many ideas in this revision. His sensitive and keen observations on the nature of the man-woman relationship in America have influenced this author's thinking and writing, and his use of the family as a context in which human relatedness unfolds has contributed significantly to the views contained in this book.

Eloise Snyder wishes to express her deep and everlasting gratitude to Jessie Bernard, who played a significant role in the author's orientation to sociology and who has been a constant source of inspiration and encouragement as a teacher and friend. This author expresses her deep gratitude to Seth Russell for his faith in her and for his consistent help as adviser and teacher.

Both of us express our very sincere appreciation to Al Clarke and Mark Flappan for their constructively critical analysis of the first edition; hopefully, they will approve of the revision.

To Professor Ronald Hanson, to members of the Graduate Research Committee of Southern Illinois University, and to Dean Roger Beyler of Southern Illinois University we are deeply grateful for the aid provided to finish this revision.

We thank Charles R. Snyder, chairman of the sociology department, for his helpful comments on the overall orientation of this book.

We also thank Sid Aronson for his evaluation and comments on the new section dealing with the history of the family, and Doris Hoye of Bradley University and Margaret Britton of Kentucky Wesleyan College for their overall comments.

We owe a great debt to Mrs. Judith Lantz, who typed the manuscript and did a considerable part of the editorial work. She gave unselfishly of her time and energies. Her helpful and critical comments added greatly both to the content and to the communication of ideas. She helped to organize the revision.

We would like to add a note of thanks to Richard Herman, Linda Taylor, Susan Babbitt, and Pam Elder for research and typing in connection with the revision.

Finally, a special word of thanks to the students who have used this book, both for their patience with the imperfections and for their insights that we have tried to employ.

Carbondale, Illinois   *Herman R. Lantz*
December 1968   *Eloise C. Snyder*

Contents

xi

MARRIAGE

Chapter One

INTRODUCTION

THIS BOOK deals with the man-woman relationship as it is found in dating, courtship, marriage, and family life among the middle class in contemporary America. We have oriented our treatment toward the middle-class family for several reasons. First, the middle-class family is becoming almost a model type; many of its values and orientations are rapidly permeating all groups in our society. Second, the majority of readers of this book either come from the middle class or aspire to membership in it. Thus a discussion of the behavior patterns and attitudes that characterize people in the middle class is pertinent. It is essential to bear in mind, however, that the extent to which all groups in our society accept middle-class values is open to question. Some interesting and significant studies of working-class and lower-class subcultures clearly reveal a set of norms not in accordance with middle-class values. Mirra Komarovsky, for example, has done a very insightful depth study of the marital habits and patterns of the working class, including sex, communication, goals, and values. The work of Rainwater also contributes substantially to our understanding of the different values in the lower-class subculture. Certainly, the present book's orientation toward the middle class does not mean that its values are in any sense more desirable than those of the lower class or the working class; it suggests only that we have chosen to write about them.[1]

[1] Mirra Komarovsky, *Blue-Collar Marriage*, Random House, New York, 1964. Lee Rainwater, *And the Poor Get Children*, Quadrangle Books, Chicago, 1960. Lee Rainwater, Richard P. Coleman, and Gerald Handel, *Workingman's Wife*, Oceana Publications, New York, 1959. Bennett M. Berger, *Working-Class Suburb, A Study of Auto Workers in Suburbia*, University of California Press, Berkeley, Calif., 1960. Mirra Komarovsky, *The Unemployed Man and His Family*, Dryden Press, New York, 1940. S. N. Miller and Frank Reisman, "The Working-Class Subculture, A New View," *Social Prob.*, 9 (Summer 1951), pp. 86–97.

ILLUSTRATION: Noah's Ark from Germany, c. 1840. Courtesy of the Museum of the City of New York.

2

The magnitude of our task and the pursuit of our analysis are complicated for at least two reasons. First, the middle class is in a period of dynamic change, at least as reflected in the behavior of its youth. College students' rebellion, their disenchantment with higher education, and their involvement with the civil rights movement and opposition to the draft suggest that this is a period of protest, of questioning and reexamination.

In addition, there are problems in understanding the composition and origins of our middle-class population. For example, with social mobility occurring, certain segments of the lower and working classes are becoming fused with the middle class. Do these groups necessarily have traditional middle-class values or do they bring with them their own values which remain reasonably intact? [2] If the latter is true, we may have different value systems side by side. In fact, the entire notion of whether there is a distinct middle class may have to be reexamined. Thus what may have constituted a limited focus for this book, that is, our concern with the middle class, may in reality not be limited at all. Indeed, defining the limits and dimensions of the middle class may be one of the most complex problems in social science. The significance of all this is that a changing middle-class population may not view as problems what have until recently been considered problems, such as premarital sex, mixed religious marriages, and in-law relationships. Young people may not experience these areas as problem areas for other reasons as well. They may be too immature to appreciate the difficulties, or they may be sufficiently mature and sophisticated not to be caught up in the conflicts that their older siblings or parents may have experienced only a decade or two ago. Thus the middle class today represents a more heterogeneous group than many suspect, and it becomes increasingly difficult to discuss the values of the middle class without taking this into account. In this book we have attempted to deal with the complexity by synthesizing and assessing the most recent research and examining the implications that emerge for man-woman relationships.

A second reason why the present undertaking is complicated is that there are many directions from which the problems introduced in this book may be approached. We have therefore tried to bring to bear on each problem the materials that, in our opinion, will allow the reader the greatest amount of enlightenment. In our analysis we make use of the combined knowledge of the several human behavioral sciences and relate it to the specific problems raised in this book. Thus at times we ap-

[2] Richard F. Hamilton, "Affluence and the Worker: The West German Case," *Am. J. Sociol.,* 71 (1965), pp. 144–152.

proach a problem sociologically, psychologically, or psychiatrically; at other times we use a balance of all three approaches.

The employment of knowledge from the different behavioral sciences does not, of course, mean that we intend to deal with all problems in the man-woman relationship. Nor do we believe that it is possible to give the reader ready-made solutions for the issues raised in this book. We do intend to single out what appear to be the most significant problems in this relationship and to suggest ways in which these may be examined and more clearly understood.

As part of the orientation of this book, we should like to clarify for the reader what he may expect as he pursues the topics presented. Therefore in this chapter we present the main objectives of the book and attempt to outline certain of its basic themes to show their importance.

The Significance of the Man-Woman Relationship

The main objective of this book is to understand the man-woman relationship as it emerges, matures, and, under certain circumstances, deteriorates. No other aspect of human interaction demands more of either the social scientist or the layman; nevertheless, an understanding of this relationship is essential if we are to increase the number of marriages that are purposeful, meaningful associations. Of course, we can only begin to scratch the surface with respect to understanding these aspects of human interaction. Nevertheless, in some areas of knowledge substantial agreement exists, and it is these materials that we plan to present in this book.

When we say that we shall focus on the man-woman relationship, we suggest that much marital incompatibility is based in the interpersonal relationship between husband and wife. The variety of ways in which husbands and wives treat each other, both interpersonally and sexually, are expressions of all that is felt between the marital partners. Thus the basic attitudes of husband and wife toward each other find expression in all phases of marital life. It follows, then, that a breakdown in the interpersonal relationship between husband and wife sets the stage for subsequent marital difficulties. The marital relationship may have become meaningless to both; or one may have tired of the relationship while the other has not; or one may have emotional difficulties that make cooperative living difficult. For example, the breakdown may manifest itself in extramarital sexual relations. Consider the case of an insurance salesman and his wife, both of whom came for assistance with their marital difficulties. The wife had been involved in an extramarital affair with a friend of the family. The affair had been going on for several months before her husband discovered what was happening. His first impulse was to obtain a divorce, but on the chance that the marriage might be salvaged, he asked for outside assistance. The husband's definition of the difficulty was that his wife had become involved with another man because he was unable to support her adequately.

In talking with the wife about the marital difficulty, an entirely different story emerged. She said that her husband let the marriage deteriorate. He was aloof from her and their two children. He constantly found excuses to be away from home and never included her or the children in any of his plans. In addition, he was unnecessarily frugal, so that she and the children had to forgo even certain necessities. Their income was not substantial, but the reasons for her infidelity, she added, were rooted in her husband's consistent indifference to her and the children. She had come to believe that he was no longer interested in her or the family and therefore to feel unwanted and unloved.

In further discussions the husband revealed that his preoccupations outside the home were largely business matters, which he thought might lead to better economic opportunities. Over a period of time he came to accept his part in the difficulty and to assume his share of the responsibility for creating unfavorable attitudes in his wife and children. Needless to say, this was a complicated case, in which both partners shared in the responsibility for the poor marital relationship. For our purposes, however, the case demonstrates that the wife's extramarital involvement was not the result of sexual incompatibility as such, nor of economic stress. Rather, it was symptomatic of a basic misunderstanding and a breakdown in the interpersonal relationship between her and her husband. She saw herself as unloved; desperate, she became involved with another person. To rehabilitate this marriage, all factors in the interpersonal relationship which led to the breakdown had to be considered and understood. Treating the difficulty as a strictly sexual problem would not have produced improvement.

Although this particular illustration has a sexual component, it should be remembered that much marital incompatibility is not rooted in sex. Indeed, many experts take the position that most sexual problems in marriage are manifestations of difficulty in the interpersonal relationship. It should also be noted that in this book the treatment of the role of sex in marriage is perhaps different from treatments that the reader has encountered elsewhere. We do not concern ourselves directly with either the anatomy or the physiology of reproduction; but we include in the appendix descriptive materials, which will answer the most common questions that students have about these topics. Nor do we focus on consumer problems in marriage. However, we discuss both problems of sexual adjustment and economic difficulties as they relate to the type and quality of the interpersonal relationship between husband and wife. Thus we examine the effect of the attitudes that husband and wife have toward each other on their economic and sexual habits. For example, some people tend to control their mates through the purse strings or through sexual relations. We have approached the subject in this fashion because we believe that, as behavioral scientists, we are in a unique position to contribute to the study of the man-woman relationship by focusing on the frame of reference of behavioral science, namely the study of the human relationship.

The Complexity of Marital Problems

One major pervasive theme of this book has to do with the way in which marital relationships are viewed here. We see the relationships between men and women as being generally more involved, indeed more complex, than do persons who are not confronted with these problems daily. We, as well as other behavioral scientists, recognize that these relationships are the most complicated types of human interaction. They involve a variety of different types of people, each of whom brings into the marriage a psychological organization that has been in process of formation since infancy and has been nurtured in a complex social environment.

The untrained observer, however, often views the dynamics of the man-woman relationship in simple terms, very much as the insurance salesman did in the case cited previously. To a college student, for example, a marital problem may be an economic or an in-law problem. The most common error is the failure to see all ramifications of a problem, even though a problem invariably is the result of numerous factors, often interrelated in complex ways. The result is a lack of appreciation for the very real complexities of the man-woman relationship, which must be recognized, understood, and worked through, if a problem is to be diagnosed early and resolved. Consider the following case in point.

A college professor sought assistance for a problem with his daughter.

This father complained that his daughter was quite rebellious and insisted on dating "the wrong kinds of boys." He claimed that he could not understand his daughter's behavior, since he and his wife had always tried to "rear her properly to be a good girl." He saw the problem simply as a lack of self-discipline in the girl. He sought a counselor's assistance to try to convince the girl that she was in error and that she should date only those boys of whom the parents approved.

Obviously, this father had little understanding of the problem, seeing it simply as a lack of self-discipline. The counselor recognized more fundamental difficulties, involving the daughter's basic relationship with her parents, the parents' attempt to rigidly control the daughter's behavior, and the daughter's need to live her own life. These were all possibilities that the father was unprepared to examine, since he insisted on clinging to his one-sided, oversimplified definition of the difficulty, but unless he did, he was unlikely to achieve much understanding of the problem.

In this book we plan to analyze the involved dynamics of the man-woman relationship in detail. We shall not be satisfied with an analysis of superficial symptoms, but shall search for basic elements.

The Importance of Understanding the Motivations for Actions

A second theme of this book has to do with understanding the motives for one's own actions, as well as for those of other persons. Such understanding is, of course, never completely possible, but we think that by merely raising questions about his motives in following a particular course of action an individual makes discoveries about himself that can be of value in avoiding future difficulties. He can cope with his attitudes better if he knows what they are; this is the therapeutic value of self-examination. Let us apply the understanding of motivations to enrolling in a course in marriage.

Much of what you will derive from a marriage course will depend on your reasons for taking it. A small number of students invariably enroll because they are seeking easy credit. This is the important motivation for them. They assume that since the subject matter deals with such commonplace topics as dating, courtship, and marriage, it cannot be very difficult. In the words of one student, "This will be pleasant chit-chat about love and marriage." Such students enter the course with a lack of serious purpose and may be unwilling to put forth the effort that is necessary to come to grips with the issues. When confronted with the need for work, they frequently become annoyed and resentful. Hence they learn little. However, the student who discovers such attitudes in himself can decide that this outlook is not consistent with a desire to grow and learn and therefore try to change the outlook.

Most students enroll in a marriage course because they hope to benefit from the experience in some way. But even such well-motivated students face obstacles. Much of what they derive from the course will depend on their ability to uproot the attitudes and ways of behaving that restrict personal growth and the ability to build a sound relationship with a person of the opposite sex.

The example of a young college student illustrates our point. This girl had been dating a boy for two years. Although she had never taken the relationship seriously, the boy had. He had lavished a great deal of attention on her and had spent a considerable amount of money on gifts, more than he could really afford. He proposed matrimony several times, but was rejected by the girl. Since the boyfriend was now pressing her for a definite answer to his proposal, she felt it necessary to act and sought assistance. During several weeks of counseling it was established that the girl considered herself to be physically unattractive and lacking in poise and had deep inferiority feelings. She had no consistent feeling for or interest in the boy, except insofar as he might give her some security, even though she in turn was willing to give him nothing. The girl soon realized that her attitudes precluded a commitment to marriage. On the other hand, she was unwilling to give up the boy, preferring "to string him along" because he served certain needs.

The most interesting point, and one related to our discussion, is that this young woman was enrolled in a course in marriage and had recently completed the section dealing with immature-exploitative relationships, including the necessity to work them through. She knew what ought to be done, but was unable to integrate the material because her immature patterns still served important functions. Thus, although intellectually recognizing the immature relationship and its dangers for her and the boy, she nevertheless still committed herself to it emotionally.

In this example, the girl's motives were brought out into the open and made clear to her. She was unable to act at the time, but the issues had become obvious, making it likely that eventually she would be able to act in her own best interests, as well as those of her boyfriend.

As you read this book, many of your attitudes may be challenged. You may have immature relationships with your boyfriends or girl friends or with your parents. You may have difficulty in thinking about sex. All of these are mental blocks, which retard your ability to fully appreciate the data in this book. Furthermore, as you probe your own feelings, you may discover unpleasant attitudes that are deeply rooted in your personality. The realization that some of these ways of behaving need changing before better relationships can emerge may be frustrating and disturbing. At such times you may become hostile toward the text, its authors, or your teacher. You may subconsciously block out some new information as though it did not exist. Moreover, like many people, you may feel quite hopeless about understanding yourself and about your ability to change. All of these developments are frequent occurrences in people who attempt self-examination and change. The experience can be therapeutic, however, if you understand that your reactions are natural side effects of this self-examination and change.

We have pointed out certain unpleasant aspects of self-examination, not to create turmoil and make you uncomfortable, but to better prepare you for the experience. For we believe that change can occur only if you come to grips with inner motivations, thus removing the obstacles to growth.

A Problem-Oriented Analysis

A third major theme of this book has to do with its problem orientation. That is, we focus in this book on those areas of the man-woman relationship that are sources of disturbance. We employ this method for several reasons. First, there is certainly no need to extol the virtues of marriage, nor to describe the basic satisfactions that constructive family living provides. The cultural milieu constantly tumpets the joyful bliss of marriage and family life.

Thus, although many people undoubtedly have some understanding of what a constructive man-woman relationship can mean, probably only a few appreciate the very real work involved in building and maintaining it. To speak in clichés and say, for example, that "marriage is a partnership" is a far cry from attempting to live a partnership and to be willing to examine attitudes and feeling when the relationship fails to function properly.

Some readers may think that a problem-oriented book teaches only about the problems of marriage, not about the happiness of marriage. To these people we can only reply that happiness in marriage does not emerge from thinking happy thoughts, but from active efforts to detect and work through problem areas. No human relationships are ever immune from problems, and probably no human relationship can ever reach a mature level without the active efforts of the persons involved. Though this may seem to be an essentially negative view of the man-woman relationship, it is not. Indeed, we are both realistic and optimistic. We believe that if man can destroy his relationships, he also possesses the power to construct and improve them.

A Final Word to the Student

The course of study that you are about to undertake will undoubtedly offer you tremendous possibilities for personal growth. In many ways the course is different from any you have ever had. It examines topics with which you are all concerned, but which you most frequently treat with some neglect and a lack of appreciation. There can be no greater challenge to any man or woman than that of attempting to build a successful marital relationship; yet we recognize that it is perhaps more difficult to build sound, creative, marital relationships than to succeed in other endeavors. We all know persons in the artistic, professional, and business fields who are successful in their occupational endeavors, but whose marriages are poor and neglected. Is it a matter of intelligence? If it were, these people would all be likely to have successful marital relationships. Rather, it requires both knowledge of what it takes to build a good marital relationship and the ability to emotionally integrate this knowledge into one's life. How this can be accomplished is a major preoccupation of the book.

As teachers we recognize that it is sometimes difficult to tell which student has achieved the greatest amount of integration from his exposure to these materials. The student will undoubtedly be preoccupied with his grade, but the teacher knows that grades are not the only criterion for judging how much the student has benefited from the course.

Some students, with excellent grades, make gross errors in judgment when they marry; some students, who rated poorly, choose wisely. Moreover, it is not uncommon for the student to integrate an insight that enables him to drop a poor relationship or find his way into a good one. How may such a result be graded? Is the grade A, B, C, or D equivalent to such an experience or to the growth of the personality? Can the grade really convey what the person has derived?

Grades are part of the university system, and it is unrealistic to expect that we can eliminate formal grading in the near future. Nevertheless, in this instance, as teachers, we wish to appeal to the better judgment of the student with the hope that, in addition to his concern with grades, he can become sensitive to the ever-present possibility of integrating material that will be significant for personal growth.

Summary

The main objective of this book is to understand the man-woman relationship as it emerges, matures, and, under certain circumstances, deteriorates. In pursuing this objective, we shall deal with several themes. First, marriage and family problems are viewed as being more involved and complex than they might seem to the untrained observer. Frequently, for example, problems that superficially appear to be financial or sexual are in reality expressions of a breakdown of the interpersonal relationship. Thus to treat such problems as financial or sexual is to treat the symptoms and not the causes of the basic difficulties.

Second, an emphasis is placed on understanding the motivations for behavior. This is a difficult task, but only through such an understanding can people learn to cope with basic attitudes, thus minimizing difficulties in the man-woman relationship in the future.

Third, a problem-oriented analysis is employed. Thus the focus is on selected areas in the man-woman relationship that appear to be the greatest sources of difficulty. We use this approach because we believe that meaningful man-woman relationships can exist only when problems have been constructively resolved. Needless to say, the resolution of problem areas in the man-woman relationship is ultimately reflected in the personal growth and development of the individual marital partners.

Questions

1. What does this book deal with? Discuss the reasons for the selection of the middle-class orientation.

2. Discuss the reasons why the pursuit of the analysis undertaken in this book is a complicated one.

3. What is the main objective of this book?

4. Discuss the problems involved in the case of the insurance salesman and his wife.

5. Discuss the following statement: "A marital problem is seldom one thing; it is many."

6. Why is it important to understand the motivations for actions?

7. Why have you enrolled in this course?

8. Explain the following statement: "Much of what you derive from this book will depend on your ability to uproot the attitudes and ways of behaving that restrict your personal growth and your ability to build a sound relationship with the opposite sex."

9. What did the young college student derive from her marriage course? Why was she unable to derive more?

10. Explain what is meant by a problem-oriented analysis in the area of the man-woman relationship.

11. Agree or disagree with the following statement and explain your answer: "Marriage failure is usually caused by a lack of intelligence on the part of one or both of the marriage partners."

Suggestions for Research and Related Activities

1. Construct a questionnaire to discover what reasons the members of your class give for taking this course. In the same questionnaire, find out what kinds of information the members of your class expect to acquire from this course. On the basis of comparing the results you receive with the contents of this book, do you feel that your fellow class members have a realistic view of this course and its offerings? Explain your answer. If the members of your class acquire the kinds of information they expect, will they have learned enough to participate in a meaningful marriage relationship or will they still have a lot more to learn? Explain your answer.

2. Conduct a survey to determine what, in the opinion of your fellow students, are the important problems confronted in marriage. Do the men and women agree on what these problems are? If not, how do you account for the differences? Have several students submit your results to their par-

ents and find out whether or not the parents agree that the problems pointed out by your fellow students are the important ones that have to be met in marriage. If the parents do not agree, find out why they do not agree.

3. Make a checklist of certain attitudes that in your opinion would lead to difficulty in marriage. Submit this list to both single and married men and women, and have them rank the attitudes according to their importance as potential sources of difficulty in marriage. On the basis of your results, what attitudes are considered to be potential sources of difficulty? Do you agree with your findings? Why? Do both married and single people rank these attitudes in the same, or very similar, manner? If not, how do you account for whatever differences you find?

Suggested Readings

Cavan, Ruth Shonle, Ed., *Marriage and Family in the Modern World: A Book of Readings,* 2nd ed., Crowell-Collier, New York, 1965, Ch. 39, Abraham Stone and Lena Levine, "The Dynamics of the Marital Relationship," pp. 277–284.

Goode, William J., *After Divorce,* The Free Press, Glencoe, Ill., 1956, Ch. 10, "The Conflict Process: Themes of Complaint Made by the Wife."

Horney, Karen, *Self-Analysis,* Norton, New York, 1942, Ch. 2, "The Driving Forces in Neuroses."

Landis, Paul H., *Making the Most of Marriage,* 2nd ed., Appleton-Century-Crofts, New York, 1960, Ch. 1, "Values and Goals of Modern Marriage," and Ch. 2, "Shortcomings of Modern Marriage."

Magoun, F. Alexander, *Love and Marriage,* Harper, New York, 1956, Ch. 2, "The Nature of Marriage," and Ch. 11, "Emotional Adjustments."

Oliver, Bernard J., Jr., *Marriage and You,* New Haven College and University Press, New Haven, Conn., 1964, especially Part VI.

Simpson, George, *People in Families,* Crowell-Collier, New York, 1960, Ch. 2, "Biological and Psychological Orientations to Marriage and the Family."

Vincent, Clark E., *Readings in Marriage Counseling,* Crowell-Collier, New York, 1957, Reading 39, Gordon W. Allport, "The Trend in Motivational Theory," pp. 357–369, and Reading 41, Nathan W. Ackerman, "The Diagnosis of Neurotic Marital Interaction," pp. 378–391.

Winch, Robert F., *The Modern Family,* rev. ed., Holt, Rinehart and Winston, New York, 1963.

Chapter Two

MARRIAGE AND THE FAMILY IN A CROSS-CULTURAL CONTEXT

ALTHOUGH OUR primary focus is on middle-class marriage in the United States, we can best study this marital type by seeing it in an entire context of various family types in societies throughout the world. In pursuing this goal, it may be helpful to begin by defining the concept of marriage.

Marriage

Marriage is a formal and durable sexual union of one or more men and one or more women, which is conducted within a set of designated rights and duties. In looking carefully at this definition of marriage, we

ILLUSTRATION: Japanese Doll House, twentieth century. Courtesy of The Cleveland Museum of Art, Extension Exhibitions Collection, gift of Eleanor Munro.

should note that the term "formal" means socially approved and "durable" means with the intent of permanence. By "sexual union" we refer to sexual intimacies, including sexual intercourse; by "conducted within a set of designated rights and duties" we mean that in a marriage relationship there are statuses and roles.

A *status* is a position in society, such as policeman, teacher, student, mother, or friend; in a marriage relationship the specific statuses are those of husband and wife. *Role* is the term used to refer to the expectations made of a person in a specific status, both in regard to the rights permitted him and the duties expected of him. Thus marriage requires that husband and wife fulfill certain rights and duties expected of them by society and certain rights and duties they expect of each other in their roles.

It must be pointed out that the specific rights and duties that comprise the roles of husband and wife may change from time to time within any one society, may differ from grouping to grouping in the same society, and may also differ from one society to another. Indeed, it is such differences in expectations—between the lower class and the middle class, for example,—that cause some people difficulty in trying to understand the behaviors of others. Failure to grasp these existing differences tends to result in the confusing and blurring of the roles involved.

The second dimension of our definition of marriage, "union of one or more men and one or more women," implies that not all marriages are between only one man and one woman, as are marriages in the United States. The forms of marriage are as follows:

Monogamy:	One man and one woman.
Polygamy:	One person and two or more persons of the opposite sex at the same time.
Polygyny.	One male and two or more females at the same time.
Polyandry:	Two or more males and one female at the same time.
Group:	Two or more males and two or more females at the same time.

The forms that specify the possible ratio of men to women in a marriage are monogamy, polygyny, polyandry, and group marriage. Polygamy, which does not specify whether males or females occur in plurality in a marriage, is a nonspecific marital form.[1]

---

[1] For an example of a complicated marriage system that taxes not only our definition of marriage but also one's ability to classify it, see Kathleen E. Gough, "The Nayars and the Definition of Marriage," *J. Royal Anthrop. Inst.*, **89** (1959), pp. 23–24.

The most frequent form of marriage has been, as far as is known, and certainly still is monogamy. At the present time monogamy exists throughout the Western world and, indeed, large and important parts of the Eastern world, such as Russia and China. Often even in societies that permitted nonmonogamous marriages many people married monogamously—primarily for economic reasons. This was probably particularly true in nonindustrialized, polygynous societies. One example of a polygynous society in which the inability to support more than one wife was at least partly responsible for most men not marrying polygynously is Arabic Islam. Indeed, the economic limitations, together with other factors such as Western monogamous influences, have led many of these Arabic societies to outlaw polygyny in recent years.[2]

Next to monogamy, polygyny has been the second most common form of marriage. Polygyny may be sororal, which means that the wives are sisters, or nonsororal.[3] There are several references to polygynous societies in the Bible. In the United States the early Mormons were polygynous.[4]

Polyandry is a less common form of marriage. Examples of polyandry are found in the records of such people as the Todas and the inhabitants of Tibet.[5] In traditional Tibet, polyandry was fraternal, that is, all the husbands of one wife were brothers. Among the Marquesans,[6] polyandry is nonfraternal.

Group marriage is extremely uncommon. In fact, it has been said that there are no clear-cut cases of group marriage and that the examples of this type of marriage, such as those among the Todas,[7] involved little more than sexual sharing.[8]

[2] For a full discussion of changing marriage patterns in Arabic Islam, see William J. Goode, *World Revolution and Family Patterns,* The Free Press, Glencoe, Ill., 1963.
[3] For a full discussion of sororal and nonsororal polygyny, see George P. Murdock, "World Ethnographic Sample," *Am. Anthrop.,* **59,** 4 (1957).
[4] For a full discussion of polygyny, see William N. Stephens, *The Family in Cross-Cultural Perspective,* Holt, Rinehart and Winston, New York, 1963, pp. 49–56.
[5] For a full discussion of polyandry, see *ibid.,* pp. 34–49.
[6] *Ibid.,* p. 38.
[7] W. H. R. Rivers, *The Todas,* Macmillan, New York, 1906, pp. 515–530. There is said to have been a tendency for the polyandry of the Todas to be combined with polygyny in a form of group marriage.
[8] For a discussion of this point, see George P. Murdock, *Social Structure,* Macmillan, New York, 1949, pp. 24–25. For a discussion of one United States community frequently said to have had group marriage, see William M. Kephart, *The Family, Society and the Individual,* 2nd ed., Houghton Mifflin, Boston, 1966, pp. 166–180, especially p. 172.

Evolution of Marriage

A number of theories have been advanced to explain how various marriage forms evolved. Some theorists, such as Edward A. Westermarck and Herbert Spencer, claim that monogamy is the natural form of marriage for human beings and that it was the original form. Others, such as Lewis Henry Morgan and Robert Briffault, contend instead that man is not naturally monogamous and that the monogamous form of marriage evolved during a long period of man's history. They tend to place the beginning of marital evolution in a state of promiscuity; that is, they believe that early man may simply have mated, without any rules about who may mate with whom. Briffault, for example, points out that the first long-term human relationship may have been that between mother and child, with the father playing an extremely transitory role. Following this initial state of normlessness, during which man was sexually promiscuous, the first norms governing marriage may have produced a form of group "marriage." We say "marriage" because we do not know whether these early relationships imposed the obligations, beyond sexual relations, that are part of any marriage of whatever form—economic, protective, and social obligations. In this early arrangement sexual access to females within the group may have been permitted, but the males of the group together would fight off any males who were not regarded as being group members. In such a setting older males may have had to force younger males out of the group, thus prohibiting sexual access of brothers to their sisters. This is exogamy—the rule requiring that a marriage partner be selected from outside a given group. Its opposite, endogamy, requires that the marriage partner be selected from within a particular group; in today's society, for example, one may be expected to marry within his own social class, race, religion, or whatever.

It is commonly believed that either polyandry or polygyny may have emerged from some form of group marriage. It is suggested that in some areas food gathering or growing was so difficult that more than one man's work was needed to support one woman and her children if they were to survive. Thus polyandry may have grown out of sustenance needs.

After man learned to control certain aspects of his natural world and was better able to sustain himself, monogamy may have been the next logical marital form. However, just as high status was given to a man who was able to have his own wife, rather than sharing her with other men, so the man who could afford to have several wives would have an even higher status. Because of the seeking of higher status, polygyny may have emerged as the next form of marriage.

It should be noted that all these are only hypotheses; each writer, on the basis of the evidence at hand, speculates about how the marriage forms could have emerged. In no case is the evidence sufficient to *prove* a specific evolutionary pattern, either for the world as a whole or for one society.

In order to fully appreciate these views regarding the origin of marriage forms it is important to remember at least several basic ideas. First, the quest for uncovering the origins of marriage is no longer a concern of the social scientist, as it was in the past. Second, there is no agreement on how the various forms of marriage came into existence; there are only hunches. Third, the forms are seen as having emerged as a result of the survival of the fittest; that is, of a number of marriage forms, those discussed above may have survived because they fulfilled the needs and met the physical and social conditions at a given time.

Finally, theories about the origin of marriage forms frequently reflect the values of the persons proposing them. Monogamy, for example, is seen as a final form. The implication is that man, as he progressed physically, mentally, and socially, also perfected his form of marriage; hence that monogamy is the most advanced of all marriage forms. Indeed, most of evolutionary marriage theory is written by scholars who were reared in highly monogamous cultures!

Marital Choice

In discussing how marital choices are made in various parts of the world, two main aspects must be considered. The first concerns the degree to which the individual's family is responsible for arranging his marriage. In some societies the individual has little choice in selecting his mate; the family selects the mate and arranges the marriage. In other societies, however, the family has little responsibility for arranging the person's marriage. Thus the family's responsibility for marriage arrangement may vary from society to society.

The second is the principle of preferential mating. This refers to the rules in a society that regard certain persons within specific groups as being "preferred" marriage partners for given individuals while prohibiting marriage with other persons from other groups. Preferential mating thus comprises sets of endogamous (marriage within a certain group) and exogamous rules (marriage outside a certain group). All societies have endogamous and exogamous rules; the degree to which such rules dictate who may or may not marry whom in a given society will, however, differ.

Table 1[a]

Degree of Arrangement of the Marriage	Preferential Mating	
	Highly Specified Preferences, Leading to Narrow Field of Eligibles	Little Specification of Preferred Mate, Leading to Wide Field of Eligibles
High: Parents or others select one's spouse	Yaruros	Feudal Japan
Low: Principal selects his own spouse	Hottentots	Middle-class United States

[a]Linton C. Freeman, "Marriage without Love: Mate Selection in Non-Western Societies," in Robert F. Winch, *Mate Selection,* Harper, New York, 1958, pp. 20–39.

Table 1 shows examples of the differing degrees of both the family's role in arranging a marriage and of preferential mating. Among the Yaruros, the family selects the individual's marriage partner from a narrow range of eligibles. The Hottentot range of eligibles is also narrow, but the individual himself makes the selection. On the other hand, feudal Japan had a wide range of eligibles, from which the person's family, not the person himself, selected a mate. Contemporary middle-class United States also has a wide field of eligibles, but the person himself is primarily responsible for selecting his mate from this field.

The Family

The family is a group of people who (1) are related through marriage, blood, or adoption, (2) interact with one another in their designated roles of husband, wife, father, mother, son, daughter, brother, sister, uncle, aunt, cousin, or grandparent, and (3) create and maintain a common subculture.

In examining this definition, several aspects must be noted.[9] First, while it is recognized that families may exist among subhuman groups, here we are concerned with the human family.[10] Second, not all groups of people comprise a family. To be recognized as a family, a group must meet certain requirements. One requirement is that its members must be related through marriage (already defined) or through blood (i.e., physical parentage or blood lineage) or through adoption . . . (i.e., social parentage). Whatever their bloodline, however, the members must regard themselves as being related and in turn must be so regarded by the society in which they reside.

Furthermore, for a group to be regarded as a family, its members must interact in their respective roles (listed previously), fulfilling the demands and exercising the privileges and rights that accompany these roles. For example, one of the duties of a father is to provide for his family, and one of his rights is the expectation of the family's respect.

Finally, a family tends to create and maintain its own particular way of life. A family's manner of living, though certainly more similar to than different from that of the society of which the family is a part, will nevertheless be unique—in implementing the cultural norms, in interpreting the behavior of others, and in doing things together. The family patterns of doing things, such as its manner of spending weekends or vacations or of preparing for a Christmas holiday, are sometimes called family rituals. It is these family rituals, with which its members identify, that are largely responsible for the attachments, the loyalty, the *esprit de corps* (feeling of belonging) that families develop.

Family Rule

Like marriage forms, family forms also may differ from one society to another. First of all, there are differences in the manner of making decisions in a family, that is, in the authority patterns. Three major author-

[9] For the difficulties of defining family, because of cultural variability, see M. J. Levy, Jr., and L. A. Fallers, "The Family: Some Comparative Considerations." *Am. Anthrop.*, 61 (1959), pp. 647–651.
[10] David Aberle et al., "The Incest Taboo and the Mating Patterns of Animals," *Am. Anthrop.*, 65 (1963), pp. 253–265.

ity patterns exist: the patriarchal, the matriarchal, and the democratic.

In a patriarchal system the eldest male rules the family; in the matriarchal, the eldest female rules. In both systems the person rules by virtue of his status (position) based on age (i.e., the eldest) and of sex (i.e., male or female respectively). In a democratic system, however, decision-making power is given to that family member (or members) whom the other members regard as being the most capable. Thus in the patriarchal and matriarchal systems, family rule or leadership falls to a member by tradition, whereas in a democratic system for the first time we find what might be called the two C's—consensus (collective opinions of family members) and competence (the family's concern for the person's abilities)—in determining how leadership or decision making will be distributed. In the United States, for example, the patriarchal system is said to have prevailed in early times, whereas today democracy is seen as the emerging family form. This point is discussed in detail in the next chapter.

Residence Systems

The families of the world also differ in regard to where newlyweds live, that is, in their residence systems. There are three major residence systems: patrilocal, matrilocal, and neolocal. In a patrilocal system newlyweds reside in or near the residence of the bridegroom. In a matrilocal system newlyweds live in or near the residence of the wife. And in a neolocal system, such as that of the United States, newlyweds have their own "new" (different from their parents') residence. In each of the systems there are, of course, exceptions to the rule. Thus in the United States, with its neolocal residence system, some young couples live with the husband's or wife's parents or a parent may live with the young couple. But when we speak of a pattern of residence, or any other pattern, as a system, we imply that it represents the ideal or the expected behavior in that society.

Lineage Systems

There are three major lineage systems, that is, ways of determining blood relationships. In the patrilineal system a person is related only to the relatives of his father; in the matrilineal system, only to those of his mother; and in the bilateral system, to those of both mother and father. The United States has always had a bilateral lineage system, and consequently many people in our society find it difficult to conceive of any other manner of determining kin.

The Residence

The number of generations that usually make up one household also varies among the world's families. In a *restricted* system two generations of family (parents and children) make up a household. In the *extended* system three or more generations comprise a household.[11] The United States has a restricted family system, whereas the traditional Chinese family was an extended system, in which the ideal was to have five or more generations residing in one household.

Two points should be noted. First, to have an extended family system, a society must have either a patrilocal or a matrilocal residence system. The logic of this is simple: if a family is to hold several generations in one household, obviously either the sons or the daughters must reside with the family even after marriage. In a patrilocal system the family never loses the residence of its sons, who remain in the residence of their birth, whereas its daughters leave the residence of their birth upon marriage and go to reside in the household of the husbands' parents. In the matrilocal system the family keeps the residence of its daughters, but loses its sons who go to reside with their wives' parents. In either case, whether the sons or the daughters remain, the generations of one family residing in a single household in this manner build up an extended family.

Second, it should be noted that terms different from those suggested here are sometimes used to describe family types. For example, the restricted family is sometimes called the nuclear family. Such a substitution of terms can cause a great deal of confusion, because in actuality a nuclear family is a specific unit of family, namely parents and children. You and your parents, for example, comprise a nuclear family, regardless of whether you reside with your parents or have a spouse and chil-

[11] E. Burgess, H. Locke, and M. Thomes, *The Family*, American Book Company, New York, 1963.

dren of your own (which is another nuclear family unit—you and your children). That is, a nuclear family is a unit of parents and children wherever they reside, whereas a restricted family has specific reference to place of residence. The nuclear family may make up the restricted family, as it often does in the United States, but an extended family is made up of a series of nuclear families—parents and their children, their children's children (male or female, depending on whether the residence type is patrilocal or matrilocal), and their children, and so on.[12]

Thus if nuclear family is used to refer to a family unit and restricted family to the generations that make up a household, a great deal of confusion can be avoided. Moreover, if a nuclear family (parents and children) is a family unit, it may be said to be the smallest family unit. The largest family unit may then be said to be kin [13]—that is, all persons to whom an individual is regarded as being related. Throughout our discussion we have said that individuals may be members of two nuclear families, one in which they are the parents and one in which they are the children. Warner refers to the latter as an individual's family of orientation and to the former as his family of procreation.[14] That is, for you, your family of orientation consists of your parents and you (and your siblings if any), and your family of procreation includes you, your spouse, and your children.

Obligation Patterns

Finally, one other variable must be considered in order to appreciate and understand family variability throughout the world—patterns of obligation. There are two such systems. One is the conjugal system, which requires that primary loyalty and obligation be directed toward one's

[12] For a discussion of the nuclear family in the extended family, see M. F. Nimkoff, *Comparative Family Systems*, Houghton Mifflin, Boston, 1965, p. 21.

[13] Some writers refer to the family unit that includes more than the nuclear unit as extended kin, and talk about extended kinship ties. Such references are certainly acceptable as long as they are not confused with the extended family per se. To repeat, an extended family refers to the residence of three or more generations of family in a single household, whereas our concept of kin or what others might call extended kin refers to a unit involving family members beyond the nuclear unit.

[14] W. L. Warner, "A Methodology for the Study of the Development of Family Attitudes," *SSRC Bulletin*, 18 (1933).

spouse and children. In the United States family obligation patterns are conjugal.

In the second system, called consanguineal, the primary loyalty and obligations are to be directed toward one's parents. Notice that we are talking about primary loyalty—not total loyalty. In a conjugal system, for example, one's first obligation to his spouse and children does not mean that he has no responsibility for his parents, but rather that his parental concerns are second to those for his spouse or his family of procreation.[15]

Conjugal systems are rather common, particularly in contemporary Western society. Consanguineal systems are less common and may in fact be combinations of both conjugal and consanguineal systems. Among the traditional Chinese families, for example, the system tended to be conjugal for the female, her primary obligations being to her husband and children, and more consanguineal for the male, whose first and foremost obligations were to his elders.

We can hypothesize how a pure consanguineal family system might work. Suppose that a male from family A marries a female from family B. In addition to the sexual intimacies, the husband may have certain social and affectional concerns for his wife that he does not have for other females in the society; hence the society regards the couple as being formally married. However, since his primary obligation is to his family of orientation (of birth), his financial responsibilities are toward them. In other words, he provides their shelter, food, and maintenance. He does not have these responsibilities for his wife or his children. Moreover, in such a society the male would most likely not be regarded as the social father of his children; that is, he would have no responsibility toward them nor they toward him. Instead, he would be regarded as the social father of his sister's children and would be responsible for them both physically and socially. His own physical children would be cared for by his wife's brother or brothers. Anthropologists call systems in which an uncle has the responsibility of socializing his nieces and nephews an avuncular society. Notice that throughout this discussion we have distinguished between physical and social parentage, at least as far as the male is concerned. The physical father is the one who is physically responsible for the child's conception, whereas the social father is the person who is regarded as being father. In the United States, except for adoption, which we discussed earlier in this chapter, the physical parents

---

[15] For a full discussion of consanguine versus conjugal emphasis, see William M. Kephart, *The Family, Society and the Individual*, Houghton Mifflin, Boston, 1966, pp. 58–60, especially p. 58.

are also the social parents, and such combining of physical and social parentage occurs among the vast majority of the world's people.[16]

Our hypothesized consanguineal family system (although a documented case exactly like the one we hypothesized is difficult to find) would seem to have a number of advantages when compared with our system. For example, if the husband and wife decided not to remain married, the breakup would have no direct impact on the child, because the man and child share no family relationship. In a system such as that in the United States, however, a separation or divorce takes the child's father away from him; indeed, in a one-child family the child loses direct contact with one half of his family. On the other hand, our system has certain advantages; at least, it will certainly seem so to every student who has just read our description of the hypothesized society. As one young coed put it in a class discussion of the hypothesized system, "It is inconceivable that anyone would want to live that way because it's simply not right." This tendency to regard one's own societal patterns as being right and proper, which is called ethnocentrism, is very prevalent. But the student should keep in mind, in studying middle-class marriage in our culture, that there have been and are very stable societies whose norms are quite different from those of our culture. The people of Tibet, for example, not only accepted polyandrous marriage, but preferred it as right and proper. In traditional China the young bride's living with her in-laws was not only an acceptable practice, but was considered to be right and proper. In fact, the young girls eagerly awaited the day when, upon marriage, they could establish such patrilocal residence, because it symbolized womanhood and wifehood. Thus the members of a society, though they must of course be socialized to observe the marriage and family norms of their society, must also be aware of the societal norms in other cultures in order to appreciate the breadth of these norms.

Comparing the United States family system with another system such as the traditional Chinese family, to which we have already referred several times, and noting the differences or similarities can indeed help us to discuss family life in more concise terms than would otherwise be possible. The traditional Chinese family was largely patriarchal, patrilocal, patrilineal, extended, and conjugal for the female but consanguineal for the male. The early United States family tended to be patriarchal, neolocal, bilateral, restricted, and conjugal for both the male and the female. Contemporary United States family systems are still the same, ex-

---

[16] A marriage and family system that does not parallel our hypothesized case but has certain elements in common with it is discussed in A. R. Radcliffe-Brown, "The Mother's Brother in South Africa," *S. African J. Sci.,* 21 (1924), pp. 542–555.

Table 2 Major Types of Marriage and Family Systems

Authority Patterns	Residence Patterns	Lineage Patterns	Number of Generations per Household	Obligation Patterns
Patriarchal: eldest male rules	Patrilocal: newlyweds reside with or near parents of bridegroom	Patrilineal: kinship determined through father's relatives	Restricted: two generations of family residing in household	Conjugal: primary loyalty to spouse and children
Matriarchal: eldest female rules	Matrilocal: newlyweds reside with or near parents of bride	Matrilineal: kinship determined through mother's relatives	Extended: three or more generations residing in household	Consanguineal: primary loyalty to parents and siblings
Democratic: family leadership given to a member on the basis of family consensus about his competence	Neolocal: newlyweds establish their own residence apart from the parental residences	Bilateral: kinship determined through both father's and mother's relatives		

Table 3   Units of Family Analysis

Nuclear	Parents and children
Kin	All persons regarded as relatives
Family of orientation	Family into which one is born
Family of procreation	Family in which one is a parent

cept that authority patterns have tended to change from patriarchal to more democratic forms.

In the chapter that follows we discuss marriage and family life in the United States. We examine the social factors that brought about a number of changes in the authority patterns and in the expectations from marriage and from marital partners.[17]

Summary

In this chapter we have tried to present a cross-cultural view of the marriage and family systems throughout the world. The purpose was to show that the United States middle-class marriage and the United States

Table 4   Marital Choice

Marriage arrangement	Degree to which individual selects his own marriage partner or his marriage partner is selected by his family
Preferential mating	Degree to which society determines groupings from which marital selections may be made; the field of eligibles may be wide or narrow
Exogamy	Norms that require marriages to occur outside certain groupings
Endogamy	Norms that require marriages to occur within certain groupings

[17] For a discussion of the attempt to relate family types and certain economic factors, see M. F. Nimkoff and Russel Middleton, "Types of Family and Types of Economy," *Am. J. Sociol.,* November 1960, pp. 215–225. See also Neil J. Smelser, *Social Change in the Industrial Revolution,* University of Chicago Press, Chicago, 1959.

family systems are but one of many types. This knowledge may enable the reader to achieve a broader understanding of his own marriage and family system. It may also provoke some insights into United States marriage and family trends. In attempting to achieve these goals, the concept of marriage, as well as the concept of family, was defined and discussed cross-culturally. Tables 2, 3, and 4 summarize the major points.

Questions

1. What is status? What is a role? Relate the two concepts, using a number of examples of statuses.
2. Define marriage and discuss each component of the definition.
3. Discuss the relationship between the concept of the survival of the fittest and the theories concerning the evolution of marital forms.
4. What is meant by natural monogamy?
5. Describe how marriage partners are selected in a society that has a high degree of marriage arrangement and few specifications in regard to preferential mating.
6. Define family and discuss each component of the definition.
7. List and discuss the three systems of each of the following:
    a. Authority patterns
    b. Lineage patterns
    c. Residence patterns
8. What is the relationship, if any, between an extended family and a nuclear family?
9. Discuss how the role of a husband in a conjugal obligation pattern would differ from that of a husband in a consanguineal system.
10. Define ethnocentrism and discuss its implications for one's understanding of marriage and family systems.

Suggestions for Research and Related Activities

1. Hold a debate or a panel discussion on the merits of two mate-selection systems, one in which the individual selects his own marriage partner and one in which the choice is made for him by his family.

2. Poll your class members in regard to their feelings about the strengths and weaknesses of a patriarchal authority pattern and then poll your parents or other persons of that age in regard to the same point. Do you find any differences in the responses given by the two age groups? Do you find any difference between the responses given by males and those given by females? If you do, or do not, find any differences in either case (i.e., age or sex), what does this mean?

3. Invite an anthropologist to speak to your class about specific cases of marriage and family life in different cultural settings.

Suggested Readings

Boalt, Gunnar, *Family and Marriage,* David McKay, New York, 1965, especially
    Ch. 1, "Marriage and the Family: An International Perspective," and
    Ch. 3, "Selection in Marriage—Theory."

Christensen, H. T., Ed., *Handbook of Marriage and the Family,* Rand McNally,
    Chicago, 1964.

Farber, Bernard, Ed., *Kinship and Family Organization,* Wiley, New York, 1966.

Kenkel, William F., *The Family in Perspective,* 2nd ed., Appleton-Century-Crofts,
    New York, 1966, especially Part I, "The Family in Time and Space."

Kephart, William M., *The Family, Society and the Individual,* 2nd ed., Houghton
    Mifflin, Boston, 1966, especially Ch. 1, "The Study of the Family,"
    Ch. 2, "Biological Foundations of the Family," and Ch. 3, "Cross-Cultural
    Patterns."

Nimkoff, M. F., *Comparative Family Systems,* Houghton Mifflin, Boston, 1965, Ch. 1,
    "Comparative Studies of the Family," and Ch. 2, "Types of Family."

Stephens, William N., *The Family in Cross-Cultural Perspective,* Holt, Rinehart
    and Winston, New York, 1963.

Chapter Three

HISTORICAL AND CONTEMPORARY ASPECTS OF AMERICAN FAMILY LIFE

THE MAIN objective of this book, as we pointed out in Chapter One, is to analyze the man-woman relationship as it emerges, matures, and, under certain circumstances, deteriorates. We now examine the important social unit in which the man-woman relationship is found in the United States, namely the American family.

We conduct this examination by focusing our attention on certain historical and contemporary aspects of American family life. First, we attempt to analyze the typical early American family and the social milieu in which it was nurtured. Second, we point out certain major social changes and their impact on family relationships. Third, we attempt to indicate the direction of family change and to comment on emergent family values. Fourth, we comment on the contemporary American middle-class family and the problems it faces.

ILLUSTRATION: American paper dolls. Courtesy of the Museum of the City of New York.

34

The Family in Early America

To avoid oversimplification, we first discuss several diverse family types in early America, each different from the others. Calhoun speaks of family settings in New England, New York, New Jersey, Delaware, Pennsylvania, and the South.[1]

Colonial New England

New England families were almost exclusively English Congregationalists of Puritan stock, with the exception of some Scotch-Irish Presbyterians in New Hampshire and Huguenots in Massachusetts and Rhode Island.[2]

The Puritans placed much value on family life. They came to this country mostly in family units. Early marriages were encouraged and common, with social pressures against both men and women who remained single. Mate selection was controlled for the most part by parents, although some individual freedom did exist. Marriage was also controlled by law, which required publication of intent to marry, parental consent, and registration. The basis of marriage was largely economic; love and affection,[3] though not necessarily bases for marriage and though their expression was often limited, nevertheless were present; divorce was permitted.

The structure of the family was patriarchal. Women in general occupied an inferior status, but did possess some property rights and were permitted to engage in trade and commerce. Since Puritan society considered the stability of the community and that of the family to be synonymous, it prescribed by law the responsibilities and obligations of parents and children. Parents were to provide for children and instill in them the religious values of the society. Rigid discipline was imposed, and obedience was expected. Children were generally subservient; individualism was present but not markedly so.[4]

Attitudes toward premarital sex were strict, as noted by Hawthorne in

[1] Arthur W. Calhoun, *A Social History of the American Family From Colonial Times to the Present,* Barnes and Noble, New York, 1945, Vol. I.
[2] *Ibid.,* Vol. I, Ch. 2.
[3] *Ibid.,* Vol. I, Chs. 2 and 3.
[4] *Ibid.,* Vol. I, Chs. 3 and 4.

the *Scarlet Letter,* but the existence of rigid attitudes also invited deviations.[5] Premarital sexual relationships were reported in different locales
and times. The practice of bundling, which permitted an unmarried
couple, fully clothed, to spend the night in the same bed, separated by a
board in the center, unwittingly may have also encouraged deviations.
The men who came to court often traveled long distances and were unable to return home the same day. Bundling enabled the family to lodge
the guest overnight, as well as to economize on the burning of candles, a
scarce commodity in the early period.[6]

The Middle Colonies and Pennsylvania in the Colonial Period

The middle colonies of New York (Dutch), New Jersey (English and
Scotch-Irish), and Delaware (Swedish and Lutheran) were more heterogeneous with regard to religion and background than those in New England. With the exception of divorce, which was presumably somewhat
easier to obtain in New England than elsewhere, the middle colonies
have been described as generally strict but less harsh and punitive in
matters of authority, sex, and rearing of children than were the Puritans
of New England. Of special interest is the status of Dutch women in New
York. They occupied a relatively high position when compared to
women in the neighboring colonies and in New England. Though a
woman's conventional role was that of homemaker, many became skilled
as traders and some occupied important positions in the trading world.[7]

Family settings in colonial Pennsylvania have been described as cos-
mopolitan and generally tolerant. This colony was settled by Quakers of
English descent, along with Germans and Scotch-Irish. With the exception of the Quakers, who were quite strict, particularly on sexual matters, these families were like their counterparts in other colonies.[8]

The Southern Colonies

During the early period almost all the colonists were English, particularly in Virginia, Maryland, and North Carolina. There the Church of
England prevailed. Later came the Baptists, Presbyterians, and Huguenots in North and South Carolina.

The life of the Southern family on the coastal plain was different from
that in the North Atlantic colonies, since the plantation economy in the

[5] Nathaniel Hawthorne, *The Scarlet Letter,* Modern Library, New York, 1950.
[6] Calhoun, *op. cit.,* Vol. I, Chs. 5, 6, and 7.
[7] *Ibid.,* Vol. I, Chs. 7, 8, 9, and 10.
[8] *Ibid.,* Vol. I, Ch. 11.

South gave rise to an aristocracy relatively early in our history. As one would expect, marriage among this class was governed, perhaps even more than in New England, by economic considerations, but family background and ancestry were, of course, also significant. Women in this class were presumably freer from toil than elsewhere. In general, they as well as the children were subordinate in the Southern colonies, but less so among the aristocracy than in other classes. Marriage and sex were regulated, at least on the Eastern Seaboard; divorces were generally difficult to obtain.

Familism—a pattern, most frequently found in a rural society, that requires the subordination of the individual to the welfare of the family unit—was much more highly developed among aristocratic Southerners, and Southerners in general, than in other sections of the country.[9]

The Frontier

Family life on the frontier differed from that in the relatively settled communities discussed so far. Of course, all regions of the frontier were not uniform. Original settlers of the hunter-pioneer type were very mobile, often single; when married, they had a family structure that was not subject to the religious and social controls and norms found elsewhere. The proximity of the frontier settlement to larger communities was also significant. Those in Pennsylvania, for example, were influenced quite early by the existence of Philadelphia and other communities of size. Those in North and South Carolina were more isolated. Sending poorer and less privileged classes to the frontier was a common practice, especially in the South where the plantation system quickly incorporated vast amounts of land. It was also advantageous for plantation owners to have a buffer of poor whites between established settlements and the Indians on the frontier. The families of poor whites on the Southern frontier represent an interesting contrast to those in the more established settlements. In general it has been noted that the longer and more extensive the period of isolation, the greater the likelihood that marriage, sex, and family behavior had a minimum of regulation and was significantly different from family life in older settled communities.[10] We shall deal with the frontier as a factor producing social change in the family later in this chapter.

We have attempted to present some of the more relevant features of the early American family, indicating both similarities and differences.

[9] *Ibid.,* Vol. II, Ch. 13.
[10] Carl Bridenbaugh, *Myths and Realities,* Louisiana State University Press, Baton Rouge, La., 1952.

Colonial families on the Eastern Seaboard, especially within a particular section, undoubtedly were more similar than different. The common features of the early American family are summarized below.

The Typical Early American Family

The typical early American family was a rural family, with a predominantly agricultural economic base. It was mostly a self-sufficient and extremely cooperative unit, which operated within a materialistic and practical setting.

A Self-Sufficient and Extremely Cooperative Unit

The early American family was self-sufficient, that is, such basic needs as those for food and clothing, shelter, recreation, education, religious and medical care, and socialization and protection of family members were fulfilled largely within the home. The family could not depend on agencies outside the home to satisfy its needs because, in many areas, no such agencies existed. There were no bakeries, laundries, construction companies, theaters, medical specialists, furniture factories, and unemployment agencies, and very few, if any, clothing stores, food stores, churches, and schools. Therefore, if the family was to survive, it had to fulfill its own needs, and the adequate fulfillment of these needs required the active participation and full cooperation of all family members.

A Materialistic and Practical Setting

The dependence of the early American family on itself for survival required, in addition to the extensive cooperation of its members, also a setting in which materialism and practicality are highly valued. Great importance was indeed placed on material and practical concerns— marriage itself, more frequently than not, was an economic arrangement. In fact, mate selection was primarily centered on such practical characteristics of the mate as having a sturdy constitution, good working habits, and the ability to perform household duties. These were frequently the basic ingredients that men and women sought in each other.[11] Marriage for love and regard for the affectional quality of the marriage relationship were given subordinate positions in the hierarchy of family values.

In such a self-sufficient, cooperative, and extremely practical social unit as the early American family, there developed a unity based on economic ties and personal loyalties from which the purpose and meaning of family life emerged.[12]

Internal Organization of Family Relationships in Early America

The internal organization of the early American rural family was based on two important principles: familism and authoritarianism.

Familism

Familism, as used here, refers to the subordination of the individual's interests to the interests of the family as a whole. That is, a member of the early American family was expected to pursue the goals of the family as a whole, rather than those that he set for himself. Thus if a son wanted to become a musician but the family desired his services as a farmer, the son was expected to give up his musical aspirations and to serve his family as a farmer. If he persisted in becoming a musician, his ignoring of the goal set for him by his family was viewed as a disobedient and selfish act, and he was considered to be a very ungrateful and inconsiderate son.

To fit into the general goals of the family was the primary obligation of the individual. To avoid misunderstanding, it was necessary for the family to assign well-defined goals to each member and to make certain that these goals fitted into the general pattern of family goals. In such a family, the desire of one daughter to become a particularly good dressmaker may have had to go unsatisfied because another person, probably her mother or an older sister, was already assigned to doing most of the

---

[11] Calhoun, *op. cit.*, Vol. I, Ch. 3.
[12] James Truslow Adams, *Provincial Society, 1690–1763,* Macmillan, New York, 1927, pp. 10–11. See also Arthur W. Calhoun, "The Early American Family," *Ann. Am. Acad. polit. soc. Sci.,* **160** (March 1932), pp. 7–12.

family sewing. The younger girl then had little choice but to forget her interest and concentrate on other useful duties that were not exclusively claimed by other family members.

It follows, then, that the training that the early American family gave its members, in addition to providing knowledge about oneself, also had to provide knowledge about the likes and dislikes, talents, and abilities of other family members, since the behavior of one member was certainly important in determining what another might or might not be permitted to do.[13] Thus under the principle of familism, the individual's interests are secondary to the interests of the family as a whole.

Authoritarianism

Authoritarianism, as used here, refers to the family organization in which the power to make decisions and pass judgments, in effect, the power to rule, is in the hands of a person who demands immediate obedience and allows little individual freedom. In the early American family the power to rule was usually given to the eldest male, who was then looked upon as head of the household. This is patriarchal authoritarianism.[14] The power to rule emanated from the patriarch and passed down to the lower echelons of the family.[15] The effectiveness of this power in regard to the wife during the colonial period is shown in the following passage:

Do you say, the slave is held to involuntary servitude? So is the wife. Her relation to her husband, in the immense majority of cases, is made for her, and not by her. And when she makes it for herself, how often, and how soon, does it become involuntary! How often, and how soon, would she throw off the yoke if she could! O ye wives, I know how superior you are to your husbands in many respects—not only in personal attraction . . . in grace, in refined thought, in passive fortitude, in enduring love, and in a heart to be filled with the spirit of heaven. . . . Nay, I know you may surpass him in his own sphere of boasted prudence and worldly wisdom about dollars and cents. Nevertheless he has authority from God to rule over you. . . . You are bound to obey him in all things. Your service is very, very, very often involuntary from the first, and, if voluntary at first, becomes hopeless necessity afterwards. I

[13] Arthur W. Calhoun, *A Social History, op. cit.*, Vol. I, Chs. 5–6. See also Katharine DuPré Lumpkin, *The Family: A Study of Member Roles*, University of North Carolina Press, Chapel Hill, N.C., 1933, pp. xii–xvii.
[14] When the power to rule is given to the eldest female, we have matriarchal authoritarianism.
[15] Lumpkin, *loc. cit.* See also Robert Bierstedt, "The Problem of Authority," in Morroe Berger et al., Eds., *Freedom and Control in Modern Society*, Van Nostrand, New York, 1954, pp. 67–81, for an excellent analysis of the concept of authority.

know God has laid upon the husband to love you as Christ loved the church.
. . . But the husband may not so love you. He may rule you with the rod of
iron. What can you do? Be divorced? God forbid it, save for crime. Will you
say that you are free, that you will go where you please, do as you please? Why
ye dear wives, your husbands may forbid. And listen, you cannot leave New
York, nor your palaces, any more than your shanties. No; you cannot leave
your parlor, nor your bedchamber, nor your couch, if your husband commands you to stay there. What can you do? Will you run away with your stick
and your bundle? He can advertise you! What can you do? You can, and I fear
some of you do, wish him, from the bottom of your hearts at the bottom of the
Hudson.[16]

The quotation illustrates the power of the husband, but the influence
of the wife is not to be underestimated. Some behavioral scientists believe that the common assertion that the patriarch alone determined the
family's course of action may be an oversimplification and warrants critical reexamination.[17] One author, for example, states that the common
acceptance of this belief is based on what may turn out to be insufficient
evidence.[18] Thus it would seem advisable at least to qualify our statements concerning the extent to which the patriarch ruled the early
American family. To this end, it is noted that the wife-mother was frequently influential in determining the family's course of action and that
this influence was effected in at least two ways. First, the wife-mother was
frequently able to influence the patriarch's decision by employing certain persuasive tactics in her interaction with him. By persuasive tactics
we do not suggest that the wife-mother argued with her husband, nor do
we imply that she actually told him what he should do. Rather, we mean
to say that many early American wives were frequently able to influence
their husbands by subtle suggestions. In addition to this ability to weave
subtle patterns of suggestion, there was a second and perhaps more important method by which the wife-mother not only influenced, but actually determined the family's course of action—the mother-centered pattern.

A mother-centered or mother-dominated home is believed to have developed out of situations in which the continuation of the father's role

[16] Calhoun, *A Social History, op. cit.,* Vol. II, p. 96.

[17] Among others, see Michael Young and Peter Willmott, *Family and Kinship in
East London,* Routledge and Kegan Paul, London, 1957; Raymond Firth and Judith
Djamour, *Two Studies of Kinship in London, Kinships in Southborough,* Athlone
Press, London, 1956. Also, some anthropologists are of the opinion that the preva-
lence of the father-centered family in American society has been overstated.

[18] Herman R. Lantz, *People of Coal Town,* Columbia University Press, New York,
1958, Ch. 8.

was in danger. The cultural and occupational hazards of the early American society, which were constant sources of possible injury or even death for the father, produced such situations. When the husband was no longer able to perform his role adequately, many women assumed the husband's role and power. In the first half of the nineteenth century several states, particularly Tennessee and Virginia, had an excess of widows because of the high death rate of husbands as a result of hardship.[19]

Thus although the early American family was formally organized around patriarchal authoritarianism, there is reason to believe that a more critical examination of the personal interactions in the family would uncover certain important influences of the wife-mother and even certain distinct mother-centered patterns. The authoritarian nature of the family, however, was pronounced, regardless of whether the father or the mother was in control. There was no place for overt disagreement in this family, because its successful operation depended on the ability of each member to follow the goals set by the authoritarian; any goals that the individual may have had were secondary. Let us now point out certain consequences of this type of family organization.

Consequences of Authoritarian-Familistic Organization

The authoritarian-familistic organization of the early American family tended to bring about four important consequences. First, the authoritarian tended to feel a strong psychological need to be right. Second, family control tended to be based on irrational authority. Third, the family tended to be an association of unequals. And fourth, the individual family members tended to be treated as commodities.

THE AUTHORITARIAN'S NEED TO BE RIGHT. For an authoritarian family organization to operate successfully, the person designated as the authoritarian had to command immediate, complete, and unquestioning obedience. To command this obedience, it was necessary that the family view his decisions and commands as always being right. Indeed, any question raised about a decision of the authoritarian tended to threaten his position, and any hesitation in obeying his commands made it necessary for the authoritarian to wage a vigorous battle if he were to maintain his control over the family.

The weapons generally used by the authoritarian in fighting this battle were tradition and custom. He was almost always able to maintain his power by invoking customs and traditions, because they were highly valued and were not subject to critical examination or change.[20]

[19] Calhoun, *A Social History, op. cit.,* Vol. II, Ch. 13.
[20] Erich Fromm, *Man for Himself,* Holt, Rinehart and Winston, New York, 1947, pp. 12–13.

Furthermore, emotionally as well the authoritarian had a vested interest in seeing that his decisions and commands were viewed as being right. His feeling of security was intimately tied to his being right, and any implication to the contrary tended to be shattering to him psychologically.[21] Some appreciation of what it is like to interact with an authoritarian who has to be right may be gained by recalling our own associations with such people. Such individuals attempt to win a point by resorting to whatever means may be necessary, by telling people what to think, at times by berating, humiliating, or using destructive humor. Should they lose, they become hostile; they may pout and retreat from the situation. They behave so because their personal worth is tied to their being right and insecurity and self-doubt result when they feel they could be wrong.

FAMILY CONTROL BASED ON IRRATIONAL AUTHORITY. The maintenance of authoritarian family control was based on the authoritarian's ability to maintain order in his family. Although order is always a prerequisite for the adequate functioning of group life, the order brought about through authoritarianism is based on irrational authority. Persons who rule or govern by irrational authority (such as patriarchs, matriarchs, monarchs, and dictators) derive their power from the privileges that are traditionally associated with their position. That is, the authoritarian is given the power to rule not necessarily because he is the most competent, but because he occupies a certain position in the group. In the early American family, the power to rule was usually given to the person occupying the particular position of eldest male, or father. No one was expected to question whether he was the most competent family member to rule; indeed, no one was to ask whether he was competent to rule at all! He was the father and, therefore, by custom, he became the authoritarian. This, then, was irrational authority; noticeably absent was the right to govern based on the demonstrated ability to govern, which we call rational authority. The concept of rational authority is discussed in a later section of this chapter.

THE FAMILY: AN ASSOCIATION OF UNEQUALS. In an authoritarian setting the family is viewed as an association of human beings who are inferior or superior, but never equal. By saying that the early American family members were not equals, we do not refer to such characteristics as intelligence, capabilities, or experience (in which they may or may not have been equal), but to the fact that they were neither considered to be nor treated as equals. To begin with, all were treated as inferior to the authoritarian; beyond this, among family members themselves the physi-

---

[21] Richard Christie and Marie Jahoda, Eds., *Studies in the Scope and Method of the Authoritarian Personality,* The Free Press, Glencoe, Ill., 1954.

cally frail and the overtly fearful were treated as inferior. On the other hand, persons who were physically strong and those who knew no fear, save fear of the authoritarian and of God, were greatly admired.[22] Differential treatment was also given to members on the basis of age and sex, males and adults occupying a more favorable position than women and children. Such categorizing of family members presented a formidable barrier against any equal or democratic treatment.[23]

FAMILY MEMBERS TREATED AS COMMODITIES. When family members are treated as commodities, their worth is based on how much they can produce; they are not viewed as ends in themselves.[24] Members of the early American family were not primarily valued for what they themselves were, namely their intrinsic worth as human beings, but rather for their abilities to contribute to the family's economic well-being. Thus, in the most materialistic and practical sense, family members were viewed as things to be used. Indeed, often those considered to be inferior were unfairly used for the benefit of those considered to be superior. This type of exploitation was common in the early American family, as well as in other authoritarian systems. Such an attitude was largely an outgrowth of the harsh physical environment, which demanded the complete efforts of all family members if material needs were to be fulfilled.

In this connection, the high birthrate of the early American family should be noted. It resulted from the need to offset the high death rate, the disinterest in and lack of knowledge about birth control, and the tradition of large families. Mainly, however, many children meant an adequate labor supply—a necessity for survival in an economy where there was little or no mechanization. One author quotes Adam Smith on American fecundity:

The value of children is the greatest of all encouragement to marriage. We cannot, therefore, wonder that the young people in North America should generally marry very young. Notwithstanding the great increase occasioned by such early marriages, there is a continual complaint of the scarcity of hands in North America.[25]

Stability of the Early American Family

It should be apparent that the early American family was an extremely stable unit, with little divorce. Such stability arose in part out of the loy-

---

[22] A. H. Maslow, "The Authoritarian Character Structure," *J. soc. Psychol.*, **18** (1943), pp. 401–411.

[23] Harry Emerson Fosdick, *Twelve Tests of Character*, George H. Doran, New York, 1923, p. 117.

[24] Maslow, *loc. cit.* See also Lumpkin, *op. cit.*, pp. xii–xviii.

[25] Calhoun, *A Social History, op. cit.*, Vol. II, p. 17.

alties that emerged from the economic interdependence of family members. However, we must not overlook the fact that in addition to the forces within the family, the community as a whole shared certain attitudes that were highly effective in maintaining family stability. For example, it was implicitly understood that wives, formally, should obey their husbands and children should obey their parents. Hence any family conflict, regardless of the circumstances involved, was viewed by the community as being caused by an ungrateful wife or a disobedient child. This simple interpretation of family conflict by the community tended to have a stabilizing effect on the family, because few persons wanted to be wrong in the eyes of the community. Marriage itself was viewed as a permanent association, and separation or divorce was both socially and religiously unacceptable as an adjustment of marital conflict.[26] Thus, in any family, when the internal forces failed to maintain stability, community and religious attitudes and values served to retain it.

It should be noted, however, that in describing the early American family as a permanent and stable social unit, we do not imply that it was necessarily a happy configuration or one conducive to healthy emotional development. How happy one might have been as a member of this authoritarian familistic group, or how healthy one's emotional development, may well be open to question. But available evidence indicates that personal adjustment in the early American family, despite the permanence and stability, was not unlike that found in the dictatorial society, where the individual is subordinate to the demands of the leader.[27] This strongly suggests that authoritarian familism was not conducive to the realization of the individual's fullest potential, a goal with which many people are concerned today.

We now turn to the second major consideration of this chapter—the social factors that tended to influence and change these traditional patterns of family relationships.

Major Social Changes and Their Impact on Family Relationships

Several social changes influenced the early American family and brought about changes in the patterns of family relationships. We dis-

[26] Ray E. Baber, *Marriage and the Family*, McGraw-Hill, New York, 1953, pp. 443–444.
[27] Calhoun, *A Social History, op. cit.*, Vol. I, Chs. 5–6.

cuss these social changes under two major headings—the shift from a rural to an urban society and the sociohistoric factors that influenced the family.

The Shift from a Rural to an Urban Society

Within the past one hundred and fifty years, American economy has changed from an agricultural to a predominantly industrial one. This change, which involved a shift from a rural to an urban society, required the migration of large numbers of people from the country to the city. Let us look at certain factors that encouraged this migration.

INCENTIVES FOR MIGRATION. The industrialization of America offered many economic and social opportunities to those who were willing to move to the city.[28] This appeal, which gave promise of greater economic security through higher wages and more attractive working conditions, was aided by the periodic declines in agricultural prices and a reduction in the employment needs of the rural area because of the increased mechanization of agriculture.[29] In addition to these economic incentives, certain social opportunities such as more adequate educational, cultural, and medical facilities aided in encouraging urban migration.[30]

EFFECTS OF THE RURAL-TO-URBAN SHIFT. The shift from a rural to an urban society brought about many social changes, which had an impact on the pattern of family relationships. There were three important effects: the family became less self-sufficient, the authoritarian lost some of his power, and the individual tended to undergo attitudinal changes toward his family.

Decline in Self-Sufficiency. In the industrial society, the family no longer had to depend on its own resources for survival. The fulfillment of such basic needs as those for food, clothing, shelter, medicine, recreation, education, and protection was largely taken over by specialized agencies outside the home. And many of the duties that were still performed in the home such as cooking and cleaning were greatly simplified through technology and mechanization. Having been freed from performing many chores that previously were necessary for its survival,[31]

---

[28] Calhoun, *A Social History, op. cit.,* Vol. II, pp. 171–175. See also R. D. McKenzie, *The Metropolitan Community,* McGraw-Hill, New York, 1933, p. 53.
[29] Arthur Charles Cole, *The Irrepressible Conflict, 1850–1865,* Macmillan, New York, 1934, p. 106.
[30] Noel P. Gist and L. A. Halbert, *Urban Society,* Crowell-Collier, New York, 1956, pp. 90–92.
[31] William F. Ogburn, *Recent Social Trends in the United States,* McGraw-Hill, New York, 1931, Vol. II, Ch. 13.

the family could now apply the extra time and energy to other areas of family living. One result was the development of an interest in the needs of the individual. This concern for the individual is something quite different from the previously described familism of the earlier period; it is discussed more fully in later sections.

Decline in Authoritarian Power. The industrial family no longer composed the work unit, because, with the rise of factories and mills, individuals sought employment outside the home. Thus the power over the work lives of family members was now transferred from the family authoritarian to such persons outside the family as foremen, managers, and plant owners. Obviously, this decreased the authoritarian's power.

Furthermore, in addition to losing control over the work lives of family members, the authoritarian, unless he was able to establish his own business, frequently lost control over his own work situation, because employment in the factory meant taking rather than giving orders. Thus by decreasing the power of the authoritarian, industrialization tended to strike at the very core of authoritarian familism, which, in effect, was the power of the authoritarian to command.

Attitudinal Changes toward Family. In the urban society, individuals tended to undergo fundamental changes in their attitudes toward their families. In part, this attitudinal change resulted from the decline of the self-sufficiency of the family and the decline of the authoritarian's power. But it stemmed also from the exposure of family members to new and different social patterns. As the individual moved within the urban area and interacted with persons of different backgrounds, he was constantly confronted by different rules of conduct and new value systems. Such factors as working daily with nonfamily members and receiving formal education outside the home tended to increase the individual's awareness of new and different patterns. Moreover, religious and community control was no longer so binding as in the past. Thus the individual in the urban setting came to view the particular social patterns of his family as only one of many existing patterns; consequently, the patterns of his family lost their exclusive position in his framework of values. It follows, then, that the individual underwent certain attitudinal changes toward his family as his loyalty to his family's particular standards began to be challenged by new and different standards.

THE FAMILY IN ITS URBAN SETTING. The growing dependence on agencies outside the home, the decentralization of authority, and the increasing awareness of new and different value systems all tended to weaken the economic ties and the personal loyalties on which the very purpose and meaning of early American family life had been founded. Urbanism, therefore, produced a milieu that made certain changes in the family inevitable.[32]

Sociohistoric Factors That Influenced the Family

It should be noted, however, that the impact of the urban industrial milieu, though significant, is not by itself sufficient to explain changes in the family. The family had to be flexible and willing to adapt itself to industrialization.[33] Equally significant is the climate of opinion and ideas that surrounds change; indeed, it has been argued that without a conducive climate of opinion many changes would never really develop or become accepted. Thus to understand what happened to the American family, we must assess certain important sociohistoric factors that tended to weaken the very foundation of authoritarian familism:

1. Secularism
2. Humanism
3. Democracy at the political level
4. The American frontier
5. The emancipation of the female and associated competence

SECULARISM. Secularism, as used here, is the doctrine that views customs, traditions, and values as the result of man's efforts, rather than the direct result of divine intervention. This doctrine was important in two respects. First, it implied that man was becoming aware of his ability to create and modify customs, traditions, and values. Second, and more important, it implied that if one found it necessary to question the standards of the society, he was questioning man's edicts and not God's! Indeed, under secularism the individual was not only free to examine standards, but could even change them without fear of divine reprisal.

It follows, then, that under secularism the existing way of life was constantly being examined. If the prevailing patterns were found wanting, they became subject to change; continued adherence to tradition, a cardinal principle of authoritarianism, became unacceptable. By giving man the responsibility for determining his way of life, this doctrine thus challenged the very principle of authoritarianism.[34]

HUMANISM. The doctrine of humanism, which became manifest in

---

[32] Ernest W. Burgess, "The Family in a Changing Society," *Am. J. Sociol.,* **53** (May 1948), pp. 417–422. See also William F. Ogburn, "The Changing Family," *The Family,* **19** (July 1938), pp. 139–143.

[33] William J. Goode, *World Revolution and Family Patterns,* The Free Press, Glencoe, Ill., 1963.

[34] Howard Becker, "Sacred and Secular Societies," *Social Forces,* **28** (May 1950), pp. 361–376.

literary, philosophical, and political movements, proclaimed faith in the human personality and in the significance of human values. While secularism made man aware of his ability to determine social standards, humanism developed in him a trust and a faith in this ability. Thus humanism tended to further weaken authoritarian familism, which had placed trust only in custom and the patriarch.[35]

DEMOCRACY AT THE POLITICAL LEVEL. The spread of democratic values through the rise of democracies both here and abroad contributed a great deal to an undermining of authoritarian familism. Although democracy at the political level does not insure its existence at the family level, there is a strong tendency for political thinking to ultimately become a part of the individual's personal reasoning. Thus if a person believes in his ability to govern himself politically, he might well rebel against any situation in which he is considered to be incapable of self-direction. And, in effect, this is what he did. Thus democratic principles at the political level made their contribution to the undermining of authoritarian familism, because they created rebellion against the authoritarian-familistic principle that denied the individual any right to self-direction.[36]

THE AMERICAN FRONTIER. The frontier—that section of our country which lay at the very edge of organized group life—had a way of life different from that in the more heavily populated rural settlements and tended to be an important factor in changing patterns of family relationships. A husband or wife might be captured by Indians, only to return years later to find a spouse remarried. Cases of runaway wives, it is reported, were common, because of harsh treatment. There were many instances of marriages without benefit of clergy, since ministers were not always available. To determine the legality of marriage, divorce, or separation was not always easy.[37] Also, it was the young married people who frequently migrated to frontier territories, which offered them greater economic opportunities. Such migration, in removing the newlyweds from the traditional parental imposition of values, created opportunities that allowed the more experimentally inclined persons to explore new patterns of conduct.

Furthermore, for young and old alike, life on the frontier was so difficult that it frequently called forth behavioral responses that differed markedly from the traditional patterns. For example, in the process of

[35] George R. Geiger, *Philosophy and the Social Order,* Houghton Mifflin, New York, 1947, pp. 384–397.

[36] Willystine Goodsell, "The American Family in the Nineteenth Century," *Ann. Acad. polit. soc. Sci.,* **160** (March 1932), pp. 13–22.

[37] Calhoun, *A Social History, op. cit.,* Vol. II.

migration itself, as well as in the process of establishing homesteads, women and children were often required to perform tasks that previously would have been performed primarily by men.

Finally, emergencies and hardships on the frontier were so severe that the physical well-being of the frontier family was under constant threat, particularly that of the father as he attempted to defend his family against the difficult environment. And, as already noted, situations that threaten the role of the father tend to produce mother-centered patterns in the family.

These effects of the frontier—the removal of newlyweds from direct parental control, the lack of social and religious control, the difficulties that called for behavioral responses different from the traditional ones, and the hardships that threatened injury or even death to the father—all tended to create a milieu that made certain changes in the traditional patterns of family relationships inevitable. To the extent that the old patterns were tested and found wanting, new patterns developed and became the foundations of family organization on the American frontier.

Romantic love, for example, was present on the frontier—if not as a basis for marriage, at least as a basis for involvement in extramarital affairs.[38] Sexual mores changed somewhat, and there were early signs that both women and children were undergoing a change in status.[39]

It should be reemphasized, however, that basically the family facilitated social change by permitting its members to enter the labor force—but not without heavy psychic costs, nor the inevitable conflicts between the old and the new.

During this period, also, conflicts between husbands and wives and between parents and children were brought out in the open. Disagreements became patterned, and even the view that the family and home possessed aloof relationships began to emerge.

THE EMANCIPATION OF THE FEMALE AND ASSOCIATED COMPETENCE. The dissatisfaction of women both here and abroad tended to center on the subservience demanded of them in a man's world. Women, as we have noted, were a part of that category which was looked upon as inferior, and were thus frequently exploited. However, under the impact of urbanization their position changed considerably. The economic opportunities that were opening to women in industrial and professional fields gave them a bargaining power that could be used to change or improve unsatisfactory relationships. Thus urbanization and its associated doctrines not only gave women reason to expect more equal treatment, but

[38] *Ibid.*, Vol. II, Ch. 2.
[39] *Ibid.*, Vol. II, Ch. 3.

also the opportunity to obtain it. Bernhard J. Stern pointedly illustrates the effects of the emancipation of women on the family:

As the technological changes of the industrial revolution transformed the processes of production, the women of the urban proletariat and many of the artisan class were drawn into the factories, mills and mines as unskilled wage-workers. The majority of women found it necessary to work outside of the household in order to augment the family income. The leisure which the industrial revolution brought to a relatively small number of women of the upper classes was made possible in part by the labor of the women of the proletariat. The latter acquired a certain element of power within family councils by virtue of their contributions to the support of their families; and their employment away from home increased their personal contacts and released them to some extent from domestic controls and thus modified male dominance within the family. The growing urbanization and secularization of life likewise changed the status of women within the family. As the factory took over the industrial functions of the family, the state encroached upon its educational functions and this detracted from the cohesion of the patriarchal family group, which had perpetuated women's inferiority.[40]

Effects of the Civil War

Finally, it should be noted that the Civil War brought a culmination of many of the changes that had been under way. Like all wars, it shook traditional ways of living. Women and children were given work opportunities in factories, where wages were relatively high, thus offering women and children greater opportunity for emancipation and freedom from parental control. Many men failed to return from the war, which resulted in new female-centered patterns. The general impact of the Civil War thus was acceleration of change, experimentation, and a somewhat different basis for family life.[41]

Family Changes

The shift from a rural to an urban society and such sociohistoric factors as secularism, scientific humanism, democracy at the political level, the emancipation of women, and the American frontier contributed

[40] Bernhard J. Stern, "Woman: Position in Society," *Encyclopaedia of the Social Sciences*, Macmillan, New York, 1935, Vol. XV, pp. 444–445.
[41] Calhoun, *A Social History, op. cit.*, Vol. II, Ch. 14.

markedly, over time, to the creation of a new social and psychological setting. In the new setting, the early American family with its authoritarian-familistic organization could hardly survive. Family members were no longer willing to obey, and often no longer able to obey, the traditional rules of conduct imposed by authoritarian familism. After a long period of intensive conflict, the old finally gave way to the new. Here we witness the beginning of the reorganization of family relationships; in effect, the rise of new family types on the American scene.

One such major family type is the contemporary American middle-class family. This family is in a state of transition between two kinds of values: the values derived from the early American family, encompassed in authoritarianism and familism, and the values underlying democracy and individualism that emerged from urbanism and the sociohistoric factors mentioned previously. If authoritarianism and familism represent one extreme in that they value the individual in the family as unimportant, democracy and individualism represent the other extreme— the supreme importance of the individual in the family. Let us now analyze the concepts of individualism and democracy, to help us understand where the contemporary American middle-class family is moving and why it is torn with so many conflicts.

Individualism

Individualism here refers to the right of a person to be the active agent in selecting his own interests out of the array of those that are available. This means that an individual is free to pursue the goals that he himself selects, rather than being forced to accept the goals set for him by his family.

We must note here that individualism is not to be confused with indiscriminate rebelliousness. Rebelliousness operates within a framework of self-concern alone and usually fails to consider the dignity and rights of others. Individualism, however, is designed to create in the person an awareness of and respect for the rights and dignity of others. As the terms are used here, individualism may be the result of successful parent-child relationships and indiscriminate rebellion the result of unsuccessful parent-child relationships. Confusion with regard to these concepts is manifest in movements of social protest within recent years. In such activities as student protests on the campus, matters pertaining to civil rights, and reactions to military service, both individualism and indiscriminate rebelliousness may be observed. Some individuals have been able to assess the alternatives rationally, to raise questions with themselves about what they are doing, and to arrive at an ideology of protest that reflects individualism. Others protest either because someone suggested that they do, thus simply relying on someone else's opinion, or because their characteristic way of reacting is *to be against whatever is.* Both individualism and indiscriminate rebellion can be operative in *social protest,* but each stems from a different set of motives. The correlation between these patterns of response and earlier relationships within the family is noted from time to time throughout the book.

Democracy

In a democratic family the power to make decisions and pass judgments—in effect, the power to rule—is given to that member who, in the opinion of a majority of the family members, is the most competent to do so. That is, authority in the democratic family is delegated on the basis of consensus and competence. However, the family member who is the most competent to pass judgments and make decisions in certain matters may not necessarily be the most competent to do so in all matters. Therefore, authority in the democratic family tends to be delegated to more than one person at a time, each person being responsible for decisions regarding specific matters. It is entirely possible, of course, for one person in the democratic family to be given all of the authority, if the family members consider him to be the most capable decision maker in all matters. Democratic family control, therefore, is not signified by the number of family members who are given authority, but by the manner in which the authority is given.

Consequences of Democratic-Individualistic Organization

The democratic-individualistic family organization tends to lead to four important consequences.

FAMILY CONTROL BASED ON RATIONAL AUTHORITY. In the traditional family, authority was based on one's position in the family irrespective of competence, which is irrational authority. Under democratic individualism, authority is rational because it is given to that person who, in the opinion of family members, is most capable of governing.

AUTHORITY ASSOCIATED WITH THE DESIRE TO BE RIGHT. The authoritarian of the early American family tended to have a strong psychological need to be right. In the democratic family, however, the person selected to pass judgment is not led to believe that he possesses an inherent superiority, though he may certainly have a desire to be right; hence he can accept a proneness to error.

THE FAMILY: AN ASSOCIATION OF EQUALS. The democratic-individualistic family does not tend to categorize its members into superior and inferior groupings, as did the early American family. The tendency to abolish categorical treatment of family members is due to a number of factors. First, since the person who makes the necessary decisions in the democratic-individualistic family receives his authority from the family members themselves, he is viewed more as one who leads than as one who commands immediate obedience.

Second, whereas the early American family women were often treated as inferiors, today women are increasingly able to attain more equal treatment, because they have a bargaining power that early American women did not possess. Pursuits other than marriage are now available to women; consequently, if a woman finds herself in a situation not to her liking, she can use the opportunities open to her in business and industry to remove herself from it. Thus, unlike the early American woman, the woman of today has a power that she can use to her benefit in seeking more equal treatment in her family relationships.

Children were also treated as inferiors in the early American family. Today there is increasing recognition of their needs as children, as well as of the necessity to give them every available opportunity to develop their potential to the fullest extent.

FAMILY MEMBERS TREATED AS "ENDS." With the emergence of a concern for the intrinsic worth of each family member, the individual is no longer measured only in terms of what he produces. Thus the declining birthrate probably does not indicate a lack of interest in children, but the family's desire to enable each member to develop his abilities to the fullest. Such a goal, many believe, is more likely to be achieved when the family concentrates its resources on a few, rather than many children.

It must be emphasized that the middle-class family is in a state of dynamic transition. The extent of individualism within the family will undoubtedly vary from family to family. A few families are truly democratic in all spheres; many others are democratic in very limited spheres; still some others are democratic only in form, with actual control residing in the hands of one or more members. The distribution of familial power is generally complex. The variations just noted are inevitable stages and processes in social change and may be useful in identifying and understanding family rule.

Despite the complexities imposed by social change, it might be valuable to identify the major shifts with regard to authoritarianism, familism, individualism, and democracy, as shown in Table 5.

It is a mistake to assume that all of the characteristics of the contemporary middle-class family were wholly absent in earlier times. Goode, for one, questions the assumed relationship between family change and in-

Table 5 Changing Values of the American Family

Tradional Values	Emergent Values
I. Family control predominately based on authoritarian familism	I. Family control predominately based on democratic individualism
a. Authority associated with strong *need* to be right	a. Authority associated with *desire* to be right
b. Authority irrational	b. Authority rational
c. Family an association of unequals	c. Family an association of equals
d. Family members treated as commodities	d. Family members treated as human beings with inherent dignity
II. Values focused on tradition, allowing little change	II. Values focused on examination, allowing much change

dustrialization and suggests that some of the characteristics of the modern family were probably present before.[42] Recent research demonstrates that individualism in mate choice, premarital sex, the presence of romantic love, the emancipation of the female, family authority, and the problems that emerged can be traced to the early colonial period in this country. Furstenberg, who examined travelers' reports for the period 1800–1850, casts doubt on the modern origin of courtship and mating practices and points out that several characteristics of the modern family —freedom of choice, romantic love, and permissiveness in parent-child relations—were observed by travelers in this country at that time.[43] Perhaps the most significant work in this area is the study by Margaret Britton, who made a content analysis of significant women's magazines between 1741 and 1794, dividing the period into 1741–1776 and 1777–1794. She reports that a number of the family characteristics usually attributed to urbanization and industrialization existed in the early colonial period; furthermore, there was a significant increase in the concern for several of the characteristics in the later period.[44]

It should be noted that social changes stem not only from influences in the broader society, but develop also from gradual changes within the family—from the daily interactions and redefinitions of the rights and

[42] Goode, *op. cit.*, p. 6.
[43] Frank F. Furstenberg, Jr., "Industrialization and the American Family: A Look Backward," *Am. Soc. Rev.*, **31**, 3 (1966), pp. 326–328.
[44] Margaret Britton, "An Examination of the Role, Status, and Power of the American Woman from 1741 to 1794 as Reflected in Selected Magazines of the Period," M.A. thesis, Southern Illinois University, Carbondale, Ill., 1965.

obligations among the family members. *Urbanization* and *industrialization* are significant in that they accelerated the changes that were already under way.

The Contemporary American Middle-Class Family

The fourth major consideration of this chapter concerns the contemporary middle-class family and the problems it faces. As already noted, the middle-class family is in transition from authoritarian familism to democratic individualism; hence it contains a mixture of traditional and emergent values. The existence of diverse values is, however, not without its consequences, for many people who grow up in a period of transition may be thrown into confusion.[45]

Such confusion may manifest itself in different ways. With regard to the role of sex in dating behavior, in a period when social norms are changing and are no longer clearly defined the question of how involved one should become is no longer easily determined. With regard to marriage, since the basis for it has shifted from an economic arrangement to a relationship centering in satisfaction of personal needs, the characteristics that people seek in a mate have undergone change.[46] Young people today must decide for themselves such important issues as: What are the meaningful traits worth seeking in a mate? How may these traits be found? What assurance is there that these traits will not change? What is love? Will it last? Can I base a marriage on love?

At the level of family life, issues tend to center in the conflict between authoritarian-familistic values and democratic-individualistic values, not only between husband and wife but between parents and children as well. Important questions arise: What are the responsibilities and obligations of the father, mother, son, or daughter? Should a wife pursue a career? If she does pursue a career, what are her responsibilities in the home and in the community? What are the family values and goals and how shall these be determined and accomplished? [47]

[45] Robert F. Winch and Robert McGinnis, Eds., *Selected Studies in Marriage and the Family*, Holt, Rinehart and Winston, New York, 1953, pp. 18–23.

[46] Margaret Mead, "The Contemporary American Family as an Anthropologist Sees It," *Am. J. Sociol.*, 53 (May 1948), pp. 453–459.

[47] Clifford Kirkpatrick, "Inconsistency in Marriage Roles and Marriage Conflict," *Int. J. Ethics*, 46 (1936), pp. 444–460. See also Mirra Komarovsky, "Cultural Contradictions and Sex Roles," *Am. J. Sociol.*, 52 (1946), pp. 184–189.

The following conversations pointedly illustrate certain of these controversies:

A short time ago I heard a worthy lawyer remark that he disapproved of women in business and the professions. "If a woman is capable and ambitious," he said, "let her marry a good man, stick to him, and push him to success. Let her rear fine, upstanding children. A woman in business is not a woman at all. She's a half-baked man in petticoats."

This vehement statement did not go unchallenged. A mild social gathering was abruptly converted into a forum on feminism versus the home, on the nature of woman, and finally on the function of marriage. Discussion rapidly became animated to the point of violent argument. A young anthropologist maintained that he would have neither love nor respect for a woman who subordinated herself to him. He wanted a strong partner who could stand on her own feet. He wanted his wife to have her own career. Only through economic independence could she preserve her independence of spirit and avoid clinging about his neck like a millstone.

"Millstone indeed!" protested another man indignantly. "Young fellow, you don't know the first thing about marriage. You ought to be glad to look after your wife. That's the trouble with marriage these days. We blame the girls for kicking over the traces, but we ought to blame the men. Young men won't take responsibility for a family. They want to keep all their independence and they think a good wife is a millstone. Well, I say, call her an anchor instead of a millstone. Stop drifting and take care of a woman and children. You'll get more solid satisfaction out of the devotion of a fine little woman than from all the equality in the world. And you'll pay for it by bringing home the bacon yourself and being the kind of man she can trust and admire. You'll both be happy. A woman wants to be shielded and cared for, and a man who is a man wants to do the protecting."

"But we don't want to be taken care of," said a young woman. "We have brains of our own and education. I want to go on with my own life and be something myself. The masterful male was all very well so long as women didn't know how to do anything but housework. I want a love life and children as much as anyone, but I'm no hothouse flower. I know the kind of life my mother led, and I don't want one like it. My husband and I will be friends. We'll work out a life together, and it'll be *our* life, not his." [48]

Finally, the distribution of power within the family has been undergoing significant change. Such change not only produces struggles between family members, but introduces uncertainty in the entire pattern of relationships. Power in the home may be less a matter of tradition and

[48] John Levy and Ruth Monroe, *The Happy Family*, Knopf, New York, 1943, pp. 145–146.

more a function of such factors as intelligence, earnings, attractiveness, and importance of the issue.[49]

The problems and anxieties that are found in contemporary marriage and in man-woman relationships in general are well summarized by Ruth Cavan, who suggests that some of the "issues in the American family at mid-century" are as follows:

1. What is the basic meaning of marriage?
2. Should marriage be a permanent or a temporary relationship?
3. Should young people have a free hand in selecting a mate?
4. Should sex relations be limited to marriage?
5. Is it necessary for husband and wife to have complementary roles?
6. What constitutes an adequate number of children?
7. What is the family's function in personality development in children? [50]

Although the man-woman relationship in contemporary American society is undergoing a crisis, many people believe that there is promise of an integration at a new and more significant level than was possible before. This belief is based on increasing evidence that leads to hope that marriages will remain intact not only because of external social pressures, but because people will discover in them the satisfaction of their most basic needs.[51]

The problems involved in achieving such voluntary and personally meaningful relationships are indeed complex. This book has been written as an attempt to clarify and assess certain of these important problems, in the hope that its readers might come to understand more fully the man-woman relationship as it emerges, matures, and, under certain circumstances, deteriorates.

Summary

Although there were differences in marriage and family life throughout the colonies (New England, the middle colonies, the Southern colo-

[49] See Phyllis N. Hallenbeck, "An Analysis of Power Dynamics in Marriage," *J. Marr. Fam.*, **28,** 2 (May 1966), pp. 200–203; and Frances G. Scott, "Family Group Structure and Patterns of Social Interaction," *Am. J. Sociol.*, **68,** 2 (September 1962), pp. 214–228. See also Robert O. Blood, Jr., "Impact of Urbanization on American Family Structure and Functioning," *Sociol. soc. Res.*, **49,** 1 (October 1964), pp. 5–16.
[50] Ruth S. Cavan, *The American Family*, Crowell-Collier, New York, 1953, pp. 7–29.
[51] Ernest Burgess, *loc. cit.* See also Paul H. Landis, "The Changing Family, *Curr. Hist.*, **19** (September 1950), pp. 151–153.

nies, and the heterogeneous frontier areas), all colonies shared certain elements, which can thus be said to represent early American marriage and family life. The early American family was a self-sufficient, extremely cooperative, rural, and agricultural unit, which operated within a materialistic and practical setting. Its internal organization was largely based on two principles—familism and patriarchal authoritarianism. The consequences of authoritarian familism were: (1) the authoritarian had a strong psychological need to be right; (2) family control was based on irrational authority; (3) the family was an association of unequals; and (4) individual family members were treated as commodities.

However, a number of sociohistoric factors—secularism, humanism, democracy, the American frontier, the emancipation of women and associated competence, and the Civil War—created a milieu that brought about changes in the manner in which people regarded one another. These changes were felt within and outside the family and were accelerated markedly by industrialization and urbanization.

Once these changes and all that they implied were felt directly by the family, family organization began to change from one based primarily on authoritarian familism to one containing a greater degree of individualism and democracy. Individualism refers to the right of a person to be the active agent in selecting his own interests out of those that are available. Democracy in the family refers to the delegation of the power to rule to that person (or persons) who, in the opinion of a majority of family members, is the most competent to do so. The consequences of democratic individualism are: (1) family control is based on rational authority; (2) authority is associated with the desire to be right; (3) the family is an association of equals; and (4) family members are treated as ends in themselves and not merely as means to ends.

The contemporary American middle-class family is in transition between traditional and emergent values. Such transition has resulted in conflicting values regarding dating, courtship, and the goals of marriage.

Questions

1. Compare the various colonial areas, discussing their similarities and dissimilarities.
2. Explain the following statement: "The typical early American family was a self-sufficient and extremely cooperative unit, which operated within a

materialistic and practical setting." Compare the contemporary American family with the early family on each of these items.

3. Describe the organization of family relationships in the early family. List and describe the consequences of this type of organization.

4. How did the change from a rural to an urban society affect family life?

5. List and define each of the sociohistoric factors that influenced the family. Show how each was responsible for bringing about changes in family life.

6. Discuss the part that the early United States social milieu played in producing industrialization and urbanization: discuss the subsequent impact of industrialization and urbanization in accelerating the very value changes that helped to produce them.

7. Describe the consequences of democratic-individualistic family organization.

8. What are some of the issues facing the contemporary family? How, in your opinion, could some or all of these issues most effectively be resolved?

Suggestions for Research and Related Activities

1. Write and enact a scene in an authoritarian-familistic family and one portraying the same situation in a democratic-individualistic family. Have the class members list the behavioral differences in the two families and discuss the advantages and disadvantages of each family type.

2. Make case studies of several families that you know quite well. In what ways do you find these families to be authoritarian-familistic and in what ways do you find them to be democratic-individualistic? Do you find any instances in which the family members think that they are democratic-individualistic when actually, in your opinion, they are not? If so, explain why you think they are not.

3. List the expectations that one might have of an authoritarian-familistic type of marriage and those of a democratic-individualistic type of marriage. Submit this list to married men and women of different ages and have them check off their own expectations of marriage on the list. What expectations predominate? Are those expectations authoritarian-familistic or democratic-individualistic? Are or are not men more inclined than women to have had authoritarian-familistic expectations? Are or are not older people more inclined than younger people to have had authoritarian-familistic expectations? Explain each of your answers.

4. Hold a debate or a panel discussion on the merits and demerits of family living in the urban setting.

Suggested Readings

Bowman, Claude C., "The Family and the Nuclear Arms Race," *Social Prob.,* **11,** 1 (1963), pp. 30–34.

Calhoun, Arthur W., *A Social History of the American Family from Colonial Times to the Present,* Barnes and Noble, New York, 1945.

Goode, William J., *World Revolution and Family Patterns,* The Free Press, Glencoe, Ill., 1963, especially pp. 1–26.

Greenfield, Sidney M., "Industrialization and the Family in Sociological Theory," *Am. J. Sociol.,* **67,** 3 (1961), pp. 312–322.

Jaco, E. G., and Ivan Belknap, "Is a New Family Form Emerging in the Urban Fringe?" *Am. soc. Rev.,* **18** (October 1953), pp. 551–557.

Landis, Paul H., *Making the Most of Marriage,* 2nd ed., Appleton-Century-Crofts, New York, 1960, Ch. 6, "Female Roles in Transition," Ch. 7, "Male Roles in Transition," and Ch. 8, "Unsolved Problems in Role Behavior."

Lantz, Herman, Margaret Britton, Ray Schmitt, and Eloise Snyder, "Pre-Industrial Patterns in the Colonial Family," *Am. soc. Rev.,* **33** (1968), pp. 413–426.

Mace, David R., "Some Reflections on the American Family," *Marr. Fam. Living,* **24,** 2 (1962), pp. 109–112.

Ogburn, W. F., and M. F. Nimkoff, *Technology and the Changing Family,* Houghton Mifflin, Boston, 1955.

Peterson, James A., *Education for Marriage,* Scribner's, New York, 1964, Ch. 1, "Marriage in Transition."

Simpson, George, *People in Families,* Crowell-Collier, New York, 1960, Ch. 1, "Toward Analysis of Marriage and the Family in the United States."

Chapter Four

CONTEMPORARY FAMILY FUNCTIONS

IN THE preceding chapter we discussed the disappearance of several traditional family characteristics and the social changes that followed. We saw that the net effect was a change from authoritarian familism to democratic individualism, which resulted in a transformation of the group-centered family to a person-centered family. In this chapter we plan to analyze the family functions that have remained and to point out how the sociohistoric factors that produced the social changes of the past have also contributed directly to the person-centered orientation that characterizes contemporary middle-class family life.

The contemporary American middle-class family is primarily organized around three sets of functions: [1]

[1] Some writers also include the protective function. It will be mentioned here only briefly. The protective function has undergone marked change and has had numerous facets. At this time it refers to the provision for the economic and physical security of family members, including an adequate standard of living and protection against the ravages of illness. The protective function was basic to the maintenance of the traditional household in earlier times and consumed much time and energy. Changes in the role of government and its relation to the family have removed many of the protective functions from the home. Note particularly the development of programs of social security and pensions, programs for the blind and handicapped, programs of aid to dependent children, as well as police and fire protection. The economic problems caused by deficits in family funds and by value differences within a family are discussed later.

ILLUSTRATION: Seventeenth-century dolls. Copyright Foto-Commissie, Rijksmuseum, Amsterdam.

1. Procreative function
2. Socialization function
3. Affectional function

Although the family has always been concerned with these functions, their fulfillment in the past was related less to the needs of the individual than to those of the group. In a rural society in which the active efforts of all family members were required for survival, individual needs were less important. Today, however, it is clearly evident that among large sections of the middle class the family functions that remain are primarily oriented toward the needs and values of the individual.[2] This person-centered orientation will become increasingly self-evident as we proceed with our analysis. Two factors are primarily responsible for this new orientation.

The Significance of Mechanical and Technological Progress

The mechanical and technological progress that has taken place in our country has helped to reorient our thinking with respect to the needs of the individual in the fulfillment of family functions. It has enabled people to turn their attention to matters other than those of physical existence. For the greater part of our history, it must be remembered, the most formidable problem was that of staying alive. With primitive techniques and limited knowledge of agriculture, what energies the family had went into the maintenance of physical existence. The constant peril of destruction by animals and bandits helped matters little. Under the circumstances, concern for the individual did not, and could not, assume much importance.

The preoccupation with individual values emerged only when our society had evolved to a point where the energies of its people did not need to be completely consumed by physical labor or defense against destructive environmental forces. Only then did it become possible to deal with

---

[2] Some writers have made serious efforts to assess statistically the extent to which Americans are adequately fulfilling the contemporary family functions. See Jessie Bernard, *American Family Behavior*, Harper, New York, 1942.

problems of the individual, especially with the psychological and social conditions out of which he develops.[3]

The Significance of Secularism, Democracy, and Humanism

The person-centered orientation derives also from the introduction of new values, which changed man's social climate. In the preceding chapter we stressed the importance of secularism, democracy, and humanism, which influenced mental attitudes and were gradually incorporated into the thinking and actions of people. The significance of these values cannot be overestimated, since they provided the social climate within which new varieties of attitudes and human relationships could emerge. Their impact was widespread and significant in that they reoriented the individual's place in his relationships to external forces—whether the pressures of social groups or traditions. Thus the values that emanated from secularism, democracy, and humanism had much to do with creating a new conception of the role of man in his universe. Whereas before the introduction of these values man was passive in his cultural world (i.e., he felt impotent to change his status), after the advent of the social forces of secularism, democracy, and humanism man realized that he could become the active agent in his life and actively turned to an improvement of his position. Once man decided that he was not integrally bound by traditions or the pressures of social groups, he could reorient his values and behavior in ways that had not been possible under the old order. Man's realization that he could order his own life extended into patterns of family living and fulfillment of family functions.

Procreative Function

With regard to the procreative function (sometimes called the reproductive function), we note several indications of a concern with individ-

[3] Ray F. Hendrickson, "Technology: Its Advance and Implications," in *Technological Trends and National Policy*, National Resources Committee, Government Printing Office, Washington, D.C., 1937, p. 99.

ual needs and values of parents, as well as of children. For example, the size of the family formerly was determined by external factors, such as economic, social, and religious pressures, whereas today this situation is less prevalent. Indeed, in the middle class family size tends to be determined primarily by the parents' personal values, which include a smaller "ideal" family size than was traditionally found in America. Thus at the end of the eighteenth century the average American wife bore more than eight children. In the decade of the 1930s the average was less than two children per family. In fewer than one hundred and fifty years, then, reproduction in the United States decreased by more than 75 percent.[4] Table 6 shows the general decline in the birthrate.[5]

Table 6 Birthrate in the United States (Based on Estimated Total of Live Births per 1000 Population)[a]

Year	Birthrate[b]
1820	55.2
1840	51.8
1860	44.3
1880	39.8
1900	32.3
1920	27.7
1940	19.4
1950	24.1
1960	23.7
1961	23.3
1962	22.4
1963	21.7
1964	21.2

[a]Rates for 1820 to 1950 were abstracted from U.S. Bureau of the Census, *Historical Statistics of the United States—Colonial Times to 1957*, Washington, D.C., 1960, p. 23. Rates for 1950 to 1964 were abstracted from *Vital Statistics of the United States*, as reported in *Health, Education and Welfare Indicators*, Government Printing Office, Washington, D.C., April 1965, p. S-3.
[b]Lowest birthrate was 18.4, which occurred in 1933 and 1936.

[4] Robert McGinnis, "Patterns of Fertility in the United States," in Robert F. Winch and Robert McGinnis, Eds., *Selected Studies in Marriage and the Family*, Holt, New York, 1953, pp. 145–146. Inter-Agency Committee for the National Conference on Family Life, *The American Family: A Factual Background*, Government Printing Office, Washington, D.C., 1949, p. 39.
[5] For a discussion of the short-term increase in fertility that occurred in the forties and fifties and now seems to be disappearing, see Richard F. Tomasson, "Why Has American Fertility Been So High," in Bernard Farber, Ed., *Kinship and Family Organization*, Wiley, New York, 1966, pp. 327–338.

The decrease in the number of children in middle-class families is due to several factors. First, in the minds of many people large families have become associated with a lower socioeconomic status. Many middle-class families consciously refrain from having too many children in order to avoid any unfavorable stigma. Second, the decision to have smaller families reflects the personal values of middle-class parents regarding how they will spend their time. Rather than devote what seem to them to be their best years to rearing, say, six children, they decide to have fewer children, so as to have the time to pursue their own interests. Such an assertion of individual values would have been unheard-of in the traditional, rural society.

Third, the class consciousness and the concern for social mobility that characterizes the American middle class contribute to smaller family size. Middle-class people are conscious of a need to maintain their class position and feel impelled to improve it whenever possible. Upward mobility requires economic assets, however. One of the ways in which economic security can be achieved is by restricting family size.[6]

The personal values of the middle class are also reflected in familial innovations in the handling of pregnancies, as well as prenatal and postnatal care, which suggest concern for the welfare of mother and child. From the first sign of pregnancy until sometime following the birth, both mother and child are under constant medical care and supervision. All of this is facilitated by the excellent advances in medicine, but the fact that prospective middle-class mothers and fathers insist on such care is indicative of the change that has occurred.

Socialization Function

The person-centered orientation is once more in evidence in the socialization function. For the very concept itself refers to the learning process that enables the child to acquire the knowledge, values, and rules of conduct that his society expects of him. The well-socialized child is familiar with the expectations of the group and patterns his behavior accordingly. Thus behavior that is markedly deviant represents a failure in socialization at some point in the individual's life history. Although parents have always been concerned with the socialization function,

[6] Raymond J. Murphy, "Psychodynamic Factors Affecting Fertility in the United States," in Robert F. Winch and Robert McGinnis, Eds., *Selected Studies in Marriage and the Family, op. cit.,* pp. 156–170.

middle-class parents are especially sensitive to the need to fulfill this function effectively. They are, as a class, conscious of a need to do things well; hence they are greatly concerned that their children become well-socialized. This concern has resulted in marked emphasis on such problems as nursing, weaning, toilet training, teaching of sex, social values, and discipline; and it has been an important factor in the large amount of reading material now available dealing with socialization problems.[7] Such interest in problems of socialization appears not only in literature for parents but also in the research interests and professional journals of human behavior scientists. This stems from at least two important sources: a pure interest in the theory and nature of social learning, which has always been present, and a more recent development—a necessity for finding practical answers to the consequences of different socialization practices. The latter development is an outgrowth of pressures originating with the public.[8] For example, research has been designed and implemented within the last few years to test empirically the consequences of certain child-rearing practices.[9]

Interest in the problem of socialization has also become manifest in formal as well as informal discussion groups. For example, all of us have probably participated in planned or spontaneous discussions of the pros and cons of discipline or the teaching of sex. Often many of these discussions provoke lively, heated exchanges, suggesting how interested people have become in these issues.

Important among the organizations that hold planned discussions of socialization practices are Parent-Teacher Associations. These groups give parents and teachers the opportunity to conduct informative, challenging discussions, centering on the methods that are most conducive to the achievement of socialization. Similarly, there has been an increase in organized groups that are designed to improve the mental health of our citizens and to reduce juvenile delinquency, crime, and emotional instability.[10]

[7] W. A. Davis and R. J. Havighurst, *Father of the Man*, Houghton Mifflin, Boston, 1947. James C. Maloney, "The Cornelian Corner and Its Rationale," in M. J. E. Senn, Ed., *Problems of Early Infancy*, Josiah May Jr. Foundation, New York, 1947.
[8] Martha Ericson Dale, "Child-Rearing and Social Status," *Am. J. Sociol.*, 52 (1946), pp. 190–192. Robert R. Sears, "Ordinal Position in the Family as a Psychological Variable," *Am. soc. Rev.*, 15 (June 1950), pp. 397–401.
[9] Robert O. Blood, Jr., "A Situational Approach to the Study of Permissiveness in Child-Rearing," *Am. soc. Rev.*, 18 (February 1953), pp. 84–87.
[10] For example, the Judge Baker Foundation, Boston, Mass., and the Leo Potishman Foundation associated with Texas Christian University, Fort Worth, Texas, are devoted to the problems of juvenile delinquency and crime. The Auxiliary Council to the Association for the Advancement of Psychoanalysis, located in New York, was a lay group interested in educating the public about problems of emotional instability.

The Affectional Function

The affectional function may be regarded as one aspect of the total socialization process, just discussed, and, as such, it has been to some extent traditionally a part of the family's functions.[11] The emphasis that the affectional function receives in the contemporary American middle-class family, however, is so great, in comparison to that in the traditional rural family, that we have chosen to single it out for special attention by treating it as a separate function.

We discuss the affectional function theoretically in a later chapter; here we only introduce its general meaning, as it is understood by the middle class. The affectional function is the process whereby the parental concern for the development of the child is oriented toward the emergence of a personality characterized by positive feelings, which include love, emotional acceptance, and respect for oneself as well as for others. Such personal attributes enable the individual to relate to others in a meaningful way, for he possesses the capacity to accept others and to have feeling and appreciation for them as human beings. Although this capacity is a significant attribute in all human relationships, it is especially important in mate selection and marriage. Individuals who come from homes where the affectional function has been adequately fulfilled are perhaps more capable than most of establishing meaningful relationships in marriage. They are free to express love, to receive love, and to treat each other with dignity and respect.

It should be noted that the affectional function is of importance not only to individual human beings, but also to society as a whole, in that once achieved, it becomes a significant integrating force in producing greater family stability. Likewise, in marital and familial deterioration the quality of the feelings characterized by the affectional function may be regarded as having broken down, as the case of a young factory worker and his wife brings out clearly. This husband was referred for marital assistance by his pastor, with whom he had been discussing his marital difficulties. At the time he appeared for help, his wife had already initiated divorce proceedings and was awaiting the final decree. The man stated that his marriage had deteriorated; he admitted to nu-

[11] William F. Ogburn, "What Is Happening to the Family?," *J. Home Econ.*, 25 (October 1933), pp. 660–664.

merous arguments over an eight-month period and to slapping his wife on two occasions. The slapping occurred, according to him, whenever his wife had been "nagging him." This husband recognized that there was little possibility that his marriage could be rehabilitated, but he pleaded with the counselor to arrange to see his wife in order that some attempt at reconciliation be made.

The wife appeared within a few days and stated at the outset that she had come only because her husband had begged her to keep the appointment. She said that she was going through with the divorce and that her mind had been made up for some time. When asked about what considerations had gone into her decision, she stated that she no longer had any deep feeling for her husband. She found the relationship with him to be unsatisfactory. Her husband had little to do with her and would not consult her or convey his concerns or feelings; instead he kept to himself and had a marked tendency to brood. She had attempted to get close to her husband but was never successful. Furthermore, his behavior made her feel repeatedly rejected and left out of his life. She was hurt and no longer wished to try to rebuild the relationship. The slappings were, in themselves, not important, she said, but they symbolized rejection for her.

We have not dealt with all the complications in this relationship, but even the general outline of the case indicates clearly the deterioration of the affectional component of this marriage. The wife's reaction is typical of the reactions frequently encountered by the marriage counselor. Note that her complaints are not about money or sex; instead, the kinds of personal feelings, warmth, and satisfactions that she had expected were not present. In our terms, the affectional function had broken down.

Impersonality and the Affectional Function

The great emphasis placed on the affectional function today is closely related to the impersonal nature of modern life. Although impersonality was undoubtedly present in rural America, the modern large-scaie urban community symbolizes the epitome of impersonality.[12] Many of the traditional family ties have been broken. Moreover, contemporary urban life is characterized by secondary relationships, with interest in the human relationship centered on what one can market or purchase— perhaps a skill, a talent, or even a favor. Hence the individual has come to view himself and others in terms of what he and they have to offer.

[12] Paul H. Landis, "The Changing Family," *Curr. Hist.,* **19** (September 1950), pp. 151–153.

Interest in the other person as a human being, his feelings, his likes, or his tastes, becomes relatively unimportant.[13]

Out of these impersonal associations a sense of isolation emerges. Such a feeling of isolation becomes manifest in a search for human relationships that promise personal acceptance and concern, and many people throughout our society recognize this need. People have come to recognize that the family may be the most effective social unit in dealing with the problem of impersonality. At the level of child rearing we have already suggested how the adequate fulfillment of the affectional function may enable the individual to deal with the impersonal world. Moreover, many enter the marital relationship with the hope that compensations for the feeling of impersonality will emerge in the form of love and acceptance at home. Thus husband and wife when they greet each other in the evening look forward to a more meaningful relationship than the impersonality experienced outside the home. When such compensations are not present, they become dissatisfied with their marriage. Feelings of dissatisfaction become especially pronounced when husband and wife discover that within their marital relationship there are the very impersonal qualities they had hoped to avoid. One of our major tasks in subsequent chapters will be to examine impersonal qualities in the man-woman relationship, to indicate how they may disturb the marital relationship and to suggest how these might be dealt with.

An interesting and important study by Miller and Swanson bears on this problem.[14] These sociologists were concerned with the *middle-class way of life*, the involvement of middle-class people in particular occupational roles, and the way in which both sets of influence effect how their children are reared. Miller and Swanson defined two types of middle-class family settings—the individuated-entrepreneurial and the welfare-bureaucratic setting. The first is based on a view of urban life as being impersonal, segmented, superficial, and competitive, with the individual isolated and lonely. When these experiences are linked with an occupation that involves risk taking, is subject to fluctuation in the market, and is dependent on personal judgment and manipulative skill for success, the individuated entrepreneur emerges. The authors think that this type of behavior characterized older middle-class persons who put a premium on self-control, rational behavior, denial of present gratification for future gain, and active manipulation. Thus they predict that in

---

[13] Erich Fromm, *Man for Himself*, Holt, Rinehart and Winston, New York, 1947, Ch. 2; Louis Wirth, "Urbanism as a Way of Life," *Am. J. Sociol.*, 44 (July 1938), pp. 10–18.

[14] Daniel R. Miller and Guy E. Swanson, *The Changing American Parent*, Wiley, New York, 1958.

the entrepreneurial home mothers would emphasize development of internal control through *earlier bowel training, scheduled feeding, not immediately tending to a crying baby, and use of symbolic, rather than physical, punishment.*

The concept of welfare bureaucracy is based on emerging patterns in large-scale organizations which, the authors believe, are modifying the older pattern in which the individuated-entrepreneurial family emerged. Bureaucracy means a high degree of specialization and supervision governed by a coded set of rules, and welfare implies that the organization offers security to its members. The authors see the values of persons in a bureaucracy as stemming from the special demands made on the personnel of such organizations. These demands include rewards for the steady faithful performance of duty, without rewards for the exercise of imagination or initiative. Excessive drive and competition are discouraged. Employees must not be too aggressive or ambitious. In such an organization people find one another's company rewarding and lacking in threat. To fit into this world children should be warm, friendly, and supportive of others. Miller and Swanson see all of American society moving toward the bureaucratic-welfare setting, with the family becoming a means of supplying the economic system with the kinds of personalities it needs to operate. They predict that bureaucratic mothers would be more permissive of *thumb-sucking and sexual exploration, with less emphasis on independence and on male and female differences.* The sample consisted of white middle-class mothers; a total of 99 entrepreneurial mothers and 86 bureaucratic mothers were actually compared. The authors report that the predictions anticipated for each type of family were generally borne out.

This study is significant because it testifies to the relationship between modern urban life and ocupational role requirements and to the impact of both on child-rearing practices. Each type of family attempts in its own way to prepare the child to deal with and adapt to modern urban society.

The Changing Role of the Family
in Fulfilling Functions

Although the major change in the manner in which the family functions are fulfilled among middle-class United States families has been that from a group-centered family to a person-centered family, other changes have also occurred. One change has to do with the enlarging role of nonfamily agencies in the fulfillment of family functions.

As noted earlier, the subject of socializing the child is frequently a discussion topic by PTA and other groups. Although such discussions reflect an interest in discovering the best means of socializing the child, they also indicate that a great deal of responsibility is increasingly being shared with agencies outside the family; schools are quite concerned about ways of best socializing the child in order that he relate effectively to others.

The school's growing concern for broad socialization is seen in the increasing number of years that are now devoted to a child's formal education (beginning in many instances around age two). In addition, the entire field of adult education is preoccupied with ways of enriching the adult's life after given levels of education have been achieved. In regard to the latter, it is common in today's educational system for both the secondary and college-university levels to have Divisions of Adult Education and Sections of Continuing Education for Women. Finally, an array of courses designed to deal with personal-social problems of living are now found in the school curriculum. This means that a significant part of a high school or college budget may now be devoted to supporting counselors, psychologists, and advisers, who share responsibilities with "schoolteachers" for the "total" education of children at the lower levels and of adults at higher levels.

This ever-increasing responsibility for broad socialization that is being given to the school structure indicates that in modern urban society, where values are diverse, the family needs the assistance of outside agencies in educating and socializing its youth in order that they move toward maturity and the fulfillment of their potential.[15] It means also that with an increased appreciation and awareness of the complexity involved in socialization, the body of literature in these areas has grown and the number of specialists in schools has increased; social workers and psychologists seek to understand truancy, behavioral disorders, and poor school performance.

Needless to say, the use that a family may make of outside socialization

[15] For a discussion of the upgrading and increasing flexibility afforded family organization through the use of such agencies, see Reuben Hill, "The American Family of the Future," *J. Marr. Fam.*, **26,** 1 (February 1964), pp. 20–28. For a discussion of how parent-education can play a part in developing more fully the human potential, see Catherine S. Chilman, "The Crisis and Challenge of Low-Income Families in the 1960's: Implications for Parent Education," *J. Marr. Fam.*, **26,** 1 (February 1964), pp. 39–43.

agencies frequently results in opportunities for family members to pursue some of their own interests, a view consistent with the person-
centered philosophy,[16] but this may be a by-product and perhaps not the
essential reason for the use of these agencies.

Dorothy Blitsten has suggested that since parents in this country place
much emphasis on individualism and self-fulfillment, the use of agencies
outside the family in order to fulfill the basic family functions may increase.[17] Indeed, unlike some scholars who view the United States family
as representing a case of rather extreme use of outside agencies in fulfilling its functions, she suggests that the United States actually lags behind
some other countries in this regard. She notes certain Scandinavian
countries where a much greater reliance is placed on outside agencies (in
these cases a number of agencies supported by socialistic governments),
which free family members from many concerns (financial and other)
and enable them to play more individualistic family roles.

The Kibbutz

Probably one of the most extreme illustrations of an effort to turn
over the socialization function to an outside agency is found in the kibbutzim in Israel.[18]

The Kibbutzim (the singular of this term is kibbutz) are communities
located in various parts of Israel. They vary in size from 40 or 50 members in newly settled communities to more than 1000 in the more established ones. They were first founded as experimental communities,
based upon collective ownership; second and later in time, they served as
communities where many of the displaced Jews of Europe found new
homes; and lastly, these communities frequently were used as a first line
of military defense for Israel.

The separation of the family from the major socialization process of
the child was due largely to the belief that parental separation from child-
rearing functions would free parental energies for work in the kibbutz.
Thus, while children from birth lived apart from their parents, the par-

[16] Phillip Fellin, "A Reappraisal of Changes in American Family Patterns," *Social
Casework*, 45, 5 (May 1964), pp. 263–267.
[17] Dorothy R. Blitsten, *The World of the Family*, Random House, New York, 1963,
pp. 169–189.
[18] Melford E. Spiro, *Kibbutz: Venture in Utopia*, Schocken Books, New York, 1963.

ents, both mother and father, were to work fully for the development of the kibbutz.[19]

In spite of the fact that the physical maintenance, rearing, and socialization of children was the collective responsibility of the kibbutz and children lived in their own children's houses—beginning with the infant's house, then a toddler's house, and then a number of children's houses with occupancy determined by age—the children nevertheless were encouraged to visit their parents.[20] From the studies that have been made of the kibbutzim parent-child relationship, it appears that although their relationships were friendly and outgoing, they were usually not on an extremely warm and intimate basis. In many cases kibbutzim parents were referred to by their proper names, and the terms "son" and "daughter" were usually extended to all children of the kibbutz. It should be noted that the kibbutzim system has undergone many changes in the past several years. For example, there has been a major decrease in the number of kibbutzim that are in operation today. Furthermore, we are told that even in the remaining kibbutzim there has been a very gradual reemergence of kinship ties and a somewhat greater concern for the socialization of the child on the part of the family itself. The extent to which these changes resulted from dissatisfaction with the total kibbutzim system on the part of those outside the kibbutzim or from a dissatisfaction with the total kibbutzim on the part of kibbutz residents is not quite clear. Nevertheless, these communities do deserve special attention. They afford us an opportunity to understand the extent to which nontraditional means of child rearing may be successfully employed.[21]

Summary

Many of the functions originally fulfilled by the family are now largely performed by agencies outside the home. Three important sets of functions still remain, however: (1) procreation, which refers to the

[19] For a discussion of how Russia freed mothers from their child-rearing duties by establishing government child care centers, see David Mace, "The Employed Mother in the USSR," *Marr. Fam. Living*, **23**, 4 (November 1961), pp. 330–333.
[20] Melford E. Spiro, *Children of the Kibbutz*, Schocken Books, New York, 1965.
[21] Bruno Bettleheim, "Does Communal Education Work?" *Commentary*, **33**, 2 (February 1962), pp. 117–125. See also Yonina Talmon-Garber, "Social Change and Family Structure," *Int. soc. Sci. J.*, **14**, 2 (1962), pp. 468–487.

bearing of children; (2) socialization, which is the process by which the child is taught acceptable modes of behavior, thereby enabling him to become integrated into his society; and (3) the affectional function, which is the process that facilitates socialization by teaching the child to interact with others within a framework of love, warmth, and acceptance. The affectional function becomes manifest in feelings of dignity and respect toward self and others.

Although these functions were, in part, present in the family of the past, the manner in which they are fulfilled has undergone considerable change. For example, the family of the past had little time to devote to the individual needs of its members. Thus, although large families may have been rooted partly in religious values, the existence of a large number of children made it easier to fulfill the family's economic function. The socialization and affectional functions, too, were primarily directed toward fulfilling the needs of the family as a whole, with little regard for the individual's interests.

Today, however, under the influences of mechanical and technological innovations and the new values engendered by such ideologies as secularism, democracy, and humanism, it has become possible for parents to concern themselves more directly with the needs of the individual in fulfilling the three traditional functions. The restriction of the birthrate, which is reflected in the increasing value placed on the small family, is believed by many to be more conducive to the personal and social development of the individual than was the large family of yesterday. Both the socialization and affectional functions, in addition to training the individual to interact meaningfully with others, now largely center in a concern for the growth of the individual.

The concern for individual growth is so important that the family makes increasing use of outside agencies to achieve its goal. One type of community, the kibbutz of Israel, which stresses socialization outside the family context, deserves special attention as an example of a nontraditional means of socialization.

Questions

1. In what ways did secularism, democracy, and humanism affect the fulfillment of family functions?
2. In what ways did mechanical and technological progress further change the fulfillment of family functions?

3. What is the procreation function? List and discuss the factors that are largely responsible for the decreasing size of the contemporary family.

4. What is the socialization function? In what way does the manner in which this function is fulfilled today differ from the manner in which it was fulfilled in the past?

5. What is the affectional function? Illustrate how the example of the young factory worker and his wife represents a breakdown in the affectional function.

6. In what way is the impersonality of modern society related to the importance ascribed to the affectional function?

7. Explain what is meant by the following statement: "In the past the family consisted of family-centered persons, while today it is largely person-centered."

8. Agree or disagree with the following statement and explain your choice: "The person-centered characteristic of the contemporary family is indicative of a lack of concern for family stability."

9. Discuss the increasing role played by agencies outside the family in assisting in the fulfillment of family functions. Do you feel that these agencies strengthen or weaken the United States family? Explain your reasons for feeling as you do.

10. Discuss the kibbutz as a system of socialization. Do you think that socialization in the United States is moving toward or away from such a system? Support your answer with facts.

Suggestions for Research and Related Projects

1. Ask several men and women of various age groupings the following questions and in each case have them explain their answers:
   a. In what ways is the small family superior to the large family?
   b. In what ways is the large family superior to the small family?
   c. Does the family today rely too much on outside agencies in the socialization of the child?
   d. Should the family rely more on outside agencies in socializing the child? If so, on what agencies should the family rely?
   e. In what areas are children today given too much freedom in making their own decisions?

f. In what areas should children today be given more freedom in making their own decisions?

Tabulate your results. Do you find any differences between the opinions of men and women, or between the opinions of persons of different age groupings? If so, how do you explain these differences?

2. Make a list of the changing trends in the functions of the American family. Interview several members of your class to determine which of these trends they regard as being beneficial to marriage and family living and which they regard as detrimental and why. What are your results? Have several of the students submit your results to their parents in order to determine whether or not they agree with the results and what basis they offer for doing so.

3. It is generally agreed that through modern homemaking devices and reliance on outside agencies the contemporary homemaker is freed from much time previously spent in performing homemaking duties. Interview several married women to find out (1) whether or not they are aware of having more free time than their mothers and grandmothers and (2) how they spend their free time. Describe your results, showing whether or not women are aware of having more free time, how they spend their free time, and explain whether or not, in your opinion, the time could be spent more effectively than it is.

Suggested Readings

Anshen, Ruth Nanda, Ed., *The Family: Its Function and Destiny,* rev. ed., Harper, New York, 1959.

Blitsten, Dorothy R., *The World of the Family,* Random House, New York, 1963, especially Ch. 8.

Burgess, Ernest W., Harvey J. Locke and Mary M. Thomes, *The Family,* 3rd ed., American Book Company, New York, 1963, Ch. 16, "The Family in Transition," especially pp. 348–354.

Cohen, Nathan E., and Maurice Connery, "Government Policy and the Family," *J. Marr. Fam.,* **29** (February 1967), pp. 6–17.

Kenkel, William F., *The Family in Perspective,* Appleton-Century-Crofts, New York, 1960, Ch. 9, "The Family as an Institution," Ch. 10, "The Childbearing Function of the Family," and Ch. 11, "The Function of Socialization."

Parsons, Talcott, et al., *Family, Socialization and Interaction Process,* The Free

Press, Glencoe, Ill., 1955, Ch. 1, "The American Family: Its Relations to Personality and to the Social Structure," especially pp. 16–22.

Spiro, Melford E., *Kibbutz: Venture in Utopia,* Schocken Books, New York, 1963.

Spiro, Melford E., *Children of the Kibbutz,* Schocken Books, New York, 1965.

Winch, Robert F., *The Modern Family,* Holt, Rinehart and Winston, New York, 1952, Part 2, "The Family and Its Functions."

Chapter Five

MOTIVATIONS
FOR MARRIAGE

IN THE preceding chapter we discussed the kind of marital relationship that middle-class Americans desire; now we shift our attention to some of the factors that inhibit its realization. The fact that middle-class Americans search for a meaningful interpersonal relationship in marriage should not obscure the fact that they often possess personality patterns and motivations that impose obstacles to the achievement of their marital goals.

To begin with, people are torn by contradictions and often seek contradictory behavior in themselves and in others. For example, they espouse high ethical standards regarding the treatment of their fellowmen, but value material success so highly that they do not mind manipulating others in order to achieve it. Or they purport to believe in democratic values, but tend toward authoritarian and dictatorial values in relations with others. The existence of diametrically opposed expectations is certainly not new; it has been recognized and given wide attention in the human behavioral sciences for some time. Nevertheless, such contradictory values create confusion about what one wants in himself and in others.[1]

When we turn our attention to specific values that dominate our thinking, we discover that these are often the very things that make a meaningful relationship difficult to achieve. Indeed, it should be clear

[1] Read Bain, "Our Schizoid Culture," *Sociol. soc. Res.,* **19** (January-February 1935), pp. 266–276; Karen Horney, *The Neurotic Personality of Our Time,* Norton, New York, 1937.

ILLUSTRATION: A room from a Queen Anne Doll House. Courtesy of the Victoria & Albert Museum, Crown copyright.

that the impersonality of life in our society, pointed out in the preceding chapter, imposes serious limitations on the person's ability to appreciate warm and meaningful human associations. Such a way of life inculcates the value of using others as commodities and helps to create a pattern of casual and superficial concern for others, which is poor preparation for the heavy emotional commitments that modern marriage requires of a person. To be sure, many people enter marriage with the hope that in this relationship they may discover compensations for the empty, impersonal associations of their daily lives. Unfortunately, however, they frequently discover within their marriage the very same qualities of impersonality they wished to avoid. Although frustrating to the person, such a development is understandable to the human behavioral scientist, for the marital partners have been nurtured in a society with impersonal values. Thus, in spite of a desire to find a meaningful relationship, a husband and wife reared in an impersonal milieu tend to carry into their home the values that govern their lives on the outside.

Furthermore, our society is also conducive to the development of personal immaturities; in fact, it is certainly no easy task to grow up in our social order without acquiring many of these immaturities. We do not wish to deal with the very complex subject of the conditions that produce immaturity. Nevertheless, we can point out that any situation that fosters in the person a lack of confidence in himself, hence a fear of dealing with others or of assuming life's responsibilities, fosters personal immaturity. In our society there are many such situations.[2] Few parents have sufficient integration to give the child a clear, realistic set of values by which to live. Instead, most parents are confused not only about what they might expect from their children, but also about what to expect from each other in their roles as husbands or wives. This kind of familial situation does not engender in the person a sense of self-confidence, but generates patterns of overprotection or rejection, which in turn serve only to entrench immaturities and avoidance of life's responsibilities.

Immaturities are seldom confined to one segment of personality, however; instead, they find expression in the entire system of motivations for behavior. With respect to marriage, it is important to recognize that immature people possess motivations that are not only faulty in terms of fulfilling the affectional function, but which also lead to additional difficulties and impose unnecessary burdens on the stability of the marital relationship. If a person marries to escape responsibilities in the parental home, he will be frustrated in the realization of the even greater responsibilities in marriage. A person's motivations for marriage are im-

[2] Harold T. Christensen, "Why All These Young Marriages," *Nat. Parent-Teacher*, **52**, 8 (April 1958), pp. 4–6.

portant determinants of his expectations from marriage and of the kind of relationship that follows. Moreover, an understanding of why people marry enables us to understand why some relationships are better than others and why some people are happier in their marriages than are others. The value of such an understanding is brought out in the conversation one of the writers had with a young coed. In discussing this young woman's interest in marriage, she was asked, "Why do you wish to marry?"

Coed: "Well, why does anyone want to marry?"
Teacher: "Let's forget about others, why do you want to marry?"
Coed: "I want to marry—because I want to marry. Why do you think I should want to marry?"
Teacher: "I don't know, that's why I raised the question."

The young woman evidently had little insight into why she wanted to marry. Such insight, exceedingly helpful in any instance, was crucial in this case, since the young lady's motivations for marriage were directly related to some of her courtship difficulties.

This coed grew up in a home where little had been expected of her. She was markedly indifferent to making decisions or assuming responsibilities. Although the idea of marriage appealed to her, she was searching for a man with whom she might continue a dependent relationship. Her conception of a husband was a man who would take over her life and solve her problems, so that she would not have to worry about them. The boy with whom this young woman had become involved grew up with an entirely different concept of a wife and her responsibilities. He expected his wife to be more reliant and assertive than this girl's actions indicated. When the coed discovered her boyfriend would not assume her responsibilities and in fact expected her to change, she became hostile and would torment him.

One of the important motivations for marriage that this young woman had should be apparent; she was looking for a man to assume responsibility for her life. She had outgrown her parents and needed a husband to carry on as her parents had. Thus a pattern for future marital difficulty was already present in courtship. Whether these immaturities could be resolved depended to a great extent on whether this young coed was willing to examine them, their relationship to her motivation for marriage, and her resultant interpersonal problems with others.

Motivations that Disturb the Marital Union

Having outlined briefly some obstacles to the efforts of the middle-class person to build a meaningful relationship in marriage, we now discuss them in more detail. Out of many possible cases we have selected those that illustrate personal immaturities and motivations for marriage commonly found in our society. In each instance we attempt to show how the combination of personal immaturity and the specific motivation for marriage leads to marital difficulties. In some examples, the problem is a marked egocentricity; in others it is a lack of basic interest in the marriage partner; in still others it is an inability to relate to or share with another person. We have, of course, simplified our discussion, so as not to complicate our attempt to illustrate the relationship between personal immaturities and motivations for marriage. People frequently behave in contradictory ways and, moreover, only rarely do they act as they do because of a single motivation. This does not mean that it is impossible to recognize the cases in which motivations for marriage are primarily immature and those in which they are primarily mature. It does mean, however, that the distinction between maturity and immaturity is one of degree rather than of kind. Hence in the cases presented here we are concerned only with the primary motivation that these people had for marrying and are dealing thus with categories of cases rather than with complete case histories.

Escape from an Unhappy Home

Consider the type of individual who complains about being unhappy at home. He does not get along well with his parents or siblings; he may feel that he is treated unfairly, perhaps misunderstood. Sometimes the complaints may be justified, but more often than not they are expressions of the person's inability (of which he is unaware) to get along with others. This type of person looks for a relationship that would remove him from his unhappiness. His predominant motivation for marriage is to escape.

The example of a young female, age nineteen, is a case in point. The girl came to the attention of a counseling center through her mother, who was concerned with the daughter's tendency to become seriously involved with boys after a short period of acquaintance. Usually these involvements were accompanied by expressions of serious intentions, love letters, and marriage commitments. The pattern of involvement appeared to be with boys who were emotionally immature. When the girl first came to the counseling center, she was two months pregnant out of wedlock. Although the boy had previously stated he would marry her, he had recently changed his mind, and her mother was quite distraught and anxious. The girl's reaction was difficult to assess, although she appeared uncomfortable.

In analyzing the family background of the case, some important features emerged. The young woman had grown up in a home with a possessive mother. The father had died when she was a child. Relationships with her mother were never satisfactory, and the girl had followed a pattern of rebelling against the mother's constant interference in her life. Whenever the young woman developed an interest in a boy, her mother exerted all her influence to break up the relationship. In some instances the mother would demand that the boy stop seeing her daughter; in others, she would move her daughter to another community in order to terminate the involvement. Over the years this tug of war continued, with the daughter developing more and more resentment and hostility. After several sessions with the counselor, it became apparent that the young woman had no healthy interest in the father of her child-to-be. She had allowed herself to become pregnant, thinking that the boy would marry her. Thus she viewed the boy as one who might enable her to escape from a parental relationship that she did not like.

In analyzing the case of this girl, we recognize that the pregnancy is incidental to the case. Most persons who marry to escape a family background are less drastic in their actions. Nevertheless, there are many factors in the personality of this young woman that must be worked through before she can become an adequate partner in marriage. To begin with, although we can sympathize with this girl's need to get away from her mother, her methods are reckless to herself and to others. She has no real interest in the boy, since he is merely the means for getting her out of something unpleasant. This young woman is essentially self-centered, concerned with her own needs regardless of their consequences for others. She is therefore not given to sharing with others or to understanding their wishes or needs. Furthermore, there is no assurance that the pattern of rebellion that characterizes this girl would diminish in marriage. Instead, it is likely that rebellion would carry over to marital responsibilities, thus threatening the stability of the marital relationship. All of these factors suggest that the young woman would have considerable difficulty becoming part of a meaningful and stable marital union.

Escape from Feelings of Loneliness

A second type of person who frequently encounters difficulty in marriage is the person who marries to escape from intense feelings of loneliness. Often these are people who have complex personality problems and who hope that in some way life will become more comfortable if they marry. They believe that a change in the environment will make life more enjoyable and meaningful. Unfortunately, such people usually discover that marriage is not a solution for inner problems. In the following case we learn of a male who marries primarily out of a sense of desperation to avoid loneliness.

The man, one of three brothers, had been supporting and caring for his mother for fifteen years. Since he was moderately successful in business, he was able to build an attractive home in which he and his mother lived. The brothers informed both the mother and their brother that the relationship was not a good one for either, but especially for their brother, who should marry and raise a family. This man, however, expressed no dissatisfaction with the relationship, claiming that it was his duty as a son to care for his mother. Within a six-month period the mother became ill and died. After the mother's death, the son went through a period of marked anxiety and intense feelings of loneliness. He was quite hostile, as though fate had deliberately robbed him of his relationship with his mother. Soon he reached a point of desperation, and it was then that he frantically began his search for female companionship. Within a year after his mother's death, he was married.

The case of this man raises several interesting points. He is a dependent type of individual, and it is common for such people to become dependent on and cling desperately to their friends. Frequently they try to be of great service to others, from which they derive a sense of meaning and purpose to their lives. Although such dedication to others appears, on the surface, to be a fine attribute, it has its negative aspects, in that these people make claims on their relationships. That is, they come to believe that, since they are of service to others, others must not leave them or lead lives of their own. When such a relationship is terminated, the dependent individual often becomes quite disturbed, and the adjustment is tenuous. For this man, if anything happens to his wife or if she becomes separated from him, he is thrown back on his own minimal resources. Thus he is always on the verge of insecurity and loneliness.

Also, the wife would certainly have problems in such a marriage. Her husband might expect her to include him in all her plans and might become so possessive that she would have little freedom, which she might well resent.

Marriage for the Purpose of Living through Others

A third category of persons who may encounter difficulty in marriage are those who feel hopeless about finding meaning in life through their own potentialities and abilities. For them marriage means the opportunity to live through the accomplishments of the marital partner. Often these people settle for less in a marital partner than they could obtain. It is not uncommon to find gifted, talented, and attractive people who have such strong inferiority feelings that they are fearful of any form of self-assertion. Such a pattern is perhaps more prevalent with women than with men, since many women have grown up in environments that looked down on the efforts of women to realize themselves. They come to regard themselves as being less worthy than they really are and as a result are frequently torn by inner conflicts.

The nature as well as the dangers of relationships that are based on the need to live through others are exemplified in the case of a young piano teacher, female, age twenty-one. This young woman was considered attractive and had a very pleasant personality. When she came for counseling, she was quite disturbed, having recently been jilted in what she thought was a serious love affair. Although some distress after such an experience is to be expected, the general quality of this girl's reaction was unusually intense, and the counselor began to suspect some hidden causes.

The young teacher, it was found, had grown up in a home with aloof parents. The father was said to be domineering and opinionated, with a marked preference for male children. The mother appeared to be an ineffectual person, quite subservient to the father. The daughter had learned to relate to her father by giving in to all his wishes, by behaving in a subservient manner, and by repressing her own interests and identifying with his. She employed the same pattern in relationships with males outside her home. But the boy with whom she had recently been involved was uninterested in a compliant woman who seemed unable to handle her affairs properly. Consequently he dissolved the relationship. After several counseling sessions, the young woman realized that her distress about the broken love affair resulted less from having been jilted than from the realization that her lifelong pattern of relating to men in a subservient way, including various forms of self-berating of her physical appearance and intelligence, had failed. A pattern that had formerly brought her a sense of security no longer functioned, and she was utterly confused and panic-ridden as a result. Although traumatic for the moment, the disturbing events of her broken relationship became a motivating factor for change. She reorganized her thinking and feeling, and over an extended period of time she began to examine the possibility of establishing a relationship with a man on a new and healthier, as well as more realistic, basis. Needless to say, such a change involved the acceptance of herself as a person with her own set of interests, feelings, wishes, and hopes. Instead of perpetually trying to relate to men by hiding her identity, she began to realize that her identity, when brought out into the open, would become a basis for the relationship she hoped to build.

This is an interesting case, since it not only identifies the factors that would have prevented the girl from becoming an adequate marital partner, but also shows how through guidance she was able to reorient her behavior and work toward a healthy relationship with a man. Another aspect of this case that bears note has to do with the conditions that produced change—it was only after being jilted that the girl began to realize her plight. We do not recommend traumatic shock as a prerequisite for change; nevertheless, we recognize that a sense of discomfort is often a requirement for change.

Marriage for Material Possessions and Wealth

A fourth category of persons who marry for reasons that lead to difficulty are those who marry to obtain possessions and wealth. The layman tends to see these people in relatively simple terms—they are "money-mad" or they are ruthlessly ambitious, willing to do anything to get ahead. Actually, their motivations may be quite complex. Many of those who marry for material wealth and possessions do so because they have despaired of finding a good love relationship. Some are cynical and do not believe that good relationships exist. Others possess such self-doubt that they question whether anybody can love them. Whatever the cause, once they decide that love is not really to be found, they compensate by settling for material things. As one person put it, "I can't have love, but I may find wealth."

The case of a salesman, age twenty-five, illustrates many of the points we have just discussed. This man grew up in an emotionally and economically impoverished family—warmth among family members was infrequent, and his parents had to struggle desperately to provide for the family. At an early age the salesman decided that meaningful human relations were not to be had, and his goal in life became to accumulate as much money as he could as rapidly as possible through whatever means were necessary. A financially profitable marriage was part of his plan, and he began implementing it by circulating in the best places in his community where eligible girls from wealthy families would be present. Before becoming seriously involved, he would check informally into the prospective father-in-law's financial position in order to calculate the size of the wedding gift, as well as of any future inheritance.

One day this man met a young lady who seemed to meet all of his financial requirements. He went through the usual procedure of checking her family's finances. What he failed to realize at the time was that the girl's father, who had been disbarred as a lawyer for illegal practice, was aware of what was taking place. Thus the father saw to it that the young man would receive favorable financial reports. The salesman worked according to plan and when he was satisfied with what he had heard, he made a proposal of marriage. The wedding date was set and plans already made when he discovered that he had been duped by his prospective father-in-law and that the girl's family had no wealth. He promptly wired the girl that he would not marry her and asked that the diamond ring that he had given her be returned.

Although this experience undoubtedly was very traumatic to the young woman, it was probably fortunate for her that the marriage did not take place, because it is doubtful that this man was equipped to build a meaningful marital relationship or even interested in doing so. Being ruthlessly ambitious, he would hardly be concerned with the needs of others. He had demonstrated that he was self-centered, concerned with his own needs, and unable to relate in a way involving mutuality. People who deny that love is possible often find it necessary to avoid committing themselves emotionally to a relationship; in fact, they have to actively discourage a potentially meaningful relationship from developing.

Although others might not be so calculating as this particular man, it would be foolish to assume that his case is unique. For, indeed, marriage for wealth, both disguised or undisguised, is common in our culture.

Marriage on the Rebound

A fifth category of persons who may encounter difficulty in marriage are those who marry "on the rebound." These are people who have had an unsatisfactory love relationship, perhaps one in which they were jilted. They are frequently subject to feelings of unworthiness. After a relationship disintegrates, self-attacks of unworthiness become quite intense and motivate the person to prove himself. Frequently such people proceed hastily to find a marital partner.

As an illustration, let us consider the case of a nurse, female, age twenty-three, who had been engaged to a serviceman for about a year. Shortly thereafter, letters from her fiance became less frequent and less personal. Eventually, the fiancé wrote her that he had met another girl and thought it best that the engagement be terminated. The nurse was upset and quite anxious for several weeks. She consciously looked for another male and felt desperately driven to prove to her friends that she could get married. Finally, she met a young accountant, who also had serious personal difficulties, never having emancipated himself from his mother. He was, at the time of marriage, still dependent on his mother even for simple decisions. He had never been allowed to mature or to assume adult responsibilities. It was also quite apparent that the young accountant's mother planned to take an active part in managing the affairs of any marriage that her son would undertake. The nurse did not consider these problems to be serious, believing that they could be easily overcome. Two months after her initial meeting with the accountant she received a proposal of marriage from him. She accepted and they were married shortly thereafter.

This case shows how the sense of urgency about saving face drives a girl into a marriage fraught with difficulty. Being desperate, she fails to examine her relationship. Hence she marries a person who has pronounced personal difficulties and who does not possess, at the time of marriage, the basic qualities necessary to become a partner in a relationship with emotional commitments. We also note that, with a personality that includes a considerable amount of self-hate, this girl's need is for a warm, accepting male who could help her establish some sense of security in herself. In the relationship that she chose such assistance from her husband is unlikely. Instead she can only look forward to an immature relationship with him and to conflicts with her mother-in-law due to interference.

Marriage to Escape Being Unmarried

A sixth category of persons who marry for reasons that may lead to difficulty are those who marry because all of their friends are getting married. These people fear that being unmarried may cause them to lose status in the eyes of others.[3] Anyone who has ever lived in a girl's dormitory, for example, is well acquainted with the "engagement measles." One girl on the floor announces her engagement; this announcement

[3] For a discussion of marriage as a status-achieving device, see James Bossard, "Marriage as a Status Achieving Device," *Sociol. soc. Res.*, **29**, 1 (September-October 1944), pp. 3–10.

seems to result in another, and another, and still another engagement announcement, until within a short period of time an "engagement epidemic" seems to break out. The engaged are indeed "in," and the unengaged are "out." Teen-age groups, in which a high degree of conformity may be expected, are especially prone to such "epidemics." The embarrassment and insecurity that result from being unengaged or unmarried frequently lead to premature marriages. In fact, in any society that considers marriage to be the "normal" and "healthy" state for all people, not only teen-agers but single people of older ages as well may feel that they are very much out of step. Indeed, as one grows older he may become increasingly uneasy about his unmarried state; the need to marry for the sake of being married may increase to the point of taking precedence over more rational thought. When this occurs the rush to find a marriage partner is on; and the person, young or old, may compulsively throw himself into a relationship that has little chance of any meaningful development.

We now turn to an assessment of the cases that have been outlined and summarize what may be learned from them.

Case Assessment

If we synthesize the insights that the cases have afforded us, we see that the motivations for marriage that result from personal immaturities tend to share three elements, which clearly pose limitations to the building of a meaningful marriage relationship.

First, in almost all of our cases the motivations for marriage involved an escape from some personal problem. Hence they are essentially negative reasons for marrying. To the extent that this is true, the person seeking a marital partner lacks intrinsic interest in the partner as a human being and merely uses him as a tool to help in the escape from an undesirable condition.

Second, in almost all of our cases the search for the marital partner was of a compulsive nature. If the motive is to escape from a problem, a sense of urgency about finding a marital partner will develop, because of the feeling that "time is running out." Under a strain of this sort, rational judgment or evaluation of the marital partner is overlooked.

Third, in the cases that have been presented the problems were primarily inner difficulties, which were unlikely to be eased by a change on the outside—that is, by marriage. It follows, then, that people who marry for the reasons described will almost inevitably be disillusioned when they realize that marriage has not solved their difficulties. Often such realization brings with it bitterness and resentment not only toward oneself but also toward the marital partner, on whom may fall gross blame for the unhappy relationship.

We have so far dealt with motivations for marriage that result from personal immaturities. These negative motivations warrant close attention, we think, because of their subtle and complex nature. Of course, not all motivations for marriage are negative. People who marry for positive reasons regard marriage not as a means of escaping from something, but as an end or a goal in itself. That is, they are motivated to marry not by the desire to escape unpleasant conditions, but by the attractiveness of the goal itself, namely the marriage. The next chapter discusses in some detail many of the positive motivations toward marriage and the specific ends of this kind of relationship, such as companionship, emotional reassurance, emotional interdependence, freedom of communication and activity, and physical sexual fulfillment. In general, those whose motivations toward marriage are more positive than negative do not use marriage as a means of escape, but view both the marriage and the marital partner in terms of what they intrinsically represent—emotionally, intellectually, and physically. The marriage relationship as such is neither used nor exploited, but instead becomes the framework within which mutual understanding, empathy, and personal acceptance emerge. At this point we should like to introduce the idea of a personal assessment of the motivations for marriage.

Personal Assessment

Needless to say, a person should understand his motivations for marriage and the extent to which he is capable of entering into a mature and meaningful relationship. Those who work with marital problems have come to recognize that lack of such understanding is frequently at the very heart of much marital unhappiness. It would seem highly profitable, therefore, for persons contemplating marriage to undergo some self-assessment, to detect facets of the personality that may not be conducive to the building of a meaningful relationship. To be sure, this area of human experience does not lend itself easily to critical self-inspection.

One cannot always tell when his motivations and personal organization are or are not conducive to taking part in a meaningful relationship. Moreover, most of us have difficulty facing attitudes in ourselves that are unpleasant. In spite of these formidable problems, however, we do find people who, upon examining both their motivations and those of the prospective mates, gain some new, previously hidden insight. When this is accomplished, there is at least the possibility of an improvement in the quality of the relationship. Although some relationships may fall apart under the impact of examination, more often than not the elimination of a factor that constituted a hindrance leads to a better, stronger, and more lasting relationship.

Summary

An understanding of the motivations for one's actions is important in building meaningful man-woman relationships. Specifically, the motivations for marriage are important determinants of what a person expects from marriage and the quality of the relationship that follows. When motivations to marry are the result of immature personality patterns, they invariably lead to marital difficulties. Since immaturities are so prevalent in our society today, it becomes important for each person to understand more fully his reasons for marrying.

Some motivations for marriage that reflect personal immaturity and lead to poor marital relationships are (1) marrying to escape from an unhappy home, (2) marrying to escape from feelings of loneliness, (3) marrying for the purpose of living through others, (4) marrying for material possessions and wealth, (5) marrying on the rebound, and (6) marrying for the sake of being married.

These motivations for marriage may lead to difficulty because in each case the individual is escaping from some personal problem; hence the marriage partner is not regarded as an end in himself, but as a means to an end. When one marries primarily to escape, he has a sense of urgency about marrying; and when marriage is entered into with the feeling that "time is running out," rational judgment and careful evaluation of the marriage are minimized, if not completely absent. Finally, when people use marriage as a means of solving their personal difficulties, they often become bitter and disillusioned on discovering that neither marriage nor the marital partner can solve the difficulties, but that they themselves must come to grips with them.

Questions

1. How does the impersonality of life in our society hinder us in appreciating meaningful human relationships? In what manner does impersonality affect our motivations for marriage?

2. How are personal immaturities nurtured in the home? In what manner do personal immaturities affect our motivations for marriage?

3. Analyze the case of the college coed and show the relationship between her home life and her motivations for marriage. How could her difficulties have been avoided? How might her difficulties be resolved?

4. Analyze the case of the young girl who was premaritally pregnant and show the relationship between her home life and her involvements with boys. Which of this girl's personality traits would have to be altered before she might be able to participate in a meaningful relationship? Why?

5. List and describe the six motivations for marriage that tend to lead to difficulty in marriage. Why are these motivations considered to be immature approaches to marriage?

6. Describe the problems that might arise in marriages entered into on the basis of the six immature motivations.

7. On the basis of what you learned in this chapter, list and describe several motivations that in your opinion would constitute a mature basis for marriage.

8. Do you think it is necessary for people contemplating marriage to consider their reasons for doing so? Why? Is it always possible for one to know what his motivations for marriage are? If not, what should one do in order to determine his motivations?

9. If, after consideration, one discovers that his motivations for marriage are immature, what should he do?

10. If the realization that one's motivations for marriage are immature causes personal discomfort, would it not have been better to ignore them to begin with? Why or why not? Explain.

Suggestions for Research and Related Projects

1. Make a list of all the motivations you can think of that one might have for marrying. Submit this list to several married men and women of various

age groups. Have the respondent rate each motivation in terms of its applicability to his own motivations for marriage. Have the respondent give ten points to the motivations that most directly apply to his case, five points to those that have less application to his case, and no points to those that do not apply at all. Do you find any differences between the answers of men and women or between those given by the different age groups? If so, how do you explain these differences? Do the answers represent a realistic picture of what motivated these men and women to marry? Why or why not?

2. Write a short skit depicting a scene in which an engaged couple discuss their future marriage. In the skit have one person represent mature motivations for marrying and the other immature motivations. After presenting the skit to the class, have a discussion concerning what problems might arise in this marriage and how these problems might have been avoided or how they might now be resolved. You might also write six short skits as described above, each depicting one of the six immature motivations discussed in this chapter.

3. Hold a panel discussion on the following topic: "What might be done to help people acquire mature motivations for marriage."

Suggested Readings

Blood, Robert O., Jr., *Marriage,* The Free Press, Glencoe, Ill., 1962.

Bell, Robert R., *Marriage and Family Interaction,* rev. ed., Dorsey Press, 1967.

Cavan, Ruth Shonle, *American Marriage,* Crowell-Collier, New York, 1959, Ch. 3, "Personal Readiness for Marriage," and Ch. 7, "Choosing a Compatible Mate."

Horney, Karen, *Self-Analysis,* Norton, New York, 1942, Ch. 2, "The Driving Forces in Neuroses," especially pp. 54–72.

Magoun, F. Alexander, *Love and Marriage,* Harper, New York, 1948, Ch. 2, "The Nature of Marriage."

Reed, Ruth, *The Single Woman,* New York, Macmillan, 1942, especially pp. 4–35, 68–75, and 92–95.

Waller, Willard, *The Family,* revised by Reuben Hill, Dryden Press, New York, 1951, Ch. 11, "Selective Mating," especially pp. 194–200 and 206–215.

Chapter Six

LOVE IN THE MAN-WOMAN RELATIONSHIP, PART I*

W E SAW in the preceding chapter how immature motivations for marriage lead to difficulties in building a meaningful relationship. Another obstacle to the development of a meaningful man-woman relationship lies in the prevalent misunderstandings about the nature of love. In this chapter we discuss (1) the significance of love in the human relationship, (2) confusions regarding the nature of love, and (3) the nature of the love experience itself. Also, we attempt to point out how misunderstandings concerning love may result in problems within the man-woman relationship.

The Significance of Love in the Human Relationship

As indicated earlier, the American family has not always considered love to be a basis for its existence. Especially marked changes in the role

* Part II follows as Chapter Seven.

ILLUSTRATION: Doll in a Calash, c. 1810. Courtesy of the Museum of the City of New York.

98

of love in marriage have occurred within the last fifty years, as manifest not only in the changing basis for family life, but in writings that reflect the spirit of the period.[1] Thus some writers have advanced the idea that the fulfillment of love is a human necessity.[2] Other writers have been critical of love's impact on human affairs, but few have denied that it is a reality with which all people have to come to terms. Why the present concern with love? In part, it reflects the important role that love has come to assume in the marital relationship. In a more fundamental way, however, it shows that many people now realize that love is significant and necessary for personal welfare and happiness. One scholar, Evelyn Duvall, for example, studied more than 3000 teen-agers and found support for her hypothesis that love tends to be directly related to one's search for identity.[3] The need to express and receive love, therefore, is recognized not merely because our culture stresses its importance, but also because we have come to a greater understanding of the role of love in the life of the individual. As Smiley Blanton suggests:

Love's greatest glory lies in the fact that it alone provides the strength, protection and encouragement without which full growth is impossible. We are all aware of this truth when it comes to the life of a helpless infant. Unfortunately, too many of us ignore its equal applicability to humanity as a whole. Since men and women rarely die before our eyes for lack of love, we assume that they can live well enough without it. We do not stop to think that it is a form of death, when we crawl through our days in the constant shadow of talent needlessly thwarted, of all those fears, illnesses and psychological self-mutilations to which we resort when hate chokes off our normal outlets of development.[4]

Although love is essential, relatively few people find mature, stable love relationships. As we saw earlier, a good many people, markedly cynical, abandon even before they marry the belief that a mature love relationship is possible. Marriage for these persons frequently is an implicitly contractual business relationship in which husband and wife receive certain benefits in return for other benefits. To illustrate the point, let us look at one college student, a very aggressive and domineering young man who was known as a "big man on campus." The young man was a

[1] Erich Fromm, *The Art of Loving,* Harper, New York, 1956.
[2] Daniel Prescott, "The Role of Love in Human Development," *J. Home Econ.,* **44,** 3 (March 1952), pp. 173–176.
[3] Evelyn Millis Duvall, "Adolescent Love as a Reflection of Teenagers' Search for Identity," *J. Marr. Fam.,* **26,** 2 (May 1964), pp. 226–229.
[4] From Smiley Blanton, *Love or Perish,* Simon and Schuster, New York, 1956, p. 21. Reprinted by permission of the publisher.

fraternity member, he maintained membership in several other important campus organizations, and he was also active in campus politics. This student was contemplating marriage to a young lady who was markedly different from him. She could be described as being quiet, sensitive to the needs of others, unassuming, and modest. When she came for assistance, she spoke of her anxieties regarding her involvement with the young man. She complained that he was indifferent to her, would fail to show up for dates, and would explain his behavior only after several days had passed. Most often, his explanations appeared somewhat farfetched and inappropriate. He reported that he had forgotten the date or that he had been too engrossed in what he was doing to appear for the date. When he did appear on time, he seemed preoccupied with other matters, usually his campus involvements. In the actual dating relationship, this man was emotionally aloof from his girl friend. Necking and petting occurred so infrequently that the young lady found it necessary to complain. The young man appeared for help at the insistence of his girl friend. It was obvious from the first that he was uninterested in any real help. His aloofness from the counseling relationship was apparent. When questioned about problems in the relationship, he became defensive and spoke of "those silly ideas of my girl friend." He was certain that with time this girl would come to appreciate his basic qualities. He went on to point out that he had his sights set on becoming president of a large business firm. What he needed from marriage, he suggested, was somebody to add the flourishes and extras to his life. By this he meant a neat, attractive wife—not too attractive to men, just attractive enough— who could entertain socially in a way that would help advance him in his work. This young man cared little for the needs of his future wife. Furthermore, he was unconcerned with love, thought it silly, and felt that it would only get in the way of the goals he wished to achieve. The young lady finally married him in spite of his almost total unwillingness to examine himself, let alone change. We might add that the young lady has lived unhappily ever after.

Even those people who have not abandoned the possibility of a mature love relationship and who do seek mature love, face many problems. To begin with, there is a great deal of confusion about the nature and real meaning of love. Much of this confusion stems from the belief that love is fundamentally unknown and unknowable, hence rooted in magic. Persons who hold such a belief view the nature of love as being beyond human comprehension [5] and feel that any attempt to understand the phenomenon is bound to lead to disappointment and frustration.

[5] Andrew G. Truxal and Francis E. Merrill, *The Family in American Culture*, Prentice-Hall, Englewood Cliffs, N.J., 1947, pp. 121–130.

The view of love as belonging to the realms of magic and the unknowable points up an interesting contradiction in our society. It suggests that despite our emphasis on science, our thinking with respect to the nature of love is more characteristic of the primitive than of the civilized mind. We are willing to accept the teachings of science when they relate to the physical universe, but reject the possibility of scientific inquiry into such significant personal phenomena as love. This antiscientific attitude hinders scientific study of the nature of love, at the loss of the contribution such study may make.

The authors are obviously not in sympathy with the point of view that places the understanding of love in the realm of the unknown and unknowable. Indeed, it seems reasonable to state that the belief that love is unknown or unknowable is not only an expression of ignorance, but also an expression of hopelessness and of fear of facing human experiences realistically. We are reminded of the young man who reported that he wished to be in love and marry but wanted to avoid the process of falling in love. Instead, he hoped that somehow he could fall asleep, awake, and discover that he was already in love and married. Thus he might somehow magically be spared the problems of doing his own selecting, or actively entering into a relationship and resolving the problems that might exist. We sense in the reaction of this young man a desire to avoid the reality of experiencing the love relationship. Instead, his wish is to assume a passive role, letting the love experience sweep him along without any emotional involvement on his part.

This young man is not unique. There are many people, committed to the notion that love is unknowable, who possess similar attitudes of passivity and hopelessness about understanding or facing the dilemmas of the love relationship. Unfortunately, such attitudes toward love have negative consequences, in that they make an understanding or examination of one's love involvements unnecessarily difficult and at times impossible.

Confusions Regarding the Nature of Love

Falling in Love and Remaining in Love

One source of the confusion about the nature of love is the failure of many people to appreciate the differences between falling in love and remaining in love. They assume that if one can fall in love, one is also capable of remaining in love. Nothing could be further from the truth. To fall in love is relatively easy, since it is often based primarily on sexual considerations; to remain in love requires the ability to build and maintain a stable relationship. To accomplish this task, a person must know what he wants, must understand his wishes, and must be able to maintain consistent feeling and to respond to the changes and growth of the partner in the relationship. None of this is easily accomplished; the reader's personal experiences are probably replete with people who were emotionally unable to remain in love. There is the case of the married woman who felt she was in love with her husband only when she was actually with him. Whenever her husband went away, even for only a little while, she would have serious doubts about whether or not she was in love with him. When her husband entered military service and was away for a considerable period of time, her doubts about her feelings became so grave that she was considering divorce. At that point her husband came home for a furlough, and her confidence in her love for him was temporarily restored. Nevertheless, it is clear that this woman was incapable of a mature love commitment and, regardless of her feelings at the moment, found it exceedingly difficult to remain in love.

Furthermore, it is important that the basis of the love relationship, which we discuss more fully later in this chapter, rest in reality. If one's love is based on an unreal image of the partner—that is, the partner is seen as being much better than he actually is—the relationship may indeed be fragile. As contact with the loved one continues, the realities begin to break through, imperfections appear, the unreal image is shattered, and a gradual disillusionment with the love partner occurs, resulting in a diminution of love feelings.[6] Such disillusionment with the love partner is a common experience for many people. It is indeed unfortunate that many are unaware of how they construct unreal images of others; inevitably these unreal images crumble.

Some writers, in their attempt to emphasize the active participation demanded of people in the maintenance of consistent feelings in the love relationship, have made marriage appear like a tremendous chore. It is doubtful whether such attitudes were really intended. Nevertheless, for the love relationship to be successful, a sensitivity to the dynamics of the relationship is required. This requirement is no different from the requirements of other human relationships.

[6] Theodor Reik, *Of Love and Lust*, Farrar, Straus and Cudahy, New York, 1957, p. 82.

Self-Love and Love for Others

The notion that love for self negates the possibility of love for others, is a second source of confusion about the nature of love. The confusion comes from a failure to differentiate self-love from narcissism. The narcissist (with whom we deal later) is indeed in love with an idealized image of himself and therefore incapable of loving others. The prevalence of the confusion between self-love and narcissism is understandable, since certain ethical and religious values have been interpreted as requiring sacrifice without regard for self. Thus signs of personal concern have frequently been interpreted as an inability to have deep feelings for others. Although such a view is prevalent, its logic breaks down on examination. If one is expected to love his neighbor and, in fact, humanity, but not oneself, does this not constitute an inherent contradiction? If one is expected to love others, why exclude oneself, since all are members of the human race? We are not advocating narcissistic absorption with self, but a love of self that is reflected in such attitudes of self-acceptance as (1) I like what I am, (2) I am a decent person, and (3) I possess dignity and deserve respect. The significance of the capacity for self-love is seen in the now widely held professional view that genuine love for others springs from the ability to care for and love oneself.[7] When a person has developed a deep appreciation, respect, and love for what he is, he does not feel the scarcity of love that characterizes the insecure person. Instead, feeling that love is plentiful rather than in short supply, he can turn outward the energies and feelings that were formerly concerned with himself in an egocentric fashion and express them toward other people.[8]

We now turn to a consideration of the nature of the love experience.

The Nature of the Love Experience

In attempting to explain love, behavioral scientists frequently provide an extensive amount of information about love, but very little con-

[7] Fromm, *op. cit.*, pp. 57–63. Harry Stack Sullivan, *Conceptions of Modern Psychiatry*, 2nd ed., Norton, New York, 1953, pp. 14–27.
[8] *Ibid.*

cerning what love is. Such statements as "love is blind," "love is both giving and receiving," or "love is a complex emotional feeling" do tell us
something about love, but they explain little of the essential nature of
love. Such explanations are understandable, since the concept of love is
difficult and complex to deal with. All definitions are probably oversimplified; all are open to one set of objections or another. Nevertheless, it
is necessary to deal with love, and we present our views for the reader's
consideration.

Although we are primarily concerned with analyzing the types of love
that emerge in the man-woman relationship, such analysis, we believe, is
dependent on a basic understanding of love in its broader manifestations. In searching for the factors that are common to all types of love, we
find one basic element—a conscious or unconscious set of need satisfactions that one derives from a specific object or person, be it home, country, wife, mother, brother, or whatever. That is, an individual comes to
love a particular object or person because certain conscious or unconscious needs that have come to be important to him are fulfilled. Thus
the essential experience of love appears to be rooted in the needs that
individuals have, and in a general sense, therefore, love may be thought
of as an emotional feeling that arises out of a complex composite of need
satisfactions.

One way of looking at the relationship between need fulfillment and
love is that formulated by Theodor Reik.[9] Reik believes that all love
arises out of a basic dissatisfaction with oneself.[10] Such dissatisfaction results in the creation of an ego ideal, that is, an image of what one would
like to be. The ego ideal's basic characteristic is perfectionism in all
qualities deemed important, such as knowledge, manners, or power over
people. The ego ideal continuously makes demands on the individual to
measure up to these standards of perfection. Since the individual inevitably falls short of the fulfillment of the ego ideal, he has a pervasive sense
of guilt. Hence he seeks for another individual in whom he may experience the traits of his ego ideal. At first he unconsciously envies these
traits in the other person, since he desires them in himself. When this
envy turns into an identification with the other person who possesses the
traits of the ego ideal, love emerges. Reik states: "Love is in its essential
nature an emotional reaction-formation to envy, possessiveness, and hostility." [11]

---

[9] Reik, *op. cit.,* p. 32.
[10] Although we do not completely agree with Reik's point of view (see p. 103 for our
discussion of the relationship between self-acceptance and genuine love for another),
it is nevertheless a point of view that warrants mention.
[11] Reik, *op. cit.,* p. 66.

Reik's formulation of all love as stemming from dissatisfaction with self negates the possibility of other needs operating; we believe that such healthy needs as those of growth, creativity, and respect are also operative. Nevertheless, Reik does present one scheme of need fulfillment and love, which enables us to understand the basis of love for some people; as such it deserves careful consideration. Reik's analysis, of course, raises the important question of the kinds of needs that people have and of the quality of the relationship that emerges. Some may, for example, have needs that result in mature relationships, and others may have needs that result in immature relationships.

Needs and the Man-Woman Relationship

Needs are deemed to be mature when they (1) contribute to both the intellectual and emotional growth of the members and (2) are rooted in reality. With respect to the first requirement, we can assert that needs that are rooted in marked egocentricity—an excessive need for flattery, the need to use and exploit others, the need to dominate and control, the need always to be right, and the need to escape from self—are not conducive to the development of a mature relationship. Such needs do not allow for sensitivity to others and for the development of the persons in a relationship. On the other hand, the needs to be appreciated and respected, to be close emotionally, to be creative and explore, and to be understood contribute to the growth and development of the persons in a relationship, and the relationship is mature. There is an important lesson to be learned from all this. Most people, quite unaware of their needs, simply search for someone with whom they feel comfortable, which is fine as far as it goes. But why do they feel comfortable with the other person? What needs are being satisfied? Are these needs conducive to their own growth or to that of the relationship? If not, might the needs be understood and changed? Let us be specific. There are many instances in which two people with needs that are not conducive to their growth meet and experience love. The case of a man with a need to dominate and a woman who has a need to be dominated is illustrative. The needs here are complementary, and possibly a marriage based on such needs would have little overt conflict, which is certainly one measure of success. Nevertheless, we can afford to aspire to something more than an absence of overt conflict and ask ourselves whether such a relationship can contribute to the growth of the individual partners. Obviously it cannot. The dominant partner has a need to be right and to control. Hence he is afraid to learn and profit through experience. Instead, he must impose his will on others. The woman has a need to be dominated; she looks for someone to take over her life. Thus the center of gravity, so to speak, is not in her but entirely in her love object. Such people expect the love object to fulfill all their desires and to take all responsibility for the relationship itself. The presence of this type of need in a love relationship hinders the capacity to grow, to make judgments and decisions, and to participate maturely in the responsibilities of family living.

The second requirement for needs to be mature is that they be rooted in reality; that is, we must determine whether the needs are realistic in order to ascertain the degree of their maturity. For example, it is obvious that people who have needs to see love as a mystical force that solves all problems have unreal conceptions; hence their love involvements tend to be immature and childlike. People who have needs to achieve without making efforts, have needs not rooted in reality, as do people who feel entitled to being waited on hand and foot and who always seek special privileges.

We can say, therefore, that a relationship that is based either on needs rooted in unreality or on needs that are so limited that they are not oriented toward the intellectual and emotional development of the couple tends to be immature.

The following needs, which are representative of those found among many middle-class people, meet our requirements for reality and intrinsic contribution to personality growth and thus are mature: [12]

1. *Companionship.* In a mature relationship the individuals have needs to share in common interests, to explore and stimulate each other's personalities, and to have sympathetic understanding for each other.

2. *Freedom of communication and activity.* In a mature relationship the individuals have needs to be accepted for what they are. There is a minimum of pretense; thus communication and activity become spontaneous and free.

3. *Emotional interdependence.* In a mature relationship the individuals have needs to be related to each other in manifest affection, tenderness, and trust. Thus need fulfillment is reciprocated in that each party to the relationship is giving need fulfillment to the other and receiving need fulfillment from the other.

4. *Sexual strivings.* In a mature relationship the individuals have needs not only for physical demonstrativeness, but for integration of sexual strivings with the total relationship, in order that they not become overbalanced or egocentric.

---

[12] Ernest W. Burgess and Harvey J. Locke, *The Family,* 2nd ed., American Book Company, New York, 1960, pp. 322–326.

These needs fulfill our requirements for mature satisfactions, since each is rooted in realistic expectations and gives promise of contributing to the growth of both individuals and their subsequent relationship. Many love relationships, however, fall short of meeting these requirements. Adolescent love relationships, for example, are frequently fraught with confusions and misunderstandings—with parents insisting that their adolescent son or daughter cannot be in love, since he or she does not know what love is. These assertions invariably bring forth bewilderment and resentment from the person whose feelings are being diagnosed. The young person who feels an intense attraction for a member of the opposite sex has a strange reaction indeed when he is informed that he is not really in love. Actually, such experiences as puppy love, infatuation, romantic love, and platonic love are all forms of love, in that each consists of a pattern of need satisfaction that one derives from another. However, such love is immature love, in that the needs being fulfilled are unreal and are too limited to enhance intellectual and emotional development. For example, the need satisfactions found in puppy love or infatuation are not based on mature needs, but are limited to physical attraction or the wish to escape from the problems of adolescence. Furthermore, considerable idealization and distortion of reality occurs, each seeing the other as being better and more glamorous than he is. Such needs are hardly conducive to the overall emotional and intellectual development of the persons involved.[13]

An understanding of the personal needs involved also enables us to understand relationships that otherwise make little sense. For example, there is the case of an attractive young lady, intelligent and well informed, who fell in love with a young man who mistreated her repeatedly. He stood her up on dates; when he did appear, he was late. More often than not he became intoxicated on the date and was unable to get home on his own. He borrowed money from the young lady without any real interest in returning it. All signs pointed to an irresponsible individual with a very uncertain future. One would normally expect the young lady to abandon the relationship. Instead, she became more desperate and continued to pursue the relationship. Why? Obviously, the relationship fulfilled certain personal needs. The needs were deeply regressed. When they were understood, however, the young lady discovered that she had a need to belittle herself. Thus without being consciously aware of what she was doing, she set out to find a boy who would embarrass and belittle her. This situation is illustrative of many that might be presented and serves to show the significance of understanding the needs that produce particular kinds of love relationships.

[13] Erik H. Erikson, *Childhood and Society*, Norton, New York, 1950, p. 228.

Mature and Immature Love—A Continuum

The differences between mature and immature love are, of course, a matter of degree rather than kind. We can think of mature and immature love as representing opposite extremes of a continuum, with the various degrees of maturity in the man-woman relationships falling somewhere in between. Put another way, if we knew enough about the pattern of need satisfaction in a specific relationship, we could plot the degree to which the relationship approximates the characteristics of mature love, or the degree to which it does not, and place it on a continuum:

Extremely Immature	Very Immature	Moderately Immature	Moderately Mature	Very Mature	Extremely Mature

From all that we have said it should be clear that whether or not one is capable of experiencing mature love is not necessarily a matter of chronological age, but rather of emotional development. Many older people are incapable of experiencing anything other than immature love feelings. There is, for example, the extreme illustration of a couple engaged for thirty years. They were going steady, to be sure, and reported that theirs was a serious relationship. Honorable intentions on both sides were reported. Marriage had not taken place, since the man felt it necessary to support his parents and did not believe that he could support both a wife and his parents. Needless to say, this man, who was fifty-five at the time, and the woman who was fifty-three, had an exceedingly immature relationship. The man was known to be tied emotionally to his parents and to be fearful, basically, of marriage. The woman was an exceedingly dependent and insecure person, afraid to give up even this relationship lest she not find another.

Furthermore, marital status is not indicative of the degree of maturity. Many single persons are capable of mature unions; many persons, married for many years, are totally incapable of having a mature love relationship. There is the case of a couple, married for fifteen years, who have worked out a pattern of life in which there is a minimum of interaction between them. The man, a successful business executive, spends as much time as he can away from home. Whenever it is possible for him to remain at home, he consistently thinks of diversions in the form of club activities and meetings to keep him from having any interaction with his wife. So impersonal is his relationship with his wife and home that he prefers to eat in restaurants rather than at home. Left to his own devices, he would eat all three meals in a restaurant. The wife, who is likewise a success in her chosen profession, prefers more of a home life, but has given up the possibility of a meaningful relationship with her husband and has come to follow a similar pattern of noninvolvement.

Love and Motivations for Marriage

From all that has been said about mature and immature types of love it can be seen that needs on which mature love is based can readily lead to the mature motivations for marriage that were discussed in the preceding chapter. For example, needs based on reality which are conducive to personal growth are not very likely to lead to a view of marriage as an escape from some problem, nor to the urgency and haste that characterize immature motivations for marriage. Thus our analysis of love and motivations for marriage must not be regarded as being separate entities. Rather, these two analyses, as well as others that follow, must be seen in relation to each other if our understanding of the man-woman relationship is to be increased.

Finally, it must be stressed, although hopefully it is abundantly clear to the reader, that there is *no perfect love* and there are *no totally mature needs* or individuals. Attempting to achieve perfection is not only futile but frustrating and self-defeating, but working toward a mature love is both possible and rewarding. We have dealt with the concepts of love and maturity in an analytic way, since many of the problems of the man-woman relationship are caused by confusion about the meaning of love and maturity, because it is either obscured or unknown.

Summary

Although love is regarded as an extremely important aspect of the man-woman relationship, some people abandon the hope of ever finding it. To them marriage becomes a contractual business relationship in which certain benefits are exchanged.

Even those who seek love, however, are confused about its nature, because of the belief that love is mystical and magical, hence unknowable. Such an antiscientific view suggests not only ignorance but hopelessness about understanding an important aspect of human involvement.

One confusion concerning the nature of love is found in the failure to understand the difference between falling in love and remaining in love; it is frequently assumed that attaining the former automatically ensures the latter. This is an erroneous idea, since remaining in love requires the ability to build and maintain a stable relationship. Thus stability, predictability, and maturity are necessary for the individuals involved.

A second confusion concerning love is found in the notion that love for self negates the possibility of love for others. This confusion arises out of the failure to differentiate self-love from narcissism. In narcissism one is in love with a glorified image of self and is unable to love others. But self-love need not involve this complete absorption in oneself. Instead, self-love is founded in such basic attitudes as liking what one is and feeling that one possesses dignity and deserves respect. Believing these things about oneself brings about a security that enables one to feel that he is not merely a receiver in the love relationship but has something to offer in return.

In turning to the nature of love, we noted that love is an emotional feeling that arises out of a complex composite of need satisfactions. Thus the essential experience of love is rooted in the needs that individuals have. It was suggested that love relationships differ with respect to degree of maturity involved. The degree to which a love relationship may be regarded as mature or immature is described by the degree to which the needs involved are conducive to the intellectual and emotional development of the couple and are rooted in reality. A grouping of such needs as (1) companionship, (2) freedom of communication and activity, (3) emotional interdependence, and (4) sexual strivings is illustrative of a mature need pattern, since these needs are realistic and sufficiently broad to provide for the overall emotional and intellectual development of the persons involved.

Questions

1. How has the place of love in the man-woman relationship changed in the past fifty years?
2. Why do some people abandon the hope of ever finding love in their man-woman relationships?
3. Is it true that those who seek a mature love relationship may confront problems in so doing? If so, what problems do they confront?

4. What is the difference between "falling in love" and "remaining in love"?

5. How do you account for the lack of systematic study concerning love as a human experience?

6. What is the difference between narcissism and self-love? Give illustrations.

7. In its broadest sense, explain what love is.

8. What are the two basic qualities of needs that are conducive to mature love? Give examples.

9. List and fully describe the four needs found among middle-class people that are illustrative of a mature relationship. Why are these needs considered to be significant for a mature relationship?

10. What are the consequences of accepting the following point of view: "Love is an unknown and unknowable force"?

Suggestions for Research and Related Projects

1. Analyze the marital relationship of a few couples whom you know well. To the best of your knowledge and without identifying the people involved, attempt to determine the degree to which each relationship may be considered to be mature. Illustrate this by means of the kinds of needs being satisfied. For those relationships that you regard as immature (if any) show what changes would have to occur if, in your opinion, they were to become mature relationships.

2. Write two brief skits, one depicting a couple with an immature love relationship and the other a couple with a mature love relationship. After having presented both skits to the class, have the class members point out why each was considered to be immature and mature respectively.

3. Hold a panel discussion on the following topic: "The study of love as a human experience is nonsense."

4. Analyze a man-woman relationship in which you have participated. Attempt to objectively determine the needs that were being fulfilled in this relationship and the degree to which you now regard it as having been a mature relationship.

Suggested Readings

Bee, Lawrence S., *Marriage and Family Relations*, Harper, New York, 1959, Ch. 6, "The Meaning of Love."

Dean, Dwight G., "Romanticism and Emotional Maturity: A Further Exploration," *Social Forces*, **42** (1964), pp. 298–303.

Ellis, Albert, "A Study of Human Love Relationships," *J. genet. Psychol.*, **75** (1949), pp. 61–71.

Magoun, F. Alexander, *Love and Marriage*, Harper, New York, 1948, Ch. 1, "The Nature of Love."

Reik, Theodor, *A Psychologist Looks at Love*, Farrar and Rinehart, New York, 1944.

Udry, J. Richard, *The Social Context of Marriage*, Lippincott, New York, 1966, especially Ch. 7.

Waller, Willard, *The Family*, revised by Reuben Hill, Dryden Press, New York, 1951, Ch. 7, "The Sentiment of Love."

Chapter Seven

LOVE IN THE MAN-WOMAN RELATIONSHIP, PART II

IN THIS chapter we continue our analysis of love and discuss the attitudes that engender immature love relationships, the development of the capacity to love maturely, and the types of persons who are unable to love maturely.

Attitudes That Engender Immature Love

You are undoubtedly familiar with many of the beliefs associated with immature love; for example, (1) the idea of the one and only, (2) the idea of love at first sight, and (3) the idea that love solves all problems. A certain logic ties the three ideas together. The idea of the one and only suggests that destiny has ordained someone for you. If you wonder how

ILLUSTRATION: Toy model of the Broadway and Fifth Avenue Omnibus, c. 1860. Courtesy of the Museum of the City of New York.

you will recognize the person when you meet him or her, you are confronted by the second component, namely love at first sight. Here you learn that you can tell in a moment when the proper person has been met. You are told to look for inner signs, a feeling of excitement, an increase in pulse and heart rate. Finally, if you are concerned about incompatibilities, wide differences in background, and personal tastes, you learn that these are not important, since love will solve all problems. All of these ideas thus constitute a point of view that some people hold regarding the nature of love. Furthermore, once a person accepts the premise expressed in point one, he is inevitably lulled into accepting the remaining ideas.

As an example of such immature involvement, one of the authors recalls a young lady, a college graduate, reared in an upper middle-class family who claimed she was in love with a lower-class semiliterate truck driver. After a short period of acquaintance, the young lady made plans to marry. Her family was quite upset, since the relationship was not what they had hoped for and appeared to be fraught with dangers. It took no family expert to predict problems for this couple. The young lady, at the insistence of her parents, appeared for counseling. She was asked how she hoped to overcome the obvious social and personal incompatibilities.

Her answer: "Oh, they will work out."

Counselor's question: "Why will they work out—because you want them to?"

Her answer: "I just know they will, if you knew how much we loved each other, you could see that it will all work out."

The young lady was insistent that the marriage take place, and after a short period of time the couple married. Within three months the marriage was terminated by divorce.

Even more common than the belief that love will overcome marked social incompatibilities is the belief that love will overcome serious emotional difficulties. Of course, mature love relationships can sometimes alleviate problems imposed by diverse social backgrounds or emotional conflicts, but it is unrealistic to assume that they will eliminate such problems.

Origin of Immature Attitudes toward Love

Searching for the origin of immature attitudes toward love is in itself an interesting pursuit. Needless to say, our society plays an important role in their development, specifically movies, popular ballads, and certain aspects of literature. In the movies, love at first sight is portrayed as being a valid index of love. Hero and heroine meet, and in a flash it is clear that they are meant for each other. The idea that there is a one and only is frequently brought home by the introduction of discord between hero and heroine. Each attempts to find happiness with another only to return to the original love with the realization that happiness can only be found with one. This general theme is also apparent in many television programs. There is little that corresponds to reality in any of these media when it comes to dealing with love. Not only are the ideas of love unreal, even the actors and actresses are atypical and unusual, invariably being very handsome or attractive. Make-believe has a field day.

Popular ballads, with their reference to the unreal, are another excellent source of immature attitudes toward love. During the depression years, and continuing until World War II, the phenomenon of the song sheet was in vogue. As the name implies, it was a rather large sheet that contained printed lyrics for the popular ballads of the day. In the big urban centers many of these sheets were sold. Obviously, some personal satisfaction was obtained in singing the lyrics to the tune of an orchestra on the radio. It has been claimed that the sale of the song sheet was related to the need to lose oneself in fantasy and find happiness in love in the midst of a grim social and economic environment. There would certainly appear to be some truth in such an assertion.

Literary forms—novels, short stories, magazine articles—also tend to propagate immature attitudes toward love. It is frequently assumed that immature love themes are portrayed only in cheap pulp magazines. Nothing could be further from the truth. In fact, the pulp magazines may carry fewer stories involving immature love attitudes than do other publications, since many of them are sordid tales that end in disaster for all parties concerned. The so-called better ladies' magazines may actually be the more serious offenders. Immature attitudes toward love carried not only in adult literature, but also in books for children, particularly in fairy tales in which the prince marries a maid of inferior social status and both live happily ever after.

Stories that contain the basic "Cinderella theme," in which people live happily ever after and overcome all diversity, can be misleading because they suggest that life experiences prior to love are unrelated to the capacity to love and to the kind of love one may experience. Instead, we know that unhappiness in earlier life may impair one's capacity to love maturely or may produce gross misconceptions regarding the nature of love. Thus fairy tales with the happy ending may strike a positive note, but the message may have little to do with reality and may in fact lead to serious frustration and disappointment later on.

The problem of dealing with children's books is a complex matter, since the selections reflect only in part the wishes of the child. Although one might hope that authors are in touch with what children enjoy and need, they are perhaps also attuned to what will sell, which means that authors are sensitive to parental wishes. There is little doubt that such a climate reflects a need to protect the child from certain realities in life. Sometimes books with a basic "Cinderella theme" may indeed reflect parental anxieties and fears about life itself. There is a need not only to protect the child but to overprotect him. Although we do not really know how much reality about love, marriage, and the family a child can absorb, there would appear to be room for a reexamination of what the child needs and what he is capable of dealing with.

The fact that millions of dollars each year are poured into products that promote immature attitudes toward love suggests that these attitudes still have considerable appeal for the populace. Regardless of what is known intellectually, large numbers of people still find satisfaction in these immature attitudes toward love and have incorporated much of what is implied by these attitudes into both their thinking and behavior. The likelihood of this is especially apparent when we realize that from the time we were children, we have been bombarded from all sides by immature attitudes toward love. Few people indeed are completely emancipated from any of these attitudes that inevitably lead to turmoil in the man-woman relationship. Of course, some people cling to immature attitudes toward love more than do others. There are those who are so cynical that they view with disdain any concept of love. There are others who are simply lacking in knowledge. Nevertheless, aside from these kinds of people, it is likely that the person who rejects the essentially immature attitudes toward love is more secure and capable of self-acceptance than is the person who must cling to them.[1] Why this is so should not be difficult to understand. Since these immature attitudes tend to be replete with magic and unreality, they offer something special to the individual who feels insecure and unworthy. For the philosophy that underlies these attitudes states in essence that no matter how one may feel, be it homely, stupid, or awkward, there is someone destined for him—the one and only. When he meets this person, he will know, since the meeting will be associated with certain kinds of feelings and experiences—love at first sight. If there are difficulties, they will be resolved, since love solves all things. Thus for the person who feels lonely, homely,

---

[1] For an effort to deal with this question, see Dwight G. Dean, "Romanticism and Emotional Maturity: A Further Exploration," *Social Forces*, **42**, 3 (Marc' 1964), pp. 298–303.

insecure, or in general out of tune with things, there is the promise of love, marriage, and happiness through a faith and belief in these attitudes, and a very real identification with these attitudes therefore emerges.[2]

There is the case of a very attractive young lady, age eighteen, who was forced to lead a very sheltered life because of the fears of her parents who wanted to protect her from "unscrupulous men." Unfortunately the young lady came to look upon herself as a misfit. She came to believe that there must be something very wrong with her, since her parents were so insistent on keeping men away from her. With such needs to compensate for her own feelings of inferiority, she soon became committed to an immature view of love in which she conceived of a one and only who would rescue her from her turmoil.

The reassurance that immature attitudes provide is terribly important for these insecure, lonely people, since at heart they feel despised, unlovable, and unwanted. Furthermore, such attitudes of self-effacement are indeed unfortunate, since they often involve considerable personal misery, imply a fundamental rejection of self, in fact an active need to cover up what the individual is, both from himself and from others. Even when these people marry, their inability to accept themselves, as well as their fundamental lack of being in touch with reality, is bound to cause many problems and limit the personal happiness that might be achieved in the marital relationship.

Attitudes That Engender Mature Love

Attitudes that are conducive to mature love, we notice, differ markedly from those associated with immature love. To begin with, the process of falling in love is stripped of its unreality and magic. It has little to do with love at first sight or with love that solves all problems. Instead, love develops out of the attractions that people feel, and attractions emerge from human interaction. Attractions, as previously noted, are rooted in particular kinds of need satisfactions. Finally, the entire process of falling in love and remaining in love is seen as a dynamic one which involves adjustment and readjustment between the two persons. The latter view is characteristic of persons who have developed a capacity to fall in love maturely.

[2] Robert F. Winch, *The Modern Family*, Holt, Rinehart and Winston, New York, 1952, p. 367.

The Development of the Capacity to Love Maturely

The capacity to love another maturely is rooted in a wide variety of personal and social influences that begin at birth. The process of developing the capacity to love maturely is therefore not a mysterious process, for it develops out of specific types of human values and relationships that are recognized and understood as operating within the context of society. These include the family social climate and familial interpersonal involvements.

At the outset we can assert that whenever the society in which one lives espouses values that lead to superficial and shallow living, the likelihood of mature love relationships is reduced. Our society emphasizes several values that impose obstacles to the development of mature love relationships. For example, our culture stresses externals and appearances. It places more emphasis on glamour and sophistication than it does on integrity, responsibility, or the capacity to love. The accent on cosmetics, soaps, and perfumes for both men and women underscores the extent to which appearances have become significant. Whereas traditionally it appealed only to women, the cosmetics market for the male has now grown so much so that investment opportunities are being widely publicized. *Forbes,* a leading magazine for investors, carried a full-page advertisement (p. 34M) in the *New York Times* of December 28, 1966, as follows:

The American male is starting to smell like the American female.

First, the hair. Those little streaks of grey have simply got to go. That may take up to a half hour of careful tinting. Then a pick-up mask of silicone gel on the face for ten minutes to remove those fatigue wrinkles. Next, a few drops of just the right fragrance to match clothes and personality. Perhaps a little hand cream.

Now, is she ready? No she isn't. *He* is.

Does this mean that the American male is starting to turn effeminate? No.

But, says *Forbes,* he is turning past utilitarian things like aftershave lotions to more feminine items like colognes, creams, hair coloring, even make-up.

And this isn't just a passing fancy. According to sales figures, *Forbes* says the American male—not his wife, daughter, or girlfriend—is now the hottest prospect for cosmetics.

In fact, the annual volume of men's "grooming aids" is close to $500 million: about three times what it was three years ago, reports *Forbes.*

And practically everybody is selling them: old-line cosmetic houses; big detergent makers; even Sears introduced its own men's line called Stampede.

Why is everybody getting into the business?

Simply because making cosmetics for men is as profitable as making them for women.

But it doesn't matter if you're not involved in the male cosmetic renaissance. What does matter, *Forbes* feels, is that you're up on current trends and future sociological phenomena. So you can apply that awareness to whatever business you happen to be in.

Who knows, today scents. Tomorrow, skirts?

Thus our society is less concerned with the inner nature of people than it is with externals and appearances. Such attitudes are facilitated by the modern man's view of himself and others as commodities, a view in which one person gives something in order to receive something in return; here a deep emotional commitment to a human relationship is avoided.[3] Moreover, the materialistic and competitive values that characterize life in our society are hardly conducive to the development of the capacity to love maturely. Materialism, when overemphasized in the man-woman relationship, may give the erroneous impression that material possessions ensure love. This point is illustrated by the man who built his wife a beautiful home, bought her a new automobile, employed a maid, and gave her an unlimited expense account. He discovered, however, that in spite of all these material advantages, she was taking large amounts of tranquilizers and was quite unhappy in the marriage. He was at a loss to understand his wife's unhappiness, since "he had given her all the possessions a woman could desire." In terms of his materialistic values, this man had provided for his wife. Nevertheless, in the process of accumulating such wealth, he was seldom home and had an exceedingly poor interpersonal relationship with his wife.

Thus materialism and the emphasis on externals are significant values to Americans, in spite of pronouncements about the significance of spiritual matters. Materialism is apparent in virtually every aspect of life from the birth of babies to the burying of the dead. It invades many of our most basic relationships and influences our decisions about the most significant parts of our lives. In fact, it is so important that outsiders have characterized our society in terms of the pursuit of these values. It is important to see the man-woman relationship within the context of materialism and externals and to examine the consequences.

With respect to competitiveness as a value, we must note that fre-

---

[3] Erich Fromm, *The Art of Loving*, Harper, New York, 1956, Ch. 1.

quently it may be so ingrained as to result in certain destructive patterns that bring about marked egocentricity; people step on others in order to achieve certain ends. Such patterns when brought into the home are incompatible with demands of a mature love relationship.

The social values that we have described are not restricted to specific areas of living, but pervade all activities. If one lives superficially without a deep commitment to life in general, it becomes difficult to love fully and deeply. Thus at some level the values in the social order become a significant factor in the development of the individual's capacity to love.

In turning our attention to the family, we can point out that family relationships are recognized as being the most significant ones in the development of the individual's capacity to love maturely. What are the minimal family essentials necessary for the development of the individual's capacity to love? In general, the familial environment must be one in which love as a human experience is valued and in which the actions of persons within the family reflect such positive attitudes. Positive attitudes toward love are contagious and are easily incorporated into the personality. Therefore, the family's emphasis on the importance of love as a human experience is significant in determining the individual's ability to express or receive love. For example, the individual who is reared in a home where the "cult of manliness" prevails—that is, where love is looked upon as a sign of feminity and weakness, hence as undesirable—tends to internalize negative attitudes toward the desirability of love. This may lead to a rejection of love as a human experience; or, as happens more often, it may result in an ambivalent reaction—one both wishes for and rejects love. Such ambivalence invariably causes inner turmoil and produces immature love involvements.

Negative attitudes toward becoming involved in love relationships may come not only from direct indoctrination, but also from the witnessing of the disappointments that others have endured because they have been in love. The child who witnesses the lifelong frustrations of his mother, who loves an alcoholic father, may come to feel that the price one pays for love may not be worth the satisfactions derived. Neither are familial situations characterized by lifelong tensions and anxieties conducive to positive attitudes toward love. Needless to say, family experiences may also be positive in that they contribute to a healthy acceptance and a desire for love.

Perhaps more important than the familial situations just described are the personal interactions between the child and adults in the family environment, which are very significant for the development of the capacity to love.

Thus the development of the capacity to love maturely is initially nurtured by the relationships with one's parents and adult siblings. When these relationships are favorable, and of a particular order, the essential foundation for the capacity to love maturely has been laid. Let us consider three important periods in the development of one's capacity to love.

Period I: Infancy

During infancy—the first period in the development of the capacity to love maturely—the child must have a set of consistent, dependable relationships with its mother. The mother is the first adult to initiate the child into a human emotional relationship. When these initial experiences are satisfactory, devoid of inconsistency, rejection, or separation through death or divorce, the child begins to sense a feeling of trust in human relationships. The relationship between mother and child is an involved one, calling forth a high degree of maturity on the part of the mother. Both the infant's physical needs and his emotional needs for warmth and security must be satisfied. Although it is difficult to separate the two types of needs in early life, it seems reasonable to assert that at the outset of the child's life the physical needs, that is, food and protection from all the elements that create fear in the physical organism, are as important as the emotional needs. An adult cannot have a clear picture of how the child perceives the world, but it is recognized that the world must seem formidable and somewhat frightening to an infant.[4] Thus it has been asserted that the earliest fears that the child has are fears about the destruction of its physical being; [5] these fears are easily engendered when physical needs are not met. When both the physical and emotional needs are satisfied, then the earliest relationship for the infant has been one associated with social trust, that is trust in the environment.

When the infant demonstrates an ease at feeding and a depth of sleep, we have the first evidence of social trust in the environment. The fear of physical and emotional abandonment is beginning to disappear, resulting in a willingness to let the mother out of sight, without anxiety or

[4] Aase Gruda Skard, "Maternal Deprivation: The Research and Its Implications," *J. Marr. Fam.*, **27**, 3 (1965), pp. 333–343. For an excellent study dealing with maternal anxiety and infant behavior, see Antonio Ferreira, "The Pregnant Woman's Emotional Attitude and Its Reflection on the Newborn," *Am. J. Orthopsychiatry*, **30**, (1960), pp. 553–561. See also Elaine R. Grimm and Wanda R. Venet, "The Relationship of Emotional Adjustment and Attitude to the Course and Outcome of Pregnancy," *Psychosomatic Med.*, **28**, 1 (1966).

[5] Melanie Klein, *The Psycho-Analysis of Children*, Hogarth Press, London, 1954.

rage. Social trust occurs most readily when the infant can count on what will happen when it is in need. In addition it should be noted that the development of social trust is not simply a matter of pouring large amounts of food and love into the infant; social trust depends also on the manner in which these are accomplished. An essentially insensitive mother, for example, may force large amounts of food into a child and produce added discomfort and tension. A sensitive mother, on the other hand, will be aware of the infant's individual needs and behave accordingly.[6] The same principle of sensitivity applies to the demonstration of the mother's love for the infant, since it involves a delicate balance of giving enough love to avoid the problems of overprotection and/or rejection. Such sensitivity to individual infant needs is believed by some to be associated with the infant's developing a sense of identity. This means that the mother's sensitivity to the infant's needs begins to create in the infant an awareness of himself.[7]

Finally, it should be noted that once social trust has emerged in the infant, the infant develops the necessary courage to explore interactions with persons other than the mother, since he feels safe and secure in his surroundings.[8]

Blanton summarizes several important points regarding the overall reaction of the infant to the environment.

Adults have in the past been misled into assuming that the child, because it lacks the power of speech, also lacks power of perception. The truth is that the human infant, like any primitive animal, is marvelously aware of everything that affects its welfare. It has the capacity to read what one may call our "muscle tensions"—those silent, but eloquent, betrayers of our true emotional attitudes.

It is through these muscle tensions that the mother transmits her true feelings to her child. And it is through her manner and attitude while caring for it that the child learns to develop security or fear. To the adult, feeding and dressing a baby may appear as routine duties without significance. But to the infant, these apparently innocuous events are momentous adventures which enable it to discover the nature and meaning of the outside world. They represent the impact of environment, affording the child its first experiences of pleasure and pain, of gratification and frustration, of love and hate, security and fear.

[6] Erik H. Erikson, *Childhood and Society*, Norton, New York, 1950, p. 219.
[7] Erikson, *op. cit.*, pp. 221–229.
[8] Robert Wyer, Jr., "Effect of Child-Rearing Attitudes and Behavior on Children's Responses to Hypothetical Social Situations," *J. pers. soc. Psychol.*, **2**, 4 (1965), pp. 480–486.

The newborn infant is by itself unprepared to evaluate these terrifying experiences. It is torn between its own selfish instinctual impulses and the outward demands that are suddenly imposed without warning. The mother is the only one who can guide the harassed little creature through the seething emotional whirlpool. Her love is the child's only possible reward for the painful sacrifices and adjustments it is called upon to make. The infant registers her approval or disapproval as a seismograph catches the faintest tremor of the earth. The mother's confidence becomes the child's confidence; her antagonism, a shattering catastrophe.

Psychiatric research has shown that the child's success or failure in negotiating these hazardous first steps depends largely on the parent's emotional attitudes. An anxious young mother, for example, may try her best to conceal her agitated feelings, but through her muscle tensions the infant will perceive the true state of affairs infallibly. It may react by nursing badly, and indigestion will follow. If the mother's disturbed condition persists, the child may form symptoms of serious illness. I have seen infants who, at the age of only two months, had already developed real neuroses because of the way they had been handled by their mothers and fathers.

The infants had absorbed the parent's anxieties like a blotter.[9]

Period II: Childhood

A second important period in the child's development of the capacity to love maturely is the time when his concept of self develops. He begins to differentiate himself from others and to engage in active role taking, that is, taking over attitudes from others. The age at which role taking starts and a concept of the self originates is difficult to ascertain precisely, but it has been variously estimated as the second or third year of life. Although role taking is a continuous process throughout life, and is essential to much social learning, it is of special significance for our discussion, since it explains how the child takes over feelings of love that parents and adults in the environment express toward it. The feelings from others are internalized when the child can imagine itself in place of the mother or father and take over what it feels these adults feel toward it.[10]

In the process of placing itself in the position of the parent and then reacting toward itself as it assumes the parent would, the child may come to take over either positive or negative attitudes, that is, "I am lovable" or "I am unlovable" (Figure 1). These early experiences with the mother

[9] Smiley Blanton, op. cit., pp. 92–94.
[10] Charles H. Cooley, Human Nature and the Social Order, Scribner's, New York, 1902, pp. 152–153. George Herbert Mead, Mind, Self, and Society, University of Chicago Press, Chicago, 1934, pp. 135–226.

Child places himself in position of parent

Figure 1   Child takes over parental attitudes toward himself.

and other adults are generally assumed to be fairly basic in establishing the child's capacity for love. When the child feels that it is loved and lovable, the social trust previously mentioned becomes more firmly implanted. Moreover, the child comes to view the world in a light of acceptance and warmth rather than hostility and rejection. When the child has love for itself and feels that it is loved by others, it does not constantly have to search for affirmation from others. It may turn its energies outward, utilizing them for the acceptance and love of others. Thus when the child knows emotionally how it feels to be loved, this feeling may be expressed toward others.

Period III. Preadolescence and Adolescence

A third significant period in the development of the capacity to love maturely has been described as occurring in preadolescence, between the ages of eight to twelve, and extending into adolescence.[11] During this period some of the egocentricity of infancy and childhood is reduced. Thus if one's life has been characterized by love and social trust, he can now express love toward another person and derive pleasure from the fact that someone else feels secure and loved. As greater personal security evolves and egocentricity is reduced, such love grows. The expression of such love has been described as initially felt in relation to persons who are similar, such as members of the same sex.[12] This may be because a

[11] Harry Stack Sullivan, *Conceptions of Modern Psychiatry,* The William Alanson White Psychiatric Foundation, Washington, D.C., 1947, p. 20.
[12] *Ibid.,* pp. 14–27.

person is more able to identify with his own sex grouping than with the opposite sex grouping. Consequently, he initially may feel safer sharing love with those of his own sex (the known); later, however, his love is expanded to include members of the opposite sex.

In the final analysis the capacity to love another person maturely is also expressed in a capacity to have love for people in general. The process of the transfer of love from self to others is accomplished easily if love is not arrested or fixated, that is, if it does not become too tied to oneself as in narcissism, to one's parents as in parental fixation, or to one's own sex as in homosexuality.

Table 7   Periods in Developing a Capacity to Love Maturely[a]

Period	Development	Love Object
Infancy	Initial development of security or insecurity, social trust, or social distrust	Mother
Childhood	Initial development of social self	Family members
Preadolescence and Adolescence	Love objects broaden to include those outside family	Peers Phase 1—homosexual Phase 2—heterosexual

[a] The periods are not intended to include all details, but merely to present the broad outline within which the processes occur.

Thus infancy, childhood, and preadolescence-adolescence are three essential periods in the development of the individual's capacity to love maturely, and much can occur during these periods to retard this development. When the early relationships between mother and infant break down, that is, when there is too little attention or too much attention, then patterns not conducive to the development of the capacity to love maturely may appear. If the infant is neglected or rejected, insecurity or withdrawal from love involvements with human beings may result. Once social mistrust develops, there is a tendency to view relationships anxiously. Such people may be fearful of letting their feelings be known, of expressing themselves, or of committing themselves to a relationship. The fear that one may be hurt and that "others cannot be counted on" keeps people from becoming involved and is probably responsible for much of the aloofness or detachment that may be encountered. If there is overprotection, prolonged egocentricity may result, making it difficult for the person to share mature love with others.

During the period of childhood it is also necessary for the family members to extend a "balanced" love toward the child. This point is summarized by Blanton:

This is the crux of the problem that faces all conscientious parents. At what point of the child's scale will they find the "adequate" mark on which to balance their love? If they are too harsh in their demands upon the child and do not give him enough love, he will be crippled in his ability to cope with his environment. He may become sullen and backward, or rebellious and over-aggressive. In either case he will feel rejected and robbed of his due, thus creating a permanent distortion of his personality and his faith in love.

Equally harmful effects will follow if the parents lavish too much love upon the child. He may become too strongly dependent in his emotional life, requiring a constant support and protection that will weaken his capacity to face stern realities alone. He may grow to feel dominated by his parents' love, and to resent the price he is compelled to pay in return. In that case he will learn to fear love as a burden and to hate all those who make its claims upon him.[13]

Furthermore, when role taking starts and self-attitudes begin to emerge, there is always the danger that negative self-attitudes will become internalized. The individual then sees himself as being essentially unloved and unlovable. Hence he finds it difficult to believe that others are in love with him and considers any love toward him to be shaky and insecure. Moreover, it is difficult for such persons to love others, since they operate in a world in which they feel love to be in short supply. Thus they are, so to speak, "stingy with love" and keep it to themselves. When the initial stages we have described have not been passed through successfully, it is difficult to lose one's self-centeredness in order to relate to the needs of others.

The patterns of parental acceptance or rejection have still further implications for the capacity to love maturely, since they may affect the way in which one relates to the opposite sex. The girl who finds her father harsh and demanding, has difficulty in relating at a later age to a man without being fearful or intimidated. The boy who discovers that he can never please his mother, frequently finds women a source of frustration. Thus the early concepts about men and women that emerge in part from parent-child relationships are important in the individual's development of the capacity to love.

Fixations

The movement from one phase of development to another may present additional problems. Failure to transcend a given stage of devel-

[13] Smiley Blanton, *op. cit.,* pg. 97.

opment is called pure fixation. Many of the more seriously disturbed individuals fall into this category. On the other hand, there may be regression fixation, which means that under stress one may go back to more infantile behavior characteristic of earlier life. Thus many, who are adults chronologically, may, when disappointed or frustrated, engage in temper tantrums, pout, or withdraw. They cannot deal with the frustration without regressing to earlier behavior that may have proved to be rewarding—either to gain attention or to get one's way. Although the concept of regression has general application, it specifically enables us to understand problems associated with sexual development.

Fixation at the homosexual phase may result in behavior that is exclusively homosexual, both homosexual and heterosexual, or sometimes latently homosexual, in which homosexuality is deeply repressed. Nevertheless, unresolved problems in this area have to be seen in a broader context. It is unfortunate that the concept of homosexuality carries with it many negative connotations. Yet it is true that some of the contempt that men have for women and women for men stems from a feeling of greater security with one's own sex and a fear of the opposite sex. Such attitudes may be noted in the preference for one-sex group and in efforts to maintain an old one-sex group. A number of years ago there was a song for men that went, "those wedding bells are breaking up that old gang of mine." Although one might have expected the thought of marriage to take precedence, marriage here is seen primarily as involving a loss of one's male friends.

Homosexuality may also be viewed as an expression of one's inability to transcend a given stage of development and to attain full maturity. Since fixation at any stage represents an insecurity about moving on to another phase of maturity, it is first and foremost a fundamental problem of *insecurity and inadequacy* and results in a good deal of self-rejection and self-hate. Our discussion regarding homosexuality rests on the assumption that fixation at the homosexual stage of one's development is less desirable than growth to full sexual maturity. Although such a view is held by virtually all psychiatrists both in this country and elsewhere, the *social definition of homosexuality* can vary from group to group. Certainly, it varies among contemporary homosexual groups. Moreover, among the ancient Greeks and American Indians the homosexual occupied a more favorable position than is the case in our own society. Such information is important to develop a perspective on homosexuality, but it should not obscure the problems that fixation of this type presents in the American context of the man-woman relationship. Finally, the kinds of attitudes derived from one's siblings and peers may also significantly affect one's capacity to love the opposite sex. Attitudes of depreciation about members of the opposite sex are not conducive to the expression of love.

We must emphasize that in a rather fundamental way the capacity to love maturely extends into many other aspects of life. As we have pointed out, the individual who is prepared to love others is first and foremost one who has a healthy self-image, hence is not readily afraid of people. He does not fear human involvement, nor the new experiences that emerge from it. He has the capacity to grow, to expand his horizons, and in a sense to pursue the quest for continued discovery of what he is. Thus to be prepared for mature love means also to be prepared for full participation in the experiences of life.[14]

Our discussion in this chapter has centered on the essential differences between mature and immature love, as well as on the development of the capacity to love maturely. Table 8 summarizes some of the essential differences between the two types of love. Such a summary will not only synthesize many of the things we have said, but may also assist the reader who is interested in self-examination or evaluation of his own involvements. It should be clear that immature love relationships lead to instability and successive difficulties. Mature love relationships afford the greatest opportunities for stability and growth in the marital union.

Table 8 A Comparison of Significant Characteristics That Engender Immature and Mature Love

Immature	Mature
1. Love arises through the ideas of · the one and only, love at first sight, and love wins out over all.	1. Love is an emergent experience that grows out of interaction, with a realistic understanding of the relationship.
2. The love relationship is characterized by considerable ambivalence, with alternate feelings of attraction, indifference, or repulsion. Such feelings of ambivalence are frustrating for the person who feels ambivalent and perhaps even more frustrating for the person who experiences ambivalence in the partner. The person who is on the receiving end of the ambivalence frequently develops considerable hostility and resentment.	2. The love relationship is characterized by relatively consistent feelings once the relationship has been established. Although some ambivalence may exist, it is seldom a pattern in the relationship; when it is present, it is usually related to some objective change in the relationship rather than inner doubts without foundation.

[14] Erikson, *op. cit.*, pp. 228–231.

Table 8 (*Continued*)

Immature	Mature
3. The love relationship is rooted primarily in sexual attraction. The concern is with personal, sexual satisfaction. A pronounced tendency for sexual involvement to remain static is present, since the quality of the involvement is egocentric. The tendency here is for people to avoid evaluating their capability of loving another in the complete sense. Thus there tends to be little recognition that love involves a capacity to love and to be loved, both of which have to be developed like other human attributes. To be able to love another human being consistently with completeness involves an emotional commitment and a high degree of personal integration devoid of the immaturities and personal difficulties discussed in the present chapter.	3. The love relationship is concerned with sexual satisfaction as one aspect of the total relationship. Sexual involvement is not static, but takes on more meaning as the relationship evolves, since there is a pronounced tendency to be concerned with the sexual and nonsexual needs of each other. The sexual involvement is much more relationship-centered than egocentric.
4. The love relationship is characterized by considerable jealousy, insecurity, and fears regarding the continuance of the relationship.	4. The love relationship is characterized by mutual trust, feelings of confidence, and security in each other.
5. The love relationship tends to be exploitative with considerable using of each other for own ends.	5. The love relationship is oriented toward acceptance of each other as persons deserving dignity and respect. There is an absence of using each other as commodities.
6. The love relationship is characterized by considerable idealization based on fantasy, with marked tendency to distort the reality of the other person and to fall in love with the distorted image.	6. The love relationship is characterized by an identification and by pride based on the favorable qualities that have been developed and realized.
7. The love relationship is characterized by marked tendency to change the partner and to impose one's values on the partner without regard to the other's wishes.	7. The love relationship is characterized by the tendency to accept differences as potentially enriching the union.

Immature	Mature
8. The love feeling is characterized by sensing that one may be in love with more than one member of the opposite sex at one time. There is the case of a young lady who was engaged to a man who was employed in a community about 100 miles from her home. The fiance visited every weekend, and the young lady reported that she always had a wonderful time with him. Nevertheless, she was confused, since she discovered that as soon as her boyfriend left, she began hoping that the phone would ring, in order that she be asked out by another boy.	8. The love feeling is oriented toward a single member of the opposite sex.
9. The love relationship is characterized by overt competitiveness toward the other partner, as well as feelings of repressed envy and the feeling that the achievement of one partner detracts from the desirability of the other. There is the case of the woman married to a public health officer. As a result of the husband's occupation he was called upon to speak to PTA groups frequently on the role of the family in maintaining proper health. His wife accompanied him on his talks and almost always after the man had completed his talk, his wife felt compelled to get up and add to her husband's comments. When she was through, the husband felt it necessary to clear up some point his wife had made; and so they went on until the audience became bored. This kind of competitiveness characterized their marriage for several years. Finally, the husband wrote a book only to discover that shortly after his book appeared his wife discovered a need to write articles for ladies' magazines.	9. The love relationship is characterized by pride in and identification with the achievements of each other. Thus as each member achieves something new, the other member has the feeling of sharing in the new achievement.

Types of People Not Capable of Mature Love Relationships

From all that has been said so far in this book it should be apparent that there are many persons who are not capable of experiencing mature love and who, therefore, encounter great difficulty in building a meaningful man-woman relationship. Some are lacking in the essential experiences that are conducive to the development of the capacity to love. It is probably safe to assert that few people are fortunate enough to have grown up in a home in which the kinds of familial relationships necessary for the development of the capacity to love are sufficiently plentiful and consistent. When the capacity to love maturely has not been properly developed, there are, almost always, certain kinds of emotional difficulties—immaturities, egocentricity, dependency, the wish to exploit, or narcissism. All of these complicate one's love relationships. Such persons, for example, may feel secure only when they can control or dominate the partner. Or they may relinquish themselves, and their wishes and beliefs, so long as someone will promise to love them. Neither of these patterns can lead to mature love relationships, since in mature love relationships each partner preserves his integrity. There are still other kinds of people who have not developed beyond the stage of receptive hoarding; they want only to receive, not to give. They view love only as a sacrifice, as having to give up things; hence they are not prepared for relationships involving mutuality.[15]

To some extent, each person with personal immaturities and difficulties is cynical with respect to finding love. Thus he tends to be somewhat on guard and suspicious about deep emotional commitments. He tends to be exploitative, in that he uses the partner to satisfy his own personal needs with no regard for reciprocity. The predominant characteristics of the emotionally immature person is his marked self-centeredness, which makes him incapable of experiencing mature love. He is generally too busy relieving his own anxieties or fears to be able to become concerned with the needs of other people. When self-centeredness becomes pronounced, we have what is called narcissism:

The term narcissism comes from the Greek legend about Narcissus, a boy who happened one day to see his image in a pool. He fell in love with his

[15] Erich Fromm, *op. cit.,* Ch. 2.

beautiful image, couldn't leave it, pined away and died. The boy was infatuated with an image of himself, but certainly he was not in love with his true self, for he neglected his real interests and welfare. Similarly, the narcissist is not in love with his true self, but with an image of himself, shimmering in all its glory and magnificence, not in a pool of water but in his imagination [16]

This description points out clearly the extent to which the narcissist is concerned with an imagined concept of himself. The fantastic creations that the narcissist may construct about himself are illustrated in the following case history of a woman undergoing psychoanalysis:

"My pulchritude exceeds my mental endowment. I am respectable, cultured, well-behaved. I am poised, proud, quiet and refined, clean-minded and meek. I am immaculate, delicate, tender, big-hearted, lovable, unselfish, unspoiled, generous, and ambitious. I don't gossip. I'm not vengeful. I don't gamble or drink. I have rare dexterity, am supermundane, possess savoir-faire. I'm perspicacious, perceptive, euphemistic, strong, healthy, and idealistic, and I make my own clothes."

This woman seems at first glance to have a world of self-confidence; in fact, she seems to have genuine self-love. A moment's reflection makes it clear, however, that she does not have genuine affection for herself, but rather is infatuated with her imaginative concept of herself. In fact at a deeper level this woman hates herself for what she really is. Her regard for herself is excessive, and inflated out of proportion with the reality of herself. Who has ever known a woman or man with all the virtues (including such contradictory ones as "proud" and "meek") which this lady ascribes to herself ? This psychological condition, self-infatuation, is known clinically as narcissism.[17]

An analysis of this case immediately reveals some common characteristics of the narcissistic individual, including the colossal egocentricity and the disregard for the needs of others. These stem essentially from the need to realize the image of oneself that has been constructed. Thus it is relatively easy for the narcissist to become exploitative and use people in a very casual and reckless manner with little remorse or feeling of guilt. Moreover, since he feels entitled to attention from others, he uses others without any emotional commitment or interest in them as people.

Although many of the essential features of the narcissist are clearly brought out in the above case, it should be remembered that this woman reveals herself in therapy. It is not likely that one will openly reveal himself as our patient has. Nevertheless, it is important to recognize that a

[16] Ralph Slater, "Narcissism versus Self-Love," paper prepared for *Auxiliary Council to the Association for the Advancement of Psychoanalysis, 1953.*
[17] *Ibid.*

great deal of narcissism is present in our society and is found in many love involvements. Needless to say, narcissistic patterns create great problems in the man-woman relationship and make a meaningful association difficult.

Much of what we have stated here about people with personal problems and immaturities, and the ways in which these affect their relationships with others, is summarized in the following excellent quotation:

The emotionally unstable person cannot help being self-centered. He is constantly preoccupied with his personal problems: how to keep his balance, how to adjust reality to his needs, how to impress people, how to steer clear of his inner turmoil. There is little incentive left for becoming acquainted with another person. The basic foundation of a good relationship and the development of mutuality—the real knowing of one another—is quite impossible. Emotionally unstable people do not, cannot, know each other. In the person with emotional problems there is not only unawareness of oneself and resistance to knowing oneself, but also unawareness of the love partner and an aversion to knowing her.[18]

Summary

Such beliefs as the existence of "a one and only," "love at first sight," and "love solves all problems" are conducive to the development of immature love, since their acceptance leads to the formation of attitudes toward love that are rooted in unreality and magic. Our society in general plays an important role in fostering these attitudes in the minds of people. Movies, television, popular ballads, novels, advertisements, and magazine articles are replete with immature notions concerning love. The fact that millions of dollars are poured each year into products that promote these immature attitudes toward love suggests that they have considerable appeal to the populace, both men and women.

Mature love, on the other hand, has little to do with ideas of love at first sight or destiny. Mature attitudes imply that love is rooted in needs that contribute to the intellectual and emotional growth of the partners and that they are rooted in reality. Mature love thus is viewed as an integration of personalities, resulting from adjustment and readjustment of the personalities of the partners.

[18] *Ibid.*

The capacity to love maturely develops out of a wide variety of personal and social experiences. For example, a person who is reared in a home where love is viewed as a sign of femininity and weakness is likely to acquire negative attitudes toward the desirability of love. Whereas the person who is reared in a family that values love as a human experience is likely to develop positive attitudes toward the desirability of love.

There are at least three important periods of interaction, which greatly influence the development of one's capacity to love maturely. First, during infancy the individual experiences his initial interaction with adults (particularly the mother) in the environment. If this interaction evokes positive responses from others, the infant feels secure and tends to explore further interactions with others without fearfulness.

Second, during childhood the individual learns to take over the feelings that he believes others express toward him. Thus the child on the basis of his interpretations of how others feel about him comes to view himself as being lovable or unlovable. When the child regards himself as lovable, he is capable of receiving and expressing love quite easily, whereas feelings of being unlovable markedly hinder his ability both to receive and to express love.

The third period in the development of the capacity to love maturely is preadolescence and adolescence. It is during this period that the individual increases the number of his love objects. The process of broadening one's love objects begins very early in life with love for self, which then grows to include love for parents and family members, and finally, during preadolescence and adolescence, love for people in general, starting with the members of one's own sex and ultimately including members of the opposite sex. When one's life is characterized by love and security, it becomes possible for him to widen his array of love objects quite easily. However, when one's life is devoid of love and security, he may fear expressing love toward others and retain all his love for himself or express it toward his parents with whom he feels more secure. When such fixation with respect to love objects occurs, the expressing of love toward people in general becomes markedly difficult and consequently one's capacity to love maturely is greatly impaired. Indeed, there are those who, because of their interaction with others and the resulting attitudes they acquire, are incapable of participating in a mature and healthy love relationship. The emotionally immature and unstable are illustrative of this point. In such cases the preoccupation with self and with one's own problems presents too great an obstacle; consequently one's ability to relate to others in a love relationship is made markedly difficult, if not impossible.

Questions

1. List several beliefs concerning love and show how each is associated with either mature or immature notions of love.
2. In what ways does society contribute to the growth of immature love? What, if anything, can be done to correct this?
3. In what way does the "cult of manliness" hinder the development of the capacity to love maturely?
4. How do interactions during infancy affect one's capacity to love maturely?
5. Describe fully the process of role taking and show how it affects the development of one's capacity to love maturely.
6. Explain what is meant by a fixation with respect to love objects. In what way does this impair one's ability to love maturely?
7. What is narcissism? How do narcissistic patterns make meaningful love relationships difficult?
8. List several types of emotionally immature and unstable people and show how each encounters difficulty in sharing a mature love relationship.

Suggestions for Research and Related Activities

1. Write down the words of at least three currently popular love songs and analyze the ideas contained in each, showing how they contribute to mature and/or immature love.
2. Select several magazine advertisements that you feel promote products associated with immature love. Explain why you think these products contribute to the development of immature love.
3. Analyze two love stories selected from any popular magazine. Using the list of characteristics of mature and immature love presented in this chapter, show how each story represents a mature and/or immature love relationship.

4. Hold a panel discussion on the following topic: "Teen-Agers' Exposure to Mature and Immature Attitudes Concerning Love."

Suggested Readings

Burgess, Ernest W., Harvey J. Locke, and Mary M. Thomes, *The Family,* 3rd ed., American Book Company, New York, 1963, Ch. 8, "Culture and Personality," Ch. 9, "Emotional Interaction," and Ch. 10, "Expectations and Roles."

Ellis, Albert, "Some Significant Correlates of Love and Family Attitudes and Behavior," *J. soc. Psychol.,* **30** (August 1949), pp. 3–16.

Framo, James L., "Rationale and Techniques of Intensive Family Therapy," in Ivan Boszormenyi-Nágy and James L. Framo, Eds., *Intensive Family Therapy,* Harper, New York, 1965, especially pp. 185–190 concerning development of the love sentiment.

Maier, Henry W., *Three Theories of Child Development,* Harper, New York, 1965, especially pp. 46–51 concerned with ever-widening circles of love objects.

Murphy, Gardner, *Personality: A Biosocial Approach to Origins and Structure,* Harper, New York, 1947, Ch. 20, "The Origin of the Self," Ch. 21, "The Evolution of the Self," and Ch. 22, "Enhancement and Defense of the Self."

Piaget, Jean, *The Child's Conception of the World,* Harcourt, Brace, New York, 1929.

Simpson, George, *People in Families,* Crowell-Collier, New York, 1960, Ch. 13, "Problems of Infancy," Ch. 14, "Problems of Infancy (Continued)," and Ch. 15, "Self-Realization in the Family: Childhood and Adolescence."

Stoller, Robert J., in Judd Marmor, Ed., *Sexual Inversion,* Basic Books, New York, 1965, Ch. 11, "Passing and the Continuum of Gender Identity."

Chapter Eight

NECKING,
PETTING,
AND PREMARITAL
SEXUAL
INTERCOURSE

A S SUGGESTED earlier, behavior patterns of the middle class appear to be diverse and going through significant change. Therefore, it is difficult to assess the extent of agreement on sexual norms in the area of premarital sexual behavior, and to differentiate between what people say they believe and how they actually behave.

Unquestionably, some change is now taking place in this country—often termed the sexual revolution or sexual renaissance and said to be a reaction against puritanical restraint. Such a reaction, however publicized at the moment, is probably not really new. People historically have reacted against conservative premarital sexual traditions, and much of the sexual behavior in this country, past or present, would be difficult to understand adequately except as a reaction against conservative tradi-

ILLUSTRATION: French paper doll, 1822. Courtesy of the Museum of the City of New York.

140

tions. Precise measurement of the extent of change, however, remains difficult.

One difficulty is the lack of a historical base line against which to measure the present. Unless we know what existed in the past, we may misrepresent it as having been more restrictive than it was, hence make the present appear to be excessively permissive by comparison. But virtually no measurement of actual behavior is possible for the nineteenth century, and only some data are available for the twentieth. Thus although many of the older generation today are certain that the youth of our nation have abandoned any semblance of moral behavior, actually the question of whether premarital petting and premarital sexual experience have increased significantly since the 1920s is not a simple one to answer. The best evidence from Kinsey states that it has not. Others who agree argue that although behavior has not changed significantly, *attitudes and values* that were once privately held are now quite out in the open. It is the open expression of *permissive attitudes and values* toward premarital petting and coitus that is *new*, rather than the *sexual behavior*.[1]

A second difficulty in the measurement of change has to do with the heterogeneity of the middle-class population. When we describe changes in premarital sexual norms, are we talking about middle-class youth in a large urban university or community or about middle-class youth in a small denominational college or community? To what percentage or segment of the middle-class population do such changes apply? Since those who advocate change toward greater permissiveness undoubtedly receive a great deal of publicity, is it not possible that we erroneously assume that such permissiveness is more widespread than, in fact, it is?

Finally, do we know whether changes taking place are permanent or temporary? Are we simply in one phase of a larger cycle of events ranging from permissiveness to rigidity in sexual norms? There are no simple answers because the issues and the ways of determining responses are complicated. And if the data from Kinsey and others are correct, much of what we are witnessing in the form of permissive premarital sexual behavior has been taking place in more subdued forms for some time. Behavior once subdued may be more out in the open today, as a result of rebellion against the norms of conventional society, an espoused search for relationships with depth and meaning, and the need to appear more

---

[1] Alfred C. Kinsey, Wardell B. Pomeroy, Clyde E. Martin, and Paul H. Gebhard, *Sexual Behavior in the Human Female*, Saunders, Philadelphia, 1953. Robert R. Bell, "Parent-Child Conflict in Sexual Values," *J. soc. Issues*, **22**, 2 (April 1966), pp. 34–44. Robert Bell and Leonard Blumberg, "Courtship Stages and Intimacy Attitudes," *Family Life Coordinator*, (March 1960), pp. 60–63.

sophisticated about premarital sex. All of these signs may give the appearance of new attitudes.[2]

The issues we have just presented pertain to changes that are taking place in our society. Regardless of trend, however, it is still important for one to arrive at an understanding of the nature and function of necking, petting, and premarital sexual relations if one wishes to develop a meaningful man-woman relationship. This is not a simple task, since our society fails to provide an orderly way for understanding the role and meaning of sexual involvements in general. For the most part, people who work out definitions about necking, petting,[3] and premarital sexual behavior do so with half-truths, confusions, and distortions.[4] Furthermore, an understanding of this aspect of the man-woman involvement is made exceedingly difficult by the fact that our society is going through considerable social changes as previously noted.[5] Thus the rules governing acceptable and unacceptable behavior are no longer well defined. In a rural homogeneous society the codes of behavior were presumably much less ambiguous; rules for proper or improper behavior were well formulated and understood. Under such circumstances, kissing or necking may have been discouraged by the respectable young lady and not expected by the respectable young man. Today, however, the norms regarding such personal behavior are not so clearly defined.[6] The fact that there is an inevitable conflict in values between parents and their children often intensifies the confusion. Parents representing the views of their own generation assume the burden of socialization in regard to sexual behavior. Their children, on the other hand, are often the recipients of misinformation, inadequate information, at times no information. It is not surprising that it is relatively easy in a situation lacking clarity or understanding for young people to seek advice from their peers

[2] For an excellent discussion of this question, see "Premarital Sexual Behavior: A Symposium," *J. Marr. Fam.*, 24 (1962), pp. 254–278. For a discussion of confusion in sex, see Paul Goodman, *Growing Up Absurd*, Random House, New York, 1960, pp. 119–129. See also Albert Ellis, *Folklore of Sex*, Grove Press, New York, 1961.
[3] Necking and petting differ in the degree of physical involvement, the latter referring to the fondling of the breasts and genitalia.
[4] Maureen Daly, *Profile of Youth*, Lippincott, Philadelphia, 1951, pp. 64–74.
[5] Lewis M. Terman et al., *Psychological Factors in Marital Happiness*, McGraw-Hill, New York, 1938, p. 323.
[6] John McPartland, "Footnote on Sex," *Harper's Magazine*, 192 (March 1946), p. 212. Our clearly two-valued attitude toward sex is stated by McPartland: "At one level of our social existence we are the most sensual and profligate of peoples, worshippers of breast and thigh, separating the fun and frolic of sex from any bindings of family and child. At the other level of our social existence we are the prissiest of prudes, a monogamous and chaste people to whom virginity is so sacred that it cannot be mentioned on our radios."

and establish norms of their own. In spite of efforts to establish new norms, however, there is still uncertainty about what one should or should not do in dating and courtship activities. How far should one go in the necking and petting involvement? What kinds of factors should one take into account in deciding how far to go? Are couples who engage in the premarital sex act immoral or is it only a matter of another kind of morality? These are not simple questions for which simple rules are available. The fact that large numbers of people are concerned with these kinds of problems suggests their complexity and highlights the need for a point of view that will enable these people to think intelligently about the issues.

The authors do not believe that it is their task to advocate a particular code of conduct with respect to necking, petting, and premarital sexual relations.[7] Nevertheless, we plan to suggest some ideas, based in part on research findings and in part on clinical observations, that are worthy of consideration and evaluation in attempting to arrive at a mature attitude regarding these areas of human experience.

Some Essential Ideas Regarding the Nature of Sexual Involvement

Sexual Involvement as Relatedness

At the outset it is important to state that sexual involvements of any type represent one way in which men and women establish relationships with each other.[8] Thus sexual involvement is primarily a type of social relationship, and like all such relationships it tells us something about the kinds of people involved and their motivations for the involvement. It is important to be aware of the role of sexual involvement in the man-woman relationship for at least two reasons. First, as a sensitive and subtle indicator of behavior, the sexual relationship may reveal needs that could create difficulty in the overall relationship. A second and somewhat related reason has to do with the possibility of differentiating an

[7] For a listing of arguments for and against premarital sexual intercourse, see Alfred C. Kinsey et al., *op. cit.*, pp. 307–309.
[8] Lester Kirkendall, "A Viewpoint on the Premarital Sex Problem," in Clark E. Vincent, *Readings in Marriage Counseling*, Crowell-Collier, New York, 1957, pp. 117–126.

essentially immature expression of sex from one that involves a mature and healthy sex interest. Let us turn to several illustrations.

The Commodity Orientation

Within the commodity orientation, the worth of a person is measured in terms of what he has to offer.[9] Human relationships tend to be evaluated on the basis of what can be derived from them; indeed, a date may be regarded as an investment. The male invests his money and time and may expect repayment from the female in terms of physical pleasures. The female may make herself sexually available, believing that this is necessary to repay the male. Although understandable and perhaps even necessary in the commercial world, commodity orientation in the man-woman relationship creates many problems. For to the extent that the commodity orientation operates, a deep concern for the person as a person is not present. Interaction based on such an orientation is not conducive to a meaningful union.

The Exploitative Orientation

In the commodity orientation there is usually an element of reciprocity, narrow though it may be; that is, value is given for value received. In the exploitative orientation, however, there is a need to manipulate others without any regard for their wishes; that is no value is given, but a value is sought.

An examination of some man-woman relationships reveals a pervasive need to use another person sexually. The reader has undoubtedly encountered the man or woman who enjoys involving others in amorous adventures without regard for their feelings. Such a person often derives considerable pride from his ability to manipulate others so that necking or sexual relations will take place.

Consider the example of a young man whose history of involvements with women appeared to be patterned. When first meeting a young lady, he would be polite and charming in every conceivable way. His goal of having the girl become sexually involved with him necessitated a considerable amount of planning and effort on his part. His friends noticed that whenever the young lady resisted his advances, he would become even more interested. When asked about this, he replied, "It's not the sexual pleasure that I enjoy as much as the thrill of the chase." For this man it was the thrill involved in manipulating and using another person that found expression in the sexual relationship.

[9] Erich Fromm, *Man for Himself,* Rinehart, New York, 1947.

Insecurity

The insecure person may employ erotic relationships as compensation for insecurity. Insecurity may motivate both sexes. In the male, the desire for necking and petting may be as much a desire for acceptance and security as it is for erotic satisfaction.[10] In a research project conducted by a student of one of the authors, it was reported that the majority of men felt that personal acceptance as exemplified by necking or petting was even more important to them than the sexual pleasures derived from these activities.

For women, erotic involvements may also serve needs for personal acceptance and security, especially since a woman, perhaps to a greater extent than a man, finds her personal security intimately tied to her physical attractiveness. Whereas the man who is physically unattractive has other compensations in the form of physical or athletic prowess, prestige in clubs or fraternal orders, and occupational success, these are not readily available to a woman. For some women the need for security may be so great that they are driven into a series of indiscriminate necking and petting involvements with many men, suggesting promiscuity.[11] But simply calling it promiscuity tells us little; in terms of psychological needs we can say that there are women whose needs for security are so excessive that they must have the demonstrativeness of every man with whom they are involved. Thus, in some instances, women who are sufficiently insecure may become indiscriminate in their necking and petting habits.

Organic-Tension Needs

Finally, the physical involvement may take the form of a quest for biological satisfaction, sometimes referred to as organic-tension needs. The search for biological satisfaction need not have negative connotations. Both male and female may simply be interested in the satisfaction of sexual tension and may be explicit about it. Relationships in which the desire for such satisfaction is present may, however, possess an egocentric quality. A misunderstanding of the nature of such needs creates difficulty, especially if the individuals cannot accept their basic biological impulses as natural and healthy. Under these circumstances people

[10] For a discussion of sexual intercourse motivated by factors other than physical satisfaction, see F. Alexander Magoun, *Love and Marriage*, Harper, New York, 1948, pp. 94–95.

[11] Norman E. Himes and Donald L. Taylor, *Your Marriage*, rev. ed., Rinehart, New York, 1955, p. 35.

often attempt to repress the significance of organic-tension needs in their relationships by unconsciously overemphasizing the importance of other nonsexual qualities and then tend to see these as the real bases for their relationships. Indeed, in the majority of such relationships these other nonsexual qualities are probably not even present. Consequently, by imagining that they are present or by overemphasizing their importance if they are present, one is distorting the relationship and may make commitments to become engaged or married when in reality there is no stable basis for such commitments. Needless to say, many relationships of this type could be based on a more realistic foundation if it were possible to assess the significance of the organic-tension component. If viewed realistically, these relationships could be accepted for what they are, and unwise commitments might be avoided.

The organic-tension component in the man-woman relationship is so powerful that it becomes formidable and difficult to deal with. The difficulty in even recognizing its existence in a relationship, as has just been discussed, illustrates this point. Without a doubt, the inability to recognize the importance of such needs in a man-woman relationship has resulted in marriages where each partner is quite sure that a mature love is present only to discover within a few months following marriage that such is not the case.

Healthy Relatedness

The negative components that we have just suggested need not necessarily be present in the erotic relationship. Sexual involvement may also be an expression of a mature and healthy love. We saw earlier that mature relationships are rooted in needs based on reality and needs that contribute to the intellectual and emotional growth of the members. Unfortunately, relationships in which the necking, petting, and premarital sexual involvement are an expression of a mature love are not particularly prevalent in our culture today.

Lester Kirkendall, who is much concerned with these problems, raises another significant issue when he speaks of the consequences of the *premarital sex act* for the *interpersonal relationship*. Does the act contribute to a lessening of egocentricity and to an understanding of and insight into the other person, as well as to responsibility, or does it have the opposite result? Premarital intercourse must be evaluated within the context of these kinds of consequences.[12]

[12] Lester Kirkendall, *Pre-Marital Intercourse and Interpersonal Relationships,* Julian Press, New York, 1961. See also Winston Ehrmann, *Premarital Dating Behavior,* Holt, New York, 1959; Michael Schofield, *The Sexual Behavior of Young People,* Longmans Green, London, 1965.

In dealing with the necking and petting relationship it is important to recognize that since people vary with regard to stages of maturity, the nature of the erotic involvement has to be carefully appraised. Necking and petting for the uninitiated or inexperienced may mean curiosity; but for a mature and integrated individual it means something else again. Finally, it is apparent that one ought to be alert to the immature personality pattern that may appear in the erotic relationship.[13] It may reveal tendencies that will cause difficulties not only in subsequent erotic unions but also in the overall relationship. Moreover, such an awareness of the immature aspects in erotic relationships may enable one to avoid premature commitments and involvements in relationships that have no stable basis. It is, of course, terribly difficult to deal with oneself in such objective terms. Few of us like to recognize the several facets of personality that may be expressed in the erotic involvement, but there is no more sober experience than the realization, without illusions and without distortions, of what a particular relationship really means.

Now that we have examined certain general considerations concerning the nature of sexual involvement, we move to another phase of inquiry—the degree of sexual involvement and its meaning for the man-woman relationship

A Continuum of Necking, Petting, and Premarital Sexual Intercourse

The degree of sexual involvement may be examined by looking at necking, petting, and premarital sexual intercourse in terms of a continuum. The continuum is simply a convenient way of describing the degrees of sexual involvement, with necking blending into petting and petting blending into premarital sexual intercourse. The sequence in such a continuum is as follows:

Absence of necking   Involvement increases ⟶   Indiscriminate premarital
(----/----/----/----/----/----/----)
⟵Involvement decreases   sexual intercourse

The basic question for most persons is how far on the continuum one ought to go and what factors one should take into account in reaching

[13] Lawrence S. Bee, *Marriage and Family Relations,* Harper, New York, 1959, pp. 80–81.

this decision. However, let us deal first with the two extremes of the continuum. Those who refuse to engage in any form of necking are at one end of the continuum, and those who pursue sexual relations with anyone are at the other end. For both extreme groups the question of how involved they should become would appear to be already answered. However, this is not necessarily true; indeed, in the authors' experience many of the individuals in these categories have considerable inner turmoil and anxiety because of unresolved conflicts about physical involvements. Those who refuse to engage in any necking often possess a rigidity and fear of physical involvement, which suggests emotional conflicts.[14] One of the predominant characteristics of these people is their emotional distance from others; since they have some basic fears about intimate human contact, sex becomes very frightening and any emotional closeness is disturbing. Many of them rationalize such aloofness as stemming from superior moral standards. On closer inspection, however, it is frequently found that they use a moral code to justify a fear of becoming involved with others.

Those who engage in sexual relations indiscriminately may have an equally serious problem: they may have failed to develop a sense of discrimination and appropriateness. As with all things—art, food, or sex—the mark of a mature, integrated person is the presence of discrimination. It is out of discrimination that things come to have a special meaning and significance. If anyone can be a friend, then the meaning of a friendship is obscure, since this implies that one can establish a friendship with any type of individual, even a destructive person. Likewise, if an individual can have sexual relations with any member of the opposite sex, then sex loses much of its meaning. Persons in this category, rather than being driven, in a sense, to run from the opposite sex, are indiscriminate in sex and engage in what we term compulsive sexual behavior. This does not necessarily mean that they are driven by sexual needs, but rather by some need to prove themselves. For example, a man, to prove his manliness, may become a Don Juan. Or a narcissistic woman may have a goddesslike image of herself and thus be driven to prove that no man whom she desires can resist her. That such people are beset by inner problems should be clear, and it is also obvious that those who engage in compulsive sex behavior use sex as a means of trying to resolve their problems.

For perhaps a majority of people, however, the basic question is neither one of completely refraining from physical involvements nor one of becoming indiscriminately involved in sexual relations. Instead, it is a

[14] Walter R. Stokes and David R. Mace, "Premarital Sexual Behavior," *Marr. Fam. Living*, 15 (August 1953), pp. 234–249.

question of deciding how involved they wish to become in the erotic relationship. At this point, therefore, we would like to introduce to the reader a frame of reference from which necking and petting may be viewed. We suggest that a meaningful point of view can be found in the examination of three crucial ideas:

1. The personality organization of the individuals involved.
2. The meaning of the erotic involvement for the partners.
3. The nature of the relationship.

We believe that these ideas are significant for two reasons. First, they offer a frame of reference from which one can examine his attitudes and develop a point of view. Second, they permit a maximum of respect and consideration for the needs and values of the partners in the relationship.

The Personality Organization of the Individuals Involved

An understanding of what each person is capable of experiencing in the physical relationship without anxiety and guilt is essential. The range of variability among persons is considerable,[15] and in mature relationships the people involved develop an understanding about what each is capable of experiencing before anxieties are aroused. If one or both partners are dissatisfied with the extent of the erotic involvement, whether it is too little or too much, the differences can be explored and perhaps an understanding obtained through discussion by consulting a counselor. As a rule, it is poor practice to manipulate a partner into more physical intimacies than he is capable of accepting, especially when there are well-entrenched personal taboos. To the extent that each person knows what the other can handle and accepts these facts, the air is cleared, so that each is acting in his own best interests as well as in the best interests of the other person.

That an understanding can be reached in regard to erotic intimacies is illustrated in Table 9. It shows confusion regarding appropriateness of necking and petting on the first date, as well as on the regular or steady date. However, when pinning or engagement have occurred, little offensive behavior is reported. It is reasonable to assume that in the latter relationships there has been an attempt to understand the erotic needs of the partners and to assess how far each can move toward erotic need fulfillment.

[15] Paul H. Landis, *Making the Most of Marriage,* 2nd ed., Appleton-Century-Crofts, New York, 1960, pp. 336–341.

Table 9   Relationship Involvement and Erotic Intimacy Level at Which Offensiveness Occurs, by Episodes[a]

	Necking and Petting above the Waist		Petting below the Waist		Attempted Intercourse and Attempted Intercourse with Violence			Total (Percent)
	N	Percent	N	Percent	N	Percent		
Ride home, first date or occasional date	411	55.0	60	31.4	25	30.1	496	48.5
Regular or steady date	295	39.4	104	54.5	43	51.8	442	43.3
Pinned or engaged	42	5.6	27	14.1	15	18.1	84	8.2
Total	748	100.0	191	100.0	83	100.0	1022	100.0

[a] From Clifford Kirkpatrick and Eugene Kanin, "Male Sex Aggression on a University Campus," *Am. soc. Rev.*, **22** (February 1957), p. 55.

The Meaning of the Erotic Involvement for the Partners

An understanding of what the physical involvement means is also important for those who wish to develop a frame of reference for necking and petting. The basic question is whether the erotic involvement has been defined, so that each person recognizes its meaning in the particular relationship. Heavy petting, for example, may define the relationship as serious to one person, but not for the other person. Such definitions appear to be important, since unwarranted assumptions about the meaning of heavy petting can create misunderstanding and resentment. The total relationship will be on a more realistic, honest foundation when the erotic involvement has been defined. The manner in which the meaning of necking and petting is made clear obviously involves tact, discrimination, and judgment; nevertheless, this usually can be accomplished to the very real satisfaction of both persons. We recognize, of course, that such a recommendation constitutes a very real challenge from several points of view. There are those who refuse to define the meaning of necking and petting in order to avoid the risks of losing the pleasures of the necking and petting relationship. Furthermore, there are those who purposely mislead others into assuming that the erotic involvement is indicative of a more serious relationship than in fact it is. Often, of course, it is impossible to define the meaning of necking and petting, since the people involved are confused. Even in these cases, however, it is of value to the couple to know that confusion exists as to the meaning of erotic involvement.

The Nature of the Relationship

The third significant variable to be considered in deciding how far to continue the erotic involvement has been partly suggested in our second point and has to do with the nature of the relationship. Here we are talking about the degree of meaningfulness, which includes the relative absence or presence of mature love. We are not primarily concerned with whether a particular relationship will result in marriage, but instead with its overall quality. With this in mind we would like to suggest the possibility of viewing the extent of erotic involvement as a function of the kind of relationship present. The more meaningful and mature the relationship, the greater the physical involvement—although the exact degree of involvement must, in the final analysis, be an individual matter. For those who are interested in developing meaning for the erotic involvement beyond the satisfaction of pure lust, our point may be of some significance.

The point of view just developed is sometimes expressed as a philosophy of *permissiveness with affection,* suggesting that petting and premarital coital behavior are reserved for serious and meaningful relationships.

Reiss, who used a scale to measure Premarital Sexual Permissiveness, reports that highly permissive groups give less relative support to *affectionless* kissing and petting behavior, and more to coital behavior associated with meaning and affection.[16] It is interesting to note that parents and youth in this country do not differ about the necessity for emotional involvement, petting, and coital behavior to be integrated. They differ only about the specific time when heavy petting and coital behavior should take place, with parents regarding these behaviors as activities associated with marriage.[17]

The notion of permissiveness with affection is characteristic of some cultures outside our own. Christensen, who studied a sample of college students in Denmark and compared them with samples in this country

[16] Ira L. Reiss, "Scaling of Premarital Sexual Permissiveness," *J. Marr. Fam.,* **26** (1964), pp. 188–198.
[17] Robert Bell and Jack V. Burkle, "Mother and Daughter Attitudes to Premarital Sexual Behavior," *Marr. Fam. Living,* **23** (1961), pp. 390–392.

from the Midwest and from a Mormon county in Utah, reports that Danish students are the most permissive. They are not promiscuous, however, nor are they involved in a wide range of affairs as some popular accounts would lead one to believe, since heavy petting and coitus are limited to one partner, usually the fiance or steady, and the relationship is expected to terminate in marriage. Thus permissiveness in Denmark carries with it *responsibility*—responsibility in the sense of commitment to a love relationship and responsibility in accepting the consequences of parenthood.[18]

Finally, it should be pointed out that the view of *permissiveness with affection* is probably most characteristic of middle- and upper- rather than lower-status groups. In the middle- and upper-status groups permissiveness poses greater threats to ongoing family prestige and continuity. They are also immersed in a set of traditions that are less subject to change from transient social norms.[19]

In contrast, in our society many people consider love and sexual involvements to be separate entities, having no real connection.[20] These people often look at sexual involvements in the most derogatory terms, as unclean and indicative of man's most depraved nature.[21] In the grossest form this attitude may be seen in the man who exalts his wife as the epitome of virtue and therefore is unable to have sexual relations with her. Thus he may be able to enjoy sexual relations with women for whom he has little regard, sometimes only prostitutes. The result of such attitudes, both before and after marriage, is that many people become intimately involved with those they care least about and remain aloof from those for whom they have great feeling. There is the case of the boy who was asked how far he "was able to go" with his girl. His reply was, "That's the girl I'm going to marry, I wouldn't try anything like that." Or the case of a girl who wanted to point out how much her boy friend

[18] Harold T. Christensen, "Scandinavian and American Sex Norms: Some Comparisons with Sociological Implications," *J. soc. Issues*, **22**, 2 (April 1966), pp. 60–76.
[19] Hallowell Pope and Dean D. Knudsen, "Premarital Sexual Norms, the Family and Social Change," *J. Marr. Fam.*, **27**, 3 (1965), pp. 314–323. Ira Reiss, "Premarital Sexual Permissiveness among Negroes and Whites," *Am. soc. Rev.*, **29**, 5 (1964), pp. 688–698. Ira Reiss, "Social Class and Premarital Sexual Permissiveness: A Re-Examination," *Am. soc. Rev.*, **30**, 5 (October 1965), pp. 747–757. See also Samuel H. Lowrie, "Early Marriage; Premarital Pregnancy and Associated Factors," *J. Marr. Fam.*, **27**, 1 (1965), pp. 48–58.
[20] Allan Fromme, *The Psychologist Looks at Sex and Marriage*, Barnes and Noble, New York, 1955.
[21] Sigmund Freud, "Contributions of the Psychology of Love: The Most Prevalent Form of Degradation in Erotic Life," *Collected Papers*, Vol. 16, Hogarth Press, London, 1934.

thought of her. She stated, "He has the highest regard for me. He won't even touch me."

In each of these cases there are distorted notions regarding the place of physical involvement in the man-woman relationship. In each instance, the greater the love, the less the physical involvement; and by implication, the less the love, the greater the physical involvement. Table 10 shows one way of illustrating this point—by using as a frame of reference the need areas discussed in Chapter 6.

Table 10   Need Fulfillment and Degree of Sexual Involvement[a]

	(minimum)	(maximum)
Companionship Freedom of communication—activity Emotional interdependence Sexual strivings		

[a]The solid line profile signifies little need involvement in three areas but a heavy sexual involvement, as in the case of lust; the profile consisting of a broken line signifies a heavy need involvement in three areas but only a slight sexual involvement, as in the cases of the young man and young woman mentioned in text.

To be sure, there are situations in which a boy's refusal to become involved physically may be indicative of respect. This is especially so in cases where the girl may have been sexually exploited earlier and where the male in question wishes to respect her wishes for limited physical involvement. But to the extent that this results in the notion that physical involvement and love are two separate things it may well prove to be damaging to the relationship as a whole.

Premarital Sexual Relations and the Man-Woman Relationship

Many people who can accept the viewpoint that the degree of physical involvement ought to be a function of the kind of relationship a couple have, frequently wonder if such a philosophy does not invariably lead to premarital sexual relations. The answer to this realistic and important question is that this philosophy need not necessarily lead to premarital sexual relations but that it certainly may.[22] Thus no mature couple can afford to become erotically involved without a clear understanding of the implications of their behavior. They would certainly have to assess, in addition to the pleasurable and what they may consider to be positive aspects, the very real problems associated with the premarital sex act. What, for example, are the responsibilities that each has toward the other? Is the sexual involvement likely to result in harm to one or both persons? [23]

Obviously, there are couples who have considered the consequences, and many of them perhaps have become convinced that their evaluation of the problems is realistic. Some couples believe that the premarital sex act makes their relationship closer and more meaningful, since now there is both an intellectual and a sexual union. Many also believe that participation in premarital sexual relations will facilitate their sexual adjustment in marriage. There is no doubt that many of these people are sincere in what they believe, and their views represent one approach to this question. It is difficult, however, to tell how valid these views are. Research is necessarily scanty, but in at least one study the majority of couples who admitted having premarital intercourse did claim that it strengthened their relationship.[24] With respect to the question of whether premarital intercourse facilitates marital success, Kanin and Howard report that sexual intercourse between engaged couples was associated with a higher degree of sexual adjustment (measured by orgastic capacity of the female) on the honeymoon than was found for a control group who had no previous sexual relations.[25] Both of these studies are

[22] For a discussion of the petting complex, see Alfred C. Kinsey et al., *op. cit.,* Ch. 16. For a discussion of the petting complex as an ingenious compromise between moral demands and sexual needs, see E. E. LeMasters, *Modern Courtship and Marriage,* Macmillan, New York, 1957, pp. 199–206.

[23] One study of how premarital intercourse affects the quality of the relationship is reported in Lester Kirkendall, *op. cit.,* pp. 119–123.

[24] Ernest W. Burgess and Paul Wallin, *Engagement and Marriage,* Lippincott, Philadelphia, 1953, pp. 361, 371–376. However, couples who refrained from having premarital intercourse were not asked whether abstinence strengthened or weakened their relationship. They might have reported unanimously that their relationship had been strengthened by their restraint. This study also found (p. 361) that those couples who had premarital intercourse had only slightly lower engagement success scores than those who did not.

[25] Eugene J. Kanin and David H. Howard, "Postmarital Consequences of Premarital Sex Adjustments," *Am. soc. Rev.,* **23** (October 1958), p. 562. Other studies that also show a relationship between premarital sexual orgasm and orgasm in marriage are Alfred C. Kinsey et al., *op. cit.,* pp. 385–390; Lewis M. Terman et al., *op. cit.,* p. 383; and Ernest W. Burgess and Paul Wallin, *op. cit.,* pp. 362–363. However, it is also noted that those who had premarital intercourse are more likely than others to

interesting and perhaps significant; they certainly indicate the very real need for additional studies in this area, since they run counter to what many would have anticipated.

Furthermore, Hamblin and Blood, who evaluated research on the relation between premarital sexual experience and the wife's sexual adjustment, report that the significant factor is not whether premarital sexual experience occurred or not. Instead, a more basic factor, *generalized scruples against all sexual pleasure,* accounts largely for the observed tie-in between the two. This study casts doubt on whether premarital sexual intercourse per se is related to marital orgasm rates.[26] It suggests that the underlying factor is not whether premarital sexual experience *did* or *did not* occur. Marked inhibition about sexual pleasure was the factor responsible for both lack of *sexual experience* before marriage and *sexual adjustment* in marriage as evidenced by orgasm capacity.

These findings, however, would have to be weighed against other research on premarital sexual relations and on overall marital success, as opposed to the less inclusive sexual adjustment.[27] For the most part, the studies that do deal with the effect of premarital sexual relations on overall marital adjustment show that couples who have not had premarital intercourse have a slightly better chance to attain overall marital success than do those couples who have had premarital relations with their mates and with others.[28] As to whether the chances of marital success are better for persons who had intercourse only with their future mate, as opposed to those who had sexual relations with additional individuals, the evidence is quite unclear.[29]

In evaluating the research on the effect of premarital sexual intercourse on the man-woman relationship, we must conclude that the findings, being based on a small number of studies, employing different methods, and using restricted samples of people, are extremely limited in their scope. Hence the research findings are regarded as suggestive and not as conclusive.[30]

engage in extramarital intercourse as well; see Alfred C. Kinsey et al., *op. cit.,* p. 427.

[26] Robert L. Hamblin and Robert O. Blood, "Premarital Experience and the Wife's Sexual Adjustment," *Social Prob.,* 4 (October 1956), pp. 122–130.

[27] Harriet R. Mowrer, "Sex and Marital Adjustment: A Critique of Kinsey's Approach," *Social Prob.,* 1 (April 1954), pp. 147–152.

[28] Burgess and Wallin, *op. cit.,* pp. 368–371. Lewis M. Terman et al., *op. cit.,* p. 329. Harvey J. Locke, *Predicting Adjustment in Marriage: A Comparison of a Divorced and a Happily Married Group,* Holt, New York, 1951, p. 133.

[29] Burgess and Wallin, *op. cit.,* p. 371.

[30] Ehrmann states that whether one enters marriage as a virgin or nonvirgin may not be a sufficiently discriminating measure of the effect that premarital intercourse has

Finally, to understand more fully the impact of premarital sex on a relationship, at least two other important considerations must be taken into account: (1) the conditions under which premarital sexual relations occur and (2) the possibility of pregnancy.

Conditions under Which Premarital Sexual Relations Occur

The conditions under which the premarital sex act occurs may lead to difficulty between the persons.[31] For example, there is the need for a place where the couple can feel relatively safe and secure. This frequently involves leaving the community and going to another where the roles of husband and wife are assumed for registry at hotels or motels. Even under these conditions the anxiety about discovery continues to be a problem. Furthermore, many couples find the need to hide, to disguise one's identity, and the duplicity involved personally repugnant. All of this, which is a by-product of the premarital sexual involvement, may become associated with sexual relations with a particular person. Thus these negative reactions may destroy a good relationship, because one or both partners are not really emotionally prepared for all that the premarital sexual involvement entails. Under these circumstances, couples who are perfectly capable of good adjustments, sexual and other, may abandon the relationship because of its identification with things unpleasant.[32]

Although there is the real possibility of negative aftereffects, they do not, of course, occur in all cases, since people vary in their personal and social experience. Thus for many there seem to be no observable problems associated with premarital involvement. Some may come from homes that have very permissive views, some may be well integrated into a peer group in which premarital coitus is accepted.

Premarital Sexual Relations and Pregnancy

Of all the difficulties associated with premarital sexual relations, pregnancy is the most serious, in the opinion of the authors. To be sure,

---

on marital success. He suggests, for example, that more attention be given to the meaning that the premarital sex act has for the person. Winston Ehrmann, "Premarital Sexual Behavior and Sex Codes of Conduct with Acquaintances, Friends and Lovers," *Social Forces*, **38** (December 1959), pp. 158–164.

[31] James A. Peterson, *Education for Marriage*, Scribner's, New York, 1956, pp. 101–102.

[32] For a discussion of how premarital sex may hinder or aid personal adjustment, see Allan Fromme, *op. cit.*, pp. 80–82.

it is difficult to ascertain the likelihood that pregnancy will occur in any particular case.[33] Furthermore, since modern contraceptive devices are readily available today, one might assume that the chances for pregnancy are limited.[34] All of this is offset, however, by the fact that the conditions under which the premarital sex act occurs are such that frequently proper precautions are not taken. Moreover, the age range of the unmarried often coincides with the years of high fertility. Thus whenever sexual relations occur, the persons involved have to be emotionally ready to accept the possibility of pregnancy. There are those persons who feel that their relationship has progressed to the point where they would go ahead with marriage plans if pregnancy occurred. Although both persons in the relationship may have good intentions at the time when such declarations are made, feelings may change. The boyfriend who was eager and willing to become married may suddenly resent the coercion that he feels impinging when the premarital pregnancy is discovered. Even if marriage occurs, it has less likelihood of success than have nonpregnancy related marriages.[35]

In turning our attention to the actual plight of the woman, we must note that the woman bears the biological consequences of pregnancy and carries the burden and stigma in our culture.[36] The middle-class woman

[33] Harold T. Christensen, "Studies in Child Spacing: I—Premarital Pregnancy as Measured by the Spacing of the First Birth from Marriage," *Am. soc. Rev.*, 18 (February 1953), pp. 53–59. By checking marriage and birth records in an Indiana county, Christensen conservatively estimated that about one fifth of all first births within marriage were conceived before marriage. He presents conditions (age, occupation, etc.) that may cause this rate to vary.

[34] Although in fact Vincent reports that increases in the rate of illegitimacy between 1938 and 1957 were more than four times greater among age groups 25–29 and 30–34 than 15–19. From 1957 to 1963 the greatest increase was in groups 20 years and older. The rate for 15–19-year-olds actually decreased in comparison with the older group. Clark E. Vincent, "Teen-Age Unwed Mothers in American Society," *J. soc. Issues*, 22, 2 (April 1966), pp. 22–34.

[35] Harold T. Christensen and Hanna H. Meissner, "Studies in Child Spacing: III—Premarital Pregnancy as a Factor in Divorce," *Am. soc. Rev.*, 18 (December 1953), pp. 641–644. These authors found that chances of unsuccessful marriage are related (from most to least) to the following: (1) delayed marriage following pregnancy; (2) early marriage following pregnancy; (3) early pregnancy following marriage; and (4) delayed pregnancy following marriage. Harold T. Christensen, "Cultural Relativism and Premarital Sex Norms," *Am. soc. Rev.*, 25 (February 1960), pp. 31–39. However, when comparing samples from Utah, Indiana, and Denmark, Christensen found that sexual permissiveness (in Denmark) was associated with higher incidences of premarital pregnancy but lower negative effects of premarital pregnancy. The study is significant in indicating the importance of the overall cultural milieu as a variable.

[36] Ruth Shonle Cavan, *American Marriage*, Crowell-Collier, New York, 1959, pp. 210–212.

in this situation often must move from the community and have her baby in another environment.[37] Frequently she must do so without the essential emotional support of those close to her. This is followed by decisions concerning what to do with the infant and the problem of reestablishment of the mother in the community. The psychic scars produced by the fears and anxieties often remain as unpleasant reminders of events that might best be forgotten. As the reader well knows, our culture has not yet resolved the inconsistencies in its handling of the unwed mother. On the one hand, it inadvertently encourages intimacies by glorifying sex through ads, movies, and popular ballads; at the same time, there is a mixture of pity and contempt for the unwed mother. The young lady who may have been the pride of a community is treated like a pariah when it is learned that she has become pregnant out of wedlock.

Conclusion

We have certainly not exhausted all of the ways in which the premarital sex act may be viewed. It is well recognized, for example, that large numbers of premarital sexual relationships occur in our society. And certainly there are those who would argue that no real harm comes to these people as a result. Furthermore, people with an essentially individualistic philosophy believe that mature love, or meaningfulness, need not be an important criterion for premarital sexual involvement. They assert that indulgence in the sexual act is a personal prerogative, so long as it is not harmful to the persons involved. These are all points of view to which many people subscribe; they are therefore determinants of action and conduct.

We have tried to assess some of the basic considerations in the matter of erotic involvement. Out of this assessment the reader may be able to formulate and crystallize an approach to premarital sexual relations that makes sense to him. Ultimately, of course, questions of this type are found to be deeply woven into the morality and the system of ethics in which one has been nurtured. But ethics and morality need not stand apart from knowledge. In some instances knowledge may fortify one's moral and ethical position; in others, it may lead to a reassessment. The reader has the opportunity inherent in this challenge.

[37] Clark E. Vincent, "The Unwed Mother and Sampling Bias," *Am. soc. Rev.*, **19** (October 1954), pp. 562–567. This study reports that unwed motherhood is more prevalent than we know and claims that we have a distorted concept of unwed motherhood (as lower-class, poor, uneducated) because our information comes largely from social agencies.

Summary

An objective understanding of changes that are allegedly taking place in contemporary premarital sexual norms is made very difficult for several reasons. Among them are differences between what people say they believe and how they actually behave; an inability to compare present sexual standards with those of the past because of lack of appropriate measuring devices; and finally the fact that it is simply not known whether changes that may be taking place are permanent, temporary, or simply a phase of a larger cycle of events pertaining to premarital sexual behavior. Furthermore, an objective understanding of the role of sexual behavior in the man-woman relationship is frequently impaired by two factors: (1) the difficulty that individuals have in coming to grips realistically with the meaning that sex holds for them and (2) the presence of half-truths and distortions in our society concerning sexual involvement. Although sexual involvement may be regarded as one means by which a man and a woman relate to each other, the meaning that this relatedness has may not only be different for each person involved in the relationship, but may also be very narrowly oriented. Some people, for example, may be sexually motivated by commodity, exploitative, insecurity, or lust orientations, whereas for others sexual involvement may be an expression of healthy and meaningful relatedness. It is important, therefore, that people make every attempt to understand the sexual motivations operating in their relationships. If the motivations are based on lust, the partners should be explicit about this and understand the consequences that this has for them. If, on the other hand, the motivations are the results of deep and meaningful relatedness, this should be known, because the consequences that such motivations have for the relationship will be different.

Without attempting to establish a code of sexual conduct to be indiscriminately followed by all, we suggest that couples give serious attention to the role that sexual involvement plays in their specific relationships by considering the following: (1) the personality organization of the individuals involved, (2) the meaning of the erotic involvement for the partners, and (3) the nature of the relationship.

Viewing sexual involvement as something apart from love can impair the development of a meaningful relationship. Indeed, sexual involvement is a part of the total love relationship and may serve as a reflection of the general quality of the total love relationship; this may be true of permissiveness with affection. Unfortunately, few love relationships of unmarried couples have developed sufficient meaning and depth to warrant deep sexual involvement. Couples, in attempting to determine the extent to which they should become sexually involved, should consider the effects on the relationship of the conditions under which the premarital sexual act occurs and of the possibility of pregnancy.

Questions

1. Why is it difficult to obtain an objective understanding of changes that may be taking place in premarital sexual norms? Explain your answers in full.
2. What is meant by "sexual involvement as relatedness"? Define the following and give one example of each:
   a. Commodity orientation
   b. Exploitative orientation
   c. Insecurity and sexual relatedness
   d. Lust and sexual relatedness
3. In what way are those people who refuse to engage in any necking or petting activities similar to those who engage in indiscriminate necking and petting?
4. List and describe the three crucial ideas involved in establishing one's own sexual code in a man-woman relationship. Why are these ideas significant?
5. What is the danger in the following statement: "I wouldn't try anything sexual with her, because she's the girl I'm going to marry"? For what reasons might such thinking become prevalent in the American society?
6. What is the difference between sexual adjustment in marriage and overall marital success? What do research findings tend to show concerning the relationships between premarital sexual intercourse and sexual adjustment and conerning premarital sexual intercourse and overall marital success? Can these findings be regarded as conclusive? Why?
7. What effect might the conditions under which premarital sexual involvement takes place have on the total man-woman relationship?
8. Is the American society prepared to deal with premarital pregnancy? If so, explain how. If not, explain why not.

Projects

1. Have a panel discussion concerning the pros and cons of granting social approval to premarital sexual intercourse in the United States today.
2. Read one of the current books concerning premarital sexual behavior and compare the advice it offers with what has been discussed in this chapter.

Suggested Readings

Bell, Robert R., *Premarital Sex in a Changing Society*, Prentice-Hall, Englewood Cliffs, N.J., 1966.

Burgess, Ernest W., and Paul Wallin, *Engagement and Marriage*, Lippincott, Philadelphia, 1953, Ch. 12, "Assessing Premarital Intercourse."

Clothier, Florence, "The Unmarried Mother of School Age as Seen by a Psychiatrist," *Mental Hyg.*, 39 (October 1955), pp. 631–646.

Drucker, A. J., Harold T. Christensen, and H. H. Remmers, "Some Background Factors in Socio-Sexual Modernism," *Marr. Fam. Living*, 14 (November 1952), pp. 334–337.

Ehrmann, Winston, "Marital and Non-Marital Sexual Behavior," in Harold T. Christensen, Ed., *Handbook of Marriage and the Family*, Rand McNally, Chicago, 1964, Ch. 15.

Kanin, Eugene J., and David H. Howard, "Postmarital Consequences of Premarital Sex Adjustments," *Am. soc. Rev.*, 23 (October 1958), pp. 556–562.

Kirkendall, Lester A., *Premarital Intercourse and Interpersonal Relationships*, Matrix House, 1966.

Krich, Aron, Ed., *The Sexual Revolution*, Vol. 2, Dell Publishing Company, New York, 1965.

Levy, Dorothy, "A Follow-up Study of Unmarried Mothers," *Social Casework*, 36 (January 1955), pp. 27–33.

Magoun, F. Alexander, *Love and Marriage*, Harper, New York, 1948, Ch. 4, "The Pre-marital Sex Problem."

"Sexual Behavior: How Shall We Define and Motivate What Is Acceptable?" A Symposium, *J. soc. Hyg.*, **36** (April 1950), pp. 129–161.

Stokes, Walter R., et al., "Premarital Sexual Behavior," *Marr. Fam. Living,* **15** (August 1953), pp. 234–249.

Chapter Nine

THE ROLE OF
DATING IN THE
MAN-WOMAN
RELATIONSHIP

THE DEVELOPMENT of a meaningful man-woman relationship is closely related to patterns of dating. Dating, of course, had little or no importance in the past, when young people began the man-woman relationship by "courting" rather than dating. Courting, which was expected to result in marriage, was under the rigorous control of family, neighborhood, and church. Their combined influence operated so as to demand that every step in the premarital man-woman involvement follow a well-defined pattern. Courtship was formal and strictly defined. Such behaviors as a kiss, a declaration of love, or the attendance of a young man with the same young woman at the "Thursday night prayer-meeting for two consecutive weeks" were viewed by all as definite commitments toward marriage. And if any doubt existed in the young people's minds, they were quickly reminded that this was the case and their intentions were immediately asked for in no uncertain terms.[1]

Today, however, this formal courtship pattern has largely given way

[1] Niles Carpenter, "Courtship Practices and Contemporary Social Change in America," *Ann. Am. Acad. polit. soc. Sci.,* **160** (1932), pp. 38–44.

ILLUSTRATION: Circus toys, c. 1910. Courtesy of the Museum of the City of New York.

to a more informal pattern known as dating. Just as courtship was considered to be the prelude to marriage, dating has come to be viewed as the prelude to courtship.

In the informal dating pattern, the behaviors of the unmarried are no longer under the binding controls of family, neighborhood, and church. Instead, young people have demanded and have largely received the right to set their own limitations on dating behavior. In addition, young people today work out their own definitions of behaviors that are or are not commitments to marriage. This informal dating pattern (which, incidentally, is predominantly American) is largely a result of certain social changes that have taken place.[2]

The Emergence of Dating

The replacement of the formal courtship pattern by the informal dating pattern as a means of initiating man-woman relationships was made necessary, first, by the urbanization of American society and, second, by the increasing demands that young people began to make on marriage.

The urbanization of society and the resulting variety of people and points of view tended to reduce the homogeneity that had existed in the rural setting. Similarity of background or interests could no longer be taken for granted, and the extent of a couple's differences or similarities could be discovered only through repeated, informal encounters—the pattern that came to be termed dating.

Moreover, as we saw earlier, the urban environment and the person-centered orientation that it ushered in brought about greater individuality in mate selection. Young people no longer wished to have their choices dictated or controlled by the church, the family, or the neighborhood. Hence dating patterns were developed that provided a means of initiating the man-woman relationship without the conventional constraints of the church or family.[3]

A second and perhaps more important reason for the emergence of the informal dating pattern was the increasing search by young people for personally more fulfilling marriage relationships. Indeed, marriage,

[2] John F. Cuber, "Changing Courtship Customs," *Ann. Am. Acad. polit. soc. Sci.*, **229** (1943), pp. 31–34.
[3] Marvin R. Koller, "Some Changes in Courtship Behavior in Three Generations of Ohio Women," *Am. soc. Rev.*, **16** (June 1951), pp. 366–370.

which was once viewed predominantly as an economic arrangement, came to be viewed more and more as a means of fulfilling such personal needs as being loved, appreciated, and respected, as well as a means of expressing interpersonal compatibility, which involved the sharing of interests and values. So long as the basis of marriage centered in economic and practical concerns, there was little need for determining compatibilities or interests. It is only when the very basis of what was sought in marriage underwent change that it became necessary to establish new ways of discovering whether or not these more personal values were present in the relationship.[4]

The Significance of Dating in Building a Meaningful Man-Woman Relationship

Dating, when conducted with maturity and realism, is unquestionably an essential stage in the development of a meaningful man-woman relationship. Every date offers an opportunity to acquire knowledge about a particular member of the opposite sex and about the nature of man-woman involvement in general. There is indeed much to be learned about the sexes, and although many of us pride ourselves on our assumed knowledge of the opposite sex, this knowledge is generally limited and faulty.[5] Why is this so?

To begin with, it is questionable whether our society prepares us adequately to understand or to get along with persons of the opposite sex. All of us, by virtue of our sex, are reared for many years in "closed societies." Until adolescence, interactions with the opposite sex are few indeed. Thus, during the formative period of our development, our associations and experiences are restricted largely to members of our own sex. The tendency for each sex to interact with its own grouping helps to orient us in terms of how we are to behave and think as boys or girls. Thus we normally acquire the ideology, the point of view, or the set of attitudes that members of the sex to which we belong possess.[6]

[4] James A. Peterson, *Education for Marriage*, Scribner's, New York, 1956, pp. 120–125.
[5] Samuel Harman Lowrie, "Dating Theories and Student Responses," *Am. soc. Rev.*, 16 (June 1951), pp. 334–339.
[6] Mirra Komarovsky, *Women in the Modern World*, Little, Brown, Boston, 1953, pp. 53–67.

The same process that teaches us to become like those of our own sex is often the source of distortions and erroneous notions about the opposite sex. Such distortions impose obstacles to free and spontaneous interaction between the sexes, since men and women do not see each other as they are, but as distorted perceptions make them appear. Although in some instances we may come to idealize members of the opposite sex and view them as being better than they are, there is also the converse pattern of viewing the opposite sex as being worse than they are. Some distortions are conscious, such as "women are impractical, overemotional scatterbrains," "men are motivated only by sexual pleasures," or "men are really big boys who haven't grown up." At a deeper, unconscious level women may feel that men are gross and insensitive, and men may feel that women are exploitative. Such deep-seated attitudes frequently arise out of particular personal experiences in the life history of the individual. For example, one boy who grew up with a mother who exploited his father came to feel that all women were exploitative. He stated that his mother had been seriously ill during her adolescence. Although she recovered quite well, she insisted on presenting herself to others as sickly and ill. Whenever possible, she took advantage of her presumed state of ill health in order to shift her responsibilities to her husband. Frequently the husband had to rise early and dress and feed the children before going to work. On his return for lunch he would feed the children, do the dishes, and return to work. Often he prepared the evening meal and did the laundry. This young man, who had observed the exploitation of his father by his mother, categorized all women as exploitative and feared involvement with them.

Although some men may be crude or insensitive and some women exploitative, it is obviously inaccurate to categorize men or women simply as being specifically one thing or another. Each man, and each woman, is essentially different and has to be evaluated individually. A failure to do so results in distortion and prejudice, a prejudice no less disruptive for its being based on sex rather than on religious or racial affiliation. There is little doubt that all of us have acquired distortions about the opposite sex which serve to hinder our ultimate adjustment and understanding of it. Since such distortions have developed over long periods of time and out of experiences that have been forgotten and repressed, they are not easily removed. Like any other habit system, they tend to resist change. Furthermore, once such stereotypes about women or men develop, they become well-entrenched ways of thinking and feeling about the opposite sex. Some people, for example, may even prefer to avoid interaction with the opposite sex in order to avoid exposing their attitudes to reality. There is the case of a young lady who at the age of eighteen had a traumatic involvement with a man who was ten years older. Although sexual relations did not occur, the man apparently initiated the girl into heavy necking and petting. All of this happened so suddenly during a date that the girl became hysterical and felt that she was fortunate to have escaped sexual involvement. Ever since this experience the young lady insists on seeing men as essentially crude and insensitive. She refrains from dating, since to her all men are the same, and prefers to cling to her views rather than to expose them to reality.

We would like to emphasize that the most significant benefits that come from extensive dating are those that promote a breakdown of the prejudices and distortions about the opposite sex and facilitate the understanding of the nature of men and women. The dating relationship may afford an opportunity to change preconceived notions about men or women. With a breakdown of acquired distortions, it becomes possible to have a clearer picture of the opposite sex and to develop a concept of what one wants in a husband or wife out of interaction rather than distorted fantasy. In this way dating may, under the most favorable conditions, lead to meaningful relationships, that is, relationships that involve deep emotional commitments, based on mature needs, interests, and feelings for one another.

You may wonder, at this point, why the sexes pursue one another if each has certain negative views toward the other. In spite of all that has been said, there are very real erotic and emotional needs that most persons can satisfy only in a relationship with the opposite sex. Unfortunately, the distortions we have described create ambivalence toward the opposite sex; they result in tendencies to limit one's commitment to a relationship and therefore thwart the fulfillment of expectations.[7]

Although we have devoted several pages to a discussion of the potential fruitfulness of dating, we immediately recognize that frequently the values of dating are thwarted. If dating nurtures maturities, it can lead to meaningful man-woman relationships; if it nurtures immaturities, however, it may lead to meaningless relationships. Ruth Cavan summarizes very well the latter alternative with respect to marriage by stating that

. . . dating develops some attitudes that are opposed to those needed in marriage. The grasping after individual ego-satisfaction, the exploitation, the noncommittal attitude that takes little or no responsibility for the welfare of the partner, and the constant playing with sex on a superficial basis are all contrary to the relationship that underlies a harmonious marriage.[8]

[7] For a discussion of other positive functions of dating, see Evelyn M. Duvall and Reuben Hill, *Being Married*, D. C. Heath, Boston, 1960, pp. 4–5.
[8] Ruth Shonle Cavan, *The American Family*, Crowell-Collier, New York, 1953, p. 307.

Dating Problems That Interfere with the Building of a Meaningful Man-Woman Relationship

Motivations

Some motivations for dating can constitute serious obstacles to the development of a meaningful man-woman relationship. If the predominant motivation is simply "to put in time," with little or no sensitivity to the actual dating involvement, then little that is of potential value can be realized. When students in a marriage and parenthood class were asked why they dated, the immediate responses were somewhat as follows: "I date because . . . well, I don't know, I never really tried to figure it out. I date because everybody dates. I don't ask myself why, I just date." On pressing for more concrete reasons, however, the writers found that young people apparently date for several reasons.

The first, and most frequently given, reason is that "dating is fun, nothing more. It's just fun and I enjoy it. It's relaxing." Second, young people sometimes date because they feel they have to. "Where can a guy go on a Saturday night without a date? To a dance, to the movies, for a walk in the park, yeah, then everybody says what's wrong with him that he doesn't date? If you want to attend the important social events you must date. They're set up for couples, not for stags." Or as a coed pointedly asked, "Did you ever sit in the dorm on a date night?" Third, young people sometimes date in order to retain or achieve popularity. "It's simple, if you want to be popular you have to date. Otherwise, you're nobody. It's through dating certain fellows that I came to be accepted by this crowd. They're the popular set here, and without dating fellows from their group, I don't know how I could have become one of them."

Admittedly, these are probably but a few of many motives that young people have for dating. And each person may have different reasons for dating different people. Some people are dated because they are fun to be with, some because the individual was "stuck for a date," some because they maintain or even add to popularity, and still others, we might add, for purposes of financial or sexual exploitation. The important point here is that dating for the purpose of fostering an understanding of the opposite sex and of developing meaningful relationships is only one of many reasons. It is frequently overlooked by young people as a motive for dating and is apparently regarded as not too important a reason at that! This is not to say that dating cannot or should not be fun, nor that such considerations as popularity should not play a part. However, when the factors of fun and popularity become the predominant motives behind dating patterns, they tend to mask interest in the dating partners themselves; hence the potentiality of developing a sincere concern for understanding the opposite sex, and oneself for that matter, through dating is grossly diminished. It is in this sense that the meaning of fun within the context of the man-woman relationship must be understood. Many young people fail to receive the full benefits that the dating experience can afford them, because of their shortsighted view of dating. Some even consider dating and marriage to be unrelated activities. A young lady reported:

It's common sense that when I marry it will be to someone whom I've dated casually at first. But here I think I have a problem because although each of the fellas I date is my idea of a good dating partner, he is not my idea of a good marriage partner. Let me tell you what I mean. I date fellas who are considered to be the top daters, that is, those who are acknowledged as the men about campus—good-looking, smooth dancers, popular as athletic heroes, adventurous, and the life of the party. However, I know that none of these fellas is the one that I would want to marry because for marriage I want someone who is very ambitious, serious, and offers security, most of the things which my dates are not.

This young lady recognizes her dilemma and realizes that her dating practices are inconsistent with her marital goals. Moreover, since she has presumably not dated serious and ambitious men, she must be assuming that they will not possess many of the qualities that she enjoys in a dating partner. Many other people, however, put up an argument when told that their motivations for dating are not designed to contribute to the development of a meaningful man-woman relationship. They insist, instead, that dating does prepare them for meaningful relationships.

Let us stop for a moment to clarify some of the points we have made. It should be clear that in stressing the more purposeful aspects of dating we are not suggesting that dating couples become preoccupied immediately with marriage. On the contrary, if dating is to be fully utilized as preparation for marriage, people should share dating experiences with many persons of the opposite sex. Our point is that one's dating should not be motivated only by such short-range considerations as getting out of the dorm on a date night or having lots of dates merely for the sake of being considered popular. Instead, dating should include the long-range considerations that we have indicated. When young people regard dating merely as a means of "killing time" until marriage becomes more feasible, they are ignoring the very real opportunities for understanding one another that dating holds for them. The following statement by a young man pointedly illustrates the complete exclusion of long-range consideration:

I've dated quite a few girls and will probably date a lot more before I am ready to think about marriage. I enjoy dating, of course, but the thing that troubles me is the interest which many of my dates have in marriage. It seems that just when we're having a good time my date starts to ask me things like— what do I think about a wife working after marriage; or whether I think the husband and wife should share decision making in marriage? When I hear this I know it's time to get out because maybe my dates are ready to talk about these things, but I'm not. I've got a lot to do before I even start to think about that little gal who will look good in an apron.

This young man obviously views dating merely as a means of killing time until marriage and regards any mention of marriage as an attempt to commit him to marriage. Both attitudes show his exclusive concern with short-range motivations in his dating. They also prevent his learning about women, since he grows impatient so readily.

Clearly, a radical change in the motivations of people with respect to dating will have to occur if meaningful man-woman relationships are to result. When it becomes possible for people to approach the dating involvement with greater seriousness of purpose than is currently manifest, then the basic understandings about the sexes which produce successful marriages may develop more readily.

Premature "Going Steady"

A second pattern that thwarts the development of a meaningful man-woman relationship is premature "going steady." [9] In recent years, many lay groups representing the different religious orientations have become alarmed at the prevalence of the going-steady pattern among the youth. Although their apprehension is related to fears about becoming involved in premarital sexual relations, our concern is primarily with other problems.

Premature steady dating prevents the individual from gaining meaningful knowledge about members of the opposite sex, because it re-

[9] We are concerned at this point only with the implications of this particular pattern for those who have had relatively little dating experience. See also Robert D. Herman, "The Going Steady Complex: A Re-Examination," *Marr. Fam. Living*, 17 (February 1955), pp. 36–40.

stricts his interactions. Furthermore, since premature steady dating is frequently entered into without careful consideration, relationships fall apart and terminate abruptly, often with considerable misunderstanding on the part of one or both persons. The reasons for becoming involved in going together prematurely are several, among them the social pressures of the group and the need to be popular. The factor that interests us most, however, is the personal insecurity that characterizes many of the persons who become involved in this pattern. For these people the premature going-steady relationship is frequently a compensation for the insecurity they feel, and it becomes personally important, since it signifies that they are capable of attracting another person. The anxiety and the fear of rejection that attend the carrying on of a conversation and getting acquainted appear to be quite intense in these insecure people.[10]

Consider a hypothetical case of an insecure individual wishing to date. He (we shall assume him to be a male) must first muster up the courage to ask for a date. He worries about getting turned down, once or several times, before he finds a date. On a date, he often worries about how he looks, whether or not his conversation interests the girl, and whether the girl is having an enjoyable time. Finally, it is entirely possible that after all his worrying, the girl will in fact not wish to date him again. The experience we have described is for many people a recurrent one, and one fraught with a good deal of personal stress.

Under such circumstances many people prefer not to experience the discomfort involved in dating different people. Going together as early as possible appears to them to be a solution to their problem. Such insecurity may at times become so intense that it relentlessly drives a person to repeat the same mistakes. There is the case of a male college student who was intelligent, handsome, and well-mannered, but very insecure. Usually after a second or third date with a girl he would ask her to date only him. Once the girl agreed, the student began to monopolize her time. He would walk her to class in the morning, meet her after class whenever possible, walk her back to the dormitory, study with her in the evening, and call her on the telephone in his spare time. This pattern was personally so repulsive to the girl that within a week the student found himself jilted and without a girl friend. This accentuated his insecurity, and he would be driven to seek another girl, repeating the pattern and making the same error. Only when this student was able to understand his fundamental insecurity, and the way in which this dis-

---

[10] For a discussion of arguments for and against going steady, see Francis E. Merrill, *Courtship and Marriage,* rev. ed., Holt, New York, 1959, pp. 104–106.

turbed his dating relationships with women, was he able to change his behavior.

Thus for those who discover tendencies to become involved with the premature going-together pattern, an understanding of the reasons for their involvement may prove to be exceedingly fruitful, since it may provide them with leads for changing their behavior.

Normative Marital Status

A third problem that tends to interfere with the building of a meaningful man-woman relationship lies in certain of our social norms, which admonish young people, particularly girls, to be married by their late teens or at least early twenties while also admonishing them to have happy marriages. Statistics showing that the probability of one's ever marrying decreases after his early twenties account for much of what in colleges is referred to as "senior panic"—the anxiety of the college coed who reaches her senior year without a marriage prospect. When the expectation that one be married at an early age is coupled with the expectation that the marriage be a happy one, the question arises whether such marriage norms are altogether realistic. Although the dating experience usually begins in the early teens, it is doubtful whether emotional seriousness and maturity have developed to a point where one can reasonably be expected to make good judgments concerning his marital choice by the age of 18 or 19. We give young adults only a short time in which to decide on a marriage partner—a decision that will ostensibly be binding upon this young adult for the remaining forty or fifty years of his life. Such social expectations may have been reasonable during the period of our history when the marital bond was largely based on economic considerations, but probably not today, given the many personal demands made upon marriage.

In spite of the structural strain, however, most people do not question these marital norms, but with all good intentions encourage young people to follow them—a course of action that makes the building of a meaningful relationship difficult for many.

Meaningful and Meaningless Interaction in the Dating Relationship

Perhaps the most serious of the dating problems that hinder the development of a sound man-woman relationship is that which arises out of meaningless interaction. By meaningless interaction we refer to patterns of behavior that are designed to hide the identity of the dating partners and restrict their understanding of each other. This type of interaction serves little purpose either in educating the dating partners about themselves or in enabling them to build a relationship with some stability. Meaningful interaction, on the other hand, is one that allows the partners to reveal themselves—their basic feelings, interests, opinions, attitudes, fears, and life goals.[11]

The patterns of meaningless interaction are so widespread that we cannot dismiss them as chance occurrences that have no plan or purpose. Instead, we must assert that meaningless interaction is purposeful (conscious or unconscious) and is designed to keep relationships superficial by limiting the involvement between the sexes and by hiding identity and reality. Patterns of meaningless interaction are intimately tied to the broader social values that characterize life in America today. For example, our society places much value on attending social events. To receive invitations and attend social gatherings is valued highly among large sections of American society. The quality of the interaction between people at such gatherings, however, evokes much less concern. The conventional social affair often is one in which people "mill around," engaging in superficial conversation and superficial interaction.[12] In many ways we value superficiality and run away from depth in human relationships. So marked is the pattern of superficial involvement that Europeans have been known to remark that "Americans are friendly, but they are very difficult to get to know." Any dating pattern that hides the reality of what one is, contributes to meaningless interaction, since meaningful interaction can take place only when persons have the capacity and desire to reveal themselves. We now turn to specific dating practices that contribute to the hiding of one's identity.

Stereotyped Dating and Hiding One's Identity

Stereotyped dating—the practice of engaging in the same activity, at the same time, in the same way—serves to hide one's identity, since it limits what people can learn about one another. As a result, only limited aspects of the personalities may be observed. Depending on the patterns of the couple, the dating partners may glimpse the personality on the movie date or that on the concert date, but seldom the total personality.[13] Stereotyped dating is limiting not only because it reveals merely

---

[11] For an interesting study on the emergence of empathy in the man-woman relationship, see Glenn M. Vernon and Robert L. Stewart, "Empathy as a Process in the Dating Situation," *Am. soc. Rev.*, **22** (February 1957), pp. 48–52.

[12] Erich Fromm, *The Art of Loving*, Harper, New York, 1956, pp. 83–106.

[13] William M. Smith, Jr., "Rating and Dating: A Re-Study," *Marr. Fam. Living*, **14** (November 1952), p. 313.

selected segments of the personalities, but also because it tends to lend itself to circumstances in which interaction, the prerequisite for meaningful associations, is restricted. The typical movie date, for example, places many restrictions on verbal interaction between the dating partners. It is interesting to note that, when asked why the movie date is so often a pattern in our society, people say, "What else can one do?" Although many communities are limited in regard to dating activities, one nevertheless wonders whether the movie date is not in reality designed to avoid meaningful interaction and to remove the burdens of interaction from the dating partners. The movie date is not, of course, the only type of date that may be designed to minimize interaction. Some persons have a pattern of dating in groups—double-dating. Although there are undoubtedly several reasons for such dating, whenever it is a preferred pattern of an individual or a couple, one may well wonder whether the constant need for others is not based on a need to shift the burden of interaction to others in the group.

Conformity and Hiding One's Identity

The high degree of conformity that is expected in most dating behavior makes it difficult for many people to reveal themselves as they are. There is usually a pronounced effort to impress. Both persons invariably dress better than they usually do and, eager to please, have their "best foot forward." Hence each person learns very little that may be real about the other, and to the extent that such dates occur, there is in fact little opportunity for much knowledge of one another to emerge.

Furthermore, the fear of being different or of expressing opinions and beliefs that may be at variance with those of others is often so pronounced that the very impulses of people to express themselves are dampened. Such behavior leads to a minimization of the individual's real interests and ideas—aspects of personality that are basic to the development of a meaningful man-woman relationship. The dating partners may limit verbal interaction, feeling that it is better to say nothing than to say the wrong thing. They may feign interests in order to please, to give the appearance of harmony and agreement. A blotting-out of one's identity may include not only the hiding of interests, but often also a distortion of one's familial and cultural background. Conversation about one's family may be eliminated, or the family may be made to appear to be better than it is. Also, religious or cultural minority status may be hidden, particularly when one fears rejection on such grounds.

We see thus that dating relationships that are characterized by hiding one's identity—stereotyped dating and dating in which the needs to impress and conform are all-important—contribute to meaningless interaction. Interaction of this type is based on minimizing the basic attitudes and feelings of the dating partners; when the personalities are oriented toward hiding their real feelings, the interaction frequently becomes noncontroversial and mundane. Unfortunately, many daters discover that "simply talking" without regard to content is the road to popularity. Here is a case in point:

One characteristic which holds an important place in dating among my friends is bantering. This involves engaging in a rapid exchange of light remarks. Bantering was very difficult for me, particularly since it usually occurred in a group where everybody was rapidly talking back and forth. I just seemed to be dumb struck and when a remark was addressed to me, I could only manage to laugh nervously and finally, when it was too late, I'd manage to think of a clever reply. Even when I would think of something to answer right away, I was always afraid it wouldn't be witty enough. I really worried about my inability to "banter" and finally discussed it with one of the girls who is very popular in our set. Her advice to me was, when at a party I should start talking about anything at all and in a continual flow. Then eventually people would begin to direct their talk to me and they would leave with the impression that we all had carried on a terrific conversation. I tried this and it works, because under circumstances such as these, it's not what you say that counts, it's having the ability to keep talking that's important.

Relationships that rest on such meaningless interaction may hold the temporary interest of some, but both the interaction and the relationship are likely to become tedious. The boredom in such a relationship occurs because the persons involved are not fundamentally interested in what they are saying or doing. Many people abandon a relationship because of such premature boredom when the relationship might potentially be worth continuing. The relationship may be uninteresting or dull not because the personalities are intrinsically dull, but because each individual is afraid to be himself, each is afraid to express himself, or each is afraid to show his real interests. Thus depth is never reached, and the identity of each person is hidden. There are those who become acclimatized to meaningless interaction and in fact cannot cope with more serious involvements. Many marry on the basis of such superficial understandings, only to discover in marriage vast incompatibilities that plague them. One often hears, "If I'd known he was like that, I would never have married him." Although understandable, much of this could be avoided if the man-woman relationship were characterized by more meaningful interaction than is currently evident.

Even when the significance of meaningful interaction in the dating relationship is recognized, its establishment may not be simple, since there appear to be many factors in the social setting, and in our individual personalities, that work against it. Frequently the person who engages in meaningful interaction is defined as being too serious—"a square"—hence undesirable. Such views tend to discourage purposeful interaction. Indeed, much personal integrity is required for one to take a stand against such views.

Aside from these social pressures, there are personal pressures of even greater significance. If the essential purpose of meaningless interaction is to hide one's identity, then we can only assume that many of us feel that what we are is unacceptable and should be made obscure. When we use the term "what we are," we suggest the total concept of ourselves, attitudes, beliefs, interests, and opinions. If one feels unacceptable and wishes to hide what he or she may be, certain consequences emerge. One may feel that he basically knows very little and therefore has no right to express an opinion; one may feel that his interests are of such little importance that they are not worth introducing into a conversation; and so it goes. Many people feel that if they reveal themselves, they will be humiliated; having a low self-esteem, they anticipate only the disapproval of others. The negative self-esteem curbs one's spontaneity of action and expression.

One may come to prefer a pattern of meaningless interaction after many years of social conditioning and personal experiences that make hiding the identity the most rewarding procedure. Meaningless interaction may become pervasive and patterned, patterned to such an extent that it affects one's total life. For such people the extent of their involvement in any relationship is extremely limited. In spite of these obstacles, it is nevertheless essential that active efforts be exerted to remove these barriers to meaningful relationships.

As a final note to this discussion we would like to point out that one must have some sensitivity about individuals with whom (and under what circumstances) meaningful interaction is possible. To reveal oneself to some persons could well result in their using such information in a harmful manner. The girl who reveals some of her insecurities to a boy, without knowing much about him, might discover that such information is used to embarrass or injure her. Also, some people simply may not have the capacity to engage in meaningful interaction. To force such interaction on them, regardless of the distress it causes them, would destroy whatever is positive in the relationship. Nevertheless, the main point of our discussion is that meaningful interaction is an important objective in the dating relationship and is essential if the full potentialities of the relationship are to emerge.

Exploitation

The pattern of exploitation is another dating problem that hinders the development of a meaningful man-woman relationship. Although this topic was introduced briefly in a previous portion of the chapter, we wish to expand our treatment at this time. By "exploitation" we mean the using of others to satisfy our needs without regard to their needs or wishes. It follows that when relationships are exploitative, there is a lack of intrinsic interest in the other person. Thus the possibility of developing a meaningful relationship is reduced, since exploitation is always associated with marked indifference and callousness toward others, hence is hardly conducive to the development of deep, emotional commitments. Although we tend to deny the existence of exploitativeness in human relationships (since it runs counter to some of our espoused virtues), its existence is marked and is in fact fostered by the cultural milieu, the social groups in which we interact; and it becomes entrenched in the personalities that arise out of these sociocultural influences.

EXPLOITATION ENGENDERED BY OUR CULTURE. Our culture plays a significant role in the development of exploitativeness by fostering particular values and beliefs. It is exemplified in such sayings as "A sucker is born every minute" and "Only a fool fails to take advantage of a sucker." Another belief suggests that our world is a predatory one where each man must take care of himself lest another take advantage of him. The high value that our culture places on competitiveness for material possessions, social prestige, and wealth often results in exploitation, since competition may become so intense that people use one another to gain advantage. Our culture permits certain practices that foster exploitativeness. Thus the businessman who uses others for his own benefit is considered to be simply using good business sense. The employee who takes advantage of his employer by restricting his productivity and "taking it easy" is not thought of as really cheating his employer but simply taking advantage of a good opportunity.

EXPLOITATION ENGENDERED BY SOCIAL GROUPS. Although we have discussed in a general way the cultural influences that foster exploitativeness, let us now examine how these beliefs are expressed in the values and behavior of social groups.

The Role of the Family in the Development of Exploitation. The family is a crucial agency in the development of exploitative patterns. An inspection of the family backgrounds of exploitative people suggests that they are characterized by a great deal of emotional impoverishment and by a lack of positive counterinfluences. Such conditions of impoverishment cut across social-class lines; we must not assume that these are characteristic of any single segment of our society.

A family in which parents and siblings espouse exploitative values as norms on which to pattern one's life fosters such values in the individual. If one parent exploits another, one parent exploits a child, or one sibling exploits another sibling, an environment is created that fosters exploitation. There is the instance of a young girl who was given adult responsibilities of caring for the home at the age of twelve. She washed breakfast and lunch dishes, prepared the evening meal, and cleaned up the kitchen after dinner. The mother was usually visiting friends and following her personal pleasures while the girl assumed these familial responsibilities. The girl experienced great hostility and resentment toward her mother and felt that she was a fool for letting her mother take such advantage of her. She vowed that when she could, she would use others just as she had been used. Now married, she has a fully developed set of exploitative patterns which permeate her human relationships. They interfere with her marriage and cause her considerable difficulty.

Not all familial patterns of exploitation are so overt. More common, and perhaps more subtle, are those instances in which a parent exploits a child for the personal prestige and benefit the parent may derive. We are thinking here particularly of situations in which parents coerce a child to excel at school or in artistic activity not because they are interested in the child's achievement, but because they wish to brag to others about the child's accomplishments. Such exploitation on the part of parents often develops resentment in the child, which may find expression in the child's developing his own exploitative patterns.

The One-Sex Group. Most young men have experienced situations, particularly during the very popular bull session, where it becomes fashionable to brag about one's latest sexual conquest or to give a detailed account of how one was able to hand out a line to some girl so skillfully that she immediately fell for it. Indeed, to have no stories to tell frequently means that one is somewhat of a "square" and certainly behind the times, because much importance is given to these testimonies of skillful exploitation.

Undoubtedly, many of the stories told are greatly exaggerated or even completely untrue. What is significant is the apparent need of people to pass themselves off as being able to exploit others, even if they must make up stories and lie about their ability to do so.

Girls, we might add, are frequently no less involved in these exploitative strategies. Often a girl is regarded as knowing her way around if she is able to exploit or if she at least can lead her girl friends to believe that she is able to use her boyfriends and thus control her dating situations.

Many girls are aware of the personal deficiency that will be ascribed to them if they are unable to control the dating situations or, worse yet, if they themselves are exploited by their dating partners.

It is not too difficult, therefore, to understand how a group of girls came to form a club exclusively devoted to exploiting their boyfriends. In this club each girl, unknown to her boyfriend, was required to get him to buy her a certain item or take her to a certain place, agreed to in the club meeting. Her rating as a club member was based on her ability to achieve these goals. One Christmas, for example, it was decided that each club member was to manipulate her boyfriend into buying her a cashmere sweater. Those who received cashmere sweaters from their boyfriends for Christmas were regarded as successful and those who did not as failures.

Certainly, this club is not to be regarded as a typical case of female exploitation, but it is nonetheless important for us to recognize its existence because, although exploitation here is formalized and concentrated, it does not differ in kind from what we as individuals frequently attempt in our interactions with others.

Exploitative values of the type we have just described become group norms and are passed on to new members as they become part of the group. People come to internalize exploitative values which become manifest in the very basis for dating. Willard Waller was one of the earliest men to study dating phenomena. Waller regarded dating as a competitive game of premarital dalliance in which the primary objective of young people was not to build meaningful relationships, but to exploit or use the dating partner for personal benefit. This exploitative element, which makes dating a competitive game of strategies, was found to be extremely prevalent among the dating pairs Waller studied. All of this is well illustrated in his insightful analysis, "The Rating and Dating Complex." [14]

Waller discovered that young people tend to rate one another according to such criteria as physical appearance, dancing ability, access to an automobile, popularity with the opposite sex, clique membership, and having a "good line." On the basis of these ratings, some persons were considered to be class A daters, while others, not faring so well, were considered to be class B, C, or D daters. Nevertheless, in spite of one's rating, Waller found that almost all young persons tended to acquire some knowledge about where he and each of his potential dating partners fell on the rating scale. Dating invitations were then extended or withheld,

[14] Willard Waller, "The Rating and Dating Complex," *Am. soc. Rev.*, 2 (October 1937), pp. 727–734.

accepted or rejected, with the clear notion of whether or not the particular date would raise or lower one's own prestige. This type of exploitation is exemplified when one's dating of a class A person is not primarily motivated by the desire to be with that particular person, but rather by the desire to use that person's class A prestige to enhance one's own reputation.

The awareness of such exploitation makes it necessary for the young person to guard himself against becoming seriously involved, at least until he is fairly certain that the dating partner is sincerely interested in him and not merely using him as a means to some other end, or merely "stringing him along." The following comment by a young lady indicates such a fear:

I date several fellows even though I really only want to date Harry. But a girl can't afford to let her preference be known. She must wait for the boy to make the bid. You see, if I let Harry know how I feel, or if I just stop dating other guys and wait for his dates, he'd be sure to know how I feel and then he'd either lose interest or more likely he'd take advantage of his hold on me. I know this can happen because it happened to me before and I don't want it to happen again. We all know that the female gets taken advantage of by the male. So I guess I'll just have to wait and see what Harry does because if he makes the first move, I know I'm O.K., but if I do—I know he'll get smart.

Waller states that assessing the dating partner's motivations is extremely difficult because young people further tend to exploit one another by pretending serious emotional involvement in their dating relationships. This pretense was referred to as having a "good line," and its effectiveness is based on the principle that the relationship tends to be controlled by the person who is least interested in its continuance. Thus in attempting to exploit the dating partner and to control the relationship, one makes believe that he has fallen seriously in love with the dating partner. He hopes that the partner will then relax his guard and become seriously involved in the relationship. When this happens and one is able to use the partner's emotional involvement as a means of controlling the relationship, one regards himself as having been successful and in turn is viewed as "knowing his way around" in this complex dating strategy.

Waller's analysis of the dating pattern thus presents a picture of man-woman involvements as a game of the unmarried in which exploitation is paramount. Neither party is ever quite certain of the motives of the other; hence relationships are created in which exploitation is feared as well as promoted.

Waller claims, however, that in spite of all the forces that oppose it, true courtship sometimes emerges from this complex process. That is, in spite of their attempts to withstand serious involvement, young people may eventually become emotionally involved and marry. However, emotional involvements under these conditions tend to be entered into with unwillingness, which does not seem to be a satisfactory way of initiating meaningful relationships.

Waller's critical opinion of dating is shared by Burgess and Wallin who, after studying the contemporary dating pattern, found many of its standards to be adolescent, immature, superficial, and undemocratic.[15]

It should be pointed out that the notion of exploitation in the man-woman relationship has troubled many college students and suggestions of its existence have met with resistance. Students exemplify such resistance by overemphasizing altruistic and socially desirable motives in dating patterns and vigorously denying any exploitative component in dating. Professionals have also been hard at work retesting Waller's findings. Some of this concern about the validity of Waller's Rating and Dating Complex stems from the belief that the roles of men and women are undergoing change. Thus Riesman in an essay suggests that relationships between the sexes encompass a greater research for genuine freedom and equality. Furthermore, he claims that there is more desire to share today and less desire to impress; relations sought for are more searching, profound, and sincere. Riesman's points are well taken; nevertheless, since, as previously noted, the search for such relationships among some segments of the population has always been the case, we may well ask how widespread is the search that Riesman describes. Assuming, however, that Riesman is correct, we must still recognize that the problems in a man-woman relationship arise not out of the *expressed desires of people,* but out of *their real behavior,* out of what they actually do. In spite of what people say, they encounter *persistent difficulty* in building relationships based on sharing and depth, because their very backgrounds and experiences have often been responsible for egocentricities and immaturities that are difficult to transcend by oneself. Indeed, the well-meaning, but often unfulfilled, search for espoused values of shar-

---

15 Ernest W. Burgess and Paul Wallin, *Engagement and Marriage,* Lippincott, Philadelphia, 1953, p. 109. Samuel Harman Lowrie, "Dating Theories and Student Responses," *Am. soc. Rev.,* 16 (June 1951), pp. 334–339. Others, however, disagree with this critical viewpoint of dating and believe that people look on dating as a means of seeking partners with whom to build sound relationships. The reader interested in pursuing this particular aspect of the problem should see Robert O. Blood, Jr., *Anticipating Your Marriage,* The Free Press, Glencoe, Ill., 1955, p. 24. For an interesting discussion of motivations in dating behavior, see James K. Skipper, Jr., and Gilbert Nass, "Dating Behavior: A Framework for Analysis and an Illustration," *J. Marr. Fam.,* 28, 4 (1966), pp. 412–420.

ing and depth on the part of young people may represent a reaction against what was missing in their own families.[16]

Concerning research findings we note that several studies in the post-World War II period attempted to test Waller's hypothesis about the materialistic-exploitative component of the Rating and Dating Complex. Christensen, Blood, and Smith, in separate studies, reported that their student samples rejected Waller's views and instead favored "personality" factors, a sense of humor, being a good sport, and being considerate; Waller's value system did seem to be much more characteristic of fraternities and sororities, however.[17]

Reiss, who studied a student population in Virginia in the mid-1960s, reports that the rating-dating system (whether competitive or personality-based) does not block mating. He suggests that a stratification system exists, in which people select a member of their own social class; hence the dating system is integrated with marriage and is not an exploitative system unrelated to marriage.[18] Reiss's findings, however, do not rule out the materialistic-exploitative component; is it not reasonable to assume that persons whose dating behavior is controlled by a prestige system, a stratification system, will seek out persons who carry the greatest prestige and will prefer them over others even within the same rank? Such a search would seem to have exploitative ingredients.[19]

How may efforts to reexamine Waller be interpreted? First, Waller's findings are not altogether easy to reexamine. The reassessment is complicated by the fact that Waller may have studied a more homogeneous college population than we have available today. In the late thirties, many of the students came from homes affected by the Depression, and it could be that they were preoccupied with materialistic-exploitative ways. Moreover, the sex ratio at the time was six men for every woman, which may have been conducive to exploitativeness on the part of the female. Thus even if Waller's findings were completely applicable in the thirties, they may not be today because the college population has *new* and *diverse* segments.

Nevertheless, cogent arguments for not abandoning Waller's views

[16] David Riesman, "Permissiveness and Sex Roles," *J. Marr. Fam. Living,* **21** (August 1959), pp. 211–217.

[17] Harold T. Christensen, *Marriage Analysis,* Ronald Press, New York, 1958, pp. 235–243, 261–264. Robert O. Blood, Jr., "A Retest of Waller's Rating Complex," *Marr. Fam. Living,* **17** (February 1955), pp. 41–47. William M. Smith, Jr., "Rating and Dating: A Restudy," *Marr. Fam. Living,* **14** (November 1952), pp. 312–317.

[18] Ira Reiss, "Social Class and Campus Dating," *Social Prob.,* **12,** 2 (1965), pp. 193–205.

[19] For additional remarks on the *erotic ranking* of dating partners, see Hans L. Zetterberg, "The Secret Ranking," *J. Marr. Fam.,* **28,** 2 (1966), pp. 134–142.

still remain. These can perhaps best be appraised by looking at situations other than dating.

For example, in the industrial and business world, do we expect friendships to be chosen exclusively on the basis of so-called personality factors? Even though they play some part, do we not anticipate the essence of the business friendship to be in how that *friendship* can facilitate advancement in the structure of the commercial world? Indeed, would we take statements about purely *altruistic responses* for friendship seriously at all? Thus if the society in which we grow up is in many ways predicated on materialistic, competitive interaction in which exploitative norms operate, are dating relationships to be excluded? Are current student protests against alienation, "people not caring," and the concern of organized religion about man's lack of interest in fellowman really all a lot of nonsense without any basis in reality?

Finally, the work of Farber is very significant for the present discussion. Farber is not interested in testing Waller's findings as such. Instead, he is concerned with accounting for family change and has developed a theory of "permanent availability." The theory states that since fewer persons are related by blood today than was the case in the past, there are more persons eligible for marriage at any one time. "Each adult individual, regardless of his current marital status, is available as a potential mate to any other cross-sex individual at any time." Moreover, more prevalent divorce and remarriage have extended in time the number of eligibles for marriage. The significance of Farber's theory of permanent availability for our discussion of exploitation lies in the fact that with a *marked increase* in eligibles for mates, due to changes in our social structure, people are in a position to use others with less fear of the consequences, that is, of being permanently bound to them.[20] Insofar as Farber is correct, and there is every reason to assume that he is, *efforts to gain advantage over the other and exploitation* both are less subject to control today; indeed, with *permanent availability* of mates, it becomes possible for an exploitative person to run through a series of marriages whenever use of the marital partner holds no particular attraction.

The issue of the extent to which Waller's findings regarding dating are correct today is obviously not settled. And in regard to present research findings that tend to reject his hypothesis, it may be that students today are sufficiently sophisticated to cover up exploitative motives in responding to questionnaires about their dating behaviors. Different

[20] Bernard Farber, *Family: Organization and Interaction,* Chandler Publishing Company, San Francisco, 1964, Ch. 5. See also Michal McCall, "Courtship as Social Exchange: Some Historical Comparisons," in Bernard Farber, Ed., *Kinship and Family Organization,* Wiley, New York, 1966, pp. 190–200.

methods may have to be employed if a more valid testing of Waller's hypothesis is to be accomplished. However, for purposes of our discussion here this particular issue is not significant. Whenever exploitation, however small, enters a relationship, the relationship suffers and poses both a threat and a challenge for the dating partners. From this point of view Waller's observations still have much relevance for the present.

PERSONALITY ORGANIZATION AND EXPLOITATION. The prevalence of exploitation in society, including the family and the one-sex group, clearly suggests that such patterns are an integral aspect of personality. The sociocultural influences we have described are all conducive to the development of exploitative patterns within the personality. An examination of the prevalence of exploitative patterns suggests that many of us are not fundamentally disturbed by the pattern; instead, we feel a certain amount of pride and cleverness in the ability to manipulate and use people for our personal benefit. Thus people derive a feeling of strength and power from their ability to exploit. When a pattern of this sort is anchored in the personality, and indeed serves a need, it is not readily changed.

Nevertheless, though it may have a purpose, exploitation destroys the very basis of meaningful man-woman relationships. It defeats the possibility of spontaneity and freedom to be oneself in the relationship; it fosters suspicion, ambivalence, and distrust on the part of both the exploiter and the exploited. It is, therefore, essential to understand the extent to which one uses others and to exert active efforts to remove such behavior if one wishes to build a constructive marital relationship.

Summary

In the past, man-woman relationships were begun by "courting." This meant that each relationship was under the rigorous controls of family, neighborhood, and church and was expected to result in marriage. Today, however, this formal courtship pattern has largely given way to dating. Under the informal pattern of dating, the behavior of the unmarried is no longer completely in the hands of family, church, and neighborhood, but rather has largely been taken over by the dating pairs, who themselves determine which behavior is acceptable and which is not. Furthermore, each relationship is viewed as an end in itself and is not necessarily expected to result in marriage.

The emergence of dating was largely the result of urbanization and individualism and of changes that came about in the qualities desired in a marriage partner. The complexity of the urban community made it difficult for young people to learn about each other without first undergoing a period of interaction. Marriage in urban areas was rooted in such facets as companionship, mutual interests, and values, and the determination of compatibility was intimately tied to the development of dating.

There can be little doubt that dating, when conducted with maturity and realism, is an essential stage in the development of meaningful man-woman relationships. Dating enables young people to learn more about each other by helping to break down the distortions that each sex holds about the other.

The benefits of dating, however, may be greatly reduced through certain conditions that may arise in the contemporary pattern: (1) dating merely to "kill time" without giving any serious attention to the dating involvements; (2) going steady too soon; (3) normative marital strains involving expectations that are all but impossible to fulfill; (4) meaningless interaction in dating, which involves conforming to a set pattern of behavior in order to hide one's real identity; and (5) exploiting the dating partner in order to gain one's own end. Not only do these conditions limit the amount of knowledge that each sex may acquire about the other, but the circumstances under which such dating is conducted are so superficial that realistic attempts to adjust to each other are also limited.

Although some authorities do not see these dangers in the contemporary dating pattern, others do. The leading spokesman in the latter area was the late Willard Waller, who pointedly noted that dating is becoming a competitive game of premarital dalliance, in which the primary objective of young people is not to build a meaningful relationship but rather to exploit or use the dating partner for personal benefit. The more skilled one becomes at exploiting others, the more chance he has of becoming regarded as a "sharp dater." Not only does this competitive aspect of dating limit premarital training, which would undoubtedly be useful in building a meaningful marriage relationship, but it also creates a situation that leads to a fear of being exploited. Thus persons may enter courtship and marriage with feelings of ambivalence and doubt. And although it is not the purpose of this chapter to determine the extent to which Waller's hypotheses are or are not present in today's dating patterns, we do wish to point out that if dating experiences are to be used in building meaningful man-woman relationships, young people must analyze their dating behavior in order to remove the superficiality and exploitativeness that may be present.

Questions

1. What is dating? What is courtship? In what ways do they differ and in what ways are they similar?
2. How do you account for the emergence of dating in the American society?
3. What is meant by being reared in "closed societies"? How does this affect the concepts we acquire of the opposite sex?
4. List and explain the benefits offered to unmarried men and women through dating.
5. In what manner do one's motivations for dating affect what one learns through dating?
6. What is meant by premature going steady and how does it affect the benefits one can derive from dating? List and explain the types of reasons for premature going steady.
7. Discuss certain normative expectations that can interfere with the building of a meaningful marriage relationship.
8. What is meant by meaningless interaction in dating? What purpose does such interaction serve? List and explain specific dating practices that contribute to meaningless interaction in dating.
9. What is exploitation? What is the role of society in fostering exploitation? Is exploitation ever a part of the contemporary dating pattern? If so, give several examples.
10. Who was Willard Waller? Describe fully his views concerning the contemporary dating pattern.
11. Discuss the work of those who do not believe that Waller's hypotheses are applicable to today's dating patterns. Do you agree or disagree with them? Support your answer.

Suggestions for Research and Related Activities

1. Take a poll to determine the reasons young people give for dating. Classify the answers you receive and analyze them in terms of how you think

they will affect what is learned from dating. Do you find any differences in the responses? If so, how do you account for such differences?

2. Write and have your fellow students enact two brief skits: one portraying a scene from a man-woman relationship operating under the formal code of courtship, and the other portraying the same scene operating under the informal code of dating. Have your fellow students point out and discuss the differences in the behaviors between the two skits, showing the advantages and/or disadvantages of each in terms of building a meaningful relationship.

3. List several stereotypes that young people hold about the opposite sex and submit this list to both married and unmarried men and women in order to determine the degree to which these stereotypes are believed to be true. Do you find that these stereotypes are accepted? Do any differences exist between the answers given by men and women or between those given by the married and unmarried? If so, how do you explain these differences? You might also want to check the dating frequency of your unmarried respondents and determine whether or not dating tends to reduce these distortions.

4. Hold a debate on the following topic: "Men and Women Today Expect Too Much of Each Other in Marriage."

5. Hold a panel discussion concerning the prevalence of "rating-dating" at your school.

Suggested Readings

Breed, Warren, "Sex, Class and Socialization in Dating," *Marr. Fam. Living,* **18** (May 1956), pp. 137–144.

Cavan, Ruth Shonle, *American Marriage,* Crowell-Collier, New York, 1959, Ch. 5, "Dating While in College."

Ehrmann, Winston, *Premarital Dating Behavior,* Henry Holt, New York, 1959.

Kirkpatrick, Clifford, and Theodore Caplow, "Courtship in a Group of Minnesota Students," *Am. J. Sociol.,* **51** (September 1945), pp. 114–125.

LeMasters, E. E., *Modern Courtship and Marriage,* Macmillan, New York, 1957, Ch. 5, "Random Dating."

Lowrie, Samuel H., "Factors Involved in the Frequency of Dating," *Marr. Fam. Living,* **18** (February 1956), pp. 46–51.

Merrill, Francis E., *Courtship and Marriage,* Henry Holt, New York, 1959, Ch. 6, "Dating Theory," and Ch. 7, "Dating Practice."

Sussman, Marvin B., *Sourcebook in Marriage and the Family,* Houghton Mifflin, Boston, 1963, especially Ch. 2, "Dating and Mate Selection," pp. 63–124.

Waller, Willard, revised by Reuben Hill, *The Family,* Dryden Press, New York, 1951, Ch. 8, "The Social Contexts of Courtship," Ch. 9, "Bargaining and Exploitative Attitudes," and Ch. 10, "Courtship as an Interactive Process."

Waller, Willard, "The Rating and Dating Complex," *Am. soc. Rev.,* **2** (October 1937), pp. 727–734.

Chapter Ten

COURTSHIP: THE PRELUDE TO MARRIAGE

WE HAVE seen that the factors that prepare people for marriage may either lead to maladjustment in marriage, if misused, or may facilitate meaningful marital adjustment, if used to advantage. Another such premarital factor that can either aid or hinder the attainment of a meaningful marriage relationship is courtship.

This period in the man-woman relationship follows the dating period and differs from dating in that it involves a commitment to marry while dating does not. Courtship, therefore, is engagement. However, we hasten to point out that courtship consists of two important phases, the informal and the formal engagements; the difference between these two phases lies largely in their purpose.

The primary purpose of the informal engagement is to afford the couple an ample period of time to test their relationship under more serious and realistic circumstances than those found in dating. Furthermore, during the informal engagement, except for the parents and perhaps the very best friends of the couple, no public announcement of the intended marriage is made. This phase of engagement when properly used offers young people the opportunity to learn about each other before publicly committing themselves to marriage.

ILLUSTRATION: A suitor being interviewed in the Library of the Doll's House (c. 1865) made for the family of the late Lord Morley, owner of Saltram House, Devon (now National Trust Property); now in the collection of Mrs. Vivien Greene at The Rotunda Museum of Antique Dolls' Houses, Oxford.

The purpose of the formal engagement is to announce the intention to marry and to make specific plans for the actual wedding ceremony and the honeymoon.[1] In this chapter we discuss the courtship period and its two engagement phases, as well as the circumstances that are involved in breaking an engagement.

Informal Engagement—Meaning

The question frequently arises whether going steady and pinning constitute informal engagement.[2] This can be answered by stating that in each case the decisive factor in deciding whether or not these are forms of informal engagement is that of intent. If it is the serious intent of the couple that their relationship ultimately result in marriage, then call it what you may, it is informal engagement.[3] On the other hand, if going steady means nothing more than a steady dating of one person this month and another next month, and pinning nothing more than having a "claim" on a person until someone better comes along, then neither

Table 11 Answers Given by Men and Women Students to the Statement: "If a Woman Wears a Man's Fraternity Pin, It Means That They Are Engaged"[a]

Response	Men	Women
Yes	27%	44%
No	47%	28%
Undecided	26%	28%

[a] Judson T. Landis and Mary G. Landis, *Building a Successful Marriage*, 3rd ed., Prentice-Hall, Englewood Cliffs, N.J., 1958, p. 277.

[1] Harold T. Christensen, *Marriage Analysis*, 2nd ed., Ronald Press, New York, 1958, pp. 333–334. For a discussion of the fact that the functions of engagement are more undefined in our society than perhaps in any other society, see George Simpson, *People in Families*, Thomas Y. Crowell, New York, 1960, pp. 94–96.
[2] For a discussion of going steady and pinning, see E. E. LeMasters, *Modern Courtship and Marriage*, Macmillan, New York, 1957, Chs. 6–7.
[3] It should be noted, though, that inasmuch as "formal pinning" may constitute a public announcement of the intent to become "formally engaged," pinning itself does not permit the couple to make their adjustments with freedom from public commitment as does the informal engagement.

constitutes informal engagement. The widely varying response meanings attached to pinning are noted in Table 11.

Informal Engagement—Function

The informal engagement period is a significant phase of the premarital adjustment. It enables the couple to make their adjustments without the formal commitment to marry. Thus, unlike casual dating, it allows each party to become assured of the serious intentions of the other and may help to provide a milieu in which pretense and superficiality are minimized. During this phase of courtship it becomes possible not only to single out the adjustments to be made but to establish a pattern for dealing with problems.[4] To establish a pattern for dealing with problems in a relationship is indeed a worthy objective, since it acquaints the couple with the realities of human involvements and thus minimizes the panic that sometimes comes with the realization that one's relationship is in difficulty.

What kinds of problems and dilemmas ought to be resolved during the informal engagement period? Certainly issues that pertain to personality incompatibilities and differences in values, orientations, and life goals should be discussed, since these are significant areas of potential difficulty.[5] Furthermore, one or both members of the relationship may be troubled about some event of the past, which they feel could become an issue in the relationship, such as a previous erotic involvement or a serious difficulty with a family member. At this point the question of how much to reveal about the past becomes a problem in the informal engagement period. No hard and fast rules apply here. There is frequently the impulse to blurt out much of this in the hope that this will clean the slate and one will have fulfilled the rules of honesty and fair play. It is not that simple, however; one may serve himself and his relationship best by examining his motivations to tell everything about the past. To some people the impulse to confess the past, so to speak, is

---

[4] James A. Peterson, *Education for Marriage*, Scribner's, New York, 1956, pp. 198–199.

[5] Francis E. Merrill, *Courtship and Marriage*, Henry Holt, New York, 1959, pp. 166–168. Merrill suggests that some of the areas in which the couple should explore their attitudes are (1) love and marriage, (2) marriage and divorce, (3) marital roles, (4) marriage and children.

merely a form of self-inflicted punishment to relieve guilt feelings. Confessing the past may then be a way of asking the engaged partner to help carry the burden of guilt, and this may accomplish little of a positive nature for the relationship.[6] As often happens with people who feel they ought to be punished for some wrongdoing, there may even be a desire to have the other partner dissolve the relationship as a form of punishment.

There was the case of a young man who had a need to tell his girl friends about the difficulties of his past. Frequently he unconsciously so distorted these events that they tended to frighten his girl friends away. He always presented himself in the worst possible light as one who took advantage of others and who had little regard for their feelings. Finally, he met a girl who did not react as the others had. She accepted him and his past and looked on him as a challenge for her. At this point the young man became quite perplexed, without knowing why, since his unconscious plan for self-punishment had failed.

A competent counselor can help one to explore his motivations for telling about past acts, to separate those that are likely to have bearing on the marriage from those that have no bearing and to learn how to go about discussing the events that should be divulged before marriage.[7] Certainly a good rule to follow is to ask oneself whether revealing events of the past will in general help the relationship or will place additional stress on it. For one partner to reveal an erotic affair to the other partner prior to marriage would be, for some persons, sufficient reason to dissolve the informal engagement. To talk about the same experience at a later time in marriage might well bring forth a less serious reaction. Much of what one reveals has to be examined in light of the security of the relationship. In general, the more secure people are in the relationship, the more they may tell about the past without precipitating crises.

Having pointed out some of the real values that may be realized in the informal engagement period, we hasten to add that it is unfortunate that young people often tend to run these informal and formal engagement periods together and treat them as one, by attempting to work out the difficulties in their relationship after publicly announcing their engagement. When this happens, frequently there is a tendency for the couple to attempt to avoid areas in which adjustments are obviously necessary. They do this because once the engagement is announced, they are reluctant to break it, feeling that to do so would be extremely embarrassing socially. Consequently, anything that might cast doubt on the advisability of the marriage tends to be ignored. People who are caught up in this

[6] F. Alexander Magoun, *Love and Marriage,* Harper, New York, 1948, p. 187.
[7] Lawrence S. Bee, *Marriage and Family Relations,* Harper, New York, 1959, pp. 254–257.

problem often find solace in thinking that it is easier to face doubts after they are married than it is to face them now and run the risk of having to break the engagement.

The episode of a young secretary may help to illustrate the point. This woman was formally engaged to a young man who behaved in a manner that suggested considerable indifference. Although he stated that he loved his fiancee, he failed to appear for dates, broke them indiscriminately, and was emotionally aloof to a point where he failed to show any physical demonstrativeness. The young woman sought professional help and urged her fiance to do so also. After some time the counselor indicated to the couple some formidable problems that needed resolution before the couple could expect a satisfactory marriage. At this point the young woman became impatient and stated that, since wedding plans had been made, perhaps she had exaggerated the seriousness of their problems and it might be best to resolve the issues later on.

When problems are avoided during informal engagement, the period becomes one of superficial entertainment rather than of adjustment; many facets of the personalities involved go unexplored and are left to be discovered in marriage itself. Such statements as "If I had only known about these attitudes before I married her" or "He's a different person from the one I married" are frequently the result of hurried, misspent engagements and could have been avoided if the premarital interaction had been used in a more meaningful way.[8]

It should be clear that the greater length of time should be devoted to the informal phase of the engagement period; once a satisfactory adjustment is attained, a much shorter period of time is required for the formal engagement.[9] Moreover, by withholding the public announcement until the relationship has been tested, young people may make the necessary adjustments without the social pressure to marry that accompanies the formal announcement. Indeed, if these couples are unable to work out a satisfactory adjustment and wish to discontinue their relationship, they can do so with a minimum of social embarrassment.

[8] E. E. LeMasters, *op. cit.*, pp. 158–161.

[9] In regard to total length of engagement, one study showed that short engagements (under six months for men and under three months for women) had the poorest chances of resulting in happiness and success in marriage. Lewis M. Terman, *Psychological Factors in Marital Happiness*, McGraw-Hill, New York, 1938, pp. 198–199. Another study found that the happily married tended to have had longer engagements than those divorced. Harvey J. Locke, *Predicting Adjustment in Marriage*, Henry Holt, New York, 1951, p. 94. Finally, Burgess and Cottrell also found that the proportion of good adjustments in marriage increases with increased length of friendship shared by the couple. Ernest W. Burgess and Leonard S. Cottrell, *Predicting Success or Failure in Marriage*, Prentice-Hall, Englewood Cliffs, N.J., 1939, pp. 164–165.

The Formal Engagement—Meaning and Function

The public announcement of the intent to marry initiates the formal engagement period. And, although the preceding informal engagement is the period during which most major adjustments should have been made, the formal engagement also offers young people plenty of opportunity for further adjustments.

During this period it is customary to decide on a date for the wedding and also make specific arrangements for the honeymoon and the first home. Such matters as whether to be married in church or at home, how many attendants and guests to have at the wedding, and what type of reception to have should be determined largely by the specific values of the couple.[10] And the exact decisions reached are not nearly so important as that they be mutually satisfactory to both parties involved.[11]

Specific plans for the honeymoon are usually made at this time. Although a honeymoon is not essential to the success or failure of marriage, it is regarded as being a desirable part of the wedding plans.[12] The honeymoon has gained an accepted place in the American marriage pattern and as such it serves the purpose of fulfilling what has come to be an important social expectation. More importantly, however, the honeymoon serves the purpose of giving the newlyweds an opportunity to begin their actual marriage relationship without the frequently embarrassing presence of well-meaning friends and relatives. Adjusting to the new roles of husband and wife and all the intimacies of interaction that this involves is best facilitated in a milieu that does not constantly remind the couple of their inexperience in these new roles.

With respect to the honeymoon, it might be well to simply call attention to some of the common mistakes in planning. It should be clear that excessive expense and involved travel arrangements create tensions that may defeat the purpose of the honeymoon. Furthermore, the tendency to

[10] For an interesting discussion of the wedding by a clergyman, see "Of Weddings and Funerals," *Harpers Magazine,* **191** (December 1945), pp. 496–499.

[11] Lawrence S. Bee, *op. cit.,* pp. 259–260. Bee points out that not only is agreement between the couple necessary, but that disagreement between the couple and one or both sets of parents can be painful and divisive in the relationship of the couple themselves.

[12] For a discussion of the wedding and the honeymoon, see Harold T. Christensen, *op. cit.,* pp. 346–356.

go to resorts that cater to a higher social class than the one to which the couple are accustomed may also lead to strain. A novel social environment often causes anxieties about such things as proper dress and behavior in the unfamiliar setting—factors that themselves can defeat the very purpose of the honeymoon. The couple—in adjusting to the plush atmosphere—are all too often detracted from effecting a meaningful adjustment to each other in their new roles of husband and wife, which the honeymoon is supposed to facilitate by providing an environment free from artificiality and unreality.[13]

Breaking the Formal Engagement

All the factors that we have described in this book as being conducive to the building of meaningful relationships during dating and courtship are likely to minimize the probability that a formal engagement must be broken. Nevertheless, incompatibilities do emerge, and many of these cannot be resolved. Hence some couples, after having worked hard at resolving their differences, are faced with the realization that they are not likely to have a successful marriage.[14] When both partners reach such an agreement, the relationship should be broken, and, although there may be some sorrow because of what might have been, there is also likely to be a sense of relief at having an unsatisfactory relationship ended.[15]

In spite of problems, the capacity of people to adjust to frustration is always greater than we think. Studies confirm this and point to the significant number of ways that people have seized upon to lessen the difficulties associated with the broken engagement—daydreaming, remembering only pleasant things, and preserving keepsakes, to mention only a few.[16]

---

[13] For a discussion of the fact that the honeymoon is not a vacation, see Lawrence S. Bee, *op. cit.*, pp. 264–267.

[14] Many factors could lead to this difficulty. Kirkpatrick and Caplow in studying the courtship experience of university students found that, among others, such factors as jealousy, possessiveness, criticism, irritability, and dislike of friends played a large part in causing conflict in serious love affairs. Clifford Kirkpatrick and Theodore Caplow, "Courtship in a Group of Minnesota Students," *Am. J. Sociol.*, 51 (September 1945), pp. 114–125.

[15] Ruth Shonle Cavan, *American Marriage*, Thomas Y. Crowell, New York, 1959, p. 186.

[16] Kirkpatrick and Caplow, *loc. cit.*

However, when one partner is desirous of breaking the engagement and the other is not, the situation should be carefully considered before a decision is made. Is the difficulty a result of one's own immaturity, suggesting that one might have difficulty in any relationship, or is it primarily a matter of value differences in a particular relationship? If one's own immaturity is found to be the primary cause, it may be wise to defer any decision about breaking the engagement. It may be that the relationship is basically sound and what is necessary is a change in the individual's personal orientation, rather than a change in relationships. For example, many immature people are unrealistic and expect too much from a relationship. They may have immature notions about love and distortions regarding the nature of love that must be dispelled before a satisfactory relationship can develop. Unless the immature individual can assure himself that he understands his part in the deterioration of a particular relationship, he undoubtedly will confront similar difficulties in other relationships.

If, however, after seriously considering his specific role in the relationship, he is assured that he has made a serious mistake in his selection of an intended marriage partner, the engagement probably should be broken. Making a wrong choice is not an uncommon thing, and the time to recognize this is during the courtship period. Burgess and Wallin report that in their study of 1000 engaged couples, about one third of the men and one half of the women had one or more broken engagements.[17] Landis suggests that some students of marriage are of the opinion that, to weed out unstable relationships, probably more engagements should be broken than actually are.[18]

This is not to suggest that breaking an engagement is something to be treated lightly. On the contrary, it is a serious matter, which often results in personal trauma. Nor is it being suggested that a pattern of broken engagements reflects a meaningful approach to marriage, because for some people the tendency to break engagements is indicative of unstable and fickle personality characteristics, neither of which can be regarded as healthy. It is being suggested, however, that becoming engaged in the first place should be regarded as a serious step in the man-woman relationship and treated as such. But if one or both of the engaged partners develop serious doubts about their ability to adjust in the relationship, a broken engagement may well mean one less broken marriage.

Let us now consider some of the ways of dealing with the engaged

[17] Ernest W. Burgess and Paul Wallin, *Engagement and Marriage,* Lippincott, Philadelphia, 1953, Ch. 9, "Broken Engagements."
[18] Paul H. Landis, *Making the Most of Marriage,* 2nd ed., Appleton-Century-Crofts, New York, 1960, p. 312.

partner when it is necessary to break an engagement. The manner in which an engagement is to be broken might well be examined in the light of certain values in the relationship. To begin with, we can assume that the couple have tried to develop a meaningful relationship, in which the qualities of trust and respect have been present to some extent. Although perhaps difficult to maintain at the time of breaking a relationship, these qualities are worthy of consideration. They add dignity to the human relationship and have therapeutic value as well. Since the breaking of a relationship is an important aspect of one's socialization, the qualities of respect and trust enable the experience to occur with a minimum of hurt to the self-worth of the members. In light of these values, perhaps the most difficult method at the time, but the best in the long run, is to break the relationship once a decision has been reached that the problems will not be resolved successfully. The realization that one should dissolve a relationship is not without its emotional complications, however. There are those who feel guilty and dislike themselves for such a decision, since it will involve hurting another person. The fact that more hurt could result were the relationship to continue is, at the time, seemingly unimportant. Thus many people feel ambivalent, especially when the time comes for the final break, since the finality arouses severe doubts and conflicts about whether or not one has reached the proper decision.

The ambivalence and the guilt about one's decision become responsible for much inner turmoil. Under these circumstances it is easy to feel not only hostility toward oneself for deciding to dissolve the relationship, but also what is experienced as hostility coming from the other person. Thus the individual who wishes to dissolve the relationship finds his difficulties compounded. For not only does he have to move ahead with a decision about the engagement, but he has to cope with hostilities, both those from within and those he feels from the outside. Some people break through the conflicts and discontinue the relationship. A good many, however, who attempt to avoid the conflicts in breaking a relationship often end up creating additional burdens.

One example of such a situation is to allow oneself to be talked into prolonging the relationship on some trial basis, perhaps aided by pleas from the other member—"If you will only give me another chance, I'll do better." Very frequently the rationale for agreeing to prolong the relationship is the belief that one has feeling for the other partner. The real reason often is that one wishes to avoid the conflict and possible hostility involved in a definite break. Such a decision to prolong the relationship is responsible for some real difficulties. To begin with, one is giving hope to the other person when really there is no hope. Certainly, only an immature person will confront the partner with the intent to break an engagement without having thought through the implications. Thus to encourage a person to believe that things can work out when in fact one has made up his mind that they will not, is cruel to the partner and is also indicative of a gross disrespect for what the relationship meant in the past. Putting off a final decision to break the relationship is one technique used to avoid or minimize the conflicts that one feels about breaking the engagement.

A second example of the need to avoid conflict in breaking an engagement is to engage in statements designed to make it easier for the other partner, thereby minimizing the discomfort that one may feel. One may resort to cliches such as "It isn't that I don't love you, but I love you like a sister (or brother)." What is frequently lost sight of, however, is that such an explanation, far from easing the situation, may inflict unintentional pain on the partner, since he or she is not desirous of being loved as a brother or sister. Other types of cliches that may lead to misunderstandings are "If we can't continue our engagement, I do hope we can continue to be good friends" and "Now, in spite of this, I do want to hear from you often." These statements are misleading, since the person uses them, in reality, to soothe his own feelings, while the engaged partner may take them as reflecting uncertainty about the desire to break the engagement. For example, a girl on hearing her fiancé say that, although he wants to break their engagement, he wants to hear from her often and continue their friendship, may easily delude herself into believing that her fiance is really not desirous of breaking the engagement. This misunderstanding and confusion is further compounded by friends who are eager to sympathize with her and who attempt to do so by agreeing with her faulty interpretation.

A third example of the need to avoid conflict in breaking the engagement is to avoid any formal confrontation at all. Instead, there may be a lessening of the frequency of dates, and even a going away, on one pretense or another, of the person desirous of making the break. Under this method, the engagement usually is terminated with the sending of a so-called "Dear John" letter. Because of the vagueness in breaking an engagement in this manner, the personal trauma created is probably far greater than it would have been if a straightforward confrontation had taken place. We are not suggesting that the engaged partner be approached with arrogance and bitterness; rather, after several unsuccessful attempts have been made to reach mutually satisfactory adjustments, the engaged partner must be confronted tactfully but truthfully with the fact that the engagement is being broken and the exact reasons why it is being broken.

It should be clear that these techniques for the avoidance of conflicts in breaking the engagement are fraught with complications. Rather than solving the difficulties, people often find themselves caught up in additional problems that complicate their dealings with the engaged partner; this is probably quite unnecessary.

Up to this point we have been viewing the broken engagement only from the standpoint of the partner desiring the break. From the point of view of the person who does not want to terminate the relationship, the breaking of the engagement is often a major emotional crisis.[19] Among other difficulties there is the feeling of being a jilted and discarded lover, and the trauma of explaining the situation to one's friends, not to mention the frequent need of the person himself to understand exactly what happened.

When this results in bitterness and suspicion, one's interaction in future relationships may become warped. Burgess, Locke, and Thomes, however, seem to feel that these reactions to a broken engagement gradually yield to time. They go on to say that there are individual differences in the rate of recovery from a broken love affair and that these differences are due to several factors, including temperament, the number and importance of other interests, and the beginnings of a new attachment. "In retrospect," they continue, "at least after another engagement which is successful, the person tends to minimize the seriousness of the experience and to be thankful that the break took place." [20]

As already noted, each broken engagement may well be one less broken marriage. If, in addition, the person being given up can also be made to understand the difficulties that impaired the relationship and to see the folly in his running headlong into another similar circumstance, then, to the extent that he was at fault, learning about his deficiencies and doing something to alter them will be of unlimited benefit in his future attempts to develop meaningful man-woman relationships. As Cavan points out, it should be remembered that "when a love affair or an engagement breaks, it is only this love relationship that is lost. The capacity to love again and to be loved again remains." [21]

The discussion of breaking an engagement is especially significant because it highlights a problem having to do with the use of knowledge in human experience. Granting all of the limitations in the status of our knowledge about the man-woman relationship, much is actually known

[19] For a discussion of emotional reactions to the breaking up of serious love affairs, see Kirkpatrick and Caplow, *loc. cit.*

[20] Ernest W. Burgess, Harvey J. Locke, and Mary Margaret Thomes, *The Family*, 3rd ed., American Book Company, New York, 1963, p. 234.

[21] Ruth Shonle Cavan, *op. cit.*, p. 188.

about the general qualities that go into making meaningful and mature relationships—psychological, psychiatric, and sociological knowledge. One major task today has to do with the problem of enabling the person to integrate and act on the basis of useful knowledge. Put another way, how can such knowledge be employed so that two human beings will not enter into a relationship of *mutual self-destruction?* All of us have known of people who had grave misgivings about the probable success of a marriage, but were unable to bring themselves to dissolve the relationship and chose marriage instead. Although specific ways for dealing with these issues are examined in counseling and therapy, the reader should be sensitized to the problems, as well as to the necessity, of acquiring knowledge of self, either alone or with the assistance of others.

As a final note to this chapter, we would like to state that at some time during the engagement period the couple will undoubtedly consider the economic as well as the medical aspects of marriage. With respect to economic aspects, the couple will be concerned with various consumer problems to be confronted in marriage. With respect to medical aspects, they will be interested in questions of overall health, family planning, and sexual adjustment. These problems, both economic and medical, are discussed in the Appendices to this book.[22]

Summary

Courtship is that phase of the man-woman relationship which follows dating and precedes marriage. It begins when each partner clearly states to the other his intention to have the relationship result in marriage. Courtship, thus, is engagement. There are two periods in the courtship phase. The first, referred to as informal engagement, is the period during which the couple have an opportunity to test their ability to adjust to each other and to establish patterns of working through whatever difficulties they may encounter. At the successful conclusion of this period, the couple announce publicly their intention to marry; this announcement initiates the formal engagement. The formal engagement period consists largely of making arrangements for the wedding and honeymoon and preparing the home in which the newlyweds will reside. In this chapter many aspects of the informal and formal engagement pe-

[22] See also Abraham Stone and Lena Levine, *The Premarital Consultation,* Grune and Stratton, New York, 1956.

riods were discussed, and the advantage of having an informal engagement was stressed. Also considered were the conditions under which an engagement should be broken and the situations that are confronted in the breaking of an engagement. Finally, it was suggested that if people would use the knowledge about human relationships that is available, at least to some extent, mutually destructive relationships might be avoided.

Questions

1. What is the difference between dating and courtship? Name and give the purpose of the two phases of courtship.
2. Under what circumstances does going steady and being pinned constitute engagement?
3. How long should the entire engagement last? What proportion of time should be devoted to the informal engagement and what proportion to the formal engagement? Why?
4. What things should a person consider in deciding how much he should "confess" about his past to his engaged partner?
5. What are the common mistakes that people make in planning a honeymoon? Why are these considered to be mistakes?
6. Is the broken engagement an infrequent occurrence in the American society? Why do some students of marriage believe that more engagements should be broken? Does this mean that the more broken engagements one has, the more likely he is to be successful in marriage? Explain your answer.
7. What techniques do people use in attempting to minimize the conflict they feel about breaking an engagement? Do these techniques help or hinder the circumstances?
8. What did Burgess and Locke find to be the reaction of people toward their broken engagements? Do you agree with their findings? (See Project 1 of this chapter.)
9. It has been said that in a broken love relationship only the relationship is lost but the capacity to love again remains. Under what circumstances is this correct and under what circumstances might it be incorrect?

Projects

1. Have each student in the class interview three students who have experienced a broken engagement. Have them find out such things as what were the reasons for the broken engagement; to what extent do the people they interview regard themselves as having been at fault; what if anything, have they learned from the broken engagement; and, finally, what feelings do these people have toward their broken relationship. Summarize the findings in class and have the class analyze the results.

2. Make a survey to find out to what extent going steady and being pinned constitute informal engagement on your campus. Do you find any differences between the answers given by men and those given by women?

3. Take a poll on campus to find out what percentage of engaged and married couples utilized the informal engagement and what percentage went directly from dating into the formal engagement. Find out whether those who utilized the informal engagement period found it helpful and why, and also whether those who did not utilize the informal engagement think they could have benefited from it and why.

4. Interview several married couples and find out in what way engagement prepared them for marriage and in what way, if any, it did not. Ask them whether, if they could relive their engagement period, they would change anything, and if so, what would they change and why would they change it.

Suggested Readings

Johannis, Theodore B., Jr., and Karen Many, "Financing Student Weddings," *J. Home Econ.,* 51 (May 1959), pp. 362–364.

Kephart, William M., *The Family, Society and the Individual,* 2nd ed., Houghton Mifflin, Boston, 1966, especially pp. 322–328.

Kirkpatrick, Clifford, and Theodore Caplow, "Courtship in a Group of Minnesota Students," *Am. J. Sociol.,* 51 (September 1945), pp. 114–125.

Mace, David R., *Marriage,* Doubleday, New York, 1952, Ch. 2, "Are Engagements Necessary?"

Magoun, F. Alexander, *Love and Marriage,* Harper, New York, 1948, Ch. 6, "Courtship," Ch. 7, "The Period of Engagement," and Ch. 8, "The Honeymoon."

Simpson, George, *People in Families,* Thomas Y. Crowell, New York, 1960, Ch. 9, "Some Critical Notes on Weddings and Honeymoons."

Waller, Willard, *The Family,* revised by Reuben Hill, Dryden Press, New York, 1951, Ch. 12, "The Engagement: A Bridge to Marriage."

Winch, Robert F., *The Modern Family,* Henry Holt, New York, 1962, Ch. 16, "Courtship and Marriage."

Chapter Eleven

MATE SELECTION: AN ANALYSIS OF RESEARCH AND CLINICAL FINDINGS

W E HAVE seen that confusion in the areas of motivations for marriage, love, dating, and sex can become manifest in problems in
the man-woman relationship. In this chapter we analyze another problem area: mate selection. Mate selection is examined with a view toward understanding how particular factors that influence selection
may result in difficulties in the man-woman relationship. We also examine some of the research concerning (1) certain factors that tend to influence mate selection and (2) the social and personal characteristics associated with mate selection that result in successful marriages and those
that result in unsuccessful marriages.

ILLUSTRATION: Jumping jacks. Courtesy of the Museum of the City of New York.

The Role of Determinism in Mate Choice

Research in mate selection is rooted in "determinism." Stated simply, the main assumption of determinism, as used here, is that the social and psychological experiences of the past markedly influence the way people will respond and react in the future. In influences from the past we include a wide variety of experiences with members of the family and with teachers and peers at school. Such experiences may result in the acquisition of particular values or prejudices. Other experiences stemming from either favorable or unfavorable relationships may result in patterned modes of reacting or perceiving. Thus if as a result of previous experience one has learned to feel more comfortable with persons who enjoy literature and the arts, such enjoyment becomes a value to him and he may tend to marry such a person. Or if one has learned to interact comfortably with dominating parents, he may develop the feeling that he will be most comfortable with dominating persons and consequently seek such a marriage partner. On the other hand, if a man, or woman, has had unfavorable experiences with dominating parents and becomes rebellious as a result, he or she may find a domineering female or male very difficult to take, and perhaps be driven to find a submissive individual. Thus the experiences of the past can operate to move one toward or away from a given type of person. Also, the person who repeatedly has been treated with disrespect in his relationships in all probability will have little capacity to treat others with respect and will, to that extent, be a poor risk for marriage. Similarly, the person who comes from a home characterized by arguing and fighting may never develop the personal security necessary to become a stable family member, and so it goes. In this manner our likes and dislikes for certain qualities in people are nurtured; often there is little awareness of how we got that way and little awareness of the power that these past experiences may exert in determining our behavior.

Let us now examine how the past may determine the type of person we seek for marriage.

Studies in Mate Selection

Those who give much thought to marriage are frequently preoccupied with such questions as: Will I marry a person who resembles my parents? Or one who conforms to my preconceived notions of an ideal mate? Or one who is of the same social class as I, or of the same religious, racial, and ethnic group? Or will I marry someone who is quite different from me in these respects? Several approaches to these questions have been made in studies dealing with the ideal mate, parental image, assortative mating, and complementary needs.

The Ideal Mate

The first type of study that attempts to shed light on mate selection deals with the concept of the ideal mate and is concerned with discovering the degree to which the individual's concept of an ideal mate influences his choice of a mate. By "ideal mate" we mean that preconceived combination of emotional, physical, and social characteristics that is embodied in one's personal image of the kind of person he would like to marry. To be sure, one's preconceived notions about such characteristics as race, religion, nationality, education, and socioeconomic status often serve to eliminate large numbers of people from one's marital choices. But these characteristics, although important, frequently operate without the person's awareness of their importance in his concept of an ideal mate. Thus one tends to think about his "dream" partner in terms of personality and physical characteristics. In this respect one investigator, Anselm Strauss, found that the majority of men and women report that their ideal mates and their real mates are "identical," "very close," or "close" both in physical and in personality characteristics.[1] The greater similarity between real and ideal mates tended to occur in personality characteristics. Moreover, when subjects compared the mate finally selected with the one they liked next best, there was practically no difference between them in approximation to the ideal in physical traits, but

[1] Anselm Strauss, "The Ideal and the Chosen Mate," *Am. J. Sociol.*, **52** (October 1946), pp. 204–208. For another study concerning the influences of the ideal mate on one's selection of a mate, see Ernest W. Burgess and Paul Wallin, *Engagement and Marriage*, Lippincott, Philadelphia, 1953, p. 175.

marked differences in personality characteristics, with the mate finally selected more closely approximating the ideal. All of this would seem to show that a person's first concern in mate selection is to seek out those persons who meet his general physical standards; once this has been accomplished, his selection of a mate is made from this group on the basis of the specific personality characteristics that he desires in a mate. Thus physical characteristics may be the initial selective factors within which personality discrimination takes place.

Although most people in this study claim to have married their ideal mates, we cannot assume that these assertions are correct. Much more has to be known about how the concept of the ideal mate may have been revised by the presence of particular types of individuals who were available as marriage partners. Indeed, in one recent study this exact point was made when the investigator concluded that the ideal mate probably changes in response to new relationships, and, therefore, the ideal-mate images may be resultants, not determinants, of mate selection.[2] Until more is known about the ideal-mate image itself—how it emerges, how it changes, or if it exists at all—the results of ideal-mate studies should be regarded as suggestive rather than conclusive.

IMPLICATIONS OF IDEAL-MATE STUDIES FOR SELECTING A MARRIAGE PARTNER. There appears to be little doubt that many of us possess a concept of the ideal mate. Such a concept need not necessarily cause problems in mate selection. Nevertheless, several potential difficulties must be recognized. For example, to the extent that the concept of the ideal mate may be a denial of the relative worth of oneself and an exaggerated superiority of others, it represents an unhealthy approach to mate selection and is often associated with the need to live through others (already discussed in connection with motivations for marriage). Furthermore, problems arise if the concept of the ideal mate is divorced from reality. Some persons, for example, in dating and courtship fabricate a grossly distorted image of the other person, who is seen in perfectionist terms as possessing all of the qualities of their ideal and being all-knowing, all-wise, all-good, and so on. The difficulty increases for those who expect contradictory characteristics from their ideal mate—that he be both all-knowing and dependent on them for advice, for example. In light of all the demands exercised on us by our concept of the ideal mate, certain reactions often follow. If our concept of the ideal mate is overly rigid, the actual persons we are dating may come to be viewed as possessing only imperfections, hence as being undesirable or contemptible. Many

---

[2] J. Richard Udry, "The Influence of the Ideal Mate Image on Mate Selection and Mate Perception," *J. Marr. Fam.*, **27**, 4 (November 1965), pp. 477–482.

potentially good mates are overlooked in this way, and some people fail to marry precisely because they cannot adjust their concept to reality. If, on the other hand, we expect contradictory things of the partner, we are perpetually ambivalent and uncertain in our feelings and reactions toward him. Finally, many marry what they believe to be the ideal mate only to discover in marriage that the real person falls short of the ideal. Since they frequently come to believe that the mate misrepresented himself as being superior to what he actually is, much hostility may develop.

There is the case of a woman who had been married for fifteen years. At the time she married, she believed herself to be fortunate to have found a husband. She saw herself as homely, unlovable, and inferior. The husband, she thought, possessed all of the qualities of an ideal mate—he was strong, handsome, and had a mind of his own. Over the years this woman discovered that her husband did not quite fit her image; instead he was, in her terms, weak, could not make up his mind, and was easily dominated. She developed tremendous hostility and resentment toward him, felt that he had misrepresented himself, and became very vindictive toward him as a result. Her vindictiveness took the form of "browbeating" her husband, refusing any type of erotic involvement, and humiliating him in front of their children. It took much time and effort for her to understand that her concept of the ideal mate, which she had imposed on her husband, was responsible for her marital problems.

Parental-Image Studies

A second type of mate-selection study in which a limited amount of work has been done concerns the degree to which one's image of his parents influences his selection of a marriage partner. Originally it was assumed that one tended to marry a person who was similar to his, or her, parent of the opposite sex. Thus men presumably tended to select mates who resembled their mothers, and women mates who resembled their fathers. Research did not uphold this hypothesis, since little relationship was found to exist between one's mate and parent of the opposite sex, per se. It has been demonstrated, however, that a person's selection of a mate is influenced by the kind of relationship he had with his parents. Strauss reports a number of such parental influences on mate selection.[3] It appears that if one has had a rather meaningful relationship with one parent, he tends to seek a mate who is very similar to that parent. If one has had an extremely hostile relationship with a parent, the tendency is to select a marriage partner who differs markedly from that parent. Thus if

[3] Anselm Strauss, "The Influence of Parent-Images upon Marital Choice," *Am. soc. Rev.*, 11 (October 1946), pp. 554–559.

a young man's most meaningful family relationship was that with his mother, he tends to select a wife with characteristics similar to hers. If his relationships with both mother and father were equally meaningful to him, his selection of a marriage partner seems to reflect both parents. On the other hand, if the young man's relationship with his mother was ridden with hostility, his tendency seems to be to select a marriage partner who possesses characteristics that differ markedly from those of his mother.

It should be noted, however, that this connection between mate selection and parental image exists with respect to temperamental and ideational characteristics, but is apparent to a much lesser degree with respect to physical characteristics.[4] In effect this means that the kind of relationship one shares with either one or both parents tends to influence his selection of a marriage partner, but this influence is more apparent with respect to the dispositions and sets of values and less apparent with respect to physical appearances.

In counseling, in addition to the type of parental influence just described, we observe cases in which people who had a poor relationship with their parents look for a marital partner who resembles, rather than differs from, their parents. They do this in the hope of finding acceptance in a symbolic way.

Parental-image studies, like ideal-mate studies, should be regarded as suggestive rather than conclusive.

IMPLICATIONS OF PARENTAL-IMAGE STUDIES FOR SELECTING A MARRIAGE PARTNER. The concept of the parental image presents difficulties that are in certain respects similar to those encountered in the concept of the ideal mate. For example, some persons idealize their parents to such an extent that they have a distorted image of the parents. The dating partner may then be compared with an exaggerated and unrealistic view of a parent; hence he may be judged and evaluated quite unfairly.

There was a young lady who was the daughter of a successful physician. She saw her father in the most ideal terms—as a brilliant, self-sacrificing person who had surmounted serious economic and personal problems in order to become a physician. Although there was some basis in fact for the view she held of her father, much of what she believed was grossly distorted. She nevertheless insisted on comparing any boy she dated with this distorted view of her father. Needless to say, none of her boy friends could measure up to her parental image. Her problem became apparent to her father, and he had to aid his daughter in acquiring a more realistic view. Once she was able to do this, she became more accepting of her dates.

[4] Ibid.

In addition, one's parental image may include personality traits that are likely to lead to difficulties. For example, one may come to admire a parent's power to manipulate and coerce others into a decision, hence to feel that such a trait is indicative of power and strength in the marital relationship. To internalize such a parental image and to seek such traits in a mate can lead to difficulty in the marriage relationship.

Assortative-Mating Studies

The ideal-mate and parental-image studies are primarily concerned with the factors that determine the traits that individuals seek in a marital relationship. The third approach to the study of mate selection deals with another question—the extent to which people select marriage partners who are similar to them and the extent to which they select partners who are dissimilar to them. This approach is known as assortative mating and involves two major hypotheses: the first is called homogamy and postulates that like marries like; the second is called heterogamy and postulates that opposites marry each other.[5] In an attempt to shed light on these hypotheses, a number of physical, psychological, and social factors have been investigated.

For the most part research findings tend to support the homogamous hypothesis in that it appears that like tends to marry like. This is particularly true of such items as race, religion, IQ, ethnic origin, place of residence before marriage,[6] marital status before marriage, socioeconomic status, social class, occupation, height, age, attitudes, and interests.[7] With respect to attitudes and interests, the evidence does not seem to be

[5] One writer has suggested a third approach to assortative mating, namely summation theory, which postulates that each strength of a person is balanced by a weakness and that when all are added up, persons selecting each other as marriage partners tend to be on a par with one another; that is, beauty may compensate for a lack of intelligence, or wealth may compensate for neurotic behavioral tendencies. See Gunnar Boalt, *Family and Marriage,* David McKay, New York, 1965, pp. 26–28.

[6] For a discussion of the conceptual significance of residential propinquity, see William Catton and R. J. Smircich, "A Comparison of Mathematical Models for the Effect of Residential Propinquity on Mate Selection," *Am. soc. Rev.,* **29,** 4 (August 1964), pp. 522–529.

[7] For reviews of the many assortative mating studies, see Helen M. Richardson, "Studies of Mental Resemblance Between Husbands and Wives and Between Friends," *Psychol. Bull.,* **36** (February 1939), pp. 104–120. Robert F. Winch in Joseph B. Gittler, Ed., *Review of Sociology,* Wiley, New York, 1956, Ch. 11, pp. 349–352. Robert C. Williamson, *Marriage and Family Relations,* Wiley, New York, 1966, Ch. 10.

conclusive.[8] With respect to height and age, homogamy tends to occur far more frequently than heterogamy. Although women do tend to marry older and taller men, the age and height differences between them are not great. Data on personality characteristics suggest that both homogamy [9] and heterogamy [10] are involved. Homogamy is particularly apparent when we deal with certain broad categories of personality. For example, neurotics tend to marry neurotics.[11] However, the kinds of neuroses involved tend to be different.[12] An overly aggressive male, for example, instead of marrying an overly aggressive female tends to marry an overly submissive female.[13] Thus the seemingly contradictory find-

[8] Most assortative mating studies are conducted by testing people who are already engaged or married and, therefore, have had a great deal of interaction, which may have produced the similarity in attitudes and interests that is found. In other words, the similarity found among engaged and married partners with respect to attitudes and interests may be the result of their interaction in engagement and marriage and need not have been necessarily present at the outset. One of the authors conducted a study of assortative mating which tested couples not after they had become engaged or married, but rather just prior to their having met. The results of this study suggest that attitudes and interests of married people are not so similar prior to engagement or marriage as we have been led to believe, but tend to become similar after intensive interaction in engagement and marriage. For a detailed account of this research, see Eloise C. Snyder, "Marital Selectivity in Self Adjustment, Social Adjustment and I.Q.," *J. Marr. Fam.*, **28**, 2 (May 1966), pp. 188–189; Eloise C. Snyder, "Attitudes: A Study of Homogamy and Marital Selectivity," *J. Marr. Fam.*, **26**, 3 (August 1964), pp. 332–336. For another study, which claims that there is a general tendency to become more homogamous in some dimensions (education) while becoming less so in others (urbanity), see Alan C. Kerckhoff, "Patterns of Homogamy and the Field of Eligibles," *Social Forces*, **42**, 3 (March 1964), pp. 289–297.

[9] In reviewing studies on psychological characteristics, Stagner points out that homogamy is more apparent in intellectual interest and attitude scores than it is in temperament scores. Ross Stagner, *Psychology of Personality*, McGraw-Hill, New York, 1948, p. 387.

[10] Horace Gray, "Psychological Types in Married People," *J. soc. Psychol.*, **29**, Second Half (May 1949), pp. 189–200. Using Jung's psychological types, this study found heterogamy predominant.

[11] Raymond R. Willoughby, "Neuroticism in Marriage, IV. Homogamy, V. Summary and Conclusions," *J. soc. Psychol.*, **7** (February 1936), pp. 19–48.

[12] Bela Mittlemann, "Complementary Neurotic Reactions in Intimate Relationships," *Psychoanal. Quart.*, **13** (1944), pp. 479–491. In one study, however, homogamy was not only found in neurotic tendency but also in the items comprising it. See Ernest W. Burgess and Paul Wallin, "Homogamy in Personality Characteristics," *J. abnorm. soc. Psychol.*, **39** (October 1944), pp. 475–481.

[13] For a discussion of how neurotic need systems tend to become interlaced and how psychiatric assistance can clearly disrupt the neurotic equilibrium, see Thomas F. McGee and Thaddeus Kostrubala, "The Neurotic Equilibrium in Married Couples Applying for Group Psychotherapy," *J. Marr. Fam.*, **26**, 1 (February 1964), pp. 77–82.

ings of the various studies (such as finding personality to be homogamous and heterogamous by turns) are due at least in part to their being
concerned with different personality characteristics. Even when the
same characteristic is being considered, the methods of getting at similarity or dissimilarity (in other words, the methodologies of the studies) differ, which may also account for certain differences in results.

A final point that should be made in regard to assortative-mating
studies is that they tend to be concerned exclusively with the item being studied, be it education, religion, or whatever, and do not take into
account the importance of the item for the person being studied. For
example, in one case a religious likeness may be considered to be more
important than a similarity of educational background, while in other
cases this may not be true.[14] The significance of one's particular values
would seem to play an important part in determining mate choice; such
shaping is probably related to one's actual experiences within his
groups, as well as to the pressure that these groups are able to exert on
him. Hollingshead notes, for example, that the upper class, in addition
to giving one certain sets of values, also tends to exert powerful controls
over its members and in so doing keeps its marriages endogamous.[15] Social pressure toward group homogamy is also apparent among other
classes. In this respect, it can be noted that the behaviors that women admire in men may be quite different in the lower class from those admired
in the middle class. Toughness or the use of physical force, for example,
may be the mark of manliness in the lower class, whereas the same behaviors may be very much frowned upon by the middle class. Indeed, the
college campus offers numerous examples of middle-class values at work
in the dating, courtship, and mate-selection processes. Many of these can
be seen in the numerous events and rituals of a sorority, for example,
which in addition to impressing particular sets of values, also functions
to take up a girl's time, thus limiting the number and degree of her interactions with lower-status individuals.[16] It is obvious that the family
exerts a great deal of influence in shaping values and in determining
who marries whom. One study, for example, found that homogamy in
such factors as race, nationality, religion, and social class was most evi-

[14] For a discussion centering exactly on this point, see Sheila Selfors, Robert K. Leik,
and Edward King, "Values in Mate Selection: Education versus Religion," *J. Marr.
Fam.*, **24**, 4 (November 1962), pp. 399–401.
[15] August B. Hollingshead, "Class Differences in Family Stability," *Ann. Am.
Acad. polit. soc. Sci.*, **272** (November 1950), pp. 39–46.
[16] John Finley Scott, "The American College Sorority: Its Role in Class and Ethnic
Endogamy," *Am. soc. Rev.*, **30**, 4 (August 1965), pp. 514–527.

dent when both marriage partners had lived at home, but less evident when only one mate had. Moreover, when both mates had not resided at home prior to their marriage, the least amount of homogamy occurred.[17] Thus it is apparent that although a number of studies have been undertaken in the area of assortative mating, much more work is needed before we can begin to understand the dynamics behind homogamy and heterogamy, which involves determining the impact of certain groups on us at given points in our lives, an impact that is significant in influencing decisions of mate selection.

IMPLICATIONS OF ASSORTATIVE MATING FOR SELECTING A MARRIAGE PARTNER. Persons with similar backgrounds tend to get along well together, since they possess a common basis of experiences. Such experiences enable them to share sentiments and values and to communicate in ways that have meaning to them. On the other hand, we must recognize that similarity of background alone is no assurance against difficulties in the man-woman relationship. Indeed, it frequently obscures the existence of some very serious problems. Two people who come from unstable families are poor risks in marriage. Although each might believe that the difficulties that are common to their backgrounds will enable him to understand and deal with family problems, his image of the nature of family life may be extremely negative. Indeed, the very personalities that these people have developed as a result of such family background may make them very poor marital risks. In essence, one may compound his difficulties in many instances by marrying a person from a similar background.

To illustrate: a couple who were contemplating marriage had both come from homes in which the parents had been unhappily married and subsequently divorced. The couple also reported that they both had an unhappy childhood and unhappy family relations. They believed that since they knew what an unhappy family life was like, they were in a position to avoid repetition of the same errors. For them, having a happy family was simply a matter of effort. After they were married they began to fight and argue, and the immaturities of each began to appear. Soon they became very discouraged and began to think of divorce. Since they had no concept of a happy family, it was difficult for them to have much faith that their problems could be resolved.

[17] For example, socioeconomic homogamy rates were 83 percent when both resided at home, 71 percent when only one mate resided at home, and 66 percent when neither mate lived at home; see Robert H. Coombs, "Reinforcement of Values in the Parental Home as a Factor in Mate Selection," *J. Marr. Fam.*, **24**, 2 (May 1962), pp. 155–157.

Another area of study, which might be subsumed under the heterogamous hypothesis of assortative mating, should be reviewed—the area known as complementary needs.

Complementary Needs

One aspect of heterogamy, which might be regarded as a fourth approach to the analysis of mate selection, is that of complementary needs. In this area the major hypothesis is that the selection of a mate tends to be made on the basis of each person's ability to satisfy "opposite kinds of needs" in the other.

Robert F. Winch, for example, who has spent a considerable amount of time studying this question, sees mate selection as occurring on the basis of complementary needs.[18] He does not disregard the importance of the previously noted findings of homogamy studies, but claims that although homogamy operates in such a way as to cause an individual to sort out from an entire population of potential mates those who are similar to him with respect to social background, cultural interests, and values, the process of falling in love tends to occur through complementary need fulfillment. Thus a male who has a need to express hostility would be attracted to a woman with a need to have hostility expressed toward her.

Kerckhoff and Davis, in attempting to test the Winch hypothesis, delineate three phases in mate selection.[19] During the first phase homogamous values predominate; these then tend to be followed by the need for arriving at a value consensus during the second phase; and, finally, need complementarity appears during the third and last phase. These investigators thereby contend that in mate selection a "filtering process" occurs and claim that the second and third phases (namely, arriving at value consensus and showing need complementarity) are related to the progress of a man-woman relationship from its impermanent to its more permanent stage.[20]

A number of recent studies, however, have cast doubt on Winch's hypothesis, suggesting that the concept of a need complementarity is too

[18] Robert F. Winch, *Mate Selection,* Harper, New York, 1958. See also Gray, *loc. cit.;* Thomas and Virginia Ktsanes, "The Theory of Complementary Needs in Mate-Selection," in R. F. Winch and R. McGinnis, *Marriage and the Family,* Henry Holt, New York, 1953, pp. 435–453.

[19] Alan C. Kerckhoff and Keith E. Davis, "Value Consensus and Need Complementarity in Mate Selection," *Am. soc. Rev.,* **27,** 3 (June 1962), pp. 295–303.

[20] If this is true, then newlyweds should exhibit a considerable degree of complementarity. But some investigators claim that such complementarity is not found. Bernard I. Murstein, "The Complementary Need Hypothesis in Newlyweds and Middle-Aged Couples," *J. abnorm. soc. Psychol.,* **63,** 1 (July 1961), pp. 194–197.

ambiguous. In an effort to pin down the concept of need complementarity and then to relate it to satisfaction in the relationship, some researchers report that neither the Winch hypothesis nor the relationship of complementarity to marital satisfaction was confirmed.[21]

IMPLICATIONS OF COMPLEMENTARY NEEDS FOR SELECTING A MARRIAGE PARTNER. Although the findings regarding complementary needs are far from conclusive, the fact that at some phase of the man-woman relationship we may be attracted to people who complement our needs and traits should alert us to the possibility of encountering difficulties.[22] It suggests, as indicated in an earlier chapter on love, that we should concern ourselves not only with the fact that we are attracted to certain types of people, but why we are attracted to them. It becomes apparent that complementariness may not necessarily be conducive to the development of a mature relationship. Difficulties become especially apparent in relationships where one person may have a need to dominate and the other a need to be dominated or where one person has a need to be aggressive and the other a need to be submissive. This, as we saw, has apparently been found to be the case in some studies of neurotics.[23]

Finally, the reader might well make some effort to assess the extent to which the variables in the concept of ideal mate, parental image, complementary needs, and assortative mating operate to influence his or her mate selection. Such an analysis may lead to an appreciation of the factors in mate selection that can operate against finding and developing the best possible relationship.

Prediction of Success in Marriage

We now turn to a discussion of the factors in mate selection that research has shown to be related to marital success and those that are re-

[21] John A. Blazer, "Complementary Needs and Marital Happiness," *J. Marr. Fam.*, 25, 1 (February 1963), pp. 89–95. See also Jerold S. Heiss and Michael Gordon, "Need Patterns and the Mutual Satisfaction of Dating and Engaged Couples," *J. Marr. Fam.*, 26, 3 (August 1964), pp. 337–339.

[22] For still another problem—the part that one's perception of his mate plays in determining whether complementary-need theory actually operates in mate selection—see J. Richard Udry, "Complementarity in Mate Selection: A Perceptual Approach," *J. Marr. Fam.*, 25, 3 (August 1963), pp. 281–289.

[23] Bela Mittlemann, "Complementary Neurotic Reactions in Intimate Relationships," *loc. cit.* See especially Thomas F. McGee and Thaddeus Kostrubala, "The Neurotic Equilibrium in Married Couples Applying for Group Psychotherapy," *loc. cit.*

lated to marital failure. Much of the information here is based on what researchers in the area of marriage prediction have found in their numerous studies.

Marriage prediction aims at determining the probability of marital success both for those who are contemplating marriage and for those who are already married. It is rooted in the relationship between one's past experiences and future behavior, which we discussed earlier. That is, it is predicated on the assumption that one's experiences before marriage will affect his behavior in marriage.

To analyze the relationship between past experience and marital success and failure, it first becomes necessary to clarify what is meant by marital success and what is meant by marital failure. To be sure, divorce and separation are indicative of marital failure, but it is incorrect to assume that these are the only criteria of marital failure. Indeed, many marriages that are not broken by divorce or separation are constantly ridden by conflict and unhappiness, hence must be regarded as being unsuccessful. Let us look therefore at the criteria that have been used (either in entirety or in part) in defining successful marriage. A successful marriage is one in which the following conditions obtain:

1. Both husband and wife are happy and satisfied with their marriage.
2. There is a quality of permanence to the relationship.
3. There is good adjustment (including sexual adjustment).
4. The attitudes and acts of the husband and wife are in agreement on the chief issues of the marriage.
5. There is integration, which means that the personalities of the husband and wife interact in such a way as to complement each other for the mutual satisfaction and achievement of common objectives.[24]

Once the criteria of marital success have been established, a sample of marriages that meet these criteria and a sample of those that fail to meet the criteria are examined, with respect to both the characteristics of the marriages and the background characteristics brought to the marriages by the spouses. All of the characteristics are then studied in order to de-

[24] See Burgess and Locke, who also suggest that the following criteria of successful marriage have not as yet been used in constructing marriage prediction instruments: (1) Marriages in which the social expectations that are made of successful marriage by the particular social class to which the partners belong are fulfilled. (2) Marriages in which there is companionship. (3) Marriages in which the personalities of both husband and wife are allowed to develop fully; in fact, are aided in doing so by the interaction of the marriage. Ernest W. Burgess, Harvey J. Locke, and Mary Margaret Thomes, *The Family*, 3rd ed., American Book Company, New York, 1963, pp. 290–308.

termine what it is that successful marriages have and unsuccessful marriages lack, and vice versa. For example, if coming from a home in which parents were happy is reported in those marriages that are successful and coming from a home in which parents were unhappy is reported in those marriages that are unsuccessful, this background characteristic is regarded as being a significant factor in differentiating successful from unsuccessful marriages. Many other items are examined in the same way, and they together make up a marriage prediction test. Let us now consider some of these items.

Factors Associated with Success or Failure in Marriage

Analyses of both successful and unsuccessful marriages point out differences with respect to the presence or absence of specific factors within six broad areas of human experience: personality characteristics, cultural backgrounds, social participation, economic status, response patterns, and sexual factors.[25]

PERSONALITY CHARACTERISTICS. Some of the personality characteristics associated with marital success are:

1. A willingness to assume responsibility.
2. An ability to make decisions with a minimum of difficulty.
3. An ability to overcome feelings of anger in oneself.
4. A sense of humor.
5. An ability to demonstrate affection.

Some of the personality characteristics associated with marital failure are:

1. An unhappy temperament, which is indicated by the tendency of an individual to be pessimistic rather than optimistic.
2. Neurotic behaviors, which are indicated by the tendency of an individual to be touchy, grouchy, lonesome, easily hurt, and bothered by useless thoughts.
3. Dominating and domineering traits, which are indicated by the

[25] The findings reported here, unless otherwise indicated, have been taken from four leading marriage-prediction studies: Ernest W. Burgess and Leonard S. Cottrell, *Predicting Success or Failure in Marriage*, Prentice-Hall, Englewood Cliffs, N.J., 1939; Ernest W. Burgess and Paul Wallin, *Engagement and Marriage*, Lippincott, Philadelphia, 1953; Lewis M. Terman et al., *Psychological Factors in Marital Happiness*, McGraw-Hill, New York, 1938; and Harvey J. Locke, *Predicting Adjustment in Marriage: A Comparison of a Divorced and a Happily Married Group*, Henry Holt, New York, 1951.

tendency of an individual to have to get his own way even to the extent of completely disregarding the feelings of others.

4. A critical and inconsiderate attitude toward others, which is indicated by the tendency of an individual to find fault with and disapprove of the behaviors of others without regard for their feelings.

5. Lack of self-confidence (particularly on the part of the husband), which is indicated by the tendency of the individual to doubt his own ability and judgment.

6. Extreme self-sufficiency, which is indicated by the tendency of the individual to face trouble alone and to avoid asking others for advice.[26]

These findings show that the successfully married tend to be more emotionally mature than the unsuccessfully married and that they display self-control, serious-mindedness, and deliberateness.[27] There are also a number of studies that show that a favorable self-perception is related to viewing spouse favorably, hence related to a sense of marital success.[28] In this regard it appears that persons satisfied in marriage see their spouses as being personally responsible, generous, cooperative, and conventional, whereas the dissatisfied tend to see their spouses as being intensely skeptical, distrustful, blunt, aggressive, and either extremely dictatorial or extremely passive.[29] Although many studies (in spite of the

[26] In addition to these findings dealing with the relationship between specific traits and success or failure in marriage, there are others that are concerned with the combination of personality traits that result when two people are married. Examined in this light, the evidence suggests that certain combinations are more favorable for marital success than are others. Winch has done some work in this area; see Robert F. Winch, "Personality Characteristics of Engaged and Married Couples," *Am. J. Sociol.*, **46** (March 1941), pp. 686–697. It has also been suggested that more work of this type would seem to be warranted; see Ernest W. Burgess, Harvey J. Locke, and Mary Margaret Thomes, *op. cit.*, pp. 298–308.

[27] Dwight G. Dean, "Emotional Maturity and Marital Adjustment," *J. Marr. Fam.*, **28**, 4 (November 1966), pp. 454–457. John Pickford, Edro Signori, and Henry Rempel, "Similar or Related Personality Traits as a Factor in Marital Happiness," *J. Marr. Fam.*, **28**, 2 (May 1966), pp. 190–192. It is interesting to note that one study suggests that the personality traits of males play a more important role in determining marital happiness and unhappiness than do the traits of females. John Pickford, Edro Signori, and Henry Rempel, "The Intensity of Personality Traits in Relation to Marital Happiness," *J. Marr. Fam.*, **28**, 4 (November 1966), pp. 458–459. Another study claims that personality is not related to marriage adjustment for men and only moderately related for women; see Bernard I. Murstein and Vincent Glaudin, "The Relationship of Marital Adjustment to Personality," *J. Marr. Fam.*, **28**, 1 (February 1966), pp. 37–43.

[28] Kate L. Kogan and Joan K. Jackson, "Perceptions of Self and Spouse: Some Contaminating Factors," *J. Marr. Fam.*, **26**, 1 (February 1964), pp. 60–64.

[29] Eleanore Brown Luckey, "Marital Satisfaction and Personality Correlates of Spouse," *J. Marr. Fam.*, **26**, 2 (May 1964), pp. 217–220.

exceptions) show that these trait combinations tend to be related, respectively, to success or failure in marriage, it is not always clear whether the traits bring about the marital state or whether the marital state produces the personality traits.

CULTURAL BACKGROUND. The findings with respect to cultural background as revealed by research on marriage prediction indicate that likenesses in cultural background, as exemplified by similar nationality, ethnicity, race, and socioeconomic status, are related to success in marriage and dissimilarity in these areas, particularly if it is sufficiently great, is associated with failure in marriage.[30]

Furthermore, couples who possess the following characteristics are more likely to have successful marriages:

1. Couples who have been reared in the country rather than in the city.

2. Couples possessing similar levels of education, with the highest educational levels having the greatest likelihood of successful marriage.[31]

3. Couples who are similar in age, with the best adjustment occurring when the husband is a little older than the wife, the husband is at least twenty-two years old at marriage, and the wife is at least twenty.[32]

4. Couples who have had no previous marriages.

5. Couples who display a pattern of church attendance, particularly if both attend the same church.[33]

[30] John Scanzoni, "Family Organization and the Probability of Disorganization," *J. Marr. Fam.,* **28,** 4 (November 1966), pp. 407–411.
[31] One study showed that school dropouts have a lower probability for marital stability than those who complete school; see Jessie Bernard, "Marital Stability and Patterns of Status Variables," *J. Marr. Fam.,* **28,** 4 (November 1966), pp. 421–439.
[32] In one study, however, absolute and relative ages of spouses were not found to be consistently and significantly related to reported marital adjustment. Clifford Kirkpatrick and John Cotton, "Physical Attractiveness, Age, and Marital Adjustment," *Am. soc. Rev.,* **16** (February 1951), pp. 81–86.
[33] However, Locke found that the degree of actual agreement or disagreement between spouses on religion was a minor factor in marital success. See Harvey J. Locke, *op. cit.,* pp. 79, 338. Furthermore, in a study using Swedish data Karlsson found religious participation to be either uncorrelated or slightly negatively correlated with marital success. See Georg Karlsson, *Adaptability and Communication in Marriage: A Swedish Predictive Study of Marital Satisfaction,* Almqvist and Wiksells, Uppsala, 1951. This finding leads some authorities to wonder whether the difference between Karlsson's findings and the American findings, which generally report religious participation as being related to good marriage adjustment, might not corroborate the charge that American studies for the most part tend to select conservative and conforming subjects.

6. Couples who regard their childhood and the marriage of their parents as having been happy.

7. Couples who have had a strong positive feeling for their parents.

8. Couples who received firm but moderate discipline as children.

9. Couples who have had parental approval of their marriage.

10. Couples without a pattern of divorce among their relatives.

SOCIAL PARTICIPATION. With respect to social participation and successful marriage, the following factors appear to be important:

1. Both marriage partners are members of several organized social groups.

2. Both partners engage in outside activities together and share common interests.

3. Both partners are in agreement on the persons who are to be regarded as friends, each having several friends of his own and also sharing several friends with his partner.[34]

ECONOMIC STATUS. It was previously noted that similarity in socioeconomic status is related to successful marriage. When differences between the partners do exist, cases in which the husband has the higher socioeconomic background have a greater chance for success than cases in which the wife's socioeconomic background is higher.

Other economic factors that have been found to be related to successful marriage are:

1. Occupations characterized by a high degree of social control.

2. A moderate rather than high or low income at marriage.[35]

3. Gainful employment for husband and wife prior to marriage. This factor appears to be especially significant if the women were employed in certain occupations, such as professional or skilled office positions.

4. A steady work record.

5. Savings before marriage.

6. Agreement on and efficiency in spending income.[36]

---

[34] One study showed that husbands tend to initiate more of the mutual friendships than the wife does. However, this may be the result of the wife's interest in her husband's occupational endeavor rather than implying a male dominance in establishing friendship networks. Nickolas Babchuk and Alan P. Bates, "The Primary Relations of Middle Class Couples: A Study in Male Dominance," *Am. soc. Rev.,* **28** (June 1963), pp. 377–384.

[35] Low occupational levels show a much greater marital disruption than do higher levels. J. Richard Udry, "Marital Instability by Race, Sex, Education and Occupation Using 1960 Census Data," *Am. J. Sociol.,* **72,** 2 (September 1966), pp. 203–209.

[36] In a study comparing high school marriages with those of older spouses, financial problems were the most commonly mentioned problems by both groups. Rachel M. Inselberg, "Marital Problems and Satisfaction in High School Marriages," *J. Marr. Fam.,* **24,** 1 (February 1962), pp. 74–77.

RESPONSE PATTERNS. In this category we are concerned with how the couple has responded to the love relationship. The findings are:

1. Couples who "fall in love at first sight" are less likely to be successful in marriage than those whose love develops out of companionship and friendship.[37]

2. Couples who knew each other for one year or two before becoming engaged are more likely to be successful in marriage than are couples who knew each other for a shorter period.

3. Couples who were engaged for at least one year are more likely to be successful in marriage than are couples whose engagement was shorter.

4. Couples who utilize their engagement period to work out interpersonal adjustments are more likely to succeed in marriage than those who view the engagement period as a series of social events and those who "meet and marry."

SEXUAL FACTORS. Research on the relationship between sexual factors and success in marriage indicates that the following are more likely to be successful:

1. Those who received sex information from parents in a straightforward but tactful and nonembarrassed manner.

2. Those who are not shy about sex matters.

3. Wives who do not fear pregnancy.

4. Couples who desire children.

5. Marriage partners who have about the same degree of interest in sex, rarely, or infrequently, refusing or demanding sexual intercourse with the spouse.

6. Marriage in which there is an absence of extramarital sexual relations.

Sexual factors conducive to failure in marriage include:

1. The wife's desire to be of the opposite sex.

2. Wife's having had a traumatic sexual experience during adolescence.

3. Wife's sexual intercourse before marriage.[38]

4. Marrying because of pregnancy.[39]

[37] Paul Hilsdale, "Marriage as a Personal Existential Commitment," *J. Marr. Fam.*, 24, 2 (May 1962), pp. 137–143.
[38] One study found that when it was restricted to future spouse, results were negligible. See Lewis M. Terman, *op. cit.*
[39] For marital instability as related to pregnancy at marriage, high value on sex alone, and little interest in having children, see L. L. Geismar and M. A. LaSorta, "Factors Associated with Family Disorganization," *J. Marr. Fam.*, 25, 4 (November 1963), pp. 479–481.

Significance of Marriage-Prediction Findings for Selecting a Marriage Partner

We have presented some of the major research findings with respect to the personal and social characteristics that are involved in marital success or failure. It is important at this point to ask ourselves: what do these results tell us about what to look for in a mate? Although much is known about the factors that are associated with successful marriage, less is known about why they are so associated. For example, church attendance and success in marriage appear together, but it is difficult to say whether church attendance causes success in marriage or whether success is due to another variable—conservatism (since conservative people go to church and are likely to be successful in marriage). These are the kinds of dilemmas that arise in trying to make some sense out of the information that is available. In the analysis that follows we attempt to interpret the findings in the light of what appears to be most reasonable in view of the knowledge available at this time.

FAVORABLE FAMILY BACKGROUND. In regard to the family, the emotional climate in the home is a significant factor, and so are the parental relationship and the view of family life that parents present to their children. These factors result in models about the nature of family life, as well as images of what a father, mother, husband, or wife ought to be. When one internalizes a positive concept of family living and has a concept of a parental model or image associated with consistency and happiness, he can take these into his own marriage. Another important dimension has to do with the quality of the interpersonal relationships at home.[40] When these relationships are characterized by warmth and acceptance, the basis for a mature and emotionally stable personality has been established, which in turn lends itself to good interpersonal relationships in marriage.

It is equally obvious that unhappy family relationships and inadequate models result in disturbances in personality and role confusion about the expectations of marriage. Thus there is a chain of events in

---

[40] One study tested the hypothesis that birth order and proportion of opposite sex siblings would be related to marriage success. The thesis was that an oldest boy in a family of boys and girls is dominant and therefore would complement the younger girl in a family of boys and girls; but the hypothesis was not upheld. See George Levinger and Maurice Sonnheim, "Complementarity in Marriage Adjustment: A Reconsidering of Toman's Family Constellation Hypothesis," *J. indiv. Psychol.*, **21**, 2 (November 1965), pp. 137–145.

which poor family relationships tend to create emotionally unstable personalities, who in turn may be motivated to marry for reasons that are not conducive to building a successful marriage. Mate selection suffers since, as suggested in an earlier chapter, these people may feel desperate about the need to marry. This may result once more in poor marital relationships, unhappy families, and emotionally unstable children.

EMOTIONAL STABILITY. From what we have just said it follows that mature and emotionally stable personalities, who have healthy sexual attitudes and are sociable, are good risks in marriage, whereas immature, unstable personalities, who are isolates, are poor risks in marriage. We have indicated throughout this book that the man-woman relationship is a type of social involvement that has all of the complexities found in any human relationship plus the additional burdens imposed on the relationship by the demands of marriage. Persons who are successful in developing healthy human relationships in general also tend to be successful in marriage.

The research on marriage prediction suggests further that conservative and conventional people do well in marriage. This is probably to be expected, since marriage and the family are by nature conservative institutions.[41] Conservatism becomes manifest in the reported absence of premarital sexual activity and in relation to economic factors, such as steady work habits, savings in the bank, and employment in occupations over which society exerts social control, all of which are related to marriage success. Thus in certain occupational roles—those in which society has a stake, such as minister or teacher—society sees to it that conventional behavior is followed and deviations are discouraged. Other occupations have a low degree of social control, such as traveling salesman or unskilled laborer; society is either less concerned about them or unable to control behavior. We are, of course, unable to tell whether it is the occupation that produces the conformity or deviation or whether certain personality types are inclined to enter certain occupational areas.

Limitations of the Research Findings

The research findings derived from marriage prediction have certain limitations. First, they were obtained for the most part from a sample of people who were largely urban, white, middle-class Protestants. The extent to which these findings would hold for other groups remains questionable. Even within the scope of the sample, however, the research

[41] On the other hand, the authors in their own experience have known of numerous marriages that were not conventional but would have to be considered successful by most any criteria.

findings in marriage prediction are limited in that they tell us much about conventional marriages, but very little about nonconventional ones. Indeed, the implication is that nonconventional marriages are unsuccessful. This may be valid in a broad sense, but it fails to take into account the many exceptions to the rule. It conveys the erroneous impression that if one is not conventional, he is doomed to marital failure.

In this connection it should be pointed out that virtually all counselors have encountered marriages that were in difficulty precisely because one or both partners were conventional to the point where they did only what was expected of them, personally and socially. They never permitted themselves deviations and thus found themselves either in conflict or generally unhappy and bored.

It is apparent that the entire notion of conventionality and nonconventionality in marriage must be studied further if understanding is to be acquired. How nonconventional can one be, and in what areas, before a marriage is threatened? In this regard, it will be remembered that although the majority of studies show religious participation to be related to good marriage adjustment, not all studies found this relationship. In fact, one Swedish study found religious participation to be unrelated to good marriage adjustment and in a number of cases to be even negatively related to good marital adjustment.[42] Such findings would seem to support the view that more inquiries are necessary before we can draw very many conclusions about the relationship between conventionality and marital success.

Provided that one recognizes their limitations, the research findings derived from marriage-prediction studies can be an aid in understanding in a broad sense some of the important factors in marital success or failure.

In pointing out that our behavior in the future is determined by what has come before, which is the underlying theme of this chapter, we do not wish to present the reader with a hopeless view about the future. Those who may be motivated to choose a mate unwisely as a result of, say, a rigid concept of an ideal mate or those who are concerned that their backgrounds do not lend themselves to success in marriage, will discover that a knowledge of these facts may enable them to examine critically and perhaps to gain an understanding of those facets of their backgrounds that are involved in the potential difficulty. When one understands the potential areas of difficulty and is prepared to deal with them, the possibility for success in marriage increases.

[42] See, for example, Georg Karlsson, *loc. cit.* See also Harvey J. Locke and Georg Karlsson, "Marital Adjustment and Prediction in Sweden and the United States," *Am. soc. Rev.,* **17** (February 1952), pp. 10–17.

Summary

An individual's previous experiences result in his ability or inability to accept certain personal and social characteristics in other people; hence they play an important and influential role in the selection of a marital partner. Several types of studies have been undertaken in the attempt to shed light on specific factors that seem to be the most influential in mate selection. The areas covered are (1) the ideal mate, (2) the parental image, (3) assortative mating, and (4) complementary needs. The findings of these studies and their implications for mate selection were discussed in this chapter.

Also discussed was the area of marriage prediction. It is important to note that, while mate selection studies are primarily concerned with determining the existence of a pattern in who marries whom, marriage prediction studies concentrate on what types of persons tend to be most successful and what types tend to be least successful in marriage. The findings of marriage-prediction studies and their implications for mate selection were discussed under six categories: (1) personality characteristics, (2) cultural backgrounds, (3) social participation, (4) economic status, (5) response patterns, and (6) sexual factors.

It was suggested that an understanding of these findings concerning mate selection and marriage prediction, when assessed in terms of their impact on individual behavior, might provide the reader with a basis from which to begin to explore his own involvements in selecting a mate and in attempting to build a sound marriage relationship.

Questions

1. How exactly does one's previous experience affect his choice of a marital partner?
2. State the major purpose of each of the following areas of scientific inquiry and discuss the major findings of each area:
   a. Ideal-mate studies
   b. Parental-image studies

     c. Assortative-mating studies

     d. Complementary-needs studies

3. In what ways might the knowledge that one acquires through the findings of each of the four areas of marital selection studies help him in selecting a marriage partner?

4. What is the difference between the purpose of mate-selection studies and the purpose of marriage-prediction studies?

5. Discuss the Kerckhoff and Davis study in regard to the Winch hypothesis. In what ways does it uphold the hypothesis and in what ways does it refute it?

6. Are one's perceptions of his mate related to marital success? If so, how are they related? Discuss one's perception of his mate as being a cause or an effect of satisfaction or dissatisfaction with marriage.

7. Exactly how are the findings from marriage prediction derived? Explain in full.

8. List the six areas of human experience into which the results of marriage prediction studies can be classified. Discuss the major findings of each of these six areas.

9. List and discuss the major limitations of marriage-prediction findings.

10. How might marriage-prediction findings be useful to individuals contemplating marriage? Give examples.

Projects

1. Interview a group of young married couples and a group of older married couples in an attempt to determine whether the two groups differ and, if so, in what ways in regard to the criteria they used in selecting their marriage partners.

2. Invite a marriage counselor to talk to the class about counseling young people in regard to marriage. If there is no marriage counselor at your school, invite a clergyman to speak on the same topic.

Suggested Readings

Burgess, Ernest W., and Leonard S. Cottrell, Jr., *Predicting Success or Failure in Marriage*, Prentice-Hall, Englewood Cliffs, N.J., 1939.

Burgess, Ernest W., Harvey J. Locke, and Mary Margaret Thomes, *The Family,* 3rd ed., American Book Company, New York, 1963, especially Chs. 12, 14, and 15.

Kennedy, Ruby Jo Reeves, "Premarital Residential Propinquity and Ethnic Endogamy," *Am. J. Sociol.,* 48 (March 1943), pp. 580–584.

Kephart, William J., *The Family, Society, and the Individual,* 2nd ed., Houghton Mifflin, Boston, 1966, especially pp. 256–308.

Kirkpatrick, Clifford, "A Statistical Investigation of the Psychoanalytic Theory of Mate Selection," *J. abnorm. soc. Psychol.,* 32 (October–December 1937), pp. 427–430.

Locke, Harvey J., *Predicting Adjustment in Marriage: A Comparison of a Divorced and a Happily Married Group,* Henry Holt, New York, 1951.

Mangus, Arthur Raymond, "Relationships between the Young Woman's Conceptions of Her Intimate Male Associates and of Her Ideal Husband," *J. soc. Psychol.,* 7 (November 1936), pp. 403–420.

Strauss, Anselm, "The Influence of Parent-Images Upon Marital Choice," *Am. soc. Rev.,* 11 (October 1946), pp. 554–559.

Strauss, Anselm, "The Ideal and Chosen Mate," *Am. J. Sociol.,* 52 (November 1946), pp. 204–208.

Terman, Lewis M., et al., *Psychological Factors in Marital Happiness,* McGraw-Hill, New York, 1938.

Udry, J. Richard, *The Social Context of Marriage,* Lippincott, New York, 1966, especially pp. 269–350.

Chapter Twelve

THE MIXED RELIGIOUS MARRIAGE: A CULTURAL AND PSYCHOLOGICAL DILEMMA

IN THE preceding chapter we noted that people with similar backgrounds confront fewer obstacles in attaining successful marital relationships than do those with divergent backgrounds. This is particularly true in regard to such background traits as race, nationality, ethnic group, and religion. Marriages in which the partners are dissimilar with respect to these traits are frequently called mixed marriages.

Although *racial* intermarriage is still the exception, a trend toward more such marriages has been reported.[1] The degree of acceptance of

[1] See David M. Heer, "Negro-White Marriage in the United States," *J. Marr. Fam.*, **28,** 3 (1966), pp. 262–273. See also Larry D. Barnett, "Interracial Marriage in California," *Marr. Fam. Living*, **25,** 4 (1963), pp. 424–427.

ILLUSTRATION: Bride Doll. Courtesy of the Museum of the City of New York.

such marriages by other Negroes and whites is difficult to ascertain, but greater acceptance among some is evident. In many of our large urban communities dating between members of different racial groups has been quite common for several years. College campuses, with both a protective and a permissive atmosphere, are also conducive to social mixing of students from different racial backgrounds.

Reports indicate that racial intermarriages are homogeneous educationally, at least as much so as marriages in general.[2] This suggests that quite apart from racial differences mate selection takes place within a common core of values. Apparently the qualities that attract people in an interracial union are not basically different from attractions in other, conventional unions. It suggests also that lower-class mixed racial marriages may be quite different from middle-class mixed racial marriages. Therefore, especially in view of their increasing acceptance, interracial campus marriages would seem to warrant study, in order to determine whether the findings on these marriages differ from those that we already have on mixed racial marriage.

Although there may be a wide variety of mixed marriages, based on differences in race, nationality, or religion, we shall concentrate our discussion in this chapter on the mixed religious marriage. We limit our discussion for several reasons. To begin with, in comparison with racial intermarriage, mixed religious marriages are by far more numerous in our society,[3] hence are of the greatest immediate concern to the majority of readers.[4] Furthermore, the problems encountered in a mixed religious marriage are in many ways similar to those encountered in mixed racial

---

[2] Jessie Bernard, "Note on Educational Homogamy in Negro-White Marriages, 1960," *J. Marr. Fam.*, **28**, 3 (1966), pp. 274–276. John H. Burma, "Interethnic Marriage in Los Angeles, 1948–1959," *Social Forces*, **42**, 2 (December 1963), pp. 156–165. Todd H. Pavela, "An Exploratory Study of Negro-White Intermarriage in Indiana," *J. Marr. Fam.*, **26** (May 1964), pp. 209–211.

[3] See Ruth Shonle Cavan, who says: "The most frowned upon mixed marriage and one rarely occurring in the U.S. is that between whites and nonwhites." Cavan, *American Marriage,* Thomas Y. Crowell, New York, 1959, p. 162. See also August B. Hollingshead, who states: "Although inter-racial marriages are legal in Connecticut, they are extremely rare." Hollingshead, "Cultural Factors in the Selection of Marriage Mates," *Am. soc. Rev.*, **15** (October 1950), pp. 619–627.

[4] Many college students claim that if other aspects of the relationship were satisfactory, they would be willing to marry persons of another faith. However, not all would be willing to change their faith. One study, for example, found that although 72 percent of Catholics and 51 percent of Protestants would marry outside the faith, only 11 percent and 37 percent respectively would be willing to change their religious affiliation in so doing. Judson T. and Mary G. Landis, *Building a Successful Marriage,* 3rd ed., Prentice-Hall, Englewood Cliffs, N.J., 1958, pp. 241–242.

and mixed ethnic marriages.[5] There are, for example, the problems of ethnic or racial incompatibilities between husband and wife, and the question of ethnic or racial affiliation for the children. Thus by dealing with the mixed religious marriage, we can in effect deal with some problems that apply to other types of mixed marriage.

One should not, however, oversimplify the basic similarities between the religious and racial intermarriage. In the latter, there may be observable physical differences. Moreover, many in our society, white and nonwhite, respond with greater intensity to the interracial marriage. Hence the problems of where the couple will live and of the identification and affiliation of children are more serious and complex in the mixed racial marriage than in the mixed religious marriage.

Social Concern for the Mixed Religious Marriage

The concern about the mixed religious marriage is not new. Throughout history different religious groups, Jewish, Protestant, and Catholic, have been concerned with and have applied sanctions and threats against persons who married out of their faith, especially those who gave up their own religion in this process.[6] The mixed religious marriage historically has been an ideological dilemma as well as a threat to the different religious groups. It has been a dilemma because each religion espouses the doctrine of brotherly love and acceptance of others, but such a doctrine, when carried to its logical conclusion, often results in marriages outside the faith, with the ever-present danger that many will lose their original religious affiliations. The abandonment of one's

[5] For a study that dealt with interracial marriages between whites and nonwhites, see Ray E. Baber, "A Study of 325 Mixed Marriages," *Am. soc. Rev.*, 2 (October 1937), pp. 705–716.

[6] Ray E. Baber, *Marriage and the Family*, 2nd ed., McGraw-Hill, New York, 1953, p. 119. Judson T. and Mary G. Landis, *op. cit.*, pp. 237–258.

For statistics and discussion of the divorce rates in mixed and nonmixed religious marriages, see Judson T. Landis, "Marriages of Mixed and Non-Mixed Religious Faith," *Am. soc. Rev.*, 14 (June 1949), pp. 401–407. Although one study found no significant differences between the happiness of couples in mixed and nonmixed religious marriages, the couples studied were in the early years of marriage. Ernest W. Burgess and Leonard S. Cottrell, Jr., *Predicting Success or Failure in Marriage*, Prentice-Hall, Englewood Cliffs, N.J., 1939, pp. 87–88.

See also John L. Thomas, S.J., *The American Catholic Family*, Prentice-Hall, Englewood Cliffs, N.J., 1956, pp. 148–153.

religious faith in order to accept another in marriage constitutes a threat to the organized religious bodies, since it means an eventual loss of followers.[7] In the United States today, despite their teachings none of the major religions advocates an involvement with a member of another faith, especially if such marriage necessitates adoption of a different religion.

Indoctrination against Marital Involvement with Outsiders

One of the ways in which religious bodies have dealt with the potential loss of followers and the dissolution of their religious traditions is to foster attitudes and beliefs that enable their members to differentiate themselves from members of other religious groups.[8] Such attitudes often involve an element of ethnocentrism—that is, the belief that one's ways are superior to the ways of others.[9] Although many people may be consciously indoctrinated with the superiority of their own religious beliefs, unconscious, informal methods are also evident. One learns a great deal through informal means, gestures, jokes, reactions of parents and peers. Furthermore, one comes to perceive the attitudes of those around him toward, and their definitions of, people who are different, be they

[7] "The number of interfaith marriages is large, and it is increasing. . . . It is unfair to argue, however, that the concern of the church is purely one of self-interest, growing out of fear of losing members. It is true that persons contracting mixed marriages tend to drop away from their respective churches and are somewhat less concerned than usual with the religious rearing of their children. But there are other reasons for the attitude of the various churches. Their leaders, for example, have long known what recent sociological studies verify concerning the high divorce and separation rates found among such marriages." James H. S. Bossard, "Eight Reasons Why Marriages Go Wrong," *New York Times Magazine,* June 24, 1956, pp. 5, 20–23.

[8] A priest allegedly is distressed by the signs that he sees as indications of the possibility that many Catholics may gradually abandon the teachings of their Church and accept the customs of the secular society in which they live. His solution: an "open ghetto," in which Catholics should avoid intimate contact as far as possible with non-Catholic culture. Mixed marriages are out of the question. "I don't think a Protestant should seriously date a Catholic, and vice versa. Of course we want to get to know and do business with persons of other faiths, but I wonder if a devout person should bring someone of another faith into his home, into his family surroundings. Catholics should not have close associates who are in a different religious situation. You soon compromise with a cultural pattern." Quoted by *Time,* July 4, 1960, p. 38.

[9] For a discussion of this point, see John L. Thomas, *op. cit.,* p. 148.

Jews, Catholics, or Protestants. Thus over a period of time one comes to believe, not necessarily knowing how or why, that some religious views and groups, especially one's own, are superior to others. The development of such attitudes is not without its logic and usefulness. Indeed, these attitudes are very functional and necessary from the point of view of a religious group. They are a means of perpetuating the religious values of a particular group and constitute an aid in the survival of the group. This is clearly pointed out by David Kirshenbaum, who claims that the lack of teaching Jewish children to be Jews, or the lack of maintaining group consciousness, is largely responsible for the increasing rate of Jewish-Gentile marriage, a factor that, according to Kirshenbaum, may well prove detrimental to the future of Judaism itself.[10] Catholicism and Protestantism also are not unaware of the need to guard against the potential threat of the mixed marriage. Formerly all non-Catholics, when marrying a Catholic, had to sign prenuptial contracts guaranteeing that the faith of the Catholic partner will not be "perverted" and that all children born to the union will be baptized and brought up in the Catholic faith.[11] Today the question whether or not the signing of contracts is necessary is usually decided by the diocese, although often the local priest may have some part in the decision. The various Protestant denominations strongly advise their members against committing themselves to these agreements:

> My advice to young Christian people is never date a Roman Catholic and you will never marry a Roman Catholic. If you will want to marry a Roman Catholic because you love him or her above all else, you can prevent a mixed marriage by helping the Catholic person find the true Saviour through studying and accepting the Scriptural truths in the Holy Bible before marriage. If, however, you have already married a Roman Catholic, and have signed the Pre-Nuptial document, it then becomes your sacred duty to amend by helping your Roman Catholic partner, and your children, if any, to find and accept the true way of salvation.[12]

The Episcopal Church issued a pamphlet warning its young members that in signing the antenuptial agreement they are denying the validity

---

[10] David Kirshenbaum, *Mixed Marriage and the Jewish Future*, Bloch Publishing Company, New York, 1958.

[11] A copy of the antenuptial agreement of the Catholic Church, which must be signed by the non-Catholic party, the Catholic party, the witnesses, and the pastor, appears in James A. Peterson, *Education for Marriage*, Scribner's, New York, 1956, pp. 402–404.

[12] Dr. Joseph Zacchello, "A Priest on Mixed Marriage" (A Tract), *The Convert*, P.O. Box 90, Clairton, Pa.

of their own faith in the upbringing of their children. Similarly, the West German Conference of Lutheran Bishops, aware of the growing number of interfaith marriages in West Germany, objected sharply to what it called Catholic "pressure" on Protestant partners to solve the problem. The bishops' statement concluded with a plea to Lutherans to "remain loyal" to their own church and to "insist" that their children be brought up as Protestants.[13]

In addition to these attempts to keep members of a particular faith loyal to that faith, other factors enter. The individual, in the course of growing up, identifies religious values with parents, siblings, and other loved ones. Hence he may experience his interfaith involvement not only as turning away from his faith, but as an abandonment of his group affiliation. Under these circumstances the need to identify with the group may be a more powerful pressure than the religious ideas as such and is then the conflict-causing factor. It is always a moot point whether the problems in the interfaith marriage stem from differences in religion or from differences in cultural background.[14] This would seem to be a question that must be raised repeatedly in the interfaith involvement.

If the socializing experiences that tend to perpetuate the strength of the several religious groups were completely effective, people would never marry outside their religious faith. However, in a society, such as our own, with a wide diversity of influences, people are exposed to values and points of view that are often at variance with the pressures that their own background may bring to bear. On the one hand, there are the beliefs regarding the inherent superiority of one's own religious background and people; on the other hand, these ideas may conflict with democratic values and the ideas of the equality of people and the right of the individual to make personal choices even when these conflict with group pressures. Thus people do become involved with members of other religious groups. The question, of course, is what happens to many of these relationships.

[13] United Press International, "Mixed Marriages a Problem for Catholics, Protestants," *The Daily Register* (newspaper), November 19, 1958, Harrisburg, Ill.
[14] One author, for example, states that some of the problems in Protestant-Catholic marriages may result from social-class differences rather than religious differences as such. He also discusses and cites a case history, to show that religion is only one of the several cultural factors that determine marital adjustment in interfaith marriage. E. E. LeMasters, *Modern Courtship and Marriage,* Macmillan, New York, 1957, pp. 331, 346–350. "A marriage between members of different religious groups is not merely a union between two persons who happen to 'go to different churches.' . . . It is, instead, a supposedly permanent relationship between people who have been reared with fundamental differences in ways of living and thinking." James H. S. Bossard and Eleanor Stoker Boll, *The Sociology of Child Development,* 3rd ed., Harper, New York, 1960, p. 415.

Intellectual and Intellectual-Emotional Commitments

The dilemmas raised by religious ethnocentrism vis-à-vis democratic values are difficult to resolve adequately and lead, in the mixed religious involvement, to a good deal of ambivalence, contradictory attitudes toward spouse, or spouse to be, repression of negative feelings, and potential conflict. The most common expression of these conflicts is seen in the ever-present tendency for people to commit themselves verbally to a mixed religious marriage without really being aware of all that it involves.[15] We term commitments of this type intellectual, as distinguished from the intellectual-emotional commitment. The difference between the intellectual and intellectual-emotional commitment can first be illustrated by certain common experiences. For example, many times we have all promised ourselves that we would do something that we knew we should do, and had every intention of doing, only to discover when the appointed time arrived that we were unable to fulfill our good intentions. College students promise themselves that they will spend the major part of the holiday vacation studying for finals, only to discover that when the vacation arrives they are unable to forgo its attendant events and frequently do very little, if any, serious studying. The difference is one between wishing to follow a course of action and having the ability to follow a course of action. As to commitments, they are intellectual when they contain only an intent, with a minimum of awareness about the underlying feelings and attitudes, which may or may not be consistent with the intent. A commitment becomes intellectual-emotional when it not only includes the intent to follow a course of action, but the intent is integrated with underlying attitudes and feelings. When both thinking and feeling are in agreement about a course of action, then a commitment that has consistency and predictability has been reached.

When applied to mixed religious marriages, understanding the difference between a commitment that is primarily intellectual and one that is intellectual-emotional is significant, since it is precisely this confusion that results in the failure of people to fulfill the promises and agreements about the issues in the mixed religious marriage, be they

[15] Lawrence S. Bee, *Marriage and Family Relations,* Harper, New York, 1959, pp. 234–235.

questions of religious faith for parents or religious faith for children.[16] The pertinence of this can be appreciated in the following illustration.

A very devout Catholic girl was dating a Protestant from a religiously liberal background. As the relationship became serious, the question of religious differences was raised by the girl. She pointed out the importance of her religion and the difficulty that she might have were she asked to abandon her religious views. The boy reported that he was not really concerned about the question of religion. He offered to become Catholic himself and to sign the required contract with respect to the rearing of his children. Since he had come to such a decision with a minimum of contemplation or difficulty, suspicions arose in the minds of the girl's parents and the boy's parents. They asked him over and over again whether he was certain about his decision. He gave every indication of having made up his mind. One evening prior to undertaking instruction in Catholicism, the boy casually asked how long a process this entailed. The girl could give no definite answer and asked why he raised the question. At that point the boy simply stated, "I hope it doesn't take too long because I get mad when I'm around priests." This casual remark was the first indication of ambivalence about Catholicism. The girl began to probe and discovered at this point a series of latently hostile attitudes toward Catholicism, attitudes that might well have become serious problems for the couple. Further analysis of this relationship revealed serious religious incompatibilities, which eventually resulted in breaking the engagement.

In this case it is clear that the boy was capable of an intellectual commitment, but his thinking and feelings were inconsistent; this ambivalence and repressed hostility emerged when the circumstances permitted. These people were fortunate in being able to locate their sources of stress before marriage. Probably the vast majority of couples in relationships of this type become aware of their unsolved problems only after the marriage.

Conflict Areas in the Mixed Religious Marriage

In the previous section of this chapter we have tried to present a framework within which problems in the mixed religious marriage may

[16] Many people who intellectually commit themselves in agreeing to have their children reared in the religious faith of the partner, find that they are unable to do so when the time arrives. For a discussion of this point and a case history, see Lawrence S. Bee, *op. cit.*, pp. 226–228.

be examined. At this point we wish to relate that framework to the difficulties encountered. For example, some common problems in the mixed religious marriage are raised by questions of the religious affiliations of the husband, the wife, and their children, as well as the consequences of these dilemmas for the interpersonal relationship between the spouses. Such difficulties, as previously suggested, are outgrowths of socialization experiences and the ethnocentrism and rigidity that follow. Furthermore, the experiences of each partner impose obstacles to what is acceptable as a solution. In this regard it should be noted that no particular solution for any of these problems appears to be inherently best. Instead, it becomes a matter of being able to commit oneself intellectually and emotionally to a given course of action. Satisfactory marriages can result from any possible combination of faiths and from any number of solutions to the problems inherent in mixed religious marriages. The problems that do arise in any of these choices stem from the failure on the part of persons involved to resolve their ambivalence, their doubts, and their repressed resentments, which are rooted in inconsistent attitudes and feelings acquired from the past.

Specific Problems of the Mixed Marriage

The objective in discussing specific problems of the mixed religious marriage is to identify the main sources of these problems and to point out alternative solutions to them. Through such a procedure we can best call attention both to the potential benefits and to the potential psychological and interpersonal difficulties associated with each alternative solution. A knowledge and understanding of these alternative solutions may enable the individual to resolve his doubts more adequately, so that whatever solution he chooses, the decision will have been made in a relatively undivided and wholehearted manner.

RELIGIOUS AFFILIATION OF THE SPOUSES. One of the most common problems in a mixed religious marriage concerns the religious affiliation of the spouses. Several approaches are possible.

Both Identify with a Single Religion. Many people believe that a greater degree of religious and marital unity results when one partner gives up his religion and adopts the religion of the other.[17] Others point out, however, that although unity may emerge, serious problems are frequently encountered. For example, there are those who feel that it is exceedingly difficult for people to give up their religious back-

---

[17] One study showed that marriages in which one spouse changes to the faith of the other do not have as high a divorce rate as mixed religious marriages in which each partner retains his own faith. Judson T. and Mary G. Landis, op. cit., p. 249.

ground without serious internal conflict as well as conflict with the mate.[18] Such conflict may occur even if the individuals have not had a formal religious affiliation and have not attended services prior to their marriage, since, as previously suggested, the issues are not necessarily restricted to religion, but also involve a commitment to one's familial and cultural background. Under these circumstances considerable resistance to giving up one's religious identification may emerge, especially if an abandonment of ties to one's background is experienced.

Also, it is important to recognize that what is frequently interpreted as a lack of interest in religion when one fails to attend religious services may in reality be a rebellion against religious affiliation and indoctrination. The danger here is that the rebellious partner may not have worked out adequately his religious views. Later in life such an individual may come to regret his rebelliousness and seek a return to the former religious affiliation. Needless to say, the failure to appreciate fully such a possibility may result in much difficulty in the marital relationship.

Each Identifies with His Own Church. A second solution to the religious affiliation of the spouses is agreement to attend separate churches. The following observations are frequently made with respect to this solution. Some believe that such an approach is desirable, since it is consistent with unity and the right of the individual to maintain his own beliefs. Others point out, however, that participation in different religious groups further entrenches value differences, especially since differences in religious values may relate to other basic aspects of family patterns and family planning, particularly planned parenthood and contraception.[19]

Other Approaches. To be sure, there are other attempts at resolving this issue. Some couples decide on a church that is presumably different from their own, but may in a sense represent a compromise. Thus a Baptist and a Methodist may decide to affiliate with a Presbyterian church. Some Jews and Protestants have attempted to affiliate with a Unitarian church.[20] Furthermore, there are those who become tired of the conflicts

---

[18] Paul H. Landis, *Making the Most of Marriage,* 2nd ed., Appleton-Century-Crofts, New York, 1960, pp. 230–232.

[19] Even where each partner retains his faith, Thomas lists reasons for the Catholic Church's opposition to mixed marriages as consisting of ideological differences between (1) contraceptives and divorce; (2) sending children to Catholic schools if they are available; (3) religious training of children; (4) loyalties to the Catholic Church; (5) spiritual ideologies. John L. Thomas, *op. cit.,* pp. 152–153. See also Larry D. Barnett, "Research in Interreligious Dating and Marriage," *Marr. Fam. Living,* 24, 2 (1962), pp. 191–194.

[20] It is interesting to note, however, that when Jewish-Gentile marriages do occur, the chances for success are greatest for the Protestant-Jewish marriage and the

and attempt to resolve them by refusing to identify with any religious body.[21] These along with other solutions may be satisfactory, but only to the extent that people understand themselves and their basic values well enough to commit themselves to a course of action that minimizes their ambivalence. Ambivalence is responsible for many of the conflicts in a marriage of this type.

RELIGIOUS AFFILIATION OF CHILDREN. Another problem in the mixed religious marriage is the religious affiliation of the children. To the extent that the parents have committed themselves to a course of action and have resolved any ambivalence, the problem may be minimized.[22] The difficulties loom large, however, in those instances where the choice is still to be made and the parents are still confused regarding a solution. Some believe that the child should make his or her own selection at the proper time. Such an approach has considerable appeal for those with a democratic orientation. Others argue that individual selection of this type can probably best take place only in an environment that is relatively unconcerned with the necessity of identifying people in terms of categories of religious affiliation. This argument indicates that few segments of our society permit children such freedom. Usually through the influence of adults, children acquire definitions of themselves as Protestants, Catholics, or Jews and come to expect that other children will be so identified. All of this creates confusion for the child of a mixed religious marriage, confusion as to where he belongs and with whom he belongs. It is further indicated that only the most favorable familial environment can overcome these difficulties.

Parents who are satisfied that they can deal with the factors that im-

chances for success are least for the Catholic-Jewish marriage; this combination, Catholic-Jewish, is only a slightly better risk than the Protestant-Catholic marriage. Ray E. Baber, *Marriage and the Family*, 2nd ed., McGraw-Hill, New York, 1953, pp. 100–107. On infrequency of Jewish-Gentile marriage, see Ruby Jo Reeves Kennedy, "Single or Triple Melting Pot: Intermarriage Trends in New Haven, 1870–1940," *Am. J. Sociol.*, **49**, 4 (January 1944), pp. 331–339.

[21] Although there are exceptions, marriages in which the spouses have no religion tend to have a higher divorce and separation rate than those in which one spouse converted to the other's religion or those in which each retained his own religion; see Judson T. Landis, "Marriages of Mixed and Non-Mixed Religious Faith," *Am. soc. Rev.*, **14** (June 1949), pp. 401–407. Paul H. Landis, *op. cit.*, p. 232.

[22] For a discussion of the effect of the mixed religious marriage on the development of the child, see James H. S. Bossard and Eleanor Stoker Boll, *op. cit.*, pp. 415–416. In one study of Protestant-Catholic marriages in which each partner maintained his original faith it was found that 50 percent of the children were reared in the Protestant faith, 45 percent in the Catholic faith, and 5 percent had no faith. The most common tendency seems to be for children to follow the faith of their mother. Judson T. and Mary G. Landis, *op. cit.*, pp. 246–247.

pinge on the child's freedom to choose a religion, still have other problems to examine. Many, in spite of what they claim, find it difficult to allow the child any real freedom in the selection of a religion. Indeed, there is almost the implicit assumption on the part of each parent that the child will probably select his faith. Thus when marriage partners agree to allow their children to select their own religious affiliations, they often feel that the child will select his (the parent's) particular religion. This indicates that regardless of the intellectual commitments made, the appropriate emotional response necessary to make the plan work may not be present. Furthermore, it suggests that the parents themselves possess attitudes that will defeat the plan to allow the child individual choice of religious affiliation. In the case that follows we note the husband's ambivalence about his original commitments to have his child reared as a Protestant and his wife's reaction to this situation.

When this husband, who was reared as a Catholic, became involved with his future wife, a Protestant, he was so desirous of marrying her that he readily agreed to join her church and to have their children reared as Protestants. He considered himself to be a rather objective man, capable of recognizing that "in the long run all religions actually have the same goals." As a result he was able to fulfill his promise to accept his wife's religion with little obvious difficulty until, after two years of marriage, their first child was born. At this time the husband began to feel quite uncomfortable about having given up his religion and having promised to allow his children to be reared as Protestants. He mentioned this to his wife. The wife appreciated her husband's feelings, but she would not agree to rearing their child in the Catholic faith. Considerable tension emerged in the spousal relationship, and the whole pattern of family life was disturbed.

It is important to recognize that to the extent that there is parental ambivalence about the child's right to choose his religious identification, the child may be bombarded, directly or indirectly, by both parents to join a particular church at a time when the child has little or no understanding of religious views or of the nature of religious experience. Such confusion results in little clarification of religious affiliation. What the child does understand, however, is that any tendency to favor the church of one parent may result in hurting the other parent and that parental love may be dependent on how he chooses. All of this may be extremely terrifying to the child, who, as a means of escaping this threatening situation, may come to reject both religions. Without being aware of what he is doing, each parent is contributing to the child's insecurity, in that the child is always uneasy about his relationship to his parents.

Needless to say, exploitation of the child is fostered under these circumstances, and in some cases the child himself comes to recognize his own exploitative powers and develops a pattern of favoring one or the other of the two religions, whichever the case warrants, as a means of manipulating his parents to gain his own wishes.

The mixed marriage of one couple, a Protestant husband and a Catholic wife, is interesting from this point of view. One day during a family discussion the wife stated that she did not think that their daughter, who was then seven years old, should be permitted to attend the local movie with other neighborhood children. Her husband, on the other hand, stated that he thought it would be all right. The daughter, immediately sensing her father's approval of something that she wanted very much to do, set out to reward him by stating that she thought her father was right. Indeed, her desire to attend the movie was so great that without actually understanding any of the values involved she went on to reward her father further by announcing that she no longer wanted to be a Catholic like her mother, but instead wanted to be a Protestant like her father!

Such exploitation on the part of the child is most likely to emerge in the midst of parental indecision and ambivalence. The exploitative power that a child can come to experience may well wreck any plan for integrated living and is something that bears watching in families where it develops.

IMPACT OF RELIGIOUS DIFFERENCES ON MARITAL INTERACTION. The third type of problem that may arise in a mixed religious marriage relates to the impact of religious differences on the marital relationship. This difficulty expresses itself in several ways. It may result in a lack of freedom and spontaneity in many areas of the relationship. The areas of the marriage that relate to religion may become topics to be avoided. Despite previous claims to be accepting of the other's faith, a fear of expressing oneself on any topic that directly or indirectly deals with religious issues sometimes develops. This awareness of the need to avoid areas that may embarrass the marriage partner, or lead to overt conflict, tends to inhibit the responses of the partners and makes it necessary for each to constantly guard against any expressions that can provoke arguments and misunderstandings.[23] Needless to say, the restrictions that people place on themselves under these circumstances are not conducive to the mutual sharing that is essential in a meaningful man-woman relationship. In some cases one may become so preoccupied with the need to avoid hostility that the interaction between husband and wife is marked with tension, superficiality, and pretense.

A second expression of difficulty that results from the impact of reli-

[23] F. Alexander Magoun, *Love and Marriage*, Harper, New York, 1948, pp. 259–260.

gious differences on a marriage is that hostility may be displaced on the marriage partner. Such hostility comes about, at least in a general way, from the fact that the persons involved in a mixed religious marriage, who have not really committed themselves emotionally to the relationship, invariably find themselves in conflict with themselves. They worry about whether their choice was a wise one and about the opinions of relatives and friends. All of this produces discomfort, with the ever-present tendency to blame the other partner for the discomfort.

For couples who repress discomfort about the marital union there are other considerations. These stem from the fact that the repressed hostility may appear in what seems to be an unrelated form. Much of this occurs with a minimum of conscious awareness on the part of the partners; the repressed hostility may take such forms as nagging or faultfinding, which seem to have little to do with religious incompatibilities.

Thomas points out both dimensions of the problem of hostility in a mixed marriage—the desire to avoid hostility and displaced hostility:

Religious beliefs by their very nature involve the emotions to such an extent that it is impossible for most people to argue about them with any degree of calm or objectivity. As a result, after a few attempts, most couples give up trying to talk over their religious differences. Finding this approach rather hopeless, they silently agree to disagree. Hence, the unstabilizing effects of religious differences develop in more subtle ways.[24]

In the case that follows we find an instance of displaced hostility. A woman who was involved in a mixed religious marriage, was quite unhappy about her marital relationship, although she showed no desire to discontinue it. According to her, the unhappiness of the marriage had nothing to do with the fact that she and her husband held quite opposite views concerning religion. Both she and her husband, according to her, were too objective to quarrel over such intangible things as religious beliefs; rather, she stated, the dissatisfaction with her marriage resulted from the fact that her husband never did anything right! It seemed that when the husband smoked his pipe, she found the odor to be extremely offensive, and when he did not smoke it, she would state that she considered pipe smoking to be a desirable masculine trait. Indeed, when her husband spent Sunday afternoon caring for the lawn, he was regarded as ignoring her, but when instead he spent his time attempting to converse with her, she would claim that he was lazy and unlike others who took an interest in their homes. Nothing this husband did was ever quite right. After a gradual deterioration of the marriage, the couple sought profes-

[24] John L. Thomas, S.J., *op. cit.,* p. 161.

sional help. Over a period of time this woman came to learn that her resentments concerning the husband's religion and background were indeed a source of great hostility for her. These resentments were being expressed in nagging and faultfinding.

Social-Psychological Preparation for a Mixed Religious Marriage

The fact that there are serious problems to be resolved in mixed religious marriage should not obscure the fact that a solution of these problems is possible. It is again important to note, however, that one's probability of resolving these problems is not dependent on which specific solution he chooses, but rather on his ability to fully accept and follow through with whatever solution he chooses. This is to say that the attainment of a meaningful relationship in mixed religious marriage is largely dependent on the ability of the marital partners to commit themselves intellectually and emotionally to a course of action. Such an intellectual-emotional commitment, however, requires a high degree of personal maturity and integration. Consequently, it is advisable for persons contemplating mixed religious marriage to attempt to assess their personal maturity and integration. In attempting such an assessment, particularly as it pertains to mixed religious marriage, the following two factors might be considered: (1) one's prejudice and (2) one's motivations for the mixed religious involvement.

Prejudice is significant because it is frequently a hidden factor which is nevertheless present and makes the development of a meaningful marriage relationship virtually impossible. The motivations are important because, like prejudice, true motivations for mixed religious involvements are also frequently hidden and, when ultimately discovered, may reveal reasons for becoming involved in the relationship that are not conducive to the development of a meaningful relationship. Let us consider each of these two factors in greater detail.

Prejudice

With regard to prejudice, it should be clear that to agree to be accepting or even sympathetic toward the religious views of an intended marriage partner does not insure the absence of difficulties, religious or other. For, as we have already pointed out, people are frequently so desirous of continuing the pleasurable aspects of dating and courtship that they are likely to delude themselves into believing that they are less prejudiced than they are.

These matters may be hidden. This is especially true of college people who believe that it is academically fashionable not to have prejudices. Thus a thought such as "I should not be prejudiced" frequently develops into the notion that "I'm not prejudiced." Under these circumstances it is possible for one to become quite broad-minded intellectually and still remain prejudiced emotionally.

One way of assessing one's prejudices is to learn to be aware of the responses to certain occurrences. When someone whom you know to be Jewish steps into the checker's line in front of you at a crowded supermarket, does your irritation usually include such thoughts as "What can you expect of a Jew"? If, during a lively discussion, you cannot get the other person to see your point, is it easier for you to dismiss the resulting anxiety when you can think "Well, what can I expect from a narrow-minded Catholic" or "That's a Protestant for you, none of them actually know what they do believe"? If under these circumstances the religion of the person enters your thinking, there is indication that in spite of the fact that you may think that you have no religious prejudice, when called on to behave in a nonprejudicial manner, you are unable to do so—a clear indication of an intellectual commitment to be nonprejudiced and of a lack of the intellectual-emotional ability to follow through.

Another occurrence, worthy of attention, pertains to those who feel that they are able to place the religion of their partner and their own religion side by side and treat them equally. Without a doubt there are some people who are capable of doing this. There are others, however, who, although they think they are able to view each religion equally, experience considerable discomfort in any circumstance that forces them to confront the religion of their partner. One young woman, for example, stated that when she and her date were among a group of friends and someone told a joke about her date's religion, she would become extremely embarrassed and think, "Why couldn't the joke have involved my religion," even though her date seemed thoroughly amused by the joke. She stated further that although she tried to avoid any discussion involving a comparison of the two religions, whenever such a discussion arose in the group she seemed compelled to bend backwards in supporting her date's religion, although she really did not believe what she was saying.

Although this may seem to be an attempt to build a relationship in which both religions are treated equally, failure is inherent, because at least one of the partners is categorizing the two religions and treating them differently. Before any equal treatment of the religions is possible, an attempt must be made to discover why this young woman finds it so necessary to protect her date's religion. Analysis may uncover that she has some very negative attitudes toward her date's religion, and the question arises, "Is this woman capable of an intellectual-emotional commitment?"

A second way to assess one's prejudices about members of another faith is to interact in a variety of circumstances with the friends and family of the spouse to be. Such interaction makes it possible for one to observe the religious values of the group, to participate in their religious practices, and to note attitudinal differences that may be present. This interaction may result either in the insight that one could adjust very well to members of another religion or in the discovery that one is less able to accept the differences in religion and background than he had thought. Some persons, on recognizing their inability to accept the differences, tend to dismiss any further consideration of this potential problem by assuming that their intended mate is different from his friends and family, hence that their feelings toward his friends and family do not apply to him. What must be realized is that during dating and courtship one is likely to twist the reality of the situation and see the person apart from the underlying prejudices that one might have about the person's group.[25] Indeed, one may be surprised to discover later that the criticism of the person's religious group applies to the person as well.

Motivations

In addition to prejudice, which may interfere with one's ability to build a meaningful relationship in a mixed religious marriage, motivation for the involvement also deserves careful examination, because it is frequently complicated and not necessarily based on a mature love. Several illustrations follow.

One category of persons who become involved in an interfaith marriage are those who do so primarily because they are ashamed of what they are—ashamed of themselves and of their family, friends, relatives, and religion. This involves a rejection of self. Holding negative attitudes toward their background, they have a need to make their own religion worse than it is and other religions perhaps better than they are. Such distortion serves the belief that rejection of oneself and acceptance of other values will make things better. These people, like those who

---

[25] F. Alexander Magoun, *op. cit.*, p. 239.

think that marriage will solve all problems, are running away from themselves and from their own religion and looking to an outside source, in this case a union with a member of another religion, to solve their problems. In situations of this type a mixed religious marriage may have much greater appeal than does a marriage with a person of one's own religion. As with all attempts at self-rejection and attempts at making life better by avoiding inner problems, however, disappointment and frustration are inevitable.

A second category of persons gravitates toward mixed religious marriages because they are essentially rebellious. Usually the mixed religious marriage is only one aspect of their rebellion. Some are also in rebellion against parents; often they have a need to hurt or get back at parents. Others like to think of themselves as nonconformists and frequently take considerable pride in the mixed religious marriage as a sign of rebellion against their group.

Finally, some people are motivated to become involved in a mixed religious marriage by a missionary zeal to change others. This "Pygmalion complex" finds its greatest fulfillment in a relationship where differences exist, thus allowing the person to bring about great changes in his partner. Without regard for the feelings of the other person, the individual sets out to remake his partner, and the existence of differing religious views offers him a very desirable challenge.

The motivations that we have just discussed have certain elements in common. None of them treat marriage as the end goal, but instead use it in an attempt to fulfill needs that are external to marriage. The first category of motivations relates to self-rejection and the need to escape, the second to rebel and get back at people, and the third to change and impose one's values on others. Two important points become apparent. (1) In marriages of this type there is little basic interest in the marriage or the marriage partner. Instead, the marriage is viewed as a means of solving certain personal difficulties and as such is not likely to result in a meaningful relationship; indeed, it is likely to produce, not solve, problems, a point that we discussed when we examined motivations for marriage. (2) In marriages of this type it is also quite impossible to make intellectual-emotional commitments, because the necessary personal maturity and integration are lacking. Consequently, an examination of the motivational factors in mixed religious marriage as well as an assessment of one's deep-seated prejudices would appear to be extremely important for all couples contemplating mixed religious marriage.

Before concluding, we hasten to add that there are many mature and meaningful mixed religious marriages. In fact, the case against intermarriage has probably been overstated.

Vernon, for example, points out that statistical reports on divorce emphasize the higher divorce rate for mixed unions when compared with conventional relationships. Such reports *fail to emphasize* that the overwhelming number of mixed religious marriages (80 to 85 percent) have been and are *in fact* successful as measured by divorce or separation criteria.[26]

Also, it should be emphasized that American society is undergoing basic change. Certainly in the area of mixed religious marriages, one senses not only less self-consciousness among youth about such arrangements, but greater acceptance of them among parents as well. Organized religions, although still generally opposed to mixed religious marriages, are not so rejecting of the individuals as they may have been in the past. To the extent that these changes are emerging, individuals are brought up with greater acceptance of such unions and find themselves with significant social support, support that may prove crucial in decisions to marry and may be a significant aid during marital crises.

In the past, many mixed marriages were vulnerable essentially because of background differences. Mutual suspicion and intolerance were added to the basic problems of marriage. Much of the difficulty that arose was in part related to the fact that many Catholic and Jewish youth were not far removed from their European origins; hence intermarriage posed many problems. The native Protestant, on the other hand, often viewed both groups negatively. This is no longer necessarily the case, since parents and children of minority groups have become assimilated and the differences between these people and those from larger native religious groups have become minimized. Thus the social context in which interreligious unions occur has changed considerably.

To the extent that our remarks are valid, the increasing success of mixed religious unions becomes a distant possibility.

Summary

Although today there is greater acceptance of mixed marriages than in the past, the problems that are confronted in such marriages frequently arise from differences in the cultural background of the partners. Each religious group, for example, shares a way of life which to a greater or

[26] Glenn M. Vernon, "Bias in Professional Publications Concerning Interfaith Marriages," *Relig. Educ.*, 55, 4 (July–August 1960), pp. 261–264.

lesser degree differs from that of other religious groups. Moreover, each religious group tends to view its own way of life as being somewhat better than that of others. This ethnocentric quality frequently makes it difficult for marriage partners who come from different religious backgrounds to accept realistically the differences in each other.

In a democratic society it is often quite easy to delude oneself into thinking that he is less ethnocentric than he is. However, in committing oneself to accept differences in other people, particularly in relation to a mixed religious marriage, it is important to be certain that one is not merely making an intellectual commitment, that is, a commitment based on the desire to accept these differences, but that one is capable of making an intellectual-emotional commitment, that is, a commitment based not only on the desire to accept differences but also on the ability to follow through emotionally and behave in accordance with the desire. Once one is capable of making an intellectual-emotional commitment to a mixed religious marriage, it is more likely that he will be able to solve effectively the basic problems that will arise, such as deciding on the religious affiliation of the spouses, deciding on the religious affiliation of the children, and dealing with the impact that the religious differences may have on the total marital interaction.

An objective examination of his prejudices and an analysis of his motivation for becoming involved in a mixed religious relationship are often quite enlightening and frequently can aid the individual in ascertaining his ability to make an intellectual-emotional commitment to a mixed religious marriage.

Apparently there are people who are not capable of making such commitments in mixed religious marriages, because the divorce and separation rates of these marriages tend to be higher than those of nonmixed religious marriages. However, the fact that the vast majority of mixed religious marriages (80 to 85 percent) do not result in divorce or separation must not be overlooked.

Questions

1. What in your opinion is the major obstacle confronted in all types of mixed marriages? How exactly does this apply to a mixed religious marriage?
2. Does socialization adequately prepare us to accept differences in people?

Explain. Does religion adequately prepare us to accept religious differences in a marriage partner? Explain.

3. In what way do social groups depend on ethnocentrism for survival?

4. What is an intellectual commitment? What is an intellectual-emotional commitment? Give an example of each. Explain how an intellectual commitment can cause difficulty in a mixed religious marriage. How might this be avoided?

5. Is it always possible to commit oneself intellectually-emotionally? What makes this particularly difficult for those contemplating a mixed religious marriage?

6. What are the main problems confronted in a mixed religious marriage? Explain each.

7. What are the dimensions of hostility found in mixed religious marriage? Explain each.

8. What might a person who is contemplating a mixed religious marriage do to attempt to discover whether he has religious prejudice? Consider also other types of prejudice which would apply to other types of mixed marriage.

9. List and explain the motivations that people sometimes have for a mixed religious marriage. Are people usually aware of their motivations? If not, how may one find help in determining his motivations for a mixed marriage?

10. Explain fully what is meant by the statement that the case against mixed religious marriages may have been overstated.

Projects

1. Select a mixed religious marriage which you know well and which, in your opinion, is an unsuccessful marriage. Without identifying the parties involved, write a paper explaining the following: (a) why you regard this marriage as unsuccessful; (b) what, aside from the couple not having married in the first place, could have been done to avoid the problems of this marriage; (c) what, in your opinion, would be necessary to make this a successful marriage; and (d) what chances for success do you feel this marriage has.

2. Select a mixed religious marriage which you know well and which, in your opinion, is a successful marriage. Without identifying the parties in-

volved, write a paper explaining (*a*) why you regard this as a successful marriage and (*b*) how you account for the success of this marriage.

3. Invite a minister, priest, or rabbi to class to present his views on mixed religious marriage. Or you may wish to interview all three on the topic of mixed religious marriage and present your findings to the class.

4. Interview several students to determine under what conditions they would consider marrying outside their religious group. Write a paper concerning what you have found. Do you find that the answers given are realistic or superficial? Do you believe that these people are more or less prejudiced than they think they are?

Suggested Readings

Bossard, James H. S., and Eleanor Stoker Boll, *One Marriage, Two Faiths*, Ronald Press, New York, 1957.

Bossard, James H. S., and Harold C. Letts, "Mixed Marriages Involving Lutherans," *Marr. Fam. Living*, **18**, 4 (November 1956), pp. 308–310.

Cahnman, Werner J., Ed., *Intermarriage and Jewish Life*, Herzl Press, 1962.

Golden, Joseph, "Characteristics of the Negro-White Intermarried in Philadelphia," *Am. soc. Rev.*, **18**, 2 (April 1953), pp. 177–183.

Golden, Joseph, "Patterns of Negro-White Intermarriage," *Am. soc. Rev.*, **19** (April 1954), pp. 144–147.

Gordon, Albert I., *Intermarriage: Interfaith, Interracial, Interethnic*, Beacon Press, 1964.

Kephart, William M., *The Family, Society and the Individual*, 2nd ed., Houghton Mifflin, New York, 1966, pp. 262–270.

Landis, Judson T., and Mary G. Landis, *Building a Successful Marriage*, 3rd ed., Prentice-Hall, Englewood Cliffs, N.J., 1958, Ch. 12, "Mixed Marriages."

Mayer, John E., *Jewish-Gentile Courtship: An Exploratory Study of a Social Process*, The Free Press, 1961.

Pavela, Todd H., "An Exploratory Study of Negro-White Intermarriage in Indiana," *J. Marr. Fam.*, **26** (May 1964), pp. 209–211.

Peterson, James A., *Education for Marriage*, Scribner's, New York, 1956, Ch. 17, "Achieving Religious Togetherness."

Slotkin, J. S., "Adjustment in Jewish-Gentile Intermarriages," *Social Forces*, **21** (December 1942), pp. 226–230.

Chapter Thirteen

SEXUAL
INTERACTION
AND
ADJUSTMENT

W<small>E HAVE</small> already devoted a considerable amount of time to discussing the issues involved in building a meaningful relationship. The more diligently one pursues the problems that have been pointed out, the less likely that serious marital difficulties will emerge. Nevertheless, the conditions of intimate and continuous interaction in marriage may bring out aspects of personality and differences in views that were not apparent in the relationship simply because the circumstances that produce them were not present. Although marital partners establish a relationship prior to marriage, it is of necessity limited. In marriage a lifetime of habits, attitudes, and values with respect to the daily patterns of existence emerge. The interaction of these and the attempt to integrate them are an inevitable source of difficulty. Thus it becomes necessary to see marital adjustments and conflicts as emerging out of daily interaction, when habits, attitudes, and values are expressed in the interactions of married persons.

I<small>LLUSTRATION</small>: Bride and groom dolls, French, c. 1870. From the private collection of John Noble, Curator of Toys, Museum of the City of New York.

Sexual Adjustment

The sexual relationship is one such aspect of marital adjustment.[1] In a study a number of years ago, it was found that fewer couples reported satisfactory adjustment in sex relations than in other adjustment areas.[2] The same is probably true in the present. To be sure, there are couples who have initiated their sexual adjustments prior to marriage. However even for these people attitudes and feelings will emerge that had no opportunity to appear previously, and these may affect the marital sex union. For example, some persons who seemed to enjoy the sex act before they were married no longer do so after they are married. The reason may lie in their view of sex. If they looked on sexual relations before marriage as bad and if they were rebels against conventional ideas, their enjoyment of the act may have been based on taking part in something that is forbidden. When such people marry, however, and sexual relations become a normal, healthy, and conventional aspect of their lives, the enjoyment diminishes.

In still other situations, persons who were sexually active with the spouse to be or others may become relatively inactive in marriage. One example is a young woman who had led a very active sex life with her fiancé prior to marriage, but virtually refused to have sexual relations with him after they were married. It turned out that she had never really enjoyed the sex act, but had used it as a means of "getting a husband."[3] As marital difficulties increased because of her sexual inactivity, she began to realize that some assessment of her behavior was necessary, both for her own well-being and for the good of the relationship.

These are only a few of many possible illustrations of the new and different attitudes toward sex that may emerge in marriage, because marriage itself represents a new relationship involving new dimensions of

[1] For a discussion of the sex problems of American wives and husbands, see E. E. LeMasters, *Modern Courtship and Marriage,* Macmillan, New York, 1957, pp. 376–384.
[2] Judson T. Landis, "Length of Time Required to Achieve Adjustment in Marriage," *Am. soc. Rev.,* 11 (December 1946), pp. 666–677.
[3] One writer points out that, among other uses, the sex act can be employed as a coin to buy affection, protection, or the like from another person. Lawrence S. Bee, *Marriage and Family Relations,* Harper and Brothers, New York, 1959, p. 81.

behavior.[4] An understanding of the various possibilities is especially important in considering the types of problems that may appear when the couple are first married.

Initial Sexual Relations in Marriage

Much has been written about the significance of initial sexual relations in marriage, and indeed there is much to be said on this point.[5] The initial sexual experiences in marriage are important for at least two reasons. First, they reveal the approach to the lovemaking process, which is important in determining attitudes regarding the sex act. Second, and at a deeper level, behavior in the sex act is indicative of the attitudes and feelings that husband and wife express toward each other. We pointed out earlier that the erotic involvement is but one way in which we relate to others. Thus it comes as no surprise that the basic attitudes and feelings about another person find expression in the sexual feeling toward that person. Thus contempt, hostility, love, and respect may be expressed in the act. The initial expressions are especially important in their effect on the subsequent sexual, as well as interpersonal, adjustment of the couple.

One of the problems frequently encountered during initial sexual adjustment is a feeling of disappointment about the erotic experience itself. Both partners may experience less than they expected; there is simply a letdown—"It's less pleasurable than I thought it would be." There may be a lack of orgasm or incomplete orgasm for either the wife or husband.[6]

Actually, a great deal of distortion is perpetrated about the nature of sexual experience. We recognize that some views may emphasize the discomfort, but a potentially more disturbing distortion arises from great expectations, so great that the real experience appears insignificant and frequently disappointing. Indeed, there may be a direct relationship between a person's need to distort sex, that is, to overevaluate sex, as com-

---

[4] For a discussion of the use and misuse of love in the man-woman relationship, see Eugenia Elliott, *Growth Through Love and Sex,* (article of) Auxiliary Council to the Association for the Advancement for Psychoanalysis, New York, 1952.

[5] For a discussion of the initial sexual experience, see F. Alexander Magoun, *Love and Marriage,* Harper and Brothers, New York, 1948, pp. 194–199.

[6] In regard to lack of orgasm, 75 percent of the married women in Kinsey's sample reported that they had experienced at least some orgasm by the end of the first year of marriage. However, 10 percent reported not experiencing orgasm by the fifteenth year of marriage, while others reported experiencing their first coital orgasm after 28 years of marriage or more. Alfred C. Kinsey et al., *Sexual Behavior in the Human Female,* Saunders, Philadelphia, 1953, p. 383.

pensation for shortcomings elsewhere and the *actual disappointment* experienced in sex. There was the case of a woman who had led a somewhat unhappy life before marriage. She came to expect that such unhappiness would disappear with love and sex. Her expectations and demands were so unrealistic that she experienced intense disappointment in sex after marriage.

An adequate understanding of how people respond to such disappointment in sexual relations is essential, since there is considerable involvement of the ego and feelings of self-worth that should be examined. One of the responses to be watched and understood when the act is not satisfactory is the tendency to hold the other partner responsible for the lack of pleasure. Often one may feel that the partner failed to respond adequately, especially if the partner did not react in a wholehearted fashion, and a feeling of having been rejected sexually may follow. For example, the husband who suffers disappointment in sexual relations may blame the difficulty on his wife's reticence or inadequacy in the sex act. Such reticence may then be viewed by the husband in a personal way and be experienced as rejection. He may react negatively, by becoming overly aggressive and pursuing sex to demonstrate manliness or by withdrawing, which may take the form of pouting. This in turn may bring a counterreaction from the wife. She may come to sense a kind of inconsiderateness for her feelings, and if, in addition, she has grown up believing that men are, after all, preoccupied with sexual satisfaction without regard for the woman's feelings, such marital experience may confirm this stereotype in her mind; numerous difficulties can result.

Similarly, the wife, if she experiences less in sexual relations than she had anticipated, may attribute her failure to enjoy sex to her husband's inability to respond properly to her and to see this as a sign of rejection. She may then berate or belittle her husband. This in turn may confirm the stereotype held by some men that women have little rational control over their behavior and may thus precipitate an argument of significant proportions.

Although rejection of the partner may in fact be involved, it should be recognized that disappointment in sexual relations usually is the result of lifelong attitudes and would in all probability occur with any marital partner. Most of us are too ego-involved, however, to accept this fact easily; hence reactions become overreactions, intensely personal and often hostile.

The tendency to blame the other person and refuse to assume responsibility for one's role in the sexual disappointment is easily come by, since most people find it painful to accept the fact that they might in some way be sexually inadequate. Furthermore, as mentioned in Chapter 7, our society places considerable emphasis on physical attractiveness. Hence to be sexually desirable is important to members of both sexes and perhaps especially important to women, since their status and role are more closely tied to marriage. For the wife the feeling of sexual rejection may be devastating, in that it causes fear of losing the husband.

There is the case of a married woman whose husband was reluctant to have sexual relations as frequently as she expected. Whenever the husband refused sexual relations, the wife felt rejected and became belligerent, aggressive, and abusive. She stated quite frankly that she felt so rejected that she had to try to prove that she was not "that horrible." Actually her husband's reluctance to have sexual relations had little to do with rejection of her. Instead it was based on the fact that he was a very cold and aloof person.[7] Intimate contact with any woman, emotional or physical, disturbed him; hence the basic sexual union was repulsive to him.

The pattern of berating each other about inadequate sexual performance is very destructive to the relationship and may lead to negative attitudes not only toward sexual relations but toward other marital aspects as well.

BACKGROUND FACTORS IN THE INITIAL ADJUSTMENT. What are the background experiences that give rise to these sexual disappointments and difficulties at the outset of marriage? They include a variety of personal and social experiences with which people have grown up and which become manifest in the sexual area of the man-woman relationship. Probably one of the most common reasons given by men and women for disappointment or difficulty in the sex act is the notion that one has acquired negative attitudes regarding sexual involvement.[8] This explanation has been used so often and in so general a way as to make it a cliché. Nevertheless, when fully examined and understood, it becomes useful in explaining some sexual disappointments in marriage. Moreover, negative attitudes toward sex take on the most meaning when we can

---

[7] For a discussion of aloofness and sexual behavior, see Abe Pinsky, *Love and Sex in Resigned People*, (article of) Auxiliary Council to the Association for the Advancement of Psychoanalysis, New York, 1951.

[8] For a discussion of the relationship between a person's attitudes and his ability to love, see Antonia Wenkart, *Healthy and Neurotic Love*, (article of) Auxiliary Council to the Association for the Advancement of Psychoanalysis, New York, 1952. One study, however, which attempted to determine the causes of the failure of women to achieve orgasm, was unable to find any association with early sex conditioning, type of birth control techniques used, husband's sex technique, or any of the other factors that one would expect to be involved. This study finally postulated a neurological factor as the usual cause. Lewis M. Terman et al., *Psychological Factors in Marital Happiness*, McGraw-Hill, New York, 1938.

see how they have evolved out of certain types of experiences and how they have become integrated into one's orientation toward sex. An understanding of any person's reaction to sex is dependent on precisely this type of analysis. At this point let us deal with some common experiences in our culture that contribute to a negative orientation regarding sexual involvement.

What do we mean when we say that the individual has acquired negative attitudes about sex? We mean, first, that in the process of growing up in our culture he (or she) has had a variety of experiences which have resulted in attitudes that inhibit sexual pleasure and foster disappointment. To appreciate these kinds of experiences, which are common in our culture, it is necessary to examine some of the values of our society and their influence on human relatedness and sex. It is probably impossible to grow up in a society that stresses some of the values that ours does and expect that healthy attitudes toward sexual relatedness will develop. As indicated earlier, the development of mature love is thwarted by the impersonality in society, the commodity orientation, the high degree of destructive competitiveness, and the shallow mode of living. It is safe to say that whenever there are patterns that operate against human relatedness and in fact reduce the worth of the human being as such, difficulties regarding love and sex are bound to be present in the population. An examination of contemporary American family life suggests that the values just mentioned may pervade the entire pattern of relationships in the home. These markedly affect husband-wife relationships, making it difficult for them to understand or relate to each other in any positive way. (See Chapter 7.) Such social and familial influences fail to foster a cultural atmosphere that facilitates a satisfactory sexual relationship.

Parental Response to Sexual Curiosity in the Child. Shifting our attention from general social values to the specific reaction of parents, we note that the early signs of sexual curiosity that children of both sexes manifest may be misinterpreted by overly anxious, sexually inhibited parents. The child who openly displays his or her sexual organs may be severely reprimanded. Masturbation may be met with threats and fears, which can be terrifying to the child. His hugging and kissing of another child may be discouraged or regarded with anxiety by some parents. These are frequently the reactions of parents who are themselves confused about erotic involvements; they become very upset about the child's sexual activity, since it may arouse in them conflicts and anxieties because of their own unresolved difficulties in this area. It would be a mistake, of course, to assume that the child comes to learn about the negative aspects of sexuality only from the overt negative reactions of parents. Parents may convey a great deal by gestures, by the tone of their voices, and by other acts that reveal their reactions to the child's behavior. For the child, sexual interests are inevitably the result of healthy curiosity and growth and of a desire for relatedness, whereas parents all all too often interpret them as signs of sexual precociousness, thus seeing that which is healthy and natural as an indication of the perverse.

What is the effect of such experiences on the child?[9] The child whose early sexual curiosity is misunderstood may generalize from the undesirable sexual conditioning to other areas of life. Such generalizations occur because the child does not possess the intellectual maturity to separate experiences, but tends to extend the results of one experience to others. Such extension of unfortunate experiences in the sexual area to other areas is often manifest in the following attitudes:

1. To expose feelings means to invite criticism from others.
2. The experiencing of pleasure is followed by punishment.

There are numerous clinical histories of adults who suffer sexual disappointment because they still react as they did when they were children. People with such faulty sexual conditioning are anxious about sex, as though parental punishment were forthcoming. They are afraid to let their feelings go and to participate wholeheartedly in the sex act. They may realize in an intellectual way that their behavior is childlike, but are helpless to deal with the problem because they do not fully understand the impact of their early sexual conditioning.

One young woman came to the marriage counselor because she had great difficulty responding sexually to her fiance. She regarded their relationship as satisfactory in every other respect, but was considering breaking their engagement because of the sexual difficulty. She stated that whenever demonstrations of affection "bordered the least bit on the sexual" she would become extremely uncomfortable, feeling "trapped" and "stifled," and would try desperately to free herself from the situation. In discussing the problem with this young woman, it became apparent that although she had obtained considerable information about sex from reading and college courses, she had previously acquired many unwholesome attitudes from her mother, who regarded sex as "something which men need and which women must put up with." The mother not only implanted this and similar ideas in her daughter's mind, but reinforced each attitude by alluding to negative religious interpretations of sex. In such an atmosphere, this young woman, even as a

---

[9] For a discussion of the relationship between the child's experiences within the family and his psychosexual development, see Paul H. Landis, *Making the Most of Marriage,* 2nd ed., Appleton-Century-Crofts, New York, 1960, p. 411.

child, soon learned not to ask questions about, or show interest in, anything pertaining to sex, and she learned never to regard sex as pleasurable.

Finally, negative attitudes toward sex may be aided by misunderstandings of religious teachings, unwholesome reading, or some traumatic sex experience, either observed or participated in.

Religious Teachings. The influence of religion in the sexual area is not altogether clear. Some scholars claim that the early Christian view of marriage was essentially negative.[10] Others believe that this was never the case and that such a view is the result of a misinterpretation of early religious teachings. What most church scholars would assert, however, is that religious teachings as interpreted by some churches and some ministers have aided the development of a negative view toward sex. There are studies that suggest that married women who have a low degree of sexual satisfaction in marriage are high on scales of religiosity.[11] Having pointed this out, we wish to remind the reader that many churches cognizant of this problem have set about to correct negative views of sex through educational programs.

Unwholesome Reading. Unwholesome reading materials can also be a factor in negative attitudes toward sex. Here we are confronted with a large mass of literature, some of which is current, some fairly old. As late as the early part of this century there was a considerable body of sex literature, authored by physicians, which fostered an unhealthy view of sex. Irrespective of training, these physicians passed on to the public a distorted view of sex, with the implicit notion that sexual feelings, though inevitable, arose from the less desirable components of man. The purpose of knowledge about sex in this framework was to enable one to understand how to deal with man's negative nature.

Sexual indoctrination of this type, emanating from professional sources, is less likely today, but there are other types of literature that are equally negative. Perhaps the most important in this regard are the published sordid tales of love and violence that reveal the most destructive components of human nature and portray sexual relations that are devoid of feeling and tenderness. To be sure, such a picture is applicable to some relationships, but it presents a distorted view of sex, and the indi-

---

[10] Stuart A. Queen, Robert W. Habenstein, and John B. Adams, *The Family in Various Cultures*, 2nd ed., Lippincott, Philadelphia, 1961, pp. 183–185.
[11] Paul Wallin and Alexander L. Clark, "Religiosity, Sexual Gratification and Marital Satisfaction in the Middle Years of Marriage," *Social Forces*, **42** (March 1964), pp. 303–309. Robert L. Hamblin and Robert O. Blood, "Premarital Experience and the Wife's Sexual Adjustment," *Social Prob.*, 4 (October 1956), pp. 122–129.

vidual who sees sex in such a manner almost invariably feels a need to develop protective techniques and mistrust, which are manifested indiscriminately.

Sexual Trauma. The role of sexual trauma is difficult to assess. Although it is entirely possible that traumatic sexual experiences are crucial determinants of sexual difficulty, their significance is almost certainly exaggerated. Those who suffer sexual disappointment invariably point to a dramatic period in their lives when they witnessed or were involved in an unpleasant sex experience. In fact, it is more than likely that the impact of such experiences has been distorted. Far more important perhaps is what they do not remember, the daily, ongoing, nondramatic processes of sexual conditioning that are really at the bottom of most sex problems.

INTERNALIZATION OF NEGATIVE VIEWS TOWARD SEX. These negative views, which create sexual disappointment, are internalized and become part of the psychic equipment with which people attempt to relate sexually to one another. If one has learned that sex as a human activity is essentially a bad activity, it tends to remain so, unless serious efforts are made to deal with it. The fact that one is legally and religiously wed does not automatically affect such basic attitudes. Hence some people are never able to view sexual relations in marriage as a "proper activity." [12] Probably few married people overtly or consciously experience sex as an evil activity. What they do experience repeatedly are the symptoms of negative attitudes in the form of disappointment or dissatisfaction with sex. The large amount of sexually oriented literature and films and the wide audiences that these hold are suggestive of the American's frustration and preoccupation with sex. The problem is even more complex for middle-class people, with whom we are primarily concerned, since on the basis of their education they believe that they should know better—that sex is normal and healthy. At the level of feeling and attitudes, however, they may have contradictory attitudes.

Some of these negative views toward sex could be minimized with the help of the school system. Although many school programs make noble attempts to counteract negative attitudes toward sex, not all are successful. Thus some courses stress the anatomy of male and female genitalia and the process of reproduction; such knowledge, though important, probably has little to do with basic sexual attitudes and feelings.[13]

[12] Francis E. Merrill, *Courtship and Marriage*, Henry Holt, New York, 1959, pp. 300–301.
[13] For a discussion of the implications of a psychosociological perspective for a program of sex education in high schools, see Jerome Himelhoch, "Sex Education in Sociological Perspective," *Social Hygiene Papers*, November 1957. We are indebted

For some people their early negative associations regarding sex will diminish, especially if the marriage on the whole is a good one. In such a marriage people discuss their fears and come to understand each other. Perhaps in a majority of marriages people are not so fortunate. They simply plod along with their confusions, expecting little and probably experiencing even less.

Overt Behavior and Inhibitions

The preceding remarks suggest inhibition in the sexual area; yet, with the overt emphasis placed on sex in our society by many youth, the question of the extent of this inhibition seems an interesting one to raise. Indeed, many parents wonder whether young people, as overt as they are with displays of affection, have any inhibitions at all. In fact, the essence of inhibition is not to be found in public displays of love and affection, as noted in parks and on the lawns of college campuses. Indeed, in some instances such behavior may suggest a rebelliousness against more conventional norms rather than real emancipation. The essence of *sexual inhibition* is probably more readily found in the incapacity to *experience orgasm* and enjoy sexual relations. Many people capable of engaging in open displays of affection are still incapable of achieving basic satisfaction in the sexual act. It is at this point that basic inhibition manifests itself.

Sexual Compatibility as a Process

Sexual compatibility in marriage is an emergent process.[14] The length of time required to achieve sexual compatibility varies, depending in general on the soundness of the marital relationship and on the couple's

to Robert A. Harper for suggestion and clarification of three related terms: sexual conditioning, sexual knowledge, and sexual therapy. Harper points out that sexual conditioning refers to the experience and attitudes toward sex that have emerged in the process of growing up; sexual knowledge consists of formal instruction received in school; and sexual therapy refers to the undoing of faulty sexual conditioning. Harper correctly states that what we need is much more sexual therapy, if problems in these areas are to be resolved.

[14] Total sexual compatibility may be defined in terms of both partners' experiencing orgasm within the sex act. It is clear that a majority of couples only approximate total compatibility.

Table 12 Length of Time Required to Adjust in Sex Relations and Happiness in Marriage (409 Couples)[a]

Length of Time Required	Very Happy	Happy	Average
Satisfactory from beginning	53%	36%	11%
1 to 12 months	61%	30%	9%
1 to 20 years	43%	38%	19%
Never satisfactory	11%	36%	53%

[a] Judson T. Landis and Mary G. Landis, *Building a Successful Marriage*, 3rd ed., Prentice-Hall, Englewood Cliffs, N.J., 1958, p. 378.

ability to deal with the problems in their relationship, as shown in Table 12. A meaningful marriage, devoid of serious incompatibilities, is conducive to sexual compatibility. A meaningful relationship tends to facilitate sexual compatibility also by fostering attitudes that allow the partners to express themselves sexually with a maximum of freedom and spontaneity, consistent, of course, with the well-being of the relationship. It follows that a meaningful relationship will impose few obstacles on the spontaneous expression of sexual behavior, which is basic for sexual compatibility.

Frequency of Erotic Experience

In a meaningful relationship there will be few rules regarding the frequency with which the sex act should, or should not, occur. Such rules lead to frustration, for in addition to disturbing the spontaneity, they frequently result in individuals' evaluating themselves as being either oversexed or undersexed. When people feel that they are undersexed or oversexed, they may develop negative self-attitudes and try in some desperate fashion to change their behavior. Such rules may be the result of literature containing statistics on frequency in sexual relations that have been misunderstood or of unconscious ideas that have been acquired from others. What is forgotten is that statistics on the frequency of sex relations for married people are based on limited samples. Furthermore, the range of differences among people may be, and usually is, considerable.[15] To impose rules and restrictions based on artificial or unreal standards is simply to promote frustration. The most sensible measure to use, if one is so inclined, is the satisfaction of the couple. This may mean

[15] Kinsey pointed out that a great variance of coitus frequency exists among couples. Taking this variance into consideration, however, he presents statistics concerning averages of coitus frequency; see Alfred C. Kinsey et al., *op. cit.*, pp. 348–349.

a high or a low frequency, depending on individual differences, needs, and attitudes toward each other. To be sure, in any marriage there may be at the outset considerable difference with respect to frequency of interest, with one person desiring sexual relations more, or less, frequently than the other.[16] If there are no deep-seated personality problems, this difficulty is often easily resolved, especially if the partners are sensitive to each other's needs and spontaneous in their sexual behavior and if a good interpersonal relationship is maintained, that is, if basic personal satisfactions in the marriage are maintained.

Lovemaking

In a meaningful relationship there will be few rigidities regarding the nature of sexual experience. By rigidities we mean a pattern of participating in the sex act at the same time in the same way with the same techniques, so that sexual relations become planned. Couples who follow such a pattern often fail to engage in sexual relations when interest develops and indeed may even feel obligated to participate at other times when there is no real interest. There are those, for example, who reject their own spontaneous sex interests because they have become so completely habit-bound in their way of life. For example, some people may engage in sexual relations only at night and in the dark. We recognize that such a procedure may be dictated by other activities in the life of the couple. However, when both the evening and the darkness are symbolic of secrecy and the forbidden, spontaneous enjoyment is restricted. Couples, of course, are never wholly free to be spontaneous and indeed all patterns, sexual and other, are dictated by other necessities. Nevertheless, the development of spontaneity in this area may enable the couple to participate in sexual relations at a time that is best for them and to avoid the periods that are not.

Regarding lovemaking practices themselves, another obstacle to spontaneity is the tendency of married partners to approach each other and to participate erotically always in the same manner. One of the problems here, of course, is the judgments that couples make about what respectable couples should, or should not, do. In fact, there are a variety of lovemaking practices that physicians and psychiatrists recognize as satisfactory for a large number of people. Appendix A by Dr. Lehfeldt could be consulted on this point. To the extent that a meaningful relationship in marriage is present, people feel free to express themselves sexually. Thus spontaneity is fostered and becomes reflected in experimentation with

[16] Most studies tend to show that husbands desire coitus more frequently than wives; see Lewis Terman et al., *loc. cit.*

lovemaking. Many of the relatively less complicated problems in sexual relations can be resolved and pleasure increased by an awareness of these potential difficulties.

The Problem of Communication

A meaningful relationship not only minimizes obstacles and fosters spontaneity, but also enables the couple to communicate difficulties about sexual matters. The importance of communication here is that it enables the partners to reveal their feelings and reactions about what each is experiencing in the sex act. Thus, when handled properly, it allows the persons to integrate their differences and build a better sexual relationship. Equally significant, however, is the fact that communication enables the marital partners to reveal those aspects of lovemaking that are disturbing, that is, those that tend to detract from the sexual satisfaction that might be achieved. Likewise, communication enables each to reveal the pleasurable aspects of lovemaking. Of particular importance in this regard is the ability to communicate the fantasies that one may have about the sources of sexual pleasure.

Fantasies are common, and by their communication to the partner a sexual relationship that is mutually enjoyable may be facilitated. Many people are fearful about communicating their wishes in the sexual area, since they feel a sense of embarrassment about them; hence they go through a lifetime of sexual frustration. We shall deal with a further aspect of communication in a subsequent chapter on handling marital difficulties.

Finally, when rigidities in the sexual relationship are minimized and spontaneity, creativity, and communication are fostered, the less complicated sexual problems may be resolved and, in addition, satisfactory erotic relations may be maintained. A good sexual relationship may have some bearing on the extramarital involvement, a problem to which we now turn our attention.

Extramarital Sex Interests

Just as a meaningful interpersonal relationship in marriage, with accompanying spontaneity, will facilitate a good sexual relationship, and vice versa, so it will also minimize the likelihood of extramarital sex interests.[17] Hence the better the marriage, the less likely the extramarital sex interests, although some such interest probably exists in most marriages. It is a mistake to assume that even the best relationship will completely insulate a couple from having extramarital sex interests at some point in their marriage. The existence of such interests is understandable in view of the powerful sexual urge, which may be controlled but seldom directed exclusively toward one member of the opposite sex. Sexual urges are biological, and the idea of marital fidelity is after all a social custom. That extramarital sex interests are considerable is shown by the Kinsey reports dealing with both men and women.[18] The presence of extramarital sex interests does not necessarily indicate marital problems, but they may at times be indicators of difficulty. Thus it becomes important to examine them more carefully.

Extramarital sex interests can be examined in terms of four broad sets of factors. First, the difficulties may be due to a breakdown of the interpersonal relationship in marriage. Basic satisfactions are no longer being realized; there is value conflict; and incompatibilities are expressed in the interpersonal relationship. Under these circumstances the marital partners may belittle each other, making the other person feel less worthy. Such a situation will often alienate people from their marriage and lead to a tendency for them to become erotically interested in others. In short, it may be necessary to evaluate the basic marital satisfactions and dissatisfactions.

There is the case of a married man who, after twenty years of happily married life, started to develop persistent extramarital interests. Although he had never pursued any of these, he became concerned about their intensity and persistence. He sought professional assistance, and both he and his wife came for help. Over a period of time it was learned that the onset of the husband's sexual interest occurred when his wife became preoccupied with furthering her education. Such preoccupation made the husband feel rejected and left out. The fact that he was a relatively uneducated person increased his anxiety and fear that his wife might no longer want him. Thus the extramarital sex interests were an expression of his fear and of a need for reassurance about his desirability.

A second reason for extramarital sex interests may be a breakdown in the erotic aspect of marriage. To find this cause, one would have to eval-

[17] Paul H. Landis, *Making the Most of Marriage*, 2nd ed., Appleton-Century-Crofts, New York, 1960, pp. 416–417.
[18] Kinsey found that about 25 percent of the wives in his sample and about 50 percent of the husbands had had at least one extramarital sexual relationship sometime during their marriage. See Alfred C. Kinsey et al., *op. cit.*, p. 416; Alfred C. Kinsey et al., *Sexual Behavior in the Human Male*, Saunders, Philadelphia, 1948, p. 585.

uate sexual relations in terms of frequency, discrepancy of interests, and pleasure obtained or absence of pleasure. Also, since general marital and sexual dissatisfactions are intertwined, it would be wise to examine how unhappiness in one area may be responsible for unhappiness in another area of marital life.[19]

A third factor in extramarital sex interests relates to personality problems and immaturities that can operate somewhat independently of the marital relationship.[20] Those who are beset by inner problems do not necessarily change in their basic patterns of life even when their marriage is a good one. One such personality type is the individual who displays a long history of insecurity. He comes to think of himself as unloved and unlovable. Thus he has a self-image that, once constructed, does not easily disappear. The fact that the marital partner shows love for him may not in itself remove his doubts. Such people, therefore, may develop extramarital sex interests, activated by their need to seek reassurance about their being lovable. The reassurance that they obtain in the new relationship seldom endures for any period of time. What is necessary, instead, is an understanding of the negative self-image that creates the insecurity.

A second personality type predisposed to marital sex interests includes individuals who have a destructive orientation toward human relationships. Put simply, this means that their lives are predicated on the assumption that good relationships do not exist, and they set out to prove it in various ways. Such people are often flirtatious when around the opposite sex. More often than not their involvement ends at the point of flirtation, since their primary purpose is to prove that no relationship can be really counted on. The presence of such types of individuals arouses anxiety in members of the more stable marital unions. The "flirt" is considered a threat to the stability of a marriage, and fear is frequently displayed by the husband or wife who sees the partner becoming ensnared in the flirtatious relationship.

Individuals who live at a shallow level of existence constitute the third personality type that is often associated with extramarital sex interests. Such people, suffering from personal deterioration and finding little meaning to life, have succumbed to a simple pleasure-and-pain principle of living. They pursue what is pleasurable and reject what may involve

---

[19] One authority clearly points out that sex adjustment is only one of the components of the overall marital adjustment; see Francis Merrill, *op. cit.,* p. 199.

[20] One student after studying sexual behavior reached the conclusion that sexual promiscuity is a response to emotional and environmental problems and as such is a psychiatric problem; see Richard A. Koch, "Penicillin Is Not Enough," *J. soc. Hyg.,* **36** (1950), pp. 3–6.

discomfort or effort. They are amoral, living outside any system of morality. Hence they are generally unconcerned about either their actions or the implications of their actions. Since much of life has lost its meaning for them, these people often thrive on the unusual and the daring, in order that the dullness of their existence be removed. They enjoy becoming involved in extramarital affairs and take special pleasure in the involvement of others and the complications and excitement that this brings.

Finally, it is important to recognize that many men and women are not necessarily socialized to accept conventional norms regarding extramarital sexual involvement and marriage. In fact, a greater internal battle to remain monogamous is perhaps waged than most people are willing to admit. The wish to avoid the social complications that may arise from extramarital involvements is probably the factor that keeps many people from becoming implicated in them. Extramarital sexual involvements need not be the result of problems within a marriage or of personality problems as such; they may represent exposure to a set of norms that differ from those associated with monogamy.[21]

When married people discover persistent extramarital sex interests, and a tendency toward involvement, a thorough evaluation of the marriage and of themselves is in order. Although discussion and communication are important, it is not recommended that married people necessarily discuss their extramarital sex interests, unless they have an unusual amount of objectivity. Ordinarily such discussions are very threatening to the marital partner, and little objectivity is likely to emerge.

On the other hand, one should not overestimate the difficulties involved. There are many relatively sophisticated couples, capable of handling threats to ego, who can face these kinds of problems. Some couples may emerge from the discussion with a much greater understanding of each other than existed before. For them, communication on these matters may be vital.

For other persons, however, it may be more desirable to deal with nonsexual marital difficulties, with the hope that an alleviation of these will result in a reduction of the extramarital interests. Such an approach may be most fruitful when the difficulties are based primarily in the relationship itself. It will probably be less rewarding when the difficulties are due to personality problems, in which case professional counseling or psychotherapy may be needed to produce any appreciable change in behavior.

[21] Gerhard Neubeck and Vera M. Schletzer, "A Study of Extra-Marital Relationships," *Marr. Fam. Living,* **24,** 3 (1962), pp. 279–281.

Role of Personality in Sexual Difficulties

The role of personality in sexual difficulties is obviously not limited to extramarital sex interests, but pervades the whole erotic relationship. It is probably true that whenever personality problems of any type are present, they express themselves in the sexual relationship. For example, there is the husband who may have a need to degrade others, in particular women, whom he views as prostitutes. He may be quite unaware of such an attitude, but nevertheless treats his wife accordingly.[22] Therefore, he may be essentially indifferent to his wife's sexual needs and wishes. She is there only to satisfy his sexual desires. He is unconcerned with her feelings. Some men of this type may try to control the budget when they are not sexually satisfied; the amount of money a wife receives thus becomes a function of her husband's sexual satisfaction. There is, on the other hand, the wife who looks on herself as a prostitute; she may expect and even suggest that her wishes be ignored. She may see herself as one without any right to wishes, as one who is there only to serve her husband. Some of these women may not even be able to enjoy the sex act unless they are treated without regard for their feelings. The husband and wife in these instances are people who enjoy sexual relations only at the expense of others or themselves. They must degrade, or they must be degraded, before enjoyment occurs.

Among other types of individuals whose personality problems in dealing with others are expressed in the sex act are those who are very inhibited and thus circuitous in their approach to sex. These people can never directly request sexual relations with the partner, but must use great subterfuge to make their feelings known. They hint, they allude, they imply; at times they are so subtle that the partner misses the cue, and disappointment is the end result. Some of them have to engage in heavy drinking before they can make their feelings known. Such deviant behavior may be frustrating to both partners, since the use of alcohol can impair sexual functioning and, if drunkenness occurs, may result in disturbance. The illustrations we have presented are only samples of the many ways in which personality is expressed in sex; these situations, nevertheless, are responsible for many of the sex difficulties in marriage.

It is interesting to note that these types of difficulties are relatively un-

[22] See Eugenia Elliott, *loc. cit.*

dramatic and frequently are not identified as a source of difficulty in sexual relations, but indeed they are serious, since they disturb not only sexual relations but other components of the relationship as well. They are involved problems, intertwined with different aspects of personality, and professional assistance is usually needed before much can be done about them.

Frigidity and Impotency

Perhaps the most complicated and involved expression of personality difficulties in sexual relationships concerns the problems of impotency and frigidity. By impotency we mean the inability to maintain an erection, and by frigidity the inability to experience orgasm, the first term applying to men and the second to women. Since some of these problems are also discussed by Dr. Lehfeldt in Appendix A, we make only a few brief remarks here. First, it should be clear that it is very difficult for any untrained observer to tell by outer appearances and behavior whether a person is impotent or frigid. Appearances are indeed deceptive. Frigidity especially tends to be disguised in diametrically different behavior. Some of the sexually most aggressive and promiscuous women may be essentially frigid. The sexual aggressiveness is both a cover-up for the real inadequacies that these people feel and an attempt to prove to themselves that perhaps it will be different "the next time."

It is, of course, necessary to recognize that it is no simple task to determine whether orgasm has been experienced by the female.[23] Physicians, in order to ascertain the presence or absence of orgasm, frequently ask the patient whether she felt relaxed or upset after coitus. When the patient reports being upset, presumably orgasm was not experienced. Kinsey at one point in his research suggested the abandonment of the term "frigidity," since the range of orgasmic experience in the female seemed to be very variable and perhaps difficult to identify precisely.[24] Some women seemed to have climactic orgasms with a definite high point in the sex act. Others seemed to have generalized orgasms, in which there was no high point, but the entire experience itself was pleasurable. In between there are many variations. Unfortunately, some women who experience the generalized orgasm think of themselves as frigid. This erroneous view creates unnecessary anguish.

The conditions termed situational frigidity and impotency are some-

---

[23] For a discussion of orgasm, both clitoral and vaginal, see George Simpson, *People in Families,* Thomas Y. Crowell, New York, 1960, pp. 175–177.
[24] Alfred C. Kinsey et al., *Sexual Behavior in the Human Female,* Saunders, Philadelphia, 1953.

what less serious and involved. They appear with the onset of some stressful situation; financial concerns, loss of a loved one, and hostility projected on the husband (or wife) are examples. When the condition is situational or temporary, it disappears once the stress is alleviated.

However, in some cases situational frigidity and impotency may persist for a considerable length of time, thus becoming serious problems. This is especially the case when they stem from unresolved difficulties in the marital relationship that have suddenly become major.[25] Marriages in which there are major attacks on the *self-worth* of the husband or wife seem to be especially vulnerable to frigid and impotent reactions. Thus persistent efforts to belittle and berate the husband or wife become particularly dangerous. For as the person is diminished in stature, he tends to withdraw from personal involvement with the partner. He may feel a need to get back and punish. Without any conscious intent to avoid sexual involvement, the person may begin to feel that sex is meaningless, which may lead to impotent and frigid reactions.

CAUSATION AND COMPLICATIONS. Impotency and frigidity are serious because they markedly impair sexual pleasure. They are complex because they have their origin in the individual's past and have been nurtured for many years. They are difficult to change because they constitute deep-seated patterns. Impotency and frigidity are conditions that have developed out of lifelong patterns and problems that have become manifest in sexual relations.[26] Probably relatively little can be accomplished by the persons themselves to remedy the conditions; the attention of an expert in psychotherapy is usually required. The need for a therapist is especially important when dealing with frigidity, since some men take a frigid response as a personal affront to their manliness and assume that the condition will be overcome if the sex act is repeated often enough. The results of such a procedure can be disastrous, since it often exposes the woman to repeated frustration and may aggravate her condition.

There are instances where serious dietary deficiencies and metabolic conditions have been responsible for impotent reactions in men and structural defects in female genitalia for frigidity in women. Nevertheless, for the most part impotency and frigidity are thought to arise out of

[25] Alexander L. Clark and Paul Wallin, "Women's Sexual Responsiveness and the Duration and Quality of Their Marriages," *Am. J. Sociol.*, **71**, 2 (September 1965), pp. 187–196.
[26] For a discussion of the relationship between impotency and personality patterns, see B. Joan Harte, "The Fear of Love and Sex," (article of) Auxiliary Council to the Association for the Advancement of Psychoanalysis, New York, 1951, p. 3.

social interaction and experience; they are the results of learning.[27] Ignorance of sexual matters, for example, can result in what is called the married virgin. One study, in which a thousand wives whose marriages had reportedly never been consummated were analyzed, reported that a major cause was a lack of sexual knowledge.[28] Among the social-psychological factors responsible for frigidity and impotency, a number of variables are frequently identified as important causative agents. Impotency has been related to the experiencing of early sex trauma, to being introduced to sex by way of prostitution and accompanying crudities, to rejection by women in interpersonal or sexual relations, which become important in the male's feeling of inadequacy about women, and to fixation on members of the same sex, expressed as latent homosexuality. Much emphasis has been placed on what Sigmund Freud termed the unresolved Oedipus complex. This refers to repressed sexual feelings that a male may have for his mother, the idea of which is so repulsive that it serves to produce impotent reactions with women in general.

The variables that may cause frigidity in women include some that are similar to and some that are different from those causing impotency in men: sex trauma, including unpleasant sex activity, rejection by the male, latent homosexuality, and an unresolved Electra complex (the opposite of the Oedipus complex; that is, the female has sex strivings for the father).

These sexual factors are considered to be some of the more significant and dramatic variables responsible for impotency and frigidity. Another view, held by many professionals, is that although faulty sexual conditioning may be a factor in producing impotency and frigidity, other important considerations—character and personality—determine how one relates sexually.[29] For example, the background experiences that make a person aloof, insecure, or sadistic determine how he relates to an-

[27] One study showed that the vast majority of sexual disturbances in marriage are related to poor social conditioning and a lack of biological and psychological knowledge, while only a minor part of the disturbances are due to biological or organic problems. Ernest W. Burgess and Leonard S. Cottrell, Jr., *Predicting Success or Failure in Marriage*, Prentice-Hall, Englewood Cliffs, N.J., 1939, p. 221.

[28] John A. Blazer, "Married Virgins—A Study of Unconsummated Marriages," *J. Marr. Fam.*, **26** (May 1964), pp. 213–214.

[29] Freud believed that sexual desire was the source of character formation; however, many modern authorities agree that character determines the particular way in which the sex urge finds expression. F. Alexander Magoun, op. cit., pp. 237–238. One authority, for example, states that "Sexual attitudes and behaviors are directed by the basic motivations which the human being acquires in the process of being socialized." John J. Honigmann, "Cultural Dynamics of Sex," *Psychiatry*, **10** (February 1947), p. 47.

other person, in all forms of expression, social and sexual. (See Chapter 8.) From this point of view impotency and frigidity at the most fundamental level are basic expressions of how one relates to the opposite sex and how one feels about the opposite sex.

Let us consider what the impotency of a male may tell us, in simple terms, about his relationships with women. The impotent reaction suggests, first, a fear of human involvement, particularly with women. Furthermore, it suggests a need to frustrate women, since in the impotent reaction one involves another person erotically only to terminate the relationship at the last moment; such behavior indicates also a need to frustrate oneself, which may indeed be present. Finally, it suggests a marked feeling of inadequacy in relation to women, which may torment the individual to such an extent that he is unable to complete the act. All these factors may be involved in impotency, although deciding which one or which combination sometimes becomes an intricate problem.

The frigid reaction in the female suggests patterns very similar to those discussed for the male. These are extensions of basic attitudes that are expressed in the sex act, as illustrated in numerous case histories of sexually disturbed people. For example, there is the case of a forty-one-year-old married female who had a pattern of frustrating herself in sex and was almost never able to achieve orgasm. The problem, as she experienced it, was that whenever sexual relations became pleasurable and whenever she seemed to be approaching orgasm, certain ideas would come up and disturb her enjoyment. The ideas in question had a pattern centering on such notions as "I should not be enjoying myself." At that point in the sex act, she felt the need to become aloof and terminate the sex act. Indeed, this woman's need for self-frustration was so deep that on the few occasions when she did experience orgasm she became extremely despondent and resentful.[30]

In the life history of this woman the following significant facts emerge. She grew up with an older, neurotic, and sadistic sister who always tormented her and gave her the feeling that somehow she was an intruder in the home, that she did not belong. When she attempted new things as a child, she was ridiculed; when she was happy, her happiness was interrupted by unprovoked attacks from her sister. This woman grew up with marked feelings of not belonging, of unworthiness, of having no right to enjoyment. In her interactions with people she was self-effacing and re-

---

[30] There are also those who, because of their need for self-frustration, on experiencing successful lovemaking feel marked depression and resentment. Thus it is an oversimplification to view the achievement of orgasm as the panacea of marital ills. See Lawrence S. Kubie, "Psychoanalysis and Marriage," in Victor W. Eisenstein, Ed., *Neurotic Interaction in Marriage*, Basic Books, New York, 1956, p. 26.

plete with self-denial. In sexual relations the same attitudes appeared in the form just described to frustrate her pleasure in sex, and these attitudes were deeply involved in her frigidity.

Therapy for Impotency and Frigidity

From all that we have said it should be clear that impotency and frigidity are deeply rooted in personality and their correction requires professional assistance. Moreover, these are difficult conditions to treat. The therapist must not only go back into the life history of the person to deal with the sexual and nonsexual factors that brought these patterns into operation, but be even more concerned with how and why these particular experiences resulted in impotency and frigidity and why they are being maintained. The latter task is especially significant and formidable. Irrespective of what combination of circumstances produced the reactions that cause frigidity and impotency, once started they are not easily reversed. They become a component of the overall makeup of the individual and are deeply imbedded in the personality organization.

Masters and Johnson in a recent book give an excellent report of the findings concerning human sexual response. The report is especially significant for the extensive treatment given frigidity and impotency. Their findings suggest that these conditions are becoming more readily understood and more amenable to therapy and that an increasing number of people with these conditions can be helped.[31]

A healthy realization of how impotency and frigidity, in their various degrees, disturb both the erotic and the interpersonal relationship is essential for any couple. Only through such a realization can a couple be motivated to receive the help that will enable them to benefit fully from the sexual and marital union.

Summary

This chapter discussed the relation between sexual compatibility and (1) background factors that affect sexual attitudinal development, (2)

[31] William H. Masters and Virginia E. Johnson, *Human Sexual Response*, Little, Brown, Boston, 1966.

initial sexual relations in marriage, and (3) patterns of sexual behavior developed in marriage. It was noted that previous experiences regarding sex can result in the internalization of either negative or positive sexual attitudes, hence either impair or aid in the development of sexual compatibility in marriage. Furthermore, it was pointed out that displays of extreme, overt sexual affection do not necessarily indicate a lack of inhibition, because such displays may result more from a rebelliousness against conventional norms than from a sense of emancipation and spontaneity of sexual expression. Also, the initial sexual approaches of the marital couple are of paramount importance in developing sexual compatibility, for it is here that one's attitudes toward the sex act and toward the sex partner are likely to emerge. The pattern of sexual behavior worked out by the marriage partners is also extremely important in developing sexual compatibility; an understanding between the spouses concerning (1) the frequency of erotic experience, (2) lovemaking, and (3) freedom of communication is a necessity. This is not to say, however, that the understanding must result in an unchangeable pattern of sexual behavior, since spontaneity in sexual behavior is of vital importance in achieving meaningful sexual compatibility.

It was noted that the emergence of concentrated extramarital sex interests may be due to any one of four broad sets of factors: (1) a breakdown in the interpersonal relationship itself; (2) a breakdown in the erotic aspect of the marriage; (3) personality problems and immaturities on the part of one or both of the marital partners; (4) the failure of some people to be socialized to accept conventional norms regarding sexual involvement and marriage. Several types of personality problems were then discussed, not only with regard to extramarital sexual interests but also with respect to frigidity and impotency. It was pointed out that although frigidity and impotency may result from physical structural aspects, it is commonly believed that, for the most part, they arise out of faulty social interaction and exposure. Concerning therapy for frigidity and impotency, it has been found that reversing these patterns tends to be a formidable task. In a recent study by Masters and Johnson, however, it is suggested that frigidity and impotency are becoming more readily understood and more amenable to treatment.

Finally, it was shown that the presence of extramarital sexual interests and frigidity or impotency in marriage might be the cause or, even more important, the result of marital breakdown.

Questions

1. In what ways are the initial sexual approaches in marriage important? Explain your answer.
2. What are some of the common experiences in American society that can contribute to negative attitudes toward sexual relations? What might be done about correcting the situation?
3. Explain how one's attitudes toward sex can aid or impair his ability to achieve a meaningful sexual relationship in marriage.
4. Discuss the relationship between public displays of sexual affection and the presence or absence of sexual inhibition.
5. Explain how a breakdown in communication between husband and wife can impair the development of a satisfactory sexual adjustment.
6. Discuss the relationship between marital breakdown and extramarital sex interests. Give examples.
7. How may personality problems be related to extramarital sex interests? Fully explain your answer and give examples.
8. In what way may impotency and frigidity be related to one's past experiences? Explain exactly how impotency and frigidity may be a cause of marital breakdown and also how it may be a result of marital breakdown. Give examples.

Projects

1. Have a panel discussion concerning the pros and cons of giving children information pertaining to sex as a means of developing healthy attitudes toward sex.
2. Write your own case history regarding how you obtained information pertaining to sex. Include the means by which you obtained attitudes toward sex that you regard as being unhealthy and the means by which you obtained attitudes that you regard as being healthy. Do you feel that your sexual information is adequate and that your attitudes toward sex will be conducive to sexual compatibility in marriage?

3. Poll your classmates on the question of whether public display of excessive sexual affection is a valid indication of freedom from sexual inhibition. Do you find any difference between the answers given by men and women or freshmen and seniors? How do you interpret the results?

Suggested Readings

Bowman, Henry A., *Marriage for Moderns*, 4th ed., McGraw-Hill, New York, 1960, Ch. 11, "Sex in Marriage."

Brenton, Myron, *The American Male*, Coward-McCann, New York, 1966.

Ellis, Havelock, *The Psychology of Sex*, Emerson Books, New York, 1938.

Fromme, Allan, *Understanding the Sexual Response in Humans*, Pocket Book, 1966.

Hastings, Donald W., *Impotence and Frigidity*, Little, Brown, Boston, 1963.

Krich, A. M., Ed., *Women, The Variety and Meaning of Their Sexual Experience*, Dell Publishing Company, New York, 1954, especially Ch. 4 by Karl A. Menninger, "Impotence and Frigidity."

Kronhausen, Phyllis, and Eberhard Kronhausen, *The Sexually Responsive Woman*, Grove Press, New York, 1964.

Landis, Judson T., and Mary G. Landis, *Building a Successful Marriage*, 3rd ed., Prentice-Hall, Englewood Cliffs, N.J., 1958, Ch. 16, "Sex Adjustment in Marriage."

Levine, Lena, and Mildred Gilman, *Frigidity*, Planned Parenthood Federation of America, New York, 1952.

Masters, William H., and Virginia E. Johnson, *Human Sexual Response*, Little, Brown, Boston, 1966.

Stone, Abraham, and Hannah Stone, *A Marriage Manual*, Simon and Schuster, New York, 1952.

Chapter Fourteen

EXTERNALIZA-
TIONS AND
MARITAL
INCOMPATIBILITY

As the reader has already observed, marital conflicts are complex; they have many dimensions and ramifications. To be sure, marital conflicts are rooted in some form of incompatibility, but incompatibility is, after all, a general term and does not specify the conditions under which marital conflicts arise. Incompatibility, for example, may arise because of different ethnic, religious, or cultural backgrounds of the partners, leading to difficulties with respect to attitudes, values, and the partners' aims in life and marriage. We recognize these as sources of marital difficulty, but there are still other marital problems, which, in the opinion of the writers, are of even greater complexity and probably less understood—the incompatibilities that arise because of the tendency to blame others for one's own tensions and to impose one's values, wishes, and goals on the marital partner. We refer to these patterns of blaming and imposition as externalizations.[1] The tendency to blame others for one's problems is a very common characteristic of many human rela-

[1] Karen Horney, *Neurosis and Human Growth*, Norton, New York, 1950, pp. 178–179.

ILLUSTRATION: The Fanny Hayes Doll House, presented to President and Mrs. Hayes in 1878 for their daughter. Courtesy of The Rutherford B. Hayes Library, Fremont, Ohio.

tionships. As pointed out earlier, many persons have considerable difficulty in assuming responsibility for their problems and, indeed, even in recognizing that most of their discomforts come from their own unresolved problems. With respect to values and goals, even persons who understand that there are different ways of viewing life discover that in their personal relationships they tend to impose their values on—and restrict the choices of—the other member of the relationship. Patterns of blaming and imposition manifest themselves in numerous ways and defeat the purpose of building a meaningful marriage relationship. In this chapter we deal with the various forms that these patterns of externalizing can assume.

Externalizations That Arise Out of Environmental Stress

Blaming the Partner for One's Tensions

Other things being equal, an individual is likely to externalize and find fault with others when the stresses and tensions that are normally present become too burdensome.[2] Some of the sources of such stress lie in the social environment, being an integral part of modern American life,[3] which subjects almost everybody to certain common stresses. There are generalized stresses, caused by worry about such matters as war, economic security, illness, and death. At other levels, the competitive nature of our society, which is evident in almost all walks of life, imposes still another series of stresses.[4] One competes for dates, for mates, for jobs, for advancement, for popularity, and for prestige.

Men are invariably immersed in competition in their occupations. There is competition for promotion, for salary increments, and for recognition. Inherent in competition is the fact that not all will succeed. Thus, inevitably, stress and frustrations can accumulate not only in the process of competing, but also as a result of losing out in the competitive process.

[2] James C. Coleman, *Abnormal Psychology and Modern Life*, Scott, Foresman, New York, 1950, p. 90.
[3] Jessie Bernard, *Social Problems at Mid-Century*, Dryden Press, New York, 1957, pp. 79–84.
[4] *Ibid.*, pp. 139–140.

There is the incident of an engineer who was anxious to get ahead and felt the competition from others in his office quite keenly. Although he worked for a conservative company in which mobility was normally slow and difficult, all the members of the staff did their very best to outdo the others in order to receive what few rewards there were. One year several openings at advanced levels became available because of retirement of older personnel. Competition at this point became intense, and the engineer for a number of months arrived home irritable and anxious. His family suffered considerably during this period, since he was difficult to get along with. When the promotions were made, the engineer was not on the list. At this point he became depressed and disillusioned and began finding fault with his marriage and his family.

Still another aspect of the competitive nature of our society which is responsible for stress concerns the ambitions and goals of power or prestige that people have and the differential outlets available to them for success. For example, people who have internalized certain concepts of success may discover that its realization is not readily possible.[5] Thus members of minority groups—racial or ethnic—find opportunities restricted because of their color or nationality. Many nonminority-group persons as well are unable to compete successfully for power or prestige because of lack of training, lack of education, or personality difficulties. Furthermore, the concept of success is subject to individual definition.[6] How much power and prestige must a person have in order to be successful? Some people who have internalized high success goals may never be at peace with themselves, since they are relentlessly driven to acquire more and more power, and they undergo considerable stress in the process.[7]

It is perhaps interesting to note that at this particular time in America there seems to be considerable discontent among youth about following conventional notions of success. Youth today appear less likely to accept traditional values; indeed, many express an unwillingness to settle for the kind of life their parents have. Thus the usual struggle and competitiveness of the business and professional world may for the moment not have special appeal. Regardless of how problems related to one's career are resolved, the very act of raising basic questions about one's life and where one is going involves a basic personal reexamination and assessment; for those undergoing such assessment, stress and anxiety may be basic by-products. Both the reexamination and the resultant stress are

[5] Robert K. Merton, *Social Theory and Social Structure*, rev. ed., The Free Press, Glencoe, Ill., 1957, pp. 170–176.

[6] Jessie Bernard, *op. cit.*, p. 76.

[7] Bud Schulberg, *What Makes Sammy Run?* Modern Library, New York, 1952.

perhaps most likely to occur early in marriage and deserve serious attention from the marital partners.

Finally, the inability to cope with the success goals through conventional competitive channels may result in socially disapproved ways of competing.[8] The man who cannot become successful honestly may turn to lying and cheating and a set of questionable ethics. Although finding dishonest patterns necessary, he may still be plagued by self-doubts, which he may wish to hide from his family, but which will nevertheless involve it.

Specialization and Resultant Stress

The organization of work in modern society is the basis of still another series of stresses. We refer here to the development of specialization and the implications of this innovation. Specialization is, of course, functional in that it results in production of better goods and services. In other ways, however, specialization produces stress for the individual. For example, a high degree of specialization is often accompanied by a reduction of basic skill required to perform particular tasks. This situation, whose presence in assembly lines is well recognized, exists also in office and managerial functions and even in some of the professions.[9] Thus a number of capable and intelligent persons are working far beneath their basic capacity. This is a potential source of considerable stress, for indeed it means that large numbers of people will for many years be so located in the world of work as not to be able to utilize fully their potentialities.

So far we have been discussing the stresses that impinge most directly on men and on those women who are involved in careers. The woman who remains at home faces other stresses. Today the demands on the housewife are perhaps greater than they were in the past.[10] The tasks often go beyond home management and involve the ability to rear emotionally stable children and to provide companionship and a favorable emotional atmosphere in the home. Thus many middle-class women today look on the emotional maturity of their children and the general quality of their marital relationship as something for which they have considerable responsibility. Indeed, they frequently compare their families with the families of other middle-class women. The achievement of

---

[8] Lawrence Guy Brown, *Social Pathology*, Appleton-Century-Crofts, New York, 1942, pp. 488–489.

[9] *Ibid.*, p. 489.

[10] Anne Morrow Lindbergh, *Gift from the Sea*, Pantheon, New York, 1955, pp. 25–27.

marital success in these terms is no simple task, and many women who were—or could have been—successful as homemakers in the past fail today because the demands are more stringent. Since all wives do not in fact have equal opportunity to be successful in this regard, because of immaturity, lack of personality integration, or education, considerable stress about failure to meet these goals may emerge.

Women who restrict their roles to basic home management tasks, without regard for contributions to the growth and development of their children, their husband, or home, and women who have no children face other tensions. One of the most formidable problems that individuals encounter is that of dealing with *time for opportunity* and self-development. Being given opportunity to do something with one's life can arouse great anxiety and feelings of futility and emptiness. Note, for example, the difficulties that some people have on vacations and their delight at getting back to a routine. Frequently the very thing proposed for a bad marriage, a vacation, can bring out the very worst in people because of their incapacity to deal with the opportunity for leisure. Instead they become anxious and quarrelsome. The problem that a woman may have in reaching out to absorb opportunity for herself is a formidable one that few can deal with. The resulting stress may manifest itself in finding fault with her life, home, and marriage, in excessive consumption of alcohol, and in compulsive work. The layman's diagnosis is usually some version of "she doesn't have enough to do," and in some very limited sense the layman is correct.

Over a period of time many people accommodate themselves to a life of little change and continue to defend this life when change creates uncertainty and anxiety. For example, persons who have placed taboos on the development of their own creativity may become frightened. A wife who is afraid that she might do well at some activity in comparison to her husband may become upset when an opportunity for growth presents itself. The problem of how to deal with opportunity is not easily resolved in any sense. It is much easier for most people to work, especially for others, be it children, a spouse, or a parent. The wife with an opportunity to pursue her real interests for self, when it is appropriate to do so, is often plagued by doubts, tensions, and stress; the feeling of emptiness can be responsible for difficulties. An additional source of stress and tension for the middle-class woman today lies in the variety of social roles that she is frequently called upon to assume, each of which may require different behavior. As already noted, social roles are culturally defined expectations of behavior. The typical married woman today, for example, may be expected to fulfill the various roles of wife, mother, companion, and partner.

1. The *wife-and-mother* role is the traditional role of the married woman. Its implied privileges are security, the right to support, alimony in the case of divorce, respect as a wife and mother, a certain amount of domestic authority, loyalty of the husband to one who has borne him children, and a more or less sentimental gratitude from husband and children. Corresponding obligations include bearing and rearing children, making a home, rendering domestic service, loyal subordination of self to the economic interests of the husband, and acceptance of a dependent social and economic status, as well as of a limited range of interests and activity.

2. The *companion* role is essentially a leisure-class phenomenon. The privileges pertaining to this role include sharing pleasure with the husband, receiving a more romantic emotional response, being the object of admiration, receiving funds adequate for dress and recreation, having leisure for social and educational activity, and receiving a certain amount of chivalrous attention. On the other hand, it also implies obligations: the preservation of beauty under the penalty of marital insecurity, the rendering of ego and libido satisfaction to the husband, the cultivation of social contacts advantageous to him, the maintenance of intellectual alertness, and the responsibility of exorcising the demon of boredom.

3. Finally, there is the *partner* role, which corresponds to a new definition of the cultural situation that is gradually emerging. This role entails the privileges of economic independence, equal authority in regard to family finances, acceptance as an equal, exemption from one-sided personal or domestic services to the husband, equal voice in determining locale of residence, and equality in regard to social and moral liberty. The obligation side of the balance sheet would include renouncing alimony save in the case of dependent children, complete sharing of the legal responsibilities of the family, willingness to dispense with any appeal to chivalry, and equal responsibility for maintaining the family status by success in a career.[11]

The existence of several roles in marriage is responsible for stress and tension on the part of the woman in several ways. First, the woman has to make choices about which role she really wishes; is it, for example, a wife-mother role or a partner role? Second, she may fulfill a role, such as the wife-mother role, out of a sense of duty and obligation, whereas in reality she may desire the partner role. One investigator found that among wives employed outside the home, marital dissatisfaction was highest for

[11] Clifford Kirkpatrick, "The Measurement of Ethical Inconsistency in Marriage," *Int. J. Ethics,* July 1936, pp. 444–460. Copyright 1936 by the University of Chicago.

women who felt forced to work because of the husband's occupational inadequacy.[12]

Third, tension arises when husband and wife disagree about the role that the woman should play in marriage.[13] One study found that the husbands and wives who scored high on marital satisfaction were exactly those couples who perceived correctly the spouses' expectations of them and who were able to fulfill these expectations.[14] In fact, the actual similarity between one's own role concept and the expectations of the spouse appeared to be the single most important factor in marital satisfaction. This was particularly true for men. A fourth source of stress lies in the woman's attempts to combine different elements from each of the three roles. Under these circumstances she may find herself faced with contradictions. Thus for women, as well as men, sources of stress and tension are commonplace in our society.

Although few people in our society can avoid completely the stressful situations just described, individual differences exist with respect to what can be tolerated. Thus some individuals are relatively less affected than others. Other things being equal, the individual with emotional difficulties and immaturities is more likely to have a lower threshold of tolerance for stress than is the person without these problems. The individual with problems already is a battleground of inner tensions, and when external stress is superimposed on the existing tensions, balance becomes precarious.

Stress and the Marital Relationship

The effects of continued environmental stress on a marital relationship are always serious and must, therefore, be examined as to their manifestations. Individuals who experience prolonged stress are inclined to function with a certain tenseness and instability; consequently they may be easily provoked, for little reason.[15] At the psychological and physiological levels these expressions become a way of releasing pent-up feelings associated with stress. Furthermore, the cause of the emotional disturbance may be externalized on the marriage partner. At this point

[12] Robert O. Blood, Jr., "Socio-Economic Differential in the Relationship between Marital Adjustment and Wives' Employment Status," (Discussion) *Marr. Fam. Living,* **25,** 4 (November 1963), pp. 456–457.

[13] Willard Waller, *The Family,* revised by Reuben Hill, Dryden Press, New York, 1951, p. 284.

[14] Robert P. Stuckert, "Role Perception and Marital Satisfaction—A Configurational Approach," *Marr. Fam. Living,* **25,** 4 (1963), pp. 415–419.

[15] Ernest W. Burgess, Harvey J. Locke, and Mary Margaret Thomes, *The Family,* 3rd ed., American Book Company, New York, 1963, Ch. 18, especially pp. 388–392.

stress, which is unresolved conflict, emerges as conflict; [16] this topic is discussed in considerable detail in the chapter on resolving marital conflicts. Under conditions of externalization, a husband may identify his irritability as stemming from what he sees as his wife's inability to care adequately for the home or from her patterns of excessive spending of family income.[17]

There is the case of a married man who had many pressures and responsibilities in his job. Whenever these became excessive, he would focus on two difficulties: his wife's cooking and her parents. At these times he humiliated her for the poor way that meals were prepared and for what he termed her ignorant and uninformed parents. His behavior was so patterned that his wife could almost predict her husband's office problems by his patterns of externalization.

In any marriage in which stress is a factor, there is the ever-present danger of incompatibilities and conflicts. Also, the partner engaged in externalizing is often not aware that his faultfinding is the result of stress. During these periods remarks are not particularly rational, nor are negative comments necessarily limited to the immediate members of the family but may include relatives and friends. One basic characteristic in marital conflict of this type is the tendency to berate, to humiliate, and to attack the self-worth of the other person. The individual reacting in this way has both the emotional release and the satisfaction of fixing blame on another, thereby avoiding any personal responsibility for the stress and the consequences of stress for the marital relationship.

It is interesting to note that people often engage in such attacks without full realization of the implications. Indeed, some persons feel that nothing they say during an argument should be taken seriously. In spite of such well-meaning pleas, we must recognize that it is difficult to attack the self-worth of another person without seriously running the risk of provoking him and bringing forth his resentment. We refer to these resentments as residues. Residues are resentments that are repressed after the argument, but become cumulative over a period of time. Thus repeated attacks on the self-worth of the marital partner are likely to lead to the partner's repeatedly trying to get back at the other in various ways. This "getting back at the partner" may occur in the form of nagging, frustrating, or taking the daily pleasure out of marriage. When this continues over a period of time, such tremendous hostility may be built up that the damage to the relationship is difficult to undo.

There is the case of a married couple who had tormented each other

---

[16] *Ibid.,* pp. 385–399.

[17] For a discussion of distortion and externalization, see Karen Horney, *op. cit.,* pp. 292–294.

with insults and berating during many arguments over a five-year period, each partner developing intense hostility and resentment toward the other. Finally, their friends prevailed on them to get professional assistance. When they appeared for counseling, they spent almost all of their time expressing resentments toward each other and trying to justify them. At this stage in their marriage, each was interested in getting back at the other; neither was concerned about understanding how to rehabilitate the marriage.

Residues may also constitute the basis for a rage that seems unprovoked at the moment. The woman who has been berated over an extended period of time may have "a very low tolerance for conflict" and may explode at her husband at the slightest provocation. Thus in many instances the explosive reaction, which many people have in particular situations, represents an accumulation of resentments and not a response to a specific situation. It is important to have some appreciation of this pattern; otherwise both husbands and wives may be bewildered when one or the other becomes markedly provoked at seemingly unimportant remarks.

Understanding Environmental Stress and Its Consequences

The stresses that are imposed by the nature of our social order require considerable understanding and handling lest they lead to a deterioration of the marriage. For over a period of time couples who are immersed in conflict that stems from their inability to handle stress may come to believe that there is something fundamentally wrong with their marriage. Some of these people become hopeless and terminate their marriage only to find similar problems in a subsequent marriage.[18] What these people fail to realize is that their tendency to find fault with each other arises out of their inability to deal with environmental stress. A first consideration, therefore, in dealing with stress is to separate the basic relationship, which might well be a good one, from the external stresses that result in the externalizations and in the blaming of one another. This is necessary in order to attain a more positive view of the

[18] An index of this problem is noted in divorce rates of the remarried; see Paul H. Jacobson, *American Marriage and Divorce*, Rinehart, New York, 1959, pp. 150–151.

marriage. When a person who feels anxious and upset outside the home discovers on arriving home that he is immersed in conflict there as well, there is almost a complete absence of any secure base in the individual's life. When one can, however, separate the sources of conflict and recognize, let us say, that it is not the marriage that is at fault, but rather one's inability to handle external stress, the security of the marriage is increased and more effective ways of dealing with stress and its complications may emerge.

We recognize, of course, that there is considerable reluctance on the part of people to accept the fact that they may be finding fault with their marital relationships simply as a means of releasing pent-up feelings of resentments caused by external environmental stress. Many people feel that to accept their inability to handle stress is to admit that they have not adequately organized their lives. Thus, since so many people are perfectionistic about the way they conduct their lives, they are subject to a good deal of self-berating when they sense a personal inadequacy. When, on the other hand, one has accepted the fact that his marital difficulties may be rooted in an inability to deal with stress from the environment, a great deal has been accomplished for the well-being of the marriage. For it is at this point that one has accepted some responsibility for problems; it then becomes easier to isolate the sources of external stress, and perhaps deal with them more effectively. Finally, the berating of the marital partners may be markedly reduced and the relationship strengthened as well as made more secure.

A second consideration that may aid a couple in dealing with environmental stress concerns the couple's values and life goals. Values and goals that are unrealistic and not likely to be attained, given the conditions and circumstances of the couple's life, will invariably be related to stressful situations.[19] In some instances it may make sense to abandon certain goals and values; in other instances more effective ways of achieving these goals may be found. Many very able individuals have set their sights so high that achievement comes only at a tremendous personal sacrifice.

There was the case of a thirty-five-year-old married man who entered college in order to become a physician. His wife was of similar age, without children, but very desirous of having a family. As the husband pursued his college work, the tensions and stress mounted. He found it difficult to study, since he had been out of school for many years. His wife had to work in order to support him, and this she resented, since she was not in favor of the sacrifices that would be entailed. All of this cre-

[19] For a discussion of values and goals and their relationship to marriage, see Ernest W. Burgess, Harvey J. Locke, and Mary Margaret Thomes, *op. cit.*, Ch. 10, pp. 191–213.

ated much stress in the marriage, and both members of the relationship fell into a pattern of arguing. After several years they reassessed their values and goals. The husband realized that at his age acceptance by a medical school was remote. Even if by chance he were accepted, he would be forty-five years of age before he could support a family. A shift to an occupation more consistent with their needs was made, and the marital tensions were markedly reduced.

A third consideration in dealing with environmental stress is concerned with commonsense remedies that are consistent with certain good health practices. We refer to the pursuit of recreational patterns and hobbies in all their forms, which can serve as outlets for stress. These are important, but probably successful only when some more basic understanding of the difficulties has been reached earlier.

Externalizations That Arise from the Need to Impose One's Values on Others

We have been discussing sources of stress and tensions that are primarily rooted in the nature of our social order. There are other stresses and tensions, which are due to personal immaturities and unresolved personality problems rather than to environmental pressures, such as those caused by value imposition.

One source of value is the belief that one's values are best, coupled with a need to impose these values on others.[20] All of us have known people who have narrow views about tastes in food and clothing or about ethnic group or religion. Such narrowness may stem from having lived in relative isolation from people with differing values and beliefs. At a deeper psychological level, however, it may stem from pronounced feelings of inferiority about oneself and one's background. The individual who feels inferior may find new and different tastes and values disturbing, since the new experiences raise questions about his own background. This often results in a need to impose one's habits on others.

A second souce of value imposition lies in failure to realize ambitions and goals. There is the case of the woman who had been urged by her parents to marry a physician. Although she had accepted these values, she failed to find an eligible physician, but instead found a teacher of

[20] Karen Horney, op. cit., p. 208.

biology. The substitute was for her never a satisfactory one, and throughout her married life she continued to socialize with physicians' families and to compare her husband with the physicians she knew. The comparison she made was always unfavorable. Since she was frustrated in achieving her values, she urged medical training on her children, tried to control their dating practices, and reminded her husband constantly of his shortcomings. This woman lived in an unreal world in which she could not appreciate the real assets of either her husband or her children. All suffered as a result.

A third source of value imposition is found in conflicting conceptions of the social roles in marriage. Social roles, as previously noted, are culturally defined expectations of behavior. Role conceptions are acquired early in life and seem to persist, once developed. With regard to marriage, roles are the parts that one expects the marital partner to play, the way in which he is expected to behave, the responsibilities he should and should not assume. One dimension of conflict arises when the concept of the role that one partner envisages for the other does not correspond with the view held by the other, a point made earlier in this chapter.[21] Under these circumstances there is frequently a tendency to impose one's expectations regarding social role on another and force him to make the necessary adjustments.

A second dimension of role conflict concerns the expectation of inconsistent behaviors from oneself or the spouse. There is the case of a young professional man who was very interested in changing his class position. Although both he and his wife had come from humble origins, the man had taken special care to equip himself with the attributes that would facilitate his mobility. He went through a university, supported by his wife who worked during this period. While the man was circulating among middle-class people with whom he identified and wished to become part of, his wife continued to work, both in and outside the home. After college the husband, who had a definite conception about how his wife could become an asset in the attainment of his goals, imposed his concept of her role on her. This concept included a variety of qualities for which she was neither intellectually nor emotionally prepared. He wanted her to be well read, informed, and intellectual, to be able to entertain well and frequently, to maintain a job, to rear children, and to care for the household. She was also to be submissive. If we examine this

[21] In fact, one writer, who feels strongly that the inability of spouses to meet each other's role expectations is a major source of marital maladjustment, suggests using a role analysis framework in order to study the dynamics of marital adjustments. See William G. Dyer, "Analyzing Marital Adjustment Using Role Theory," *Marr. Fam. Living*, **24**, 4 (1962), pp. 371–375.

man's concept of his wife's role, two things stand out. First, there are demands made here that most women would find difficult to fulfill. Furthermore, the demands are inconsistent. Thus this man expects his wife
to be well informed and to be concerned with intellectual matters, but
he also expects her to be submissive. Since this was a relatively uninformed girl of very average intelligence, who made little pretense about
what she was, the imposition of her husband's values caused considerable
conflict.

A good deal of marital difficulty is rooted in role conflict of the type
we have described. Prior to marriage or during marriage some of these
difficulties may be clarified by exploring, in the most serious and meaningful way, the concept that each has of the role of the other. Although
role concept exploration is a necessity, we recognize that few married
persons are prepared to deal with the difficulties in changing role concepts. As noted earlier, each member enters the marriage with a concept
of role, both for himself or herself and for the other. Such concepts of
role are to a lesser or greater extent woven into the fabric of personality
and are not easily changed. The reasons for the resistance to change are
rooted in several factors.

Resistance to Changes in Concepts of Role

Role concepts are difficult to change, first, because one's concepts of
husband, wife, father, or mother have emerged out of long interaction
with the adults in one's environment; indeed, they may have been derived from parental models, hence frequently have deep-seated emotional undertones. Changing a role concept about oneself or a spouse
often entails a reevaluation of a parental model from whom the role concept was derived. A husband's giving up of a patriarchal role concept, for
example, may entail the realization that his patriarchal father imposed
many undesirable decisions on those around him, and such realization
may be painful to accept.

Second, role concepts are difficult to change because they are rooted in
one's reference groups, that is, the groups with which one identifies.
Such groups may include friends, neighbors, or relatives. Reference
groups provide one with a value orientation and set of beliefs about
familial duties and obligations, and they also constitute a pressure for
conforming to group norms.

One man who entered marriage with the idea that men should not
assist their wives with chores around the home found that his wife held a
different view. After several discussions he agreed to assist his wife with
certain household tasks. However, when his friends learned about these

activities, they made remarks that cast reflections on his manliness. His need for acceptance by his group was so important that he immediately abandoned his efforts to assist his wife and returned to his privately held notions.

Third, in the process of growing up in a dynamic society, people seldom internalize merely one role concept of husband, wife, father, or mother; usually different concepts are acquired. For example, a male who has grown up in an authoritarian family will probably internalize a patriarchal concept of his role. It is equally possible that through interactions outside the home he also internalizes a democratic concept of the father's position in the home. The internalization of two diametrically opposite concepts of role results in a good deal of conflict. At times a man may be both authoritarian and democratic; and he may try to function as though there were no inconsistencies between patriarchal and democratic values. When conflict arises, he may be quite confused about what he believes, and this becomes manifest in his difficulty in understanding precisely what views have to be changed. Many men, for example, are willing to let their wives work or even pursue a career, an indication of a democratic view. Frequently such men are also quite adamant about their right to determine how such additional income should be spent. This attempt to integrate both authoritarian and democratic concepts of role without a clear understanding of how each contradicts the other lends itself to considerable difficulty and confusion.

Fourth, concepts of role are difficult to change because they reflect a person's values and represent the way in which he comes to terms with those around him. For example, the wife who views the husband's role as including major responsibility for all important decisions is expressing also her view about the position of men and women in the home. Therefore, any change in role concepts involves not only changes in a few items of behavior, such as whether one spouse or the other assumes a new responsibility, but very frequently also major changes in value concepts of men and women in general, which, being basic attitudes, are not easily uprooted.

Flexibility in Concepts of Role

The four variables that we have just discussed tend to work in the direction of minimizing change in role concepts. On the other hand, experiences of life and interactions with different persons constantly suggest different and alternative views of husband-wife relationships. In our age of mass media and marked personal mobility, almost every marital union is faced with new factors that suggest the possibility of revising what each partner expects of the other. The realization of such a likelihood is exceedingly important, for it can help orient a couple to anticipate changing views of roles as the marital union matures. Whereas in the past, in a society concerned with traditions, clinging to fixed concepts of family roles may have insured success, today such a pattern may well be responsible for failure. Hence one of the major tasks in middle-class marriage today involves the ability to maintain a flexibility in regard to concepts of role, in order that desirable changes may be integrated with a minimum of disruption to the persons and the marital union. It is particularly necessary to have an understanding of the implications of changes in concepts of role, for both the person and the family. For example, a young woman who had grown up in a patriarchal family was married to a man who was also reared in a patriarchal family. The wife, after engaging in reading and conversation with other women, announced one day that she was tired of being so subservient to a man and that she planned some changes in her home, both for herself and her husband. Rebelling against the patriarchal order, she abandoned all her responsibilities in the home—the washing, cooking, and caring for the children—and demanded that her husband perform these tasks. After a week of such rebellion she resumed her household responsibilities, but became very depressed and was sent for therapy. Her depression, as interpreted by her therapist, was caused by a sense of guilt about her actions. Although she had rebelled, she also felt that she had failed in her responsibilities to her husband and children.

This case clearly suggests that the woman, seeking a revision of role for herself and her husband, was not fully prepared to appreciate the complexities involved in producing change. She failed to work through the impact of her desired changes on others in the home and the effects that this might have on her.

Finally, it should be noted that any given marital relationship represents an accommodation between the persons and the experiences that each constantly brings into the marriage. While these external experiences may be threatening to the smooth functioning of a relationship, they may also make the marriage creative, that is, sensitive to individual needs and wishes as they emerge in a dynamic life setting.

Thus far we have dealt with three sources of value imposition: the belief that one's values are best, unrealized goals and ambitions, and the need to impose one's concept of role on the other partner.

A fourth source of imposition of values on the mate is one's idealized self-image, which is deeply anchored in the personality.[22] The idealized image develops early in life if the circumstances surrounding personal development are not conducive to the individual's acceptance of himself. The individual who as a child is rejected or not appreciated for what he is tends to create an idealized image in an attempt to make himself worthy and acceptable. He rejects what he is and creates an image of what he would like to be. The concept is not unlike Reiks' ego ideal (Chapter 6); we prefer to call it idealized image, which is a more descriptive term. An individual with an idealized image is in a constant state of anxiety, because he is both straining to fulfill the idealized image and fearful of not measuring up to it. Failure to measure up to the idealized image is of special concern, since it brings out self-contempt, contempt for what one is. The idealized image, being a concept of imagination, has a mixture of unreal components. For example, one of its major characteristics is perfection.[23] Thus the individual may think of himself as being all-knowing, all-kind, all-truthful, all-moral. Furthermore, he may demand of himself that he behave as though he were all-knowing, all-kind, all-truthful, and all-moral without regard for the circumstances involved. Such inner demands created by the idealized image are impossible to live up to, and the realization that one cannot live up to them may cause considerable anxiety and uncertainty about who and what one is. At this point the tendency is to feel that others are not living their lives properly and to find fault with them. At such times one may engage in considerable criticism of the marital partner. If, for example, the wife has an idealized image in which she sees herself as a woman of power and high status, she may focus on factors of power and status in her husband's life. Thus she may express dissatisfaction about how her husband is progressing in his work, even though objectively he may be doing quite well. She may complain that her husband has not received promotion as rapidly as he should or that he has not received salary advances as often as others. If the wife's idealized image contains the idea of being all-knowing, she may externalize this component on her husband and expect him to solve all her problems. If the husband's idealized image contains moral perfectionism, he may externalize this on his wife and expect her never to smoke or laugh at an off-color story under any and all circumstances or always to tell the truth regardless of circumstances. When the idealized image is imposed on the marital partner, shortcomings become readily apparent and criticisms are made about these.

[22] Karen Horney, *op. cit.*, pp. 24–25, 292.
[23] *Ibid.*, pp. 196–197.

In dealing with externalizations that stem from the idealized image, the couple must always assess the kinds of values that are necessary for stability in a marital union. Certain values, to be sure, are essential. In general, we can say that those values that will ultimately destroy the relationship cannot be tolerated. There must be confidence in the essential honesty, loyalty, and responsibility of the partners. Furthermore, there must be a relative commitment to the mutually agreed-on basic goals and values that the couple seek. Aside from these basic values, however, there is an entire area of life in which individual differences in values can function; and it is clearly destructive to a marital union when one imposes values on the other for the sake of maintaining certain immaturities.

The idealized image that one has constructed does not change easily or simply. It has grown out of very real needs in the development of the individual, and over a period of time it comes to give the individual a sense of significance. One will abandon the idealized image only if he feels that he will remain significant and worthwhile without it. When the marital union is characterized by acceptance of the individual, the relinquishing of the idealized image is facilitated. Barring this state of affairs, professional assistance might be sought in order that the implications of the idealized image for the stability of the marital relationship be thoroughly explored and examined.

Finally it is important to recognize that the criticisms in marriage, be they major or minor, are frequently manifestations of the externalizations that we have been describing in this chapter. Few people who externalize are aware of what they are doing; rather, they experience their behavior in terms of attempts to aid the other person to live a more effective life. They usually fail to see why they engage in externalizations and the implications of externalizations on the marital relationship.

The externalization patterns described are common in interactions both inside and outside marriage. Although they disturb human relationships of all types, they are particularly devastating for marital relationships where the intense and intimate contact brings the externalizations into operation quite early; such reactions to stress and tension can gnaw away at a marriage and make daily living a chore and a battleground for anger.

Externalizations in all their manifestations are seriously disruptive to the marital union, since they are subtle and nondramatic. They are the ongoing, recurrent complaints, accusations, and demands that can erode the basic foundation of the marital union.

Summary

Externalization is the tendency to blame others for one's tensions and to impose on them one's difficulties, values, wishes, and goals. Needless to say, externalization in marriage can create a great deal of marital conflict. Certain factors external to the marriage relationship, such as the competitive social order, a reexamination of one's goal commitments, the function of specialization, opportunities for self-development, and the social roles open to women in marriage, tend to create stress and may result in externalization. With respect to the social roles open to women in marriage, for example, it was noted that there are at least three such roles, the wife-mother role, the companion role, and the partner role. The existence of several different marital roles can produce a great deal of stress and result in externalizations when a woman (1) is uncertain about the role she would like to fulfill, (2) fulfills one role out of a sense of duty but would prefer to be fulfilling another role, (3) desires one role while her husband demands that she fulfill another, and (4) tries to combine several roles and thus confronts contradictions.

Other factors that tend to produce externalization are personality problems and immaturities. This can be seen, for example, in people whose need to impose their values on others arises out of their personal narrowness or their failure to have realized certain of their ambitions or goals.

It was suggested that individuals attempt to understand not only the part that external stress plays in their marital incompatibilities, but also the effect of the need to impose one's values on the marital partner. Once each of these leading contributors to externalization in marriage is understood, it is believed that marital incompatibilities can be dealt with more objectively and, consequently, more effectively.

Questions

1. In what ways may cultural background cause marital incompatibilities? Exemplify.

2. What is externalization? How exactly may it result in marital incompatibility? Give examples.

3. How may the role of specialization in the American society affect marital incompatibility?

4. In what way may the changing role of women in marriage bring about increased stress?

5. Some people feel that nothing they say during an argument should be taken seriously. How might such an attitude be damaging to a marital relationship?

6. What is likely to happen to a person who, not understanding the role that externalization plays in marital incompatibility, simply runs out of one marriage into another? Explain and exemplify.

7. List and discuss the three considerations in dealing with environmental stress in a marriage relationship.

8. List and discuss the four sources of value impositions. Give examples in each case.

9. What type of a marital climate may facilitate the relinquishing of the idealized image? Explain how this is possible.

Projects

1. Write and present a sociodrama about a marital conflict based primarily on externalization factors. After presenting the drama, have the class discuss it.

2. Have a debate on the following topic "The Modern American Wife-Mother Confronts More Stress Than Did the Early American Wife-Mother."

Suggested Readings

Berne, Eric, *Games People Play*, Grove Press, New York, 1964.

Burgess, Ernest W., Harvey J. Locke, and Mary Margaret Thomes, *The Family*, 3rd ed., American Book Company, New York, 1963, Ch. 18, "Family Conflicts and Accommodations."

Hill, Reuben, *Families Under Stress,* Harper and Brothers, New York, 1949.

Hollis, Florence, *Women in Marital Conflict,* Family Service Association of America, New York, 1949.

Hurvitz, Nathan, "Control Roles, Marital Strain, Role Deviation, and Marital Adjustment," *J. Marr. Fam.,* **27** (February 1965), pp. 29–31.

Jacobson, Alver Hilding, "Conflict of Attitudes Toward the Roles of the Husband and Wife in Marriage," *Am. soc. Rev.,* **17** (April 1952), pp. 146–150.

Magoun, F. Alexander, *Love and Marriage,* Harper and Brothers, New York, 1948, Ch. 10, "Emotional Adjustments."

Waller, Willard, *The Family,* revised by Reuben Hill, Dryden Press, New York, 1951, Ch. 14, "Bases of Marriage Conflict," and Ch. 15, "Processes of Conflict."

Chapter Fifteen

THE CHANGING
ROLE OF WOMEN
AND MEN

IN THE preceding chapter we noted the importance of agreement on role expectations in marriage. In this chapter we focus more directly on marital role expectations, particularly on the changes they are undergoing. Role change has been the subject of much writing over the years, with special emphasis on the changing role of women. Such emphasis, however, often results in failure to consider the implications of role changes for the total *man-woman relationship*. In this chapter, therefore, we discuss the changing roles of both women and men. We begin by examining what appear to be the roots of such role change in the United States, namely, the quest for emancipation among women.

Emancipation of Women

Women in the United States have long been rebels. In fact, the earliest women dissidents were not champions of their sex, but carried the banners of many causes. Sometimes rebellion took the form of an antireligious expression; this was especially the case with those who saw certain Biblical teachings as being responsible for much of the social and political degradation of women. Elizabeth Stanton, an early feminist who was extremely anticlerical, exemplifies the latter group; she repeatedly asked, "Why Should We Not Pray to Our Mother Who Art in Heaven, As Well As to Our Father." [1]

Other causes included antislavery, championed by the Female Anti-Slavery Societies, temperance, pacifism, slum clearance, immigrant assistance, settlement house development, and birth control. The significance of these causes for the present discussion is that they often provided opportunities for the expression of social protest. It is especially important to note that almost all of the causes themselves were unpopular among a large segment of the population, *male and female*. The fact that men were often unwilling to support these issues may have created a *vacuum* in leadership which some women readily filled.

Thus it was during participation in movements of social protest that the great debate concerning the rights of women was born, and feminist movement in the United States got under way. [2]

Women's Education

In addition to social issues, another opportunity for the expression of growing female emancipation was provided by education. [3] Formal efforts appear early in the nineteenth century. Emma Willard founded a female seminary in 1821 in Troy, New York; Mary Lyon founded Mount Holyoke in 1837. This was followed by the emergence of a number of other colleges and universities that opened their doors to women. Some of these were not coeducational, but were established for the sole

---

[1] Elizabeth Stanton, *The Revolution,* July 30, 1868.

[2] Many of the early feminists in America were Quakers. Andrew Sinclair, *The Emancipation of the American Woman,* Harper and Row, New York, 1966, p. 26. This was probably due to the fact that the Quakers traditionally gave boys and girls an equal education, and education was a major preoccupation of the feminists. Other factors associated with feminism were the Married Woman's Property Acts in the 1840s, the fight to get the vote, which was won sometime later, and the demands for equal treatment within factory unions.

[3] Mary Clay, "Arguments before the Judiciary Committee of the House of Representatives by a Committee of the Sixteenth Annual Convention of N.W.S.A.," Washington, D.C., March 8, 1884.

purpose of educating women. The establishment of women's colleges tended to be the pattern in the East, where Vassar, Wellesley, Smith, Bryn Mawr, and Radcliffe were founded; Swathmore, although Eastern, was founded on the principle of coeducation. The coeducational pattern predominated in the West during the early period. Oberlin College was the first to admit students without regard to their color or sex and as such played an important part, not only in the antislavery movement, but in the early feminist movement as well. Other institutions that permitted women to enroll included Antioch, Iowa State, Wisconsin, Northwestern, Michigan, Illinois, and Ohio State.

At first, particularly in the early women's academies, the major emphasis in educating women was on making well-to-do girls more ladylike. However, this orientation was soon changed, and the differences between education for men and that for women became increasingly more difficult to find. The shift in the content emphasis in women's education became more pronounced after strides had been made in the feminist movement; it was during the 1920s, when women were feeling their first full flush of freedom, that feminism was in its most antimale phase. To be an educated woman was now interpreted as having the opportunity to serve mankind, not through *marriage* and *motherhood,* which traditionally had been regarded as woman's primary services to society, but through a professional career. Indeed, the roots of this negative reaction to marriage and motherhood are seen as early as 1851 in the writings of Harriet Taylor:

> Numbers of women are wives and mothers only because there is no other career open to them. . . . To say that women must be excluded from active life because maternity disqualifies them for it, is in fact to say that every other career should be forbidden them, in order that maternity may be their only resource.[4]

Education and Marriage

In spite of the antimotherhood and antimarriage emphasis, marriage was far from outmoded. Nevertheless, in the 1930s it was not unusual to find letters between educated women that contained apologetic references to their having succumbed to the temptations of romance.[5] Thus began the woman's effort to combine marriage with traditional education, an education more or less equal to that of her marital partner. The

[4] Harriet Taylor, "The Enfranchisement of Women," *Westminster and Foreign Quarterly Review,* July 1851.
[5] See: Andrew Sinclair, *op. cit.,* pp. 358–359.

conflict about women's rights became increasingly expressed in marriage itself, especially in the 1940s, 1950s, and 1960s. Study after study suggests that the growing numbers of women who are receiving college and graduate educations today have every intention of marrying.[6] Today's dilemma, therefore, seems to lie not in the right of women to *receive an education,* but rather in how education is to be employed and integrated into marriage.

Part of the growing emphasis on the right of women to use their education is reflected in the trend toward greater and greater numbers of women in today's labor market. For many women participation in the labor market becomes a serial-type participation, that is, they tend to work before their children arrive and again after their children are grown and have left the home.

Implications

The changing role of women, as reflected by educational and career changes, carried with it certain potential problems in the form of differing views of husband and wife. Some studies show that many husbands accept the fact that their wives are gainfully employed,[7] and some husbands of working wives report that they have altered their own role tasks to better fit the duties of their wives.[8] In a recent book, however, it is noted that there may be a difference between how men say they respond to a wife's employment and how they actually do respond.[9] In fact, it is claimed that lower-class men tend to concede *fewer rights ideologically*

[6] More women are enrolled in college today than during any earlier period. However, proportionately speaking, fewer college enrollees today are women. In the 1920s approximately 50 percent of college enrollees were women, whereas during the 1950s this figure fell to approximately 35 percent; it has risen to around 40 percent during the 1960s. See, for example, Carol N. Doty and Ruth M. Heoflin, "A Descriptive Study of Thirty-Five Unmarried Graduate Women," *J. Marr. Fam.,* **26,** 1 (February 1964), pp. 91–94.

[7] Leland J. Axelson, "The Marital Adjustment and Marital Role Definitions of Husbands of Working and Non-Working Wives," *Marr. Fam. Living,* **25,** 2 (1963), pp. 189–195.

[8] Lois Wladis Hoffman, "Effects of the Employment of Mothers on Parental Power Relations and the Division of Household Tasks," *Marr. Fam. Living,* **22** (February 1960), pp. 27–35.

[9] William J. Goode, *World Revolution and Family Patterns,* The Free Press, Glencoe, Ill., 1963, p. 21.

than their women in fact have, whereas the more educated men are likely to *concede more rights* ideologically than, in fact, they grant. Nevertheless, even though expressing agreement in regard to their marital roles, many couples openly admit feelings of tension about their roles.

Tensions Arising Out of Changing Role Expectations

In some cases these tensions are related to differences between the husbands' and wives' expectations about the role each should be playing.[10] We discussed in the preceding chapter instances where the wife played the role of wife-mother, with its emphasis on home duties and child rearing, because her husband expected her to do so. Nevertheless, she may have preferred to continue her career and fulfill the partner role in marriage. We need not enumerate again the anxieties and problems that such disagreements can produce. Moreover, there are women who claim that they would like to fulfill a role other than the one they are fulfilling, but in reality may be frightened of the responsibilities. In one such case a woman who was trained as a teacher repeatedly stated her dissatisfaction at having to leave her career because her husband did not want her to work after marriage. In reality this woman had feelings of inadequacy about her teaching role, and she was simply using her marriage as a convenient excuse for escaping from these feelings. There are numerous instances of wives who perceive their husbands as forbidding them activities in which, in reality, they are deeply afraid to engage.[11]

In some cases the actual confrontation of opportunity may be quite devastating, particularly for those women who have to accept responsibility for themselves. Tensions here are not related to actual differences in role expectations, but rather to the need that some people have *to perceive* these differences as existing when indeed they do not exist. Thus the wife who seeks a new role and the husband who is willing to make a new role for his wife possible may each be contributing to tension and conflict if the wife is unprepared for the opportunity.

The question of why some women wish to see others as forbidding changes in role is quite complex. Such views may stem from pronounced feelings of inadequacy that have always been present. Many prefer living with the fantasy about what they might do to trying to do it, because of *a*

[10] For a discussion of the difficulties experienced by college women in attempting to accept the contradictory expectations made of them by the traditional roles and modern roles of women, see Mirra Komarovsky, "Cultural Contradictions and Sex Roles," *Am. J. Sociol.*, **52** (1946), pp. 184–189.

[11] Eric Berne, *Games People Play*, Grove Press, New York, 1964, pp. 50–58.

fear of failure. Such inner feelings can easily become externalized on the husband, who is then seen as being opposed to particular activities. Thus some women are attracted to domineering men, behind whose dominance they can hide their own inadequacies by imagining that their husbands are responsible for holding them back. These feelings of inadequacy, which sometimes force people to misperceive role expectations, have ramifications for the total man-woman relationship; some of these have been discussed in earlier chapters.

The Problem of Identity

For many women the historical changes that the roles of women have undergone have raised a fundamental problem that is far from being resolved. In a society that combines education and marriage, there is the problem of ascertaining what the role of married women should be, what it should stand for, what it should entail, and what its major responsibilities are. Also, does a woman have autonomy in selecting what she wants or is she simply the sum of what others expect? These are all problems of the woman's attempt to determine her identity. As already noted, the wife-mother, in addition to the traditional wife-mother role, now has at least two additional alternative roles: the partner role, in which the married woman is gainfully employed outside the home, and the companion role, in which the woman's primary responsibility is neither motherhood nor career, but rather being a social asset to her husband, usually through physical appearance and social behavior. Some women attempt to solve the problem of selecting a meaningful role by taking on the responsibilities of all three roles. Although a few remarkable women succeed in this, most women simply cannot; and the probability of failure increases because the demands are very great.

Indeed, the problem of women's identity and role conflict has become so acute that numerous writers have devoted their primary energies to advising women on the solution to this problem.

REMEDIES FOR THE "IDENTITY PROBLEM." Among myriad writings concerned with telling women how they can best use their fullest potential, two recent and well-known books are Betty Friedan's *The Feminine Mystique* and Phyllis McGinley's *Sixpence in Her Shoe.* These books are interesting because, when compared, they present a classic example of the polemics involved in the attempt to define the role of the married woman in today's society. Although both books claim to recognize that women may differ in their desires, abilities, and expectations, the primary message in *The Feminine Mystique* is that to make use of their fullest potential as human beings and become total individuals in marriage, women should employ their education for something other than reading recipes and children's fairy tales.

Friedan tells us that woman's intelligence and energies are to be used for some higher purpose than housework and thing-buying. "Perhaps," she says, "it is only a sick society, unwilling to face its own problems and unable to conceive of goals and purposes equal to the ability and knowledge of its member, that chooses to ignore the strength of women. Perhaps it is only a sick or immature society that chooses to make women 'housewives' not people. Perhaps it is only sick or immature men and women unwilling to face the great challenges of society, who can retreat for long, without unbearable distress into that thing-ridden house and make it the end of life itself." [12] The concept of the feminine mystique itself refers to the misconception that a woman's primary purpose in life is to concentrate her efforts on her marital and maternal roles. This misconception, according to Friedan, is internalized by most women as the ideal, while in reality most women are really interested in achieving more in their lives than marriage and motherhood. As a result, women frequently feel *extremely guilty* about having such *nonmarriage* and *nonmotherhood desires* and about not really wanting to live up to the ideal.

This problem, which Friedan sometimes refers to as the problem that has no name, is seen as significant in causing great psychological difficulties for women in our society. "We can no longer ignore the voice within women that says: 'I want something more than my husband and my children and my home." [13] Friedan suggests that women who are satisfied with the wife-mother role may be immature.[14] Upon publication the book was generally well received, and acclaim was won from important women in American society.[15] The fact that it won such wide acclaim is

[12] Betty Friedan, *The Feminine Mystique,* Dell Publishing Company, New York, 1963, p. 223.

[13] *Ibid.,* p. 27.

[14] *Ibid.,* p. 223.

[15] For example, Pearl Buck said: "Betty Friedan has, in my opinion, gone straight to the heart of the problem of the American woman." Millicent McIntosh, President Emeritus of Barnard College, said: "A serious and important book. Its implications are terrifying . . . a 'must' for all who are concerned with marriage and family life, or who care about the future of our society." Marya Mannes of the *New York Herald Tribune* said: "A damning indictment of the . . . pressures which have caused a harmful discrepancy between what women really are and what they are told they should be. . . . Mrs. Friedan charts a course for women. . . . Her suggestions are not only sensible but mandatory." It should be noted that all of these statements, which incidentally are quoted at the front of the Friedan book, are made by career women like Friedan herself. The statement of Mannes probably best uncovers the

further evidence of the extent to which women are vitally concerned with the dilemmas in the problem of identity and in role conflict.

The counterpart to this so-called remedy for the identity problem is a book that was on the *New York Times* bestseller list for months and is advertised as "the book that talks back to *The Feminine Mystique.*"

In *Sixpence in Her Shoe,* Phyllis McGinley defends the traditional woman's role:

So highly do I regard our profession and its importance to the human scheme, it seems to me occupation sufficient to fill a life, a heart. In an ideal society we would want no other work. Men would earn the bread, we would bring up the family. We should unsettle no masculine pride by competition in masculine fields, divert none of the male energy from its proper preoccupation with the business and discoveries of the public world. The two nations, male and female, would each inhabit a sphere snugly suited to its ordained capabilities.[16]

McGinley's solution to the identity problem is as follows:

I have sung then, and continue to sing, the worth of a domestic career in an age where it is terribly needed. We crave light and warmth in this century. Only the mother, the wife, can supply it for the home. To be a housewife is not easy. Ours is a difficult, a wrenching, sometimes an ungrateful job if it is looked on only as a job. Regarded as a profession, it is the noblest as it is the most ancient of the catalog. Let none persuade us differently or the world is lost indeed.[17]

Thus, we have another solution for women's identity problem—be a housewife. What has been written about this book is as interesting as the content of the book itself. The book jacket quotes the following statement from the *New York Times:* "Should be a joy and a boon to the downtrodden women of America who are being urged to get out there and land a job." To the general points made by Friedan and McGinley a third should be added. Eli Ginzberg, in his study of the life styles of educated women, reports that the educated American woman never had it so good. He argues that the American female has many choices open to her; more choices, in fact, than any man can possibly have. She can choose marriage, with or without children, higher education, career. The

major problem of the book, namely its purpose, which is that of charting a course for women to follow and then regarding this course not only as a sensible approach to achieving feminine identity but as a mandatory course.

[16] Phyllis McGinley, *Sixpence in Her Shoe,* Dell Publishing Company, New York, 1965, p. 44.

[17] *Ibid.,* p. 238.

woman today can actually do much as she pleases, without suffering criticism from anyone.[18]

Identity and Social Roles

It is clear that there are several major points of view regarding the plight of women. At least two advocate different solutions, and a third suggests that the choices are virtually without limit. Yet there is a basic confusion which must be clarified. Although the quest for identity and the search for satisfactory social roles are related, *they are not one and the same.* The search for identity is first and foremost a quest for "who am I and what am I?" Identity is present when one has answers to these questions, when one can consult with himself and know where he stands and what he believes. The woman with an identity knows what she stands for, what has meaning for her, and, ultimately, what she regards as significant in life. The problem of identity has plagued both men and women throughout history and has been an essential concern of all great religions and all significant philosophy. The question of who one is and what one stands for probably comes first and foremost out of a set of earlier human relationships in which one has developed *respect* and *regard* for one's sex, one's assets, one's qualities. The internalization of adult social roles may assist in this process, but cannot in itself overcome the deficits in personality development, a lack of identity, that may have occurred earlier in life and become manifest in *identity problems.* Social roles are only part of the drama, not its entirety. Roles are taken over, but in the process something of self is put into the role, be it wife, mother, or teacher, that produces differences in the way in which different persons fulfill it. Although all people who possess an identity are involved in taking over *social roles,* all people who take over roles do not necessarily possess an *identity.* The person who is merely a reflection of *social roles* is probably lacking an identity.

Many of the problems and much of the conflict that women experience today are *essentially issues of identity,* compounded by a rapidly changing society which has thrown even their traditional role and image into a state of uncertainty.

Implications

The implications of what we have pointed out are serious and significant, because many women who are searching for an *identity* hope to

[18] Eli Ginzberg, *Life Styles of Educated Women,* Columbia University Press, New York, 1966.

find it with a particular social role or set of roles. Herein lies the major source of disturbance. Identity has to be established first. If the problem of identity were resolved initially, several things could ensue. First, one would allow real feelings to emerge when attempting to fulfill new roles, instead of repressing feelings, as is common for persons who lack an identity. If people were in touch with their real wishes and feelings, disturbances about role conflict might be markedly reduced. The dilemma lies in *searching for an identity* by filling the vacuum with one or another role—a search that is probably doomed to failure.

Insofar as we are correct, there is no single role that is equally suitable for all women. Yet in view of the idea of democratic individualism, discussed in earlier chapters, those with an identity might feel that one has the right to make a choice of role in marriage *without the need to harbor guilt.*

Implications for Men

Since a role involves rights and duties and implies that one's rights are another's duties, unless husbands feel it their duty to recognize the rights that wives acquire, confusion reigns in marriage.

This relationship between husbands' and wives' roles means that if flexibility in role choices is permitted, women must have husbands who are able to accept the role that their wives choose. Each of the roles open to women in marriage, if it is to be effectively utilized and implemented, requires certain types of duties and rights on the part of the husband; [19] the same applies to the male role in marriage. Clark Vincent notes that the time has come for us to conceive of homemaking as a husband-wife role, rather than as a strictly wife role.[20] Such shifts in role concepts may be expected to occur at a relatively slow pace.[21]

Moreover, it is as important for men as for women to have an identity and to know what they stand for, what has meaning for them, and what is significant in their lives. Therefore, the change in the husband's role that

[19] The exception here is the husband who, even though his wife is gainfully employed outside the home, continues to regard his wife as playing only the wife-mother role and does not alter his own role at all. Consequently, the wife has the impossible job of performing all of the tasks of the wife-mother in addition to those demanded by her partner role.
[20] Clark E. Vincent, "Role Clarification for the Contemporary College-educated Woman," *J. Home Econ.,* 45 (October 1953), pp. 567–570.
[21] Leland J. Axelson, *loc. cit.;* P. G. Herbst, "The Measurement of Family Relationships," *Human Relat.,* 5, 1 (1952), pp. 3–35; Robert Blood, Jr., "Long Range Causes and Consequences of the Employment of Married Women," *J. Marr. Fam.,* 27, 1 (1965), pp. 43–47.

is necessitated by the choices presently offered women in marriage will be made more readily by men whose identity is not based on the superficial foundation of simply adhering to the "traditional male role." The degree to which identity is present in a given situation may, at least in part, help to explain why some husbands seem to experience little anxiety when performing or sharing household tasks previously regarded as being primarily female tasks, while others show a great deal of it under the same conditions. Just as in the case of women, social roles do not give men a sense of identity. Thus adaptation to the role behaviors required by a changing social setting will be effected with a minimal degree of tension and strain only to the extent that persons, male or female, have a sense of security in what they represent. A role consensus and a sense of flexibility is required; the partners must be prepared to accept changes in each other and to respond positively to constructive changes if and when they occur. Mature people encounter little difficulty under these conditions, but the less mature relationships may well be devastated by such blurring of the marital roles.

It may be that in a setting where men and women can be made to feel free to express their desires concerning their marital behaviors, fewer women and men will feel trapped by the mandatory roles set for them by society. And, perhaps, with freedom to exchange through dialogue one's ideas of the ideal role, people may come to objectify their search for roles, grasping the real expectations, responsibilities, and skills that some roles require and the rewards that they offer.

There are probably certain tasks in marriage for which either the wife or the husband is considered to be best suited, whatever role each otherwise fulfills. This can be seen most clearly in mother-infant relationship. The process of carrying the child and giving birth offers the opportunity for a very special relationship out of which the significance of trusting and loving can emerge. Although it is theoretically conceivable to remove the child from the mother after birth and turn responsibility over to the father, the norms of our society do not provide for it and considerable reshifting of roles would be needed to accomplish it. We are not arguing the question of whether adequate mother substitutes can be found, but are simply saying that our society has not yet accepted the pattern. The mature and integrated mother, who cares for her infant with sensitivity and tenderness, may well perform a task that men are in some sense incapable of. Likewise, it is doubtful that the woman can in any majority of cases expect to assume the major burden of providing for the family without some basic shifts in the orientation of American society.

Beyond such minimum requirements of both husband and wife, however, a wide range of alternatives exist from which a person can choose the manner in which to fulfill his or her role. The wife-mother role, for example, is a complex one and can be variously performed. Much of what is written by those who accept the negative view of Friedan suggests at bottom *a contempt for and a lack of understanding of* the complexities involved in the wife-mother role. Seeing the requirements of this role in light of basic household management, preparation of meals, and similar tasks, important though they are, is at best a limited view of what is involved. The job of being a mature and responsible wife and mother requires a level of integration that few possess. It involves the capacity to relate effectively to husband and children and requires both knowledge and emotional integration. Witness the extent of mental illness, alcoholism, and other forms of deviance that in some basic sense originate within the home from defective relationships. One might argue that rejection by the woman of the wife-mother role and pursuit of other roles may well be based on a combination of ignorance and self-rejection.

A woman may reject a *wife-mother* role for a variety of good reasons. The assertion that it affords the woman little opportunity for creative expression is not true. More to the point is the fact that many men and women in our society may not overtly recognize the significance of the wife-mother contribution. Such lack of recognition undoubtedly affects the woman's perception of her own place; especially the woman *without an identity* is apt to be excessively *sensitive* to this lack of recognition.

Summary

In this chapter we discussed the changes that are occurring in marital roles and related these changes to the role changes of men and women occurring in society generally. The historical changes in the role of women have created other roles for women in marriage than the traditional one of wife-mother. The choice of the additional roles of partner and companion that women now have in marriage frequently leads to tensions and anxieties between husbands and wives if they do not agree on role expectations or if one of them is confused about the marital role he or she wants to play. Note particularly that we say "he or she." This is important, because quite frequently the emphasis in considering role change in marriage is on the woman's role, without adequate attention being given to the fact that changes in the role of women in marriage entail changes in those of men as well.

The popular literature, in fact, almost ignores the changing role of men in marriage while giving a great deal of attention to the changing role of women. However, even the problems arising from the changing roles of women tend to be treated in terms of polemics. Thus some authors suggest that women would be happiest if they fulfilled their potential, not by remaining housewives, but by developing their talents for use in professional careers, which they should pursue in addition to marriage, while others suggest that the true fulfillment of women is in the role of housewife alone.

In regard to these "solutions" to women's identity problem two factors were noted. First, although identity and social roles are related, they are not one and the same. It was suggested that as a person develops a sense of identity (i.e., who am I and what do I stand for?) the role that he plays merely becomes a reflection of this identity, and not a creator of it.

Second, the need to consider the changing role of men in marriage was reemphasized. The male's sense of identity, or lack of it, may be the decisive factor in determining the degree of tension and anxiety he may experience in accepting role change in his spouse or, indeed, in achieving role change for himself.

Finally, it should be noted that role flexibility and consensus about marital role expectations require persons who have developed a sense of identity; mature, responsible persons effect mature, responsible marriages. This is particularly true in a society that is undergoing interesting and challenging changes.

Questions

1. In what ways have women in the United States been longtime rebels?
2. Discuss the historical relationship between women's education and marriage in the United States. Note specifically the impact that this relationship has had on marital roles.
3. In what way does a change in the role of women in marriage affect the role of men? Give examples.
4. Discuss and assess the suggestions that have been made by some authors for resolving the women's identity problem.

5. What is identity? What is a social role? How is identity related to social role? Give examples.

6. Discuss what you believe will occur in the future regarding the roles of men and women in society generally. Support your answer with whatever facts you can find.

7. Discuss how the roles of men and women in society generally, which you noted in your previous answer, may affect marriage and marital roles. Again, support your answer with whatever facts you can find.

Projects

1. Select two marriages with which you are acquainted, one in which the wife is successfully playing the wife-mother role and one in which the wife is successfully playing the partner role. Analyze the role tasks of the husband and wife in each of these marriages and compare your findings in the first marriage with those in the second marriage. What do you conclude from your comparison?

2. Poll your fellow students (both married and unmarried) about the expectations that they have concerning their own roles in marriage as well as those of their spouses. Do most people in your sample intend to marry? Do you feel that the expectations of their own roles take into account the impact that this will have on the role of the spouse? Do you feel that the expectations of those in your sample have an appreciation for the need for consensus and flexibility in regard to marital roles? Do you note any differences between the expectations of (a) the men and the women and (b) the married and the unmarried?

Suggested Readings

Blood, Robert O., Jr., and Donald M. Wolfe, *Husbands and Wives,* The Free Press, New York, 1960, especially Ch. 2, "The Power to Make Decisions," and Ch. 3, "The Division of Labor."

Friedan, Betty, *The Feminine Mystique,* Dell Publishing Company, New York, 1st Dell Printing February 1964.

Kirkpatrick, Clifford, *The Family as Process and Institution*, 2nd ed., Ronald Press, New York, 1963, especially Chs. 7 and 17.

McGinley, Phyllis, *Sixpence in Her Shoe*, Dell Publishing Company, New York, 1st Dell Printing October 1965.

Udry, J. Richard, *The Social Context of Marriage*, Lippincott, New York, 1966, especially Ch. 13, "Sex-Role Differentiation in Marriage."

Williamson, Robert C., *Marriage and Family Relations*, Wiley, New York, 1966, especially Ch. 6, "Differences in Sex Roles."

Chapter Sixteen

PARENTS
AND IN-LAWS

IN SEVERAL sections of this book we have dealt with the role of parents in the various stages of one's personal and social development. That parents play a crucial part in what an individual becomes should be abundantly clear. In the course of his development, parents come to deal with him in particular ways and he in turn learns to respond to them in particular ways. Thus characteristic patterns of relationships emerge between parents and children. These patterned relationships are an outgrowth of several factors, including the dependency needs of the child on the mother, and vice versa, the quality of the relationship between the parents, and the emotional maturity of the parents. In this chapter we discuss some of the implications of these parent-child relationships as they pertain to one's personal development and to the development of one's marriage.

Family Variables Affecting Relationships with Parents

In the mother-child relationship there are certain factors that almost always offer the possibility of each becoming overly dependent on the other for the gratification of needs. The human infant has probably the

ILLUSTRATION: Side view of the Brett Doll House, 1830–1840. Courtesy of the Museum of the City of New York.

longest period of dependency on its mother of all members of the animal kingdom. Under these circumstances it is inevitable that the infant becomes conditioned to depend on its mother for the gratification of its basic physical and emotional needs and that the mother looks forward to the pleasure that she may derive from being involved in the satisfaction of the infant's needs. Although the development of some dependency between mother and child is to be expected, the likelihood that the extent of such dependency will reach an unhealthy point, that is, that each will become overly dependent on the other, is increased when the husband-wife relationship is lacking in basic satisfactions.

If the husband-wife relationship is unsatisfactory for whatever reasons, one or both parents tend to compensate by an excessive preoccupation with their children. Although the husband-father may become excessively involved with his children, most often it is the wife-mother who does so; [1] before discussing this point in more detail, let us look at the problem of marital dissatisfaction.

The reasons for marital dissatisfactions may run the gamut of all types of incompatibility described in preceding chapters. A common factor in producing marital dissatisfaction among the American middle class, however, centers in the value orientation of many middle-class husbands and wives. Frequently these people are concerned with acquiring and maintaining position and wealth. The husband, who has the major involvement in these pursuits, may spend a great deal of time away from home at his business or office in the effort to consolidate his socioeconomic position and to improve it when the opportunity presents itself. Considerable time and energy may also be spent in cultivating desirable social contacts and in maintaining membership in the proper clubs, since these are important assets for the male who wishes to "get ahead." The middle-class woman, who is often not adverse to the male's orientation, faces certain consequences as a result. Frequently she finds herself living a lonely and dissatisfied life with a husband who is seldom home. When the home is located in the suburbs several hours removed from the husband's place of employment, the extent and frequency of the husband's absence may be further increased. A woman who finds herself in this plight, and who experiences marital dissatisfaction as a result, may well be at a loss to understand her difficulty. For, indeed, in terms of her own middle-class orientation, her husband's preoccupation with social status fulfills many of her own social expectations; she has often been taught that happiness is, after all, often dependent on social and material success. At a deeper interpersonal level she may sense that something has

---

[1] Geoffrey Gorer, *The American People,* Norton, New York, 1948, p. 54.

happened to her marriage, but is unable to identify the difficulty; she may also be quite confused about whether her personal dissatisfactions should be verbalized to her husband. Her husband may be equally confused if he is accused of failing in the family responsibilities, since in his own view his socioeconomic pursuits are precisely the concerns that a good husband should have. He sees himself as a self-sacrificing, hardworking husband who is trying to provide his family with all they need. Thus he may be unable to see the full impact of his behavior on his family; and he may be unresponsive and unsympathetic to complaints from his wife, or his family, about his failure to fulfill the emotional component of his role as husband and father. When these problems are compounded by personal immaturity, family life becomes even more difficult. This condition in the more economically secure families may be related to the emotional disturbances that some children growing up in these families experience.

Maternal or Paternal Overprotection—A Prelude to In-Law Difficulties

The kind of marital relationship that has just been described has certain consequences. First, the mother may become so absorbed in the lives of her growing children that she rejects, for all practical purposes, the possibility of reexamining the relationship with her husband. (To reexamine one's relationship is no simple task, to be sure, since it usually involves a drastic revision of values and perspectives; nevertheless, some people are able to make such revisions in their way of life and thereby improve the quality of their marriages.) Or she may become so preoccupied with her children that she abandons herself as a person. She may neglect her health and give up her own interests in her excessive concern with her children.

Why does the mother abandon herself and become overly preoccupied with her children? All emotionally healthy people desire recognition and a place of some importance in the lives of those dear to them. When this recognition is not forthcoming in the home, a male can turn to areas outside the home, whereas the woman's opportunities for such recognition outside the home are usually much more restricted. The male may find recognition in his occupation and profession; he is also less restricted in his personal behavior and may find socially acceptable diversions from an unhappy marriage. Of course, this does not mean that there are no overprotective fathers. Some men, in spite of other acceptable diversions from an unhappy marriage, choose, nevertheless, to ignore these diversions and to concentrate attention on their children, through whom they obtain their primary rewards. In our society, however, the middle-class mother who is unhappy and dissatisfied has fewer compensations than the father. She can pursue a career only if she is properly trained and so oriented. She may become an active "joiner" and "clubwoman," but even here the satisfactions are limited, since competition for status in these organizations may be quite intense. One of the most feasible roles, therefore, into which she can pour all her energies, is the role of mother; it is the one role in which she is most likely to achieve success and a sense of significance in the lives of her children.[2] Hence this role becomes a compensation for a poor marital relationship. Although the preoccupation with children may have healthy and responsible proportions at first, it often develops into maternal overprotection, especially if the mother herself has had an unhappy childhood.[3] Such overprotection results in a pervasive effort to restrict the child's experiences by taking over many of the responsibilities that should be the child's. Why does the mother, who has had an inadequate relationship with her husband, overprotect? First, such mothers often feel trapped in the marriage, without much understanding of its problems. Hence they tend to become quite hopeless about their ability to deal with the circumstances of life, and they come to feel that the adversities of life are so overwhelming that without excessive parental protection the child will come to some disaster. Second, these mothers tend to believe that their efforts will bring affirmation and give them a sense of importance and significance. In all of this activity on the child's behalf, there is an unconscious agreement that the mother often expects the child to fulfill. It goes something like this: "I have sacrificed for you, and it is, therefore, your responsibility to repay me by continued affirmation, by affording me a significant place in your life, and by abiding by my wishes." It is easy to see how an overprotective mother with such views can become excessively concerned with what the child does, how he performs at school, whether he eats, what he eats, and so on and on. When the child begins to demonstrate an interest in the opposite sex, more parental anxiety may be aroused, since this signifies a concern for relationships that will ultimately remove the child from the home. Thus interference in dating patterns and discouragement of involvements with members of the opposite sex are common. One study that examined the attempts of parents to interfere with the courtships of their sons and daughters found

[2] Marvin B. Sussman, "The Help Pattern in the Middle-Class Family," *Am. soc. Rev.*, **18** (February 1953), pp. 22–28.

[3] David M. Levy, "Maternal Overprotection and Rejection," *Arch. Neurol. Psychiat.*, **25** (April 1931), pp. 886–894.

not only that such interference is quite common, but that it is more likely to be done by the mother.[4]

At best, many parents, both mothers and fathers, who have not emancipated themselves from their children interpret a love interest of their son or daughter as a threat to the perpetuation of the family unit and react with apprehension. Frequently such apprehension takes the form of hypercriticism toward those with whom an involvement takes place. When a serious involvement that may lead to marriage appears, such a parent may become unusually disturbed; this requires understanding. A parent who has built his life around a child may be faced with a terrible void when the child leaves. This is particularly the case when a mother has neglected to revitalize her own relationship with her husband. Upon the marriage of her son or daughter, she may be faced with the need to reestablish a union with a husband for whom she no longer cares. She may find it necessary to undo many personal habits that have been responsible for alienating her husband. All of this may be quite formidable and painful.

Some women of the type we have described behave quite childishly when confronted with the marriage of their child. In one instance, for example, at the wedding of her daughter, a woman was told by her pastor that "this is a happy occasion for all; especially for you and your husband, since now you will have an opportunity to do many things with one another that you were not free to do before." Since the pastor was unaware of the deteriorated state of the marital relationship, he was very surprised at the hostility that this elicited from the woman. She replied rather indignantly that she had always done things with her husband and that she resented the insinuation that she had not. Having blurted this out, she sensed the inappropriateness of her reaction and apologized profusely. Those who knew the woman more intimately understood why she was so touchy and defensive. She reacted as she did precisely because she was now without any appropriate diversion and would be forced to confront the rather meaningless relationship that she shared with her husband.

The small middle-class family is particularly vulnerable to the pattern of unhealthy emotional involvement, since the overprotective mother can concentrate all of her attention on only one or two children. In a large family, maternal emotional involvements are dispersed among a greater number of children, thereby restricting the likelihood of an excessive attachment to only one child. Unless children are unusually

4 Alan Bates, "Paternal Roles in Courtship," *Social Forces*, **20** (May 1942), pp. 483–486.

astute and can see the consequences of such maternal interference, they are likely to confront two things: first, a feeling of helplessness with respect to doing things on their own and, second, a pervasive feeling of guilt when their wishes run counter to the wishes of their parents, since they have been impressed with the sacrifices that their mothers have made on their behalf. In the process of growing up, young people may deal with this problem in one of several ways. There are those who sense the unhealthy component and fight it off. Thus, after some struggle, the child emancipates himself in a healthy way. He comes to have a healthy realization of his rights and those of his parents. There are others who react with rebellious behavior and reject the parent. They become hostile in varying degrees and, in extreme cases, may decline to have anything to do with their parents. Still others accept the overprotection; they accept the idea of being helpless; they abandon their own wishes and feel perpetually guilty when they have wishes of their own that are different from those of their parents. Neither rebellion nor acceptance of overprotection is likely to lead to successful resolutions, and both cause difficulties in the person's own marriage. The rebellious person may attempt to reject his parents, but generally there is a pervasive guilt about having done this, which can plague the individual for many years. This not only creates inner conflict, but may also disturb his relationship with his spouse.

There is the case of a young married man who had openly rejected both his parents. He saw his mother as one who was interested in "tying him to her apron strings." After a series of violent arguments he left home and married without inviting his parents to the wedding. After the wedding he moved to a location far away from his parental home; he claimed that he was very satisfied with this arrangement and refused to answer mail from home. After his first child was born, he became ambivalent about his decision to reject his mother. He wanted his parents to see his first child. For a number of months he was quite depressed, anxious, and prone to pick fights with his wife. The general domestic situation had deteriorated considerably before the husband and wife both agreed that a solution to the parental problem was mandatory if the marital arguments were to diminish. At this point professional assistance was sought, which over an extended period of time aided the husband in understanding his difficulties in relation to his parents.

Accepting the overprotection without any effort to emancipate oneself is even more devastating, since it dooms one to a life of feelings of inadequacy and feelings of guilt whenever parental wishes are not adhered to. Such an existence can be quite crippling and restricts the assumption of responsibility for oneself. There are numerous cases of individuals who have learned to think of themselves as inadequate. Frequently they feel entitled to be excused from the demands that life makes. Moreover, since they feel helpless, they may consider unfair any requests that they work and support themselves or their families. They may even consider it unfair that they are expected to assume responsibility for their mistakes and errors in judgment.

It should be pointed out that once the individual feels helpless, his demands on a mother or father and others may become so excessive that the parents' life and the lives of others become increasingly chaotic.

If neither rebellion nor the acceptance of overprotection is a satisfactory solution, how does one come to terms with his overprotective parents? First, by accepting the fact that one's parents are as they are, not necessarily because of their own choosing, but because of the way in which life has dealt with them. Second, by avoiding complete rejection of one's parents through an acceptance of those things that further a mature relationship with the parent, rejecting only those aspects of behavior that restrict the development of a mature relationship. This can only be done, however, when the parents and children have some measure of autonomy; that is, when each feels that he has a right to choose the course of action that he wants rather than finding it necessary to be compliant to the wishes of the other.

Maternal or Paternal Rejection—Another Prelude to In-Law Difficulties

In our discussion we have so far concentrated on how an inadequate parental marriage may lead to parental overprotection and all the consequences thereof. However, it is important to remember that an inadequate parental marriage may also result in a parent's rejection of the child. What are the consequences here? In some instances the parent who recognizes this tendency in himself may, out of a sense of guilt, immediately attempt to compensate for this by becoming overly concerned with the child. Thus overprotection is again the result. However, even in cases where compensation is not the major mechanism involved, the rejection of a child is seldom total. Instead, it usually takes the form of ambivalence, with alternate feelings of rejection and efforts at trying to make up; this might be regarded as a partial compensation for the rejection. Needless to say, all of this can be very devastating for the child, since it leaves him with a pervasive feeling of doubt and uncertainty as to where he stands. The child who feels uncertain about his parental relationship may react with a compulsive need to please them, which results in abandonment of his own wishes. But parents who are ambivalent toward their children are, indeed, difficult to please.

In-Law Difficulties

In-law difficulties are of two types—short-term problems and long-term problems. The short-term in-law problems are usually resolved during the early years of marriage. Since they stem from the insecurities experienced by some young people in their newly-acquired marital roles, they diminish as the insecurity diminishes. However, while the insecurities are present young people can become quite upset by even the most innocent behaviors of their in-laws, whom they regard as competitors for the attention and approval of their spouses. Such a simple behavior as a mother baking her son's favorite pie and presenting it to the young couple may be regarded by the young wife as her mother-in-law's attempt to show her ineptness in baking; and many are the young men who feel very uncomfortable by manifestations of the financial success of their fathers-in-law. As these young people become more secure with each other in their marital roles, however, they are able to see the behaviors of their in-laws in a less subjective light, and these types of in-law problems tend to subside.

The second type of in-law problems are called long-term because they do not subside with time. In fact, they may even increase with time. They are caused by the interpersonal problems between parents and children that we have already discussed. For example, parental overprotectiveness when the child marries becomes an in-law problem. And when both partners have unresolved parental problems of this type, the situation becomes extremely complicated.[5]

The Nature of Long-Term In-Law Involvements

If a parent still needs to control the life of his grown, married offspring, one can expect a good deal of parental involvement in several areas of the young adult's married life. Furthermore, such involvement will actually be encouraged by the offspring who has not achieved eman-

---

[5] All of this may be aggravated by the fact that young people tend to enter marriage with extremely negative attitudes toward the mother-in-law, attitudes that may be the result of the American stereotype of a mother-in-law as being mean, meddlesome, and miserable. See Evelyn Millis Duvall, *In-Laws: Pro and Con,* Association Press, New York, 1954, Ch. 2.

Table 13 The In-Law Named Most Difficult by 1337 Persons[a]

Most Difficult In-Laws	Percent
Mother-in-law	36.8
Sister-in-law	20.3
Brother-in-law	5.4
Father-in-law	5.0
Daughter-in-law	2.8
Other female in-laws	1.6
"All in-laws"	1.5
Son-in-law	0.7
Other male in-laws	0.1
No difficult in-laws	25.8
Total	100.0

[a] Evelyn Millis Duvall, *In-Laws: Pro and Con*, Association Press, New York, 1954, p. 188.

cipation from his parents. In this regard recent studies show that the tendency to bring the mother into marital conflicts is more frequent among young wives, since they are found to be less emancipated from their mothers than are their husbands.[6]

The in-law involvements may focus on what kind of a place the couple reside in, how the home is furnished, how the couple spend their time, how they entertain their friends, how they spend their money, what style of clothes each wears, how often they visit parents, and how long they stay.

In order to fully understand the nature of long-term in-law involvements, however, it is less important to concentrate on the types of symptomatic problems they can produce than to consider the sources from which these involvements emanate. In this regard, we have already discussed at some length the relationship between faulty parental marriages and in-law involvements. There are additional sources of in-law involvements, however, which for the most part are described in the psychological and psychiatric literature. Let us look at some of these.

Mothers or fathers who are emotionally immature and are fearful about relating to people often lead very sheltered lives. Such parents become emotionally attached to a son or daughter and find it very painful to sever the psychic ties with their children. Unable to make such a break, they often regard the marriage of their child with utmost anxiety.

[6] Mirra Komarovsky, "Continuities in Family Research: A Case Study," *Am. J. Sociol.*, **62** (July 1956), pp. 42–47.

Indeed, if they are unable to prevent the marriage, they tend to keep a critical eye on the marriage and frequently make excessive demands on their daughter-in-law or son-in-law to ensure that all the wishes of their son or daughter continue to be fulfilled as adequately as in the past.

Moreover, some psychoanalysts report that an insecure mother may actually become jealous of her daughter, because she, the mother, may find herself romantically attracted to her son-in-law. Such attraction, however, is so socially unacceptable to her that she must reject it, turning it into a strong dislike for the son-in-law.[7]

Finally, a parent who has been frustrated in his professional ambitions may make excessive demands on his child whom he has come to regard as a means of vicariously fulfilling his own ambitions. When the child marries, there may be a good deal of berating of the son-in-law or daughter-in-law by the parent and a tendency to constantly remind the son or daughter about the spouse's shortcomings.

Parental dissatisfactions of this type are especially likely because of the high degree of upward mobility in our society today. The existence of social mobility in general also makes possible the selection of a mate from a different cultural background and with different values. This means that not only differences in the value patterns held by the marital partners will have to be accommodated, but also those between the individual and his in-laws.

All of these difficulties should suggest the greatest caution in deciding to live with in-laws for any period of time, since the problems that we have described may become intensely aggravated when living together.[8] Furthermore, several aspects of the newlyweds' marital adjustment may be delayed by living with parents and in-laws. The opportunity to reach independent decisions may be greatly retarded. Adjustment, in sexual relations, which require freedom and spontaneity for maximum enjoyment, may be blocked when the environment cannot be properly controlled. Thus, in general, the speed with which a couple mature in terms of marital obligations and responsibilities is reduced.

In one case a young man brought his wife home to live with his

---

[7] For a full discussion of the psychoanalytic factors involved, see John C. Flugel, *The Psychoanalytic Study of the Family*, International Psychoanalytic Press, London and New York, 1921.

[8] George Simpson, *People in Families*, Thomas Y. Crowell, New York, 1960, pp. 204–205. We do not imply that this would be true in all cultures. Indeed, one study dealing with another culture refutes the idea in that it not only reports that no association was found between living with in-laws and marital adjustment, but also suggests that in certain cases having an in-law in the house may be advantageous to the young couple. Georg Karlsson, *Adaptability and Communication in Marriage*, Almqvist and Wiksells, Uppsala, Sweden, 1951, p. 106.

mother, a woman obsessed with the dangers of sexual intercourse, since she believed that it depleted one's energies. Whenever the couple could not be found for any period of time, the mother became quite inquisitive about the cause of the absence, always being certain that her son was sexually involved. The mother so plagued the couple that within a matter of weeks the wife threatened to obtain a divorce if the husband did not make some provision for their residence elsewhere.

An Attempt to Deal with the Parent and In-Law Problem

There are those who believe that problems with parents and in-laws are less evident today than in the past, since fewer young couples reside in the community of the parents and those who do are somewhat more isolated in their interactions. Actually, however, it has been noted by Sussman in his study "The Isolated Nuclear Family: Fact or Fiction" that this suggested isolation, be it physical or social, is largely fiction.[9] Moreover, together with Burchinal,[10] he found numerous behavioral exchanges, involving aid, social interaction, and services extended, taking place within the kin group.[11] Paul Reiss suggests several reasons why these exchange patterns between parents and their married children exist, among them the increased intensities in personal relationships made possible by the existence of smaller families.[12] The intensity in personal relationships may have either supportive or destructive impact on the kin relationship, depending on the specific conditions under which they occur. They do exist, however, and the feelings that they produce, whether positive or negative, are deeply felt.

One indication of the intensity of parent and in-law relationships is seen in the fact that parents and in-laws are frequently the major source

[9] Marvin B. Sussman, "The Isolated Family: Fact or Fiction," *Social Prob.*, 6 (1959), pp. 333–340.
[10] Marvin B. Sussman and Lee Burchinal, "Kin Family Network: Unheralded Structure in Current Conceptualizations of Family Functioning," *Marr. Fam. Living*, 24 (August 1962), pp. 231–240.
[11] See also Bert N. Adams, "Structural Factors Affecting Parental Aid to Married Children," *J. Marr. Fam.*, 26, 1 (August 1964), pp. 327–331.
[12] Paul J. Reiss, "Extended Kinship Relationships in American Society," in Hyman Rodman, *Marriage, Family and Society*, Random House, New York, 1965, pp. 204–210.

of children's names in contemporary families.[13] In regard to the use of names, another interesting factor emerges—the lack of a specific term of address for in-laws. This lack frequently creates uncomfortable feelings for young people who have to decide whether to call their mother-in-law mother, Mother Smith, Mary, Mrs. Smith, or whatever. In fact, it has been suggested that this lack of a specific term for in-laws reflects the ill-defined nature of the in-law relationship itself.[14]

Without a doubt, the nature of the in-law relationship presents difficulties, and, with the possible exception of some of the short-term problems already discussed, there are no simple solutions or remedies for them. There are, however, certain considerations that are worth examining. Thus it is of the greatest importance to be able to identify prior to marriage those patterns in the parent-child relationship that are likely to result in a restriction of the young person's maturity in his marital relationship. A realization of possible restrictions and efforts to remove them by both parents and children can do much in avoiding some of the difficulties we have discussed.

A parent's acceptance of the emancipation of his grown, married child is made excessively difficult by the fact that an entire way of life, consisting of specific attitudes and a sense of significance and purpose, has become intimately rooted in his relationship with the child. To give this up, particularly when there may be no real substitute, is very disquieting. It is because of this that a son or daughter who wishes to help a parent with these problems must have considerable understanding of the parent.

The son or daughter has an equally serious problem. Emancipation from one's parents necessitates the relinquishing of some of the satisfactions that one has come to enjoy. Such satisfactions as having another person assume responsibility for one's life may be much more enticing than the goals of maturity, which require both the development of a philosophy about the meaning and responsibility inherent in living and constructive efforts to attain the goals.

Finally, it should be noted that it is questionable whether one ever gives up the satisfactions derived from immature relationships without some hope that the alternative will be more rewarding. Parents and their grown children may find such a hope in the realization that far greater stability and personal happiness can be derived from personal autonomy

---

[13] Alice S. Rossi, "Naming Children in Middle-Class Families," *Am. soc. Rev.,* **30,** 4 (August 1965), pp. 499–513.

[14] John M. Shlien, "Mother-in-law: A Problem in Kinship Terminology," *Int. J. gen. Semantics,* published by ECT., Vol. 19, July 1962, pp. 161–171.

than from the endless waste of energies tied to the maintenance of an immature way of life.[15]

Summary

The relationship between parent and child is an important factor in understanding the complexities of certain in-law problems. A mature and meaningful parent-child relationship is unlikely to produce in-law problems. An unhealthy parent-child relationship (characterized by overprotection or rejection), however, may become a major factor in bringing about long-term in-law difficulties. Overprotection, for example, unless the young adult is able to emancipate himself from his parents and in turn cause his parents to free themselves from using him as their major source of satisfaction, may become a concern in his marriage and bring about many serious difficulties in his interactions with his wife.

The nature of in-law involvements and the sources from which these involvements emanate were discussed. In addition to faulty parental marriages, such other sources of long-term in-law involvements were considered as parents' inability to sever the psychic ties between themselves and their children and parents' use of their children as a means of vicariously fulfilling their own frustrated wishes. Short-term in-law problems were also discussed. These problems are seen as emanating largely from insecurities felt by young couples early in their marriages, which may cause them to view their in-laws as competitors for their spouse's attention and approval and thus render suspect even the most innocent of their in-laws' behaviors. These types of in-law problems tend to subside as young married people grow more secure in their marital roles, hence are of short duration compared to those that stem from faulty parent-child relationships.

Whether the problems are long-term or short-term, however, it is important to recognize the complexity of in-law involvements, because the development of successful in-law relationships requires an understanding on the part of both parents and their children.

[15] Evelyn Millis Duvall, *op. cit.,* Chs. 3 and 6.

Questions

1. State briefly but clearly the relationship between child-parent interaction and in-law problems. Give examples.
2. What is parental overprotection? Discuss how, for example, a woman involved in an inadequate relationship with her husband may become overprotective with her child.
3. List and discuss the ways in which young adults may deal with parental overprotection. Which of these ways are likely to lead to successful marriage and which are likely to lead to unsuccessful marriage? Explain your answers.
4. What is parental rejection? How does this affect a parent-child relationship? What effect might it have on one's subsequent marriage? Explain your answers.
5. How do short-term in-law problems differ from long-term problems in:
   a. Their sources?
   b. Their impact on a marriage?
6. How might living with in-laws increase the possibility of in-law problems? Is this always true? Explain your answers.

Projects

1. Select two marriages with which you are acquainted, one that you regard as reflecting successful in-law relationships and one that you regard as reflecting unsuccessful in-law relationships. Make an objective analysis of each marriage, attempting to show how the successful relationships differ from the unsuccessful, and also how each type develops.
2. Write a paper concerning the circumstances under which you would consent to live with your in-laws and also the circumstances under which you would consent to have them live with you. Attempt an objective analysis of your answers.

Suggested Readings

Adams, Bert N., "Structural Factors Affecting Parental Aid to Married Children," *J. Marr. Fam.*, **26**, 1 (August 1964), pp. 327–331.

Duvall, Evelyn Millis, *In-Laws: Pro and Con*, Association Press, New York, 1954.

LeMasters, E. E., *Modern Courtship and Marriage*, Macmillan, New York, 1957, Ch. 15, "In-Laws: Friends or Enemies."

Levine, Lena, *Modern Book of Marriage*, Bartholomew House, New York, 1957, Ch. 5, "Getting Along with Parents and In-Laws."

Neisser, Edith G., *Mothers and Daughters: A Lifelong Relationship*, Harper and Row, New York, 1967.

Ostrovoley, Everett S., *Father to the Child*, Putnam, London, 1959.

Stryker, Sheldon, "The Adjustment of Married Offspring to Their Parents," *Am. soc. Rev.*, **20** (April 1955), pp. 149–154.

Wallin, Paul, "Sex Differences in Attitudes to In-Laws—A Test of a Theory," *Am. J. Sociol.*, **59** (March 1954), pp. 466–469.

Chapter Seventeen

MARRIAGE AND THE PURSUIT OF A COLLEGE EDUCATION

So far we have dealt with particular dimensions of marital difficulty, such as sexual adjustment, sources of marital conflict, role conflicts, externalizations of various kinds, and parent and in-law difficulties. In this chapter we examine marriage in a particular setting in which several of the difficulties previously discussed play a significant role.

Not so many years ago it was customary for the middle-class male to complete his education and become established in a job or profession before marrying. However, since World War II there has been a marked increase in the number of married people who are pursuing an education.[1] Many of these marriages present special difficulties, which we shall

[1] For a discussion of the role of wartime anxiety and military service in increasing the number of college marriages, see James A. Peterson, *Education for Marriage,* Scribner's, New York, 1956, pp. 175–176. For a discussion of reasons and pressures for early marriage, see James H. S. Bossard and Eleanor Stoker Boll, *Why Marriages Go Wrong,* Ronald Press, New York, 1958, pp. 103–111. See also Lester A. Kirkendall, "Married Undergraduates on the Campus: An Appraisal," *Family Life Coordinator,* 5, 2 (December 1956), pp. 54–63.

ILLUSTRATION: Doll representing a Needles and Pins Vendor, c. 1860. Courtesy of the Museum of the City of New York.

examine.[2] Before doing so, however, it should be noted that there are at least three types of college marriage: those in which the couples were married for a considerable period of time before either or both of the partners entered college, those in which the couples were married just prior to entering college, and those in which the couples married while attending college.

In this chapter our concern is with the last two types. Although there are undoubtedly some differences between them, both face two eventualities for which some preparation may be warranted. First, many of the marital conflicts may emerge much earlier than would be the case in the noncollege marriage. Second, these marital conflicts may occur with great rapidity, throwing the couple into more turmoil than usual, since they do not have an adequate opportunity to resolve one conflict before another starts. The reason why married persons attending college may be faced with conflicts in the first two years of marriage that others might not have to face for a considerably longer period of time is the unique atmosphere of the college setting. To a lesser or greater extent, institutions of higher education are dedicated to the examination of ideas and the exploration of new and different values. In such an atmosphere the opportunity for intellectual stimulation and growth and for new experiences is very great, which has a significant impact on many, if not all, of the individuals involved. The problem of coping with changes in the marital partners, for example, is more imminent in such a setting. In this sense the college atmosphere is not easily matched by any nonuniversity situations. Let us examine some of these possibilities for new experiences and trace their implications for conflicts in the marital relationship.[3]

Differential Change and Growth in Marriage

One major potential source of conflict in the college marriage lies in the possibility that one partner may change and grow more rapidly than

---

[2] For a discussion of college marriages, see Ruth M. Hoeflin, *Essentials of Family Living*, Wiley, New York, 1960, pp. 231–233. For a discussion of the special stresses confronted by college marriages, see Henry A. Bowman, *Marriage for Moderns*, McGraw-Hill, New York, 1960, pp. 490–498.

[3] For a discussion of the problems involved in the "too early" college and high school marriage, see Paul H. Landis, *Making the Most of Marriage*, 2nd ed., Appleton-Century-Crofts, New York, 1960, pp. 274–278.

the other. Such changes emerge quite early and frequently have their origin in the broad impact of the university experience on the marital partners.

The husband who attends school has an opportunity for growth through his participation in an academic program and through his interaction with different persons in the university setting who open new vistas for him. His wife, not attending school, has no such opportunity, and differential growth may be the result. This frequently presents a problem of considerable significance, since many wives under these circumstances find the husband's education and personal growth so threatening that they impose obstacles to his education.

In one instance a wife became so concerned that she might lose her husband that she exaggerated the seriousness of even her minor ailments. This resulted in her husband's staying at home, missing classes, and receiving poor grades. It was some time before the husband saw what was happening and realized the necessity of reassuring his wife of his love for her. Frequently, the woman who regards the education of her husband as a threat may become competitive and try to outdo him, either by attending school herself or by developing other skills. Competition of this type, if not recognized, may lead to serious conflict, because in addition to the wish to surpass the other there is also envy of his success without any healthy identification with his accomplishments. When, however, the achievements of the husband awaken in the wife a healthy desire for new experiences, the results may be extremely beneficial to the marriage.

Although we have assumed that it is the husband who attends school, it may be the wife who decides to do so. Here, also, the ever-present opportunity for new experiences may change the wife's entire outlook, and the husband may experience the university as a threat to his marriage. There was the case of a husband who did not possess a college education and who became very upset after his wife started to attend school. He complained bitterly about how the home had "gone to pieces." He accused her of being selfish and threatened to leave her, if she did not stop attending school.

When both partners undergo a process of change, new views may enter the marriage—views regarding what the goals in marriage should be and what values are worth pursuing. Often such reassessment of values and goals leads to a sounder and more meaningful relationship. However, even when change involves both partners, some difficulty between the spouses may still result for at least two reasons. First, both partners may not necessarily change at the same pace or in the same way. Second, change usually involves core elements of the personality, which can never be altered without difficulty. One of the core elements in the personality of each spouse has to do with perception of roles in marriage.

Role Conflict

A second major source of potential conflict in the college marriage, which is interrelated with the change and growth just described, is change in role conceptions. As a result of exposure to the academic setting, each partner in a college marriage may envision a new and different role in marriage. A subservient wife or husband may perceive new capacities. Often this may lead to a new definition of role, which may be in conflict with the role expectations of the spouse. Furthermore, frequently the realization of such new capacities may be so exciting for the moment that the individuals become narrowly selfish. Thus a husband who discovers a new talent in himself may temporarily ignore his responsibilities to his wife and children; or the wife who believes that she possesses acting ability may ignore her responsibilities in the home and spend her time at the local playhouse. The realization of capacities, although intrinsically worthwhile, is frequently associated with conflict and confusion in the home. In one situation, a woman who had discovered a new asset in herself was exploited by her friends to the detriment of her family. This young married woman discovered that she had a great capacity for organizing social affairs. She was so delighted at this discovery that she allowed her friends to shift an unusual amount of responsibility onto her. Her friends accomplished this by flattery. As a result the young lady found her time completely taken up with the organization of church picnics, school lectures, and the like. Her husband recognized what was happening and began to complain bitterly in the hope that his wife might take stock of how she was being manipulated by her friends.

In all matters dealing with realization of new capacities a sense of perspective is necessary. Personal talents and interests have to be woven into the broader fabric of the marriage; otherwise chaos and imbalance are likely to characterize the marriage.

Multiplicity of Roles

A third major source of conflict in college marriages lies in the fact that the partner may be required to fulfill several roles, each of which may be in conflict with the others. The husband, for example, may discover that he must be a husband, a father, an employee, and also a student. Thus he may have to be fairly passive in the classroom and at work, and more assertive at home with his wife and child. Furthermore, as a student he must study, but his wife may demand more social life than they have. He also may feel obligated to spend time with his children, if he has any.[4] All of this may be aggravated if the wife is also seeking to complete her education. Her potential for tension is also great, since she may be for the moment wife, mother, student, and employee.[5] The obligations inherent in each role may be equally important and none may be satisfactorily abandoned. Thus life for such couples can often become grim, with the difficulties involved in the growth of each individual, the conflict with one another, and the conflicting nature of the new social roles; tension is ever-present. The pot is always on the verge of boiling over, so to speak.

Externalizations in College Marriage

Under these circumstances externalizations of tensions may be a regular occurrence, and such externalizations constitute a fourth major source of conflict in the college marriage. As already noted, when externalizations are operating, it is easy for people to aggravate each other, to find fault, to nag and berate each other. The particular focus of the externalization—that is, what a spouse singles out as a target—will vary with the particular relationship. For example, it may be an economic

[4] For a discussion of the effect children have on a college marriage, see Theodore B. Johannis, "The Marital Adjustment of a Sample of Married College Students," *Family Life Coordinator*, 4, 4 (June 1956), p. 29.
[5] James A. Peterson, *op. cit.*, pp. 169–172.

problem, a sex problem, or an in-law problem, particularly when there already is some basis for the grievance. Indeed, all of these problems may be sources of conflict in any marriage. The point is that when a person externalizes his tension and hostility and begins to focus on problems, even minor problems are distorted, and their seriousness and significance are exaggerated. It is important that the tendency to distort the seriousness of a problem (which is a by-product of externalization) be noted, since a tremendous amount of energy can be wasted in conflict about relatively unimportant matters.

The Parent and In-Law Relations

A fifth source of conflict in the college marriage has to do with parents and in-laws. We recognize, of course, that such problems are frequently a function of the externalizations that have just been described. Thus, under some circumstances, parents and in-laws may be blamed for difficulties that they have little to do with. On the other hand, there are several factors intrinsic to the college situation that do make certain types of conflicts with parents and in-laws a common occurrence.

Parental and In-Law Ambivalence

One factor that is related to parental and in-law conflict is the fact that from the beginning of the marriage each partner may have been faced with negative reactions from his parents. Middle-class parents are generally very concerned with the social and economic well-being of their children. Thus, they may view the marriage of their children while still in college as potentially disruptive to the plans that they have for their children. Middle-class parents may fear that a son who marries while in college may become so burdened with economic responsibilities that he will abandon college or that a daughter may fail to complete her education and the years attended may be wasted. Thus often there may be a reservoir of ambivalence on the part of parents and in-laws.

Economic Difficulty and Resulting Patterns of Interaction

A second factor involved in the possible rise of conflict with parents and in-laws relates to economic difficulties, a problem fairly common in the college marriage.[6] Of significance here is not the economic problem per se, but rather the patterns that tend to be used in dealing with it. For in these patterns much about how the married pair deal with parents and in-laws and vice versa is revealed. A knowledge of such patterns may prove to be significant in enabling all of the involved persons to understand the nature of their conflicts with one another.

The economic problem, which has been singled out for analysis, may be divided into two parts; one involves the married pair,[7] the other pertains to parents and in-laws. For the married pair in need of economic help, there is often conflict about how the problem ought to be resolved. The couple may wish to be independent and solve their own problem or they may decide to seek assistance from their parents. Either of these two courses of action, however, involves calculated risks for the married pair. If, for example, one or the other member of the relationship is too independent, both may suffer from this aloofness. On the other hand, if the couple is inclined to be dependent, the economic help received from the parents may increase the dependency and involve the parents in the marriage to a greater extent than is wise. Thus the course of action that couples decide to follow when economic help is needed should be given a great deal of consideration.

The second dimension of conflict in regard to the question of economic assistance is concerned with the parents and in-laws. If they are middle-class persons, they may be concerned that their children maintain a particular standard of living. At the same time, as middle-class parents they may also feel that individualism and a spirit of self-reliance are necessary if their children are to manage their affairs properly. This conflict may be complicated by the fact that they desire a place of importance in the lives of their children and feel that economic assistance will insure such a place. Here, also, the several courses of possible action involve calculated risks. If the parents refuse to give economic help, they may endanger their relationship with the married pair and hurt their children in a very material way. If they extend help, they may encourage dependency on the part of the married pair and may become involved in the young couple's life to a degree that is detrimental to their relationship with them. This would be the case especially if parents and in-laws were led to a pattern of frequently visiting the couple, ignoring their

[6] For a discussion of economic support from parents in regard to college marriages, see Judson T. Landis and Mary G. Landis, *Building a Successful Marriage,* 3rd ed., Prentice-Hall, Englewood Cliffs, N. J., 1958, pp. 188–190.

[7] For a study of student opinion concerning financial assistance from parents in college marriages, see Rex A. Skidmore and Anthon S. Cannon, *Building Your Marriage,* Harper and Brothers, New York, 1951, pp. 226–227, 638–639.

own interests, and becoming completely absorbed in the relationship of their children. Thus for both the married pair and the parents or in-laws there are conflicting motivations that are brought into play when questions of economic assistance arise.

MASKING EMOTIONAL DEPENDENCY. The precarious balance between emotional dependence and independence may be so uncomfortable, both for parents and children, that it is often masked. One way of masking it is to act on the basis of one motivation and repress the other. When motivations are sufficiently mixed and complicated in this way, there is always the danger that they will not be fully explored or fully understood either by parents and in-laws or the married pair. For example, a son who has needs both for independence and dependence may block out momentarily his need for independence and seek the financial aid. With an equally strong repressed need to be independent, however, and without being consciously aware of what he is doing, he may become very sensitive and resentful about any advice he receives from his parents, since he already feels uneasy about depending on them for economic aid. Thus such repression brings with it added complications.

Parents and in-laws, also, may feel both a need to help their children and a need to leave them on their own. Because of this ambivalence, economic assistance is frequently accompanied by a need to control its use; parents may become moody and pout when they are not consulted on purchases that the married pair make. In one instance a married daughter, who borrowed money from her mother, found her mother very unhappy whenever she was not consulted on purchases. The mother's reaction troubled the daughter so much that she cleared all purchases with her mother, a pattern that robbed the daughter of her autonomy and caused much conflict in her marriage.

APPROACHING THE NEED FOR ECONOMIC ASSISTANCE WITH HIDDEN INTENT. Situations in which economic help is being sought are frequently complicated by the fact that both the married pair and the parents or in-laws may be sensitive to rejection. Often such sensitivity may lead to the hiding of actual intent. A married son, for example, may allude to the many material possessions of his friends, hoping that his parents will pick up the cues and offer assistance. On the other hand, parents may talk about the spirit of adventure and the excitement of building one's own future, thereby indicating that they have no intention of giving help. In each of the situations, there are two points to keep in mind. First, the hiding of intent is in many instances done unconsciously, so that persons are unaware of what they are doing. Second, by hiding intent a good deal of face-saving becomes possible. If a father appears unreceptive to the idea of help, the son may hide consciously or unconsciously behind the idea that he never really wanted help. If the father recognizes that he has really hurt his son by refusing to help, he may declare that he really did not understand his son's request and at that point offer assistance.

The patterns of interaction that emerge during questions of economic assistance, including the masking of emotional dependency and the hiding of intent, make whatever problems are present between parents, in-laws, and the married pair immensely complicated. Reactions of the sort we have described keep all participants from actually dealing with their responsibilities toward one another; they can be averted only when all concerned attempt to understand the situation more clearly than is often the case.

Conflict and Sexual Adjustment

The disturbances in the interpersonal relationship that can come from all of the conflict sources just described very often find their expression in the sexual adjustments in the college marriage. Some individuals who are hostile may become indifferent to sex; they may suddenly experience less pleasure or refuse to participate, particularly if it will enable them to get back at the spouse.

Furthermore, as persons undergo changes in concepts of role, their part in sexual relations may undergo change as well. Thus a woman who believes she has no choice other than to engage in sexual relations when her husband so indicates, may come to feel that her wishes are also important and refuse sexual relations. Or a husband who feels that he has no right to indicate his interest in sexual relations may suddenly come to feel that he has every right to do so, and make such feelings known. Thus, new definitions of one's role produce conflict.

Finally, each partner may become so absorbed with the demands of college and his other responsibilities that he experiences periods of marked indifference regarding sexual activity. Here the sexual withdrawal is not a matter of expressing resentment, but stems from the fact that energies are completely absorbed by the many other demands and responsibilities.

There was a married male college student who found his academic work exceedingly difficult and had to spend tremendous amounts of time preparing for examinations. He experienced such anxiety about doing well in his exams and meeting his other responsibilities that for a couple of weeks before midterms he suffered temporary or situational impotency. Such impotency remained until the examinations were completed, after which he became sexually responsive once more.

Positive Factors in College Marriages

Although our focus has been on the problem areas in the college marriage, the reader must not conclude that beneficial aspects are not present.[8] First, both the satisfaction and the disappointments that emerge out of sharing interests and goals may provide the couple with a solid foundation for dealing with the future. Second, erotic satisfactions can be realized, devoid of the difficulties that confront the unmarried. Both of these features help to orient the individuals more clearly as to purpose in life, and may become important factors in their commitment to serious pursuits in life. There have also been assertions that married students perform better academically than single students.[9] Chilman and Meyer report that married students are more oriented toward academic achievement than are single students.[10]

Marshall and King, however, reporting on the general status of such research, note that on the whole grade-point averages do not seem to differ significantly between single and married students, although married students seem to have higher aspirations than do single students.[11]

[8] For studies involving success and happiness ratings of college marriages, see Judson T. Landis, "On the Campus," *Survey Midmonthly*, **84**, 1 (January 1948), pp. 17–19; Harold T. Christensen and Robert E. Philbrick, "Family Size as a Factor in the Marital Adjustments of College Couples," *Am. soc. Rev.*, **17** (June 1952), pp. 306–312.

[9] Svend Riemer, "Married Veterans Are Good Students," *Marr. Fam. Living*, **9** (February 1947), pp. 11–12. See also Judson T. Landis and Mary G. Landis, *op. cit.*, pp. 179–180. For a report indicating that married students do better academically, see Ralph Schroder, "Academic Achievement of the Male College Student," *J. Marr. Fam.*, **25**, 4 (1963), pp. 420–423. Laurence L. Falk, "A Comparative Study of Problems of Married and Single Students," *J. Marr. Fam.*, **26**, 2 (1964), pp. 207–208.

[10] Catherine S. Chilman and Donald L. Meyer, "Single and Married Undergraduates' Measured Personality Needs and Self-rated Happiness," *J. Marr. Fam.*, **28**, 1 (1966), pp. 67–76.

[11] William H. Marshall and Marcia P. King, "Undergraduate Student Marriage: A Compilation of Research Findings," *J. Marr. Fam.*, **28**, 3 (1966), pp. 350–359.

To be sure, conflict may also emerge out of the pursuit of marital satisfaction. Conflict, however (as will be indicated in a subsequent chapter), need not be negative. It can be quite beneficial, in that it provides many opportunities for the reassessment of values and goals and thus can contribute to the subsequent growth of the marital relationship. In college marriages, the successful are those who have been able to detect the sources of conflict, who have learned to deal with conflict, and who have been able to profit as a result.

Summary

The college marriage is much more prevalent today than it was in the past. Because of this, and because of the unique conditions that surround the college marriage, it warrants special consideration.

With respect to the conditions in which the college marriage is found, it is recognized that persons involved in college marriages not only tend to confront the "normal" marital conflicts earlier, but also more rapidly than do persons in noncollege marriages. The early and rapid conflict confrontation and the accompanying need for adjustments on the part of members of a college marriage frequently create more than the usual amount of turmoil.

In this chapter, in addition to discussing the place of conflict in college marriage, some of the sources of the conflict were also discussed. These sources of conflict are (1) differential change and growth in marriage, (2) role conflict, (3) multiplicity of roles, (4) externalizations, and (5) parents and in-laws. Special attention was given to such patterns as the masking of emotional dependency and the hiding of the intent of asking for, giving, or receiving economic assistance; it was suggested that these patterns add complications to the problems that may already be present in the college marriage.

It is not our intent to reflect negatively on college marriages—it goes without saying that many of them are happy and successful. We have intended, however, to point out very clearly the complexity of the conflict that may confront persons involved in, or contemplating, college marriage. This is done in the hope that a clearer understanding of conflict may eventuate in more successful marriages of this type.

Questions

1. Describe briefly the three types of college marriages. Analyze each type from the standpoint of probable problem areas and show how these marriages may be similar to or different from one another in regard to the amount and type of conflict confronted.
2. What is meant by differential change and growth in marriage? Is differential change and growth more likely to occur in a college marriage than in a noncollege marriage? Explain your answer.
3. Discuss role conflict in marriage. Does this potential problem area apply more to college marriages than to noncollege marriages? Explain your answer.
4. Explain how externalizations occur in college marriage. Cite examples.
5. Discuss parent and in-law relations as potential sources of marital conflict. Do you think that there is a difference between college marriage and noncollege marriage with respect to how this potential source of conflict unfolds and its probability of occurrence?
6. What is meant by masking dependency? What is meant by hiding intent? How can each of these patterns compound the difficulties in effecting adjustments in college marriage?

Projects

1. Hold a panel discussion about the pros and cons of marrying while in college.
2. Interview several married college students. Divide these subjects into two groups: those who were married before attending college and those who were married while attending college. Attempt to determine what each group regards as the advantages and disadvantages of combining marriage and college attendance. Do you find any difference between the two groups? Do you find any differences in the answers given by men and the answers given by women? If you find differences, how do you account for these differences? Report your findings and your analysis to the class.

Suggested Readings

Bowman, Henry A., *Marriage for Moderns,* 4th ed., McGraw-Hill, New York, 1960, Ch. 15, "Young Marriage Today."

Christopherson, Victor A., Joseph S. Vandiver, and Marie N. Krueger, "The Married College Student, 1959," *Marr. Fam. Living,* **22** (May 1960), pp. 122–128.

Johannis, Theodore B., "The Marital Adjustment of a Sample of Married College Students," *Family Life Coordinator,* **4,** 4 (June 1956), pp. 24–31.

Kirkendall, Lester A., "Married Undergraduates on the Campus: An Appraisal," *Family Life Coordinator,* **5,** 2 (December 1956), pp. 54–63.

Landis, Judson T., and Mary G. Landis, *Building a Successful Marriage,* 3rd ed., Prentice-Hall, Englewood Cliffs, N.J., 1958, Ch. 10, "Marriage Under Special Circumstances."

Riemer, Svend, "Married Veterans Are Good Students," *Marr. Fam. Living,* **9** (February 1947), pp. 11–12.

Chapter Eighteen

RESOLVING MARITAL CONFLICT

HAVING DISCUSSED some of the major areas of marital conflict, we now turn to examining its nature and the understandings that may contribute to its resolution.

It is obvious that no specific formula for dealing with marital difficulty exists and that any attempt to arrive at specific prescriptions in a book would invariably be superficial and limited. Instead, we focus our attention on the dynamics of conflict—that is, of what conflict consists, its different dimensions—because we believe that an understanding of conflict can move a couple in the direction of its resolution.

Some Basic Ideas Regarding the Nature of Marital Conflict

It is important to be aware of certain basic ideas about marital conflict. One common assumption is that conflict is inherently bad for a marriage. In fact, not all marital conflict is necessarily undesirable or de-

ILLUSTRATION: The Uihlein Doll House, 1893. Courtesy of the Milwaukee Public Museum.

structive.[1] Some conflict is inherent in life; and any marriage in which there has been no conflict at some period is not only atypical, but may suggest also that feelings are being repressed.

Many of the middle class have grown up with norms of conduct that value the withholding of resentments and differences. There is a tendency to view the ideal family as one in which complete consensus and harmony prevail. Such a view results in a fear to express conflict and an inability to appreciate the positive value of *some conflict*.

Whether or not conflict is destructive depends on the extent to which it involves an attack on the self-worth of the marital partner; as previously indicated, such an attack is replete with difficulties for the marital union. When the self-worth of the marital partner is not the focus of the conflict, however, there may be beneficial developments.

Conflict serves a useful purpose, first, if it leads to a redefinition of the marital difficulty. This may be achieved when issues are brought out into the open, extraneous issues are dispensed with, and misunderstandings about the real issues are clarified. As a result, each partner may be able to think more clearly about the difficulty, and a resolution for the difficulty may be found more readily.

Second, conflict serves a useful purpose if the marital partners develop a realistic understanding of each other and if the basic values of each are delineated. There was the case of a woman who saw her husband, a college student, as being much brighter than he actually was. She had an idealized image of her husband, which kept getting in the way of seeing him realistically. For several semesters the husband's grades were very average, and the wife became resentful and brooded. One day when she could no longer contain her resentment she expressed her sense of disappointment toward her husband, and this led to a series of quarrels. In the process of quarreling, the husband pointed out the strain under which he had been operating trying to live up to his own as well as her expectations. The quarrels were quite intense, but they resulted in the wife's coming to have a deeper sense of appreciation of her husband's plight. The husband, on the other hand, grew in his understanding of his wife's behavior and her needs. A closer and more meaningful relationship emerged as a result. In this instance, and in many others, conflict clarified the different values at work and reminded the marital partners of their obligations. It may well be that in any relationship some conflict is essential, if it serves to sharpen beliefs and continues to alert the partners to the expectations of the other.

[1] See Willard Waller, *The Family*, revised by Reuben Hill, Dryden Press, New York, 1951, pp. 309–312.

A third useful purpose of marital conflict is achieved if the partners come to appreciate the extent of their emotional commitment to the marriage. As disagreements leading to conflict emerge in the marital relationship, the partners tend to become alienated from each other and to assume that the entire relationship is negative. Often conflict may create an awareness of the positive emotional involvement.

There was a married couple who were engaged in conflict that had its origins at least fifteen years in the past. During the quarrels they brought up many hurts from the past: insults that had been made, interference from parents in their marriage, even difficulties during courtship. However, while remembering the many hurts from the past, they also found themselves thinking about the enjoyments: the restaurants they had eaten in, the movies they had seen, the places they had visited, and the sentiments and feelings surrounding all of these experiences. Thus they realized that not only was there much that was positive in their marriage, but that deep personal feelings were also associated with the marriage.

It is obvious that some conflict is inherent in marriage and that the basis for such conflict can lie in several quarters. In previous chapters we have mentioned major areas of conflict, and such areas of difficulty are compounded by changes in values which necessitate reevaluation.[2] In the modern world there are ever-present dilemmas. Kirkpatrick calls attention to some of these:

1. Freedom in the family versus order and efficiency in the home.
2. Career patterns and achievement versus the love-reproduction function.
3. Personal self-expression versus devoted child rearing.
4. Family loyalty versus community loyalty.[3]

It is suggested that husband and wife may be torn by ever-present changing and conflicting demands of this type.

Finally, it is important to recognize that marital conflict is not uniform throughout the history of a marriage; instead, it has to be seen in light of the *stage of development* of the family. Each period in the life history of the marriage brings with it new and different responsibilities, hence new conflicts. A newly married couple without children face a different set of problems than do families with children, and parents with small children, in turn, confront different problems than do those with children in high school and college; the conflicts and adjustments of

[2] Robert O. Blood, in Ruth Cavan, Ed., *Marriage and Family in the Modern World*, 2nd ed., T. Y. Crowell, New York, 1965, pp. 426–438.

[3] Clifford Kirkpatrick, *The Family as Process and Institution*, 2nd ed., Ronald Press, New York, 1963, pp. 89–95.

those whose children are grown and married are still different. Such differences are in part a function of the different needs and requirements of people at different stages of family growth. Moreover, people do not react in precisely the same way to a conflict at age 50 as they might have at age 25.[4] Thus the family is faced with different challenges and tasks at different times. Since all eventualities cannot be anticipated, it is the general understanding of the dimensions of conflict and their implications that can perhaps best prepare people for the future in this regard.

Forms of Marital Conflict

Much marital conflict originates in competition between the spouses about some aspect of their life. When not resolved, competition lends itself to rivalry. Rivalry brings with it tension, which, if not dealt with effectively, emerges into conflict. Conflict most often results in accommodation, each partner agreeing to grant some concession in order that an adjustment be reached. The interplay between competition, rivalry, conflict, and accommodation over an extended period of time results in each marital partner accepting some of the values of the other. When this occurs, understanding and acceptance have taken place, and the difficulties between the marital partners are minimized.[5]

Exterior Forms

In dealing with marital conflict, one must differentiate the broad exterior forms of conflict from the inner dynamics of conflict—the actual interplay between the persons. In its exterior form, conflict can be con-

---

[4] Irwin Deutscher, "The Quality of Postparental Life: Definitions of the Situation," *J. Marr. Fam.*, **26** (1964), pp. 52–59. Roy H. Rogers, "Toward a Theory of Family Development," *J. Marr. Fam.*, **26**, 3 (1964), pp. 262–270. Murray A. Straus, "Power and Support Structure of the Family in Relation to Socialization," *J. Marr. Fam.*, **26** 3 (1964), pp. 318–326. Vincent D. Mathews and Clement S. Mihanovich, "New Orientations on Marital Maladjustment," *Marr. Fam. Living*, **25**, 3 (1963), pp. 300–304. Irwin Deutscher, "Socialization for Postparental Life," in Arnold Rose, Ed., *Human Behavior and Social Process*, Houghton Mifflin, Boston, 1962, pp. 508–523. Ruth S. Cavan, "Self and Role in Adjustment in Old Age," in Arnold Rose, *ibid.*, pp. 526–535.
[5] Waller, *op. cit.*, pp. 298, 306–307.

cealed or overt, acute, chronic, progressive, or habitual.[6] In concealed conflict the feelings are kept under wraps, so to speak. Conflict takes the form of frustrating the other or dropping subtle remarks designed to belittle. A wife, for example, may develop a pattern of cooking food the husband does not like, neglect the home, or make unfair comparisons between her husband and others who are perhaps more successful in occupation or profession.

In overt conflict the difficulty is out in the open; there is no attempt to deny the problem by either of the marital partners. One form of overt conflict may be acute conflict, in which tension builds up over a period of time and then bursts forth when neither of the partners can contain it. Sometimes in patterns of acute conflict a particular problem subsides, but as new problems appear, tension mounts and acute conflict again becomes imminent.

When the basic marital difficulties are not resolved, there may be chronic conflict; it is recurrent. There may be temporary solutions, but little is resolved. The feud goes on, with nagging and belittling. Chronic conflict often emerges into progressive conflict. In progressive conflict the marriage continues to deteriorate, and each new problem is added to the unresolved problems of the past. Progressive conflict can develop into habitual conflict, in which the couple cannot, or will not, agree. The toll on the mental health of the marital partners in habitual conflict is perhaps greater than in any other form of conflict, since it is often characterized by a high degree of tension and much berating.[7] The marital partners become increasingly hopeless and demoralized.

Inner Dynamics of Conflict

Thus far our analysis has been limited to the outer dimensions of marital conflict. More important, and of greater concern for us in the present treatment, are the inner dynamics of marital conflict; that is, what actually goes on between the marital partners during conflict.

The inner dynamics in any marriage are not haphazard, but are to a large extent a function of how the couple, with their individual personalities, have come to relate to each other. Each couple during courtship and the formative period in their marriage come to understand the way in which they can best deal with each other. This learning process in any marriage involves a type of verbal sparring, some of it conscious, but a

[6] *Ibid.*, pp. 296–298. Joseph K. Folsom, *The Family and Democratic Society*, Wiley, New York, 1943, Ch. 13. Ernest R. Groves and William F. Ogburn, *American Marriage and Family Relationships*, Henry Holt, New York, 1928, pp. 85–87.
[7] Waller and Hill, *op. cit.*, p. 306.

good deal unconscious. The term "sparring," generally applied to boxing, is defined by *Webster's* as "skirmishing for advantage." The function of such verbal sparring in a marriage is to see what the opponent is like, what his points of vulnerability and sensitivity are, and what kinds of statements bring what types of reactions.

Thus a husband married to a woman who is insecure about her educational background may attempt to intimidate her with ideas he obtained in school in order to win an argument. He senses her vulnerability here and tries to take advantage of the situation. If his plan works, he has a technique for use in subsequent marital difficulties.

A strategy for dealing with each other is thus developed. An understanding of the strategies employed is important in understanding how conflict can be resolved in a particular marriage.

Whether conscious or not, strategies are designed to gain people the ends they seek. This is not to say that strategies do not misfire. In fact, some individuals persist in employing strategies that have outlived their usefulness, that is, strategies that are likely to produce failure in terms of gaining ends. People who are unaware of the strategies others possess are usually in trouble; because in order to engage in conflict successfully one must be adroit in knowing how to employ strategies and one must be sensitive to tactics, that is, when to have an orderly retreat and when a change in strategy is indicated. All of this sounds much more like a plan for *battle* than a discussion of marital conflict. Some marriages are, of course, in some psychic sense, battlegrounds. It becomes important, therefore, to emphasize that marriages based on strategies drain the energies of the partners. Over a period of time deep resentments and fears emerge, since people are always on guard. Although some element of strategy may be quite inevitable in conflict, it is only when strategies are minimized that people can be relaxed and free to react and express themselves openly.

We now turn our attention to specific strategies.

STRATEGIES. One strategy in marital conflict is the throwing out of "feelers" or "trial balloons" to see what responses will occur and then plotting further strategy from there. A husband, for example, may wish to join a country club in order to play golf, but he knows that his wife does not approve of his golf playing. In his discussions with his wife he may talk in vague generalities about people whom his wife thinks highly of, who also happen to be members of the club. The subject of golf, the most important element, may not even be introduced in the conversation. The husband's main concern is to observe his wife's response. Thus after each of his comments he waits for a reaction from his wife, for these reactions give him his cues as to which strategies to employ.

The purpose of strategy here is to win the wife over by manipulation. Failing to achieve the goal, some husbands may withdraw and become vindictive, seeking punishment for the wife in some other area of life— another strategy. Other husbands may become increasingly direct and insulting—perhaps also a strategy.

A second strategy in marital conflict is the introduction of behaviors designed to engender guilt in the marital partner in order to control his or her behavior. There was the case of a married woman who, whenever faced with marital conflict, presented herself to her husband as a sweet, innocent, misunderstood, and helpless female. In this way she aroused fears in her husband that he could be mistreating her and such guilt about it that he usually abandoned his own wishes and gave in to hers.

A third strategy in marital conflict is to "needle" the partner. This is accomplished by presenting what seem to be compliments which on reflection turn out to be insults. The purpose of the "needle" is both to berate for the purpose of berating, that is, to hurt the marital partner, and to undermine the self-confidence of the marital partner in order that he will abandon his views.

There was a married man who, when in conflict with his wife, had a habit of comparing her with other wives. He would always select a person with virtues—a hard worker or a devoted wife—and these attributes he would praise. But the women he selected for comparison also possessed some obvious limitation, such as being known for poor judgment, a tendency to gossip, or homeliness. This man's wife would at first feel complimented, but on further reflection would sense the invidious comparison. She was sensitive enough, so that her confidence was indeed undermined. As a result, she would withdraw from the conflict and give in to her husband.

There are many other strategies that are employed in marital conflict. Flirtatious behavior at social gatherings may be used to make the marital partner jealous and insecure, so that he will become more agreeable. Temper tantrums and sexual unresponsiveness are also employed as strategies.

CONSEQUENCES OF STRATEGIES. First, the use of strategies in marital conflict tends to result in a marked complication of and confusion about the real issues of the conflict. The marital partners may become so confused that they do not really know what the real issues are. Indeed, the basic points of disagreement and the strategies employed in dealing with the conflict become so intertwined, involved, and complicated that many married people do, in fact, become hopelessly bogged down because they do not know what their basic marital problems are.

Second, the use of strategies in marital conflict has a direct impact on the members of the marriage in that it diverts energies into deviant and nonconstructive channels. Each partner expends a considerable amount of energy in planning strategy, energy that perhaps could be more profitably employed in a more straightforward and constructive approach to the marital conflict.

Although strategies to some extent characterize almost any marriage, in some relationships one member employs strategies much more than does the other. Such marriages pose the interesting question of which partner is in control of conflict situations. At first glance there is some reason to suspect that the partner who relies heavily on strategy frequently controls the relationship. Nevertheless, there is a price involved. Like all people who have to rely on strategies, such a person often has a tenuous and insecure feeling about the control. This creates not only anxiety, but also the need for additional strategies to cope with the anxiety. Thus the price of control would appear to be high in terms of psychic energy. The member of the marriage who uses fewer strategies can also at times control conflict by simply being aware of the strategies of the other partner. However, such an awareness may at times usher in counterstrategies. Regardless of who controls conflict, both partners pay a price, since they have to be on guard in their dealings with each other and cannot relate to each other with their true feelings.

Third, strategies, being resistant to change, over time tend to become an integral part of the personality. Thus the strategies themselves become important, in that the person derives a feeling of pride and significance from employing them. One may come to feel, for example, that the powers of strategy and manipulation are clever, subtle, deceptive; the strategies give to the person a feeling of mastery over others. There are some persons who enjoy creating marital conflict in order to have an opportunity to employ strategies. Indeed, some marriages are held together primarily because each partner finds the use of strategies an exciting diversion. In such marriages the pride that surrounds strategies is more important than the actual issue in the conflict. Finally, we must add that being proud of the strategy not only complicates conflict, as indicated earlier, but makes the resolution of marital conflict excessively difficult.

Resistances That Interfere with Resolution of Conflict

We have discussed the nature of marital conflict, including its exterior forms, its internal dynamics in the form of strategies, and the resultant complications. We now turn to another important dimension of marital conflict—the particular tendencies that keep people from recognizing their conflicts and dealing with them effectively, which we shall call resistances.

Not Accepting the Existence of a Problem

One major resistance that interferes with a couple's abilities to handle their marital conflicts is their reluctance to admit that a problem exists.[8] Although such admission sounds simple enough, there is resistance on the part of one or both members of a marriage to admit to themselves and to each other that all is not well, even when obvious signs of difficulty are present. Almost all counselors have at one time or another encountered the husband or wife who appeared for help not because they felt any need for it, but only to satisfy their mate.[9] These kinds of people are very difficult to work with, since they find it necessary to provide a facade of marital well-being.

Furthermore, there are well-developed ways of thinking that block out a couple's awareness about themselves and their marital problems. For example, there are people with marital difficulties who state that since all couples have problems, there is little that is different or unusual about any incompatibility that they might possess. To be sure, to have marital problems is to be like other married people; problems are inherent in living. What is important here, however, is the manner in which this point of view is employed. The danger is that such a philosophy may be used to rationalize doing nothing about one's marital problems. The logic goes something like this: all couples have some marital difficulty; we also have marital difficulty; therefore, we are like others. This means that since the couple believe that they are like other couples, there is really nothing to be concerned about. If one shifts the same analysis to questions of physical illness, however, the logic no longer holds. If the average couple in our society suffered from tuberculosis, few couples would feel comfortable about the thought that they were like other couples in this regard. Instead, they would try to remedy the condition as early as possible. However, since many people view only medical problems as worthy of time and consideration, problems in interpersonal re-

[8] Paul H. Landis, *Making the Most of Marriage,* 2nd ed., Appleton-Century-Crofts, New York, 1960, p. 643.
[9] For a discussion of this point and also of the motives behind decisions to consult an analyst, see Lawrence S. Kubie, "Psychoanalysis and Marriage," in Victor W. Eisenstein, *Neurotic Interaction in Marriage,* Basic Books, New York, 1956, pp. 10–43, especially pp. 32–33.

lationships are persistently avoided and rationalized as being unimportant. It is clear that unless a couple can overcome their resistance to accepting that all is not well with their marriage, little can be done to bring about change.

The Lack of Communication

A second area of resistance that interferes with the handling of marital problems results from an inability to communicate problems, resentments, and feelings. In the most positive sense, communication between the marital partners enables feelings, resentments, and hostilities to come out into the open. Ideas, distorted or other, when brought into the open may be tested by reality. Some problems can be avoided and many can be resolved when the lines of communication between husband and wife are kept open; there is much that is positive and therapeutic in this. A breakdown in communication negates these possibilities; and the greater the breakdown in communication, the greater the likelihood that people will distort, imagine, and twist grievances, since it is so easy for the imagination to run off in all directions when a basis for testing reality in interaction is not present. It should be pointed out that regardless of the therapeutic values involved, there is considerable resistance to communication; instead, there are patterns among people that restrict the communication of marital grievances.

One such instance is found in the pattern of hopelessness, which some people use in dealing with their marital problems. They accept marital difficulty as part of fate; this is what life has "dished out." Thus they believe that there is little that they can do in order to change things; hence it makes little sense to complain about grievances.[10]

Consider this example of a married woman whose husband was an alcoholic. He usually built up to his drinking sprees slowly, but once started, they would last for about a week, climaxed by some kind of violence that necessitated imprisonment. During one of these sprees the husband came home, beat his wife, and knocked out her upper front teeth. Since such drinking and violence in some form had characterized their marital life, the woman's friends encouraged her to go to a marriage counselor. She resented the idea and became angry at her friends. Finally she consented, but came to the counselor in a very hostile and defensive mood. Her attitude was one of defending her husband, she was certain that the counselor wanted to break up her home, and in one moment of stress she blurted out: "He only knocked out my uppers, he did leave the lowers."

[10] Francis E. Merrill, *Courtship and Marriage*, Henry Holt, New York, 1959, p. 380.

This was a woman who was quite hopeless about the possibility of change and was therefore willing to put up with considerable abuse. More important, she was not only hopeless about making her life a happier one, but by avoiding professional assistance she also sentenced her husband to a life of gradual deterioration.

A second instance of a pattern that limits the communication of marital grievance is found in the person who is fearful of the conflict and hostility that may emerge if there are complains about dissatisfactions. Such persons have great difficulty in handling conflict situations and usually become anxious and upset at such times. They go to lengths to avoid conflict, even when this means withholding marital grievances from their spouses. These are often people who are self-effacing, afraid to assert themselves and to stand up against abuse and mistreatment. To avoid anxiety and conflict, some of these people are even prone to minimize the importance of their dissatisfaction and over a period of time may reach the conclusion that they attached too much significance to their grievances.

Thus there are individuals who appear for professional assistance and talk quite openly and readily about their marital problems. However, when they sense that a resolution of their difficulties may involve conflict and the confrontation of their spouse on particular issues, they often become passive. At this point they frequently terminate their counseling and indicate that they had perhaps exaggerated the seriousness of their difficulties.

A third instance of a pattern that limits communication of marital grievances is found in people who refrain from complaining because they are insecure about their marriage. These people believe that any expression of dissatisfaction with the marriage will produce rejection by the other partner, resulting in the termination of the marriage. Thus they prefer to hold on, no matter how bad things are, rather than run the risk of losing the marriage.

Fourth, we have the person who has learned that there is value to holding onto a grievance until it can be used strategically against the marital partner at some opportune time.[11] Thus grievances can be built up as ammunition to be used in an argument to attack the marital partner. These grievances may also be held back and employed later to justify demands for material possessions or for favors from the marital partner.

Here, then, we have several instances of patterns that keep people from communicating their problems. They constitute serious resistances

[11] For a discussion of the self-pitying individual and the use of marital grievance, see F. Alexander Magoun, *Love and Marriage*, Harper and Brothers, New York, 1948, p. 251.

to the solution of marital difficulties and, therefore, must be dealt with if solutions to marital problems are to be reached.

Dealing with Symptoms Rather Than Causes

A third major resistance that interferes with a couple's abilities to handle marital conflicts is their tendency to deal with superficial aspects of their marital problems; thus little is resolved. There are, to be sure, many reasons for this tendency. In some instances a problem may have many facets and thus only certain parts are seen. In other instances individuals may be genuinely ignorant or unaware of the real issues involved.[12] In a great many cases, however, there is something far more serious at work—an unconscious tendency to substitute a superficial problem for the basic problem, since frequently the real problem may be painful or difficult to face. Counselors readily report that the problems that couples present are seldom the basic difficulties and that an important aspect of counseling has to do with bringing into focus the real issues. The particular superficial problem selected as a substitute will vary with a couple or with an individual. Often people who have dabbled in psychological literature, and have encountered the belief that sexual problems are at the root of all difficulty, will assume that their marital difficulties are rooted in sex, when indeed they may not necessarily be.[13] When such people come for counseling, they may discuss sexual difficulties, giving the impression to the counselor that they are presenting significant information about their marriage. One of the authors has encountered in counseling many people who were perfectly willing to talk about sexual problems, but were quite unwilling to discuss, say, the way in which they maneuver their mates.

Very conventional people, on the other hand, may cover up a sexual problem with something more socially acceptable, such as an economic problem.[14] This tendency may be illustrated with the case of a very conventional middle-aged couple who appeared for counseling complaining about conflicts concerning economic matters. They reported that in general, aside from money squabbles, all was well in their marriage. They refused to accept the possibility that other problems could be present. Nevertheless, the counselor's impression was different. It was diffi-

---

[12] Emily H. Mudd and Malcolm G. Preston, "The Contemporary Status of Marriage Counseling," *Ann. Am. Acad. Polit. Soc. Sci.*, **272** (November 1950), pp. 102–109.
[13] One study indicated that financial problems are often the focus in marital disagreements, but usually not the cause of such difficulty. Lewis M. Terman et al., *Psychological Factors in Marital Happiness*, McGraw-Hill, New York, 1938, p. 169.
[14] *Ibid.*

cult for him to believe that a seemingly intelligent couple could not solve a budgetary problem unless there were underlying difficulties that had not been brought out. Over a period of time the underlying complications were revealed. The husband reported that for a considerable period of time he had been dissatisfied with the frequency of sexual relations but that his wife was quite unsympathetic about this. The counselor found that at this point in the marital history the husband started to nag and to complain to his wife about the amount of money she was spending. The wife in turn resented her husband's behavior, and arguments would ensue. When these patterns were brought out into the open, the question of a sexual interpretation was raised for the first time by the wife, who wondered whether her husband's concern about how much money she spent was really an attempt to get back at her for his sexual frustration. At that point, however, the wife herself rejected such an interpretation, and the husband could see little validity to it. Over a period of time the significance of the wife's interpretation emerged. The problem was sexual in nature, but not exclusively so. For there were feelings of personal rejection on the part of the husband, who was already insecure. Whenever he felt rejected by his wife, who was an emotionally aloof person, he would become vindictive; he would try to get back at her. In this particular marriage the husband's attempt to get back at his wife took the form of controlling the wife's spending habits; in other marriages a mate's vindictiveness might have another outlet.

The case we have just described illustrates several important points. The tendency to deal with the superficial aspects of a problem is frustrating and self-defeating. The people in our example could never arrive at a satisfactory solution to their problem by simply making budgetary arrangements, and yet their conventional outlook enabled them to see only an economic problem. Furthermore, dealing with a superficial dimension of their difficulty increased their frustration, since it exposed them to the same problem, or similar ones, with the likelihood that eventually they might become quite hopeless about reaching any sort of a solution.

Avoidance of Responsibility

A fourth major resistance that interferes with a couple's abilities to handle marital difficulty is the tendency to avoid responsibility for one's part in the difficulty. We hear a great deal about the need to be objective and to see all sides of a question, but often such advice, although well intended, represents an oversimplification and does not come to grips with those forces that keep people from assuming responsibility for what they do or for what they believe. There are several aspects to the problem of avoidance of responsibility. Nevertheless, an essential component found in all such people is a fear of accepting unfavorable notions about themselves. To accept patterns that may enable one to change and grow is, of course, a positive step. For many perfectionistic people, however, to accept responsibility for their part in a difficulty means to realize that they have not handled their lives with perfection; this makes them very vulnerable to self-hate and self-berating, which upsets them greatly. In order to avoid these possibilities of attack on self, such people are really fearful, and understandably so, about admitting their responsibility in the problems of marriage.

An interesting illustration of this point concerns a young wife who had become involved with other men. Although extramarital sexual relations had never occurred, they might easily have. The marriage had so deteriorated that the husband saw no point in continuing the relationship unless both of them were willing to get professional assistance. But the wife stated that she could never go to a counselor, since this would entail admitting and accepting some responsibility. She said, "I simply couldn't stand admitting I was wrong."

Overintellectualization

A fifth resistance to overcome is the tendency for couples to deal with their problems at the level of thinking only, without regard for underlying feelings. People are often told to discuss rather than argue, to be objective rather than subjective. This is not bad advice, but it often misses the point. Certainly, we can say that it is better to discuss than to argue, since in the argument one is out to win, regardless of tactics, and is not really looking for a resolution. Advising a couple to discuss and to be objective does not go far enough, however, and is therefore likely to be unrewarding. Many couples who wish to resolve their difficulties sit down with a list of cliches, believing that no problem will be insurmountable, if they maintain a reasonable, objective attitude.[15] In reality, however, the most rewarding way to deal with marital difficulties is to try to come to grips not only with the reasonable and objective remarks that people make, but also with the underlying attitudes and values of which people frequently are not aware. It is unlikely that anything that is only verbal or intellectual will bring about lasting change. But when people can emotionally integrate new views, their behavior

[15] One author calls this "discussion without communication." Henry A. Bowman, *Marriage for Moderns,* McGraw-Hill, New York, 1960, p. 317.

changes. (Our earlier discussion of distinction between intellectual and intellectual-emotional commitments developed this point of view.)

When the resistances we have described are not dealt with adequately, the quality of the marriage continues to deteriorate. Even in positive relationships some disillusionment tends to take place. When conflict is not resolved, however, disillusionment can markedly increase.[16]

It is also obvious that many unhappy associations do not end in separation or divorce. Instead, many couples prefer an accommodation of some kind rather than facing the anxieties of breaking the union. Cuber and Harroff have suggested a typology of marriages, ranging from *one* domir ..ed by conflict to *one* defined as a total relationship:

1. The conflict-habituated relationship.
2. The devitalized relationship (one devoid of zest, but without serious conflict).
3. The passive-congenial relationship (comfortable associations, but nonemotional).
4. The vital relationship (both partners share in and are indispensable to the relationship).
5. The total relationship (similar to the vital, but includes sharing in all vital aspects of relationship).[17]

It is interesting to observe that in *three* of the *five* types people have apparently accepted what seems to be a marriage with serious deficiencies.

Resolutions

It is apparent that resistances have to be overcome if marital difficulties are to be resolved. Whenever a couple can overcome the resistances that keep them from dealing with their marital difficulties, although they have not resolved their problems, they have certainly have taken an important step toward their solution. Resistances obscure difficulties

[16] Eleanore Braun Luckey, "Number of Years Married as Related to Personality Perception and Marital Satisfaction," *J. Marr. Fam.*, **28**, 2 (February 1966), pp. 44–48. George Levinger, "Marital Cohesiveness and Dissolution: An Integrative Review," *J. Marr. Fam.*, **27**, 1 (February 1965), pp. 19–28.
[17] John F. Cuber and Peggy B. Harroff, *The Significant Americans*, Appleton-Century-Crofts, New York, 1965, p. 192, Ch. 3.

and hinder solutions: resistance keeps people from admitting that anything is wrong; those who can feel that something is wrong may have a fear about communicating; those who communicate, may still avoid responsibility for the problem. Only when all these resistances are worked through can there be much hope of satisfactorily resolving marital conflicts. When resistances are removed, it is possible for a couple to develop some comprehension about the underlying attitudes and feelings that lurk beneath the surface remarks that they make about their problems. These hidden feelings and attitudes are the real indicators of motivations and go to the heart of the issues. If, in the course of a discussion about a marital problem, a couple can capture the real indicators of thinking and feeling, they can, indeed, do much about their problems. The following dispute between a husband and wife about her mother is a case in point:

Husband: Whatever you may think, I have a lot of respect for women.
Wife: I hope that's the way you feel.
Husband: Yes, you know that's the way I feel; I give them every consideration at the office and at home.
Wife: Why do you react to my mother as you do?
Husband: Your mother, well that's different. She's a woman, that's right, but she's also a mother-in-law; and that's something you don't fully understand. A mother-in-law is a special case.
Wife: Well, doesn't the idea of respect apply to her?
Husband: Yes, it does and it doesn't. It depends; now sometimes your mother is as sweet as can be; she keeps quiet and never says anything. You never know she's there. I respect her then.
Wife: You mean when she doesn't disagree, you respect her?

In this conversation, part of a lengthy discussion between husband and wife, several interesting aspects are revealed. First, regardless of what this man says, his respect for women is conditional. That is, respect depends on whether women threaten him or not. It is clear, therefore, that he can be quite inconsistent in his attitudes toward women; he behaves in different ways at different times. This husband might benefit greatly from a realization that he believes things other than what he states and, indeed, that some of his beliefs are contradictory and inconsistent. Such a realization might enable him to understand some of his difficulties in relation to women in general, as well as to his mother-in-law.

There is no intent to convey the idea that the resolution of marital conflict can be achieved through any single or simple technique. A good deal of our analysis in this book runs counter to such an idea. On the other hand, if one can assume that many marital conflicts are the result of conflicting personal views, which are neither readily known to the marital partners nor easily observable, then the ability to capture the underlying impact of marital discussions makes it possible for many couples to be of considerable assistance to each other in resolving some of their marital difficulties.

The capacity to come to grips with marital conflict through an understanding of the deeper levels of personality of the partners is perhaps one of the most essential requirements if a marriage is to develop and grow.

Summary

Marital conflict is not necessarily undesirable or destructive. Indeed, when the focus of the conflict does not involve an attack on the self-worth of the marriage partner, conflict can, and frequently does, serve some useful purposes in marriage. Conflict can, for example, (1) lead to a redefinition of the marital difficulty, (2) help the partners to develop a realistic understanding of each other, and (3) help them to appreciate the extent of their positive emotional commitments to the marriage. Some conflict is inherent in marriage and differs in degree and kind depending on the particular stage of marriage and family development.

The exterior forms of marital conflict, such as concealed, overt, acute, chronic, progressive, and habitual conflict, as well as the inner dynamics of marital conflict, were defined and discussed. In regard to the latter, it was noted, for example, that when marital conflict involves the use of certain conflict strategies, such as the "feeler" strategy, the "needle" strategy, and strategies designed to create feelings of guilt in the partner, it is least likely to serve a useful purpose in marriage. Also involved in those patterns of inner dynamics that keep people from dealing effectively with conflict are what were referred to as resistances. Resistances consist of such patterns of thinking and behaving as (1) not accepting the existence of a problem, (2) lack of communication, (3) dealing with symptoms rather than causes, (4) avoidance of responsibility, and (5) overintellectualization.

When these resistances are not adequately dealt with, the marriage shows increasing deterioration. Not all unhappy marriages result in separation or divorce, however. Some people prefer to attempt some kind of accommodation instead. It is very important, therefore, to analyze marital conflict both for people considering divorce or separation and for those seeking accommodation patterns, because an understanding of these inner dynamics of marital conflict, as well as an understanding of conflict itself, can do much to facilitate the resolution of marital conflict.

Questions

1. List and describe three useful purposes that marital conflict can serve. When is marital conflict most unrewarding and damaging to a marriage?
2. Discuss the relationship between the degree and kind of conflict and the various stages of marriage and family development.
3. Define and give an example of each of the following forms of marital conflict: concealed, overt, acute, chronic, progressive, and habitual conflict.
4. What is a strategy as it pertains to marital conflict? List and discuss the consequences of the use of strategies in marital conflict.
5. What is a resistance as it pertains to marital conflict? List and discuss the five major resistances discussed in this chapter.
6. List and discuss the patterns that impair communication of marital grievances.
7. Under what circumstances do you believe that couples can solve their marital conflicts without professional assistance? Under what circumstances do you feel that professional assistance is necessary? Discuss in full.

Projects

1. Write, and have members of the class enact, a two-part skit depicting a couple involved in a marital conflict. In the first part bring out as many of the factors as possible that impair the resolution of conflict, as discussed in this chapter; for example, an attack on the personal worth of the partner, the use of strategies, and the presence of resistances. In the second part of the skit show how these impairments might be avoided and the conflict resolved. Have the class as a whole discuss the skit.

2. Write two brief case histories involving marital conflict. For your first history use a case that involves marital conflict that you think was successfully solved; for your second history use a case involving marital conflict that you regard as unsolved. Analyze each case in terms of the discussion in this chapter.

Suggested Readings

Baszormenyi-Nagy, Ivan, and James L. Framo, Eds., *Intensive Family Therapy*, Harper and Row, New York, 1965, especially Ch. 9, "Mystification, Confusion and Conflict," by Ronald D. Laing, and Ch. 11, "Systematic Research on Family Dynamics," by James L. Framo.

Benson, Purnell, "The Interests of Happily Married Couples," *Marr. Fam. Living*, 14 (November 1952), pp. 276–280.

Bowman, Henry A., *Marriage for Moderns*, 4th ed., McGraw-Hill, New York, 1960, Ch. 10, "Adjustment in Marriage."

Duvall, Evelyn M., and Reuben Hill, *Being Married*, D. C. Heath, Boston, 1960, Ch. 14, "Coping with Conflict," and Ch. 15, "Facing Crises."

Kenkel, William F., *The Family in Perspective*, Appleton-Century-Crofts, New York, 1960, Ch. 15, "Developmental Tasks of the Married Pair."

Landis, Paul H., *Making the Most of Marriage*, 2nd ed., Appleton-Century-Crofts, New York, 1960, Ch. 21, "Marriage Adjustment," Ch. 22, "Patterns of Adjustment," and Ch. 23, "The Issues of Marriage: Happiness and Unhappiness."

Simpson, George, *People in Families*, Thomas Y. Crowell, New York, 1960, Ch. 11, "Marital Accommodation and Discord."

Chapter Nineteen

PARENTHOOD

Throughout this book we have stressed the significance of a meaningful relationship in marriage, pointing out not only how it may be nurtured, but how it may be maintained. It should be clear that the quality of the marital relationship that a couple have established is intimately related to questions regarding parenthood. In this chapter we deal with several aspects of parenthood, including motivations for parenthood, family planning, the emotional climate necessary for successful parenthood, the conditions of parenthood in America today, and finally some factors that affect a person's role as a parent.

Parenthood is highly valued in American society. Pity for those who are unable to have children and the setting aside of special days to honor mothers and fathers are but two of the indications of the importance accorded parenthood. The majority of people entering marriage desire to have children; few enter marriage expecting to have no children. Some married couples plan to have children early in their marriage, while others plan to postpone parenthood. Few couples, however, are fully aware of the factors that can disrupt their plans. For example, couples who engage in sexual relations with some frequency and regularity must face the fact that a pregnancy can occur earlier than they anticipate.

Unanticipated Early Pregnancy

Some couples have so complete a confidence in methods of child spacing that they fail to realize the limitations of such control, natural or mechanical. In this respect it is important to emphasize that in spite of widespread use of birth control methods, unplanned pregnancies in marriage do occur. They are perhaps more likely to occur during the

ILLUSTRATION: Doll and Carriage, c. 1905. Museum of the City of New York.

early period than at a later time, because of the probability of high intensity of sex desire, the probability of high fertility, and the probability of inadequate knowledge of child spacing and of birth control techniques on the part of the couple during this period. It was found, for example, that in one group of college marriages in which birth control techniques were used, two thirds of the pregnancies were unplanned.[1] Half of the unplanned pregnancies were admittedly due to carelessness in the use of the technique, but in the remainder of unplanned pregnancies the couples were unable to explain the occurrence. Consequently, young married couples, regardless of their desire not to have an early pregnancy, should at all times be prepared emotionally to accept it if it occurs. Some couples, for example, make elaborate plans for the initial years of married life, prior to parenthood. Such plans must always be made with the realization that pregnancy may not always be controllable. Couples who fail to accept emotionally the possibility of parenthood later face serious disruption in their lives and in that of a child. No couple can fully realize beforehand the demands and changes in their way of life necessitated by the birth of a child. Parenthood has been described as a crisis by some investigators.[2] In essence parenthood calls for a drastic revision of the couple's patterns, a revision that is demanded within a short period of time. Those couples who have seriously examined the social and psychological adaptation to be made are invariably in the best position to welcome the infant. When a pregnancy occurs before the marital partners are willing to accept it, they suffer, and the infant finds himself in a disturbed family atmosphere.

Although we have emphasized that marriage partners must prepare themselves for an early pregnancy, it is perhaps equally important that they give some consideration to the possibility that they may never be able to have children, and to the resolution of whatever problems they might have in regard to the acceptance of this possibility.

Childless Marriages

So much attention is given to the topic of avoiding pregnancy that the fact that some couples attempt again and again to effect pregnancy is fre-

[1] Shirley Poffenberger, Thomas Poffenberger, and Judson T. Landis, "Intent toward Conception and the Pregnancy Experience," *Am. soc. Rev.*, **17** (October 1952), pp. 616–620.

[2] Daniel F. Hobbs, Jr., "Parenthood as Crisis: A Third Study," *J. Marr. Fam.*, **27**, 3 (1965), pp. 367–372.

quently overlooked. Throughout the world 10 to 15 percent of all marriages are childless.[3] In the United States, approximately 9 percent of marriages in rural areas and 17 percent of urban marriages are childless. Admittedly, we do not know exactly what percentage of these marriages are childless by desire; but we do know that at least some of these marriages are childless despite attempts to have children. Young couples should, therefore, be prepared to face the possibility of a barren marriage, and certainly some attempt should be made to assess the attitudes of each partner toward this possibility. For many, barrenness is extremely difficult to accept. In some instances the attitudes and behavior of parents and in-laws become an important aspect of the problem. In one case of an involuntarily childless couple, the parents of the wife were certain that the inability to have children was due to some deficiency on the part of the husband. They reasoned that they, the wife's parents, had no problem having children; hence why should their daughter? The husband's mother, using the same reasoning, assured her son that the sterility was not his but his wife's. When this occurs and the desire for children is strong enough, the husband and wife may begin to blame each other for their childlessness. Thus the relationship may become disturbed.

Certainly, if either partner has knowledge of his or her sterility, withholding this information can be potentially damaging to the relationship, as it was for one woman who married late in life at the insistence of her mother, who was fearful that the woman would become "an old maid." Although the woman had known that she would be unable to bear children, her mother insisted that this not be revealed to the prospective husband, since it might bring about a change in his attitude. The woman complied and said nothing to her prospective husband. After several years of trying to have children, the husband insisted on a medical examination for each. At this point the woman revealed the fact that she could not have children. The husband became furious, accused his wife of being a liar, threatened divorce, and was on the verge of initiating proceedings. The family and friends prevailed on him to reconsider his decision. Although he has remained married, he has never forgiven his wife for withholding this important information, nor has his wife forgiven him for his hostile attitude toward her.

Whenever there is suspicion that a couple are unable to have children, it is probably best to consult a physician as early as possible. If, after proper examination and treatment, a pregnancy seems unlikely, the couple might decide whether they wish to accept their childlessness or

[3] See Abraham Stone, "World Conference on Human Infertility," *Marr. Fam. Living,* 15 (August 1953), pp. 231–233.

whether they would prefer to try to adopt a child. Adopting a child is, of course, a serious undertaking and should, therefore, be considered carefully before being attempted. The couple should recognize that complications may arise. At any one time and in any one community there can be a greater number of couples who wish to adopt than children for adoption. On the other hand, adoption of a child is probably on the whole simpler than it was in the past. For many years the law in New York required that the religion of the adopting parents and the child be the same. In August 1967 the New York State Constitutional Convention approved the revision of the "religious protection clause" in the state constitution which had been in effect for the last 36 years, by a vote of 176 to 0. The revision provides that instead of religion being the dominant consideration, "the welfare of the child shall be of primary concern" and that the religion-pairing consideration cannot be pursued if it is "inconsistent with the welfare of the child" (New York Assembly Bill 91–58). If a couple are unable to adopt a child, they must accept their childlessness and must set out to maturely build their relationship on bases other than parenthood.

Family Planning

For the majority of couples, however, plans for child spacing will be feasible and practical; their consideration will undoubtedly be given to the advantage of either having a baby during the first year of marriage or delaying the first pregnancy until sometime later in marriage.

In regard to these two possibilities, opinions differ. Some authorities claim that early pregnancy may have adverse effects on a young marriage. Such authorities believe that the adjustments to each other that husband and wife have to make are more readily achieved without the additional complications imposed by parenthood. There is some evidence that having a child during the first year of marriage does make the early period of marriage unnecessarily difficult and, according to Christensen,[4] interferes somewhat with the happiness of the couple. Furthermore, early pregnancy may detract from the spouses' initial adaptation to

[4] Harold T. Christensen and Hanna H. Meissner, "Studies in Child Spacing: III—Premarital Pregnancy as a Factor in Divorce," *Am. soc. Rev.,* **18** (December 1953). pp. 641–644. See also Harold T. Christensen, "Child Spacing Analysis Via Record Linkage," *Marr. Fam. Living,* **25,** 3 (1963), pp. 272–280.

their marital roles; this detraction may create difficulties, especially for those young couples who do not recognize and are not yet prepared to accept the responsibilities of pregnancy and parenthood.

Not all authorities view early pregnancy unfavorably, however. In fact, it is strongly favored by some. Mace,[5] for example, along with the authors, suggests that postponing pregnancy is associated with certain risks, since the likelihood of infertility increases with age; thus prolonged postponement may ultimately make pregnancy impossible. It has also been suggested that the possibility of physical complications in pregnancy increases with the age of the mother. See Dr. Lehfeldt's discussion in Appendix A.)

Indeed, because of the likelihood of a minimum number of medical complications present for the woman when births occur at younger ages, many gynecologists have even abandoned the previously held notion that children should be spaced at least two years apart. They now suggest that, in order to get the childbearing period over earlier, pregnancy can occur at more frequent intervals depending on the general health of the woman.[6]

Voluntary Childlessness

Finally, we must recognize that there are some marriages in which one or both partners do not desire a child at any time in their marriage. Some men, for example, are so opposed to becoming fathers that they refuse to accept the reality of pregnancy when it occurs in their marriages; and in so doing they may withhold the emotional support necessary to women during pregnancy. These men, when confronted with the physical signs of pregnancy during its later stages, may refuse to be seen publicly with their wives, thus making the entire period of pregnancy an unwholesome and grotesque thing.[7]

[5] David R. Mace, "Should You Have a Baby the First Year?" *Woman's Home Companion,* 76 (December 1949).
[6] Paul H. Landis, *Making the Most of Marriage,* 2nd ed., Appleton-Century-Crofts, New York, 1960, p. 504.
[7] F. Alexander Magoun, *Love and Marriage,* Harper and Brothers, New York, 1948, p. 291. Ronald Freedman and Lolagene Coombs, "Childspacing and Family Economic Position," *Am. soc. Rev.,* 31, 5 (October 1966), pp. 631–648. Charles F. Westoff and Raymond H. Potvin, "Higher Education, Religion and Women's Family-Size Orientation," *Am. soc. Rev.,* 31, 4 (August 1966), pp. 489–496.

Some of the reasons given for not wanting a child are that it limits freedom, ruins the figures of women, and, in general, does not offer rewards commensurate with the efforts involved. Some women remain childless because of an extreme fear of pregnancy and childbearing. Read points out that the fear of childbirth is not surprising in view of the fear-ridden and unwholesome attitudes that society has toward it. In fact, he goes further and states that much of the physical pain of childbirth is actually rooted in fears created by society. He describes the process by which this occurs as a fear-tension-pain syndrome—fear causes physical tension, which in turn is largely responsible for unnecessary pain during childbirth.[8]

Other authorities believe that many people who think that their motives for avoiding parenthood are simply financial or are based on fears of childbirth are really motivated by deeper psychic processes. These authorities claim, for example, that a woman who identifies with an unhappy mother, might, in avoiding parenthood, really be attempting to reject her femininity. In some instances the reluctance to have children may suggest a negative orientation toward life—that is, the reluctance to create and contribute to life. Such a deep and basic view may be related to earlier experiences in which creativity had a negative connotation. There may have been rejection or ridicule for creative efforts, or a person may have grown up feeling that what *he* or *she* creates is not of value. Under these circumstances there may be repressed fears about the creation of life itself. In other words, parenthood for some may become symbolic of conflicts with which that person is not prepared to deal.[9] Certainly, a couple should try to understand their motivations in avoiding parenthood, just as it is useful to understand the motivations for parenthood. Having said this, it should also be clear that there are many couples who refuse to have children for other kinds of reasons. Some persons have decided to pursue careers and have rationally examined the alternatives of having or not having children. Such people believe that since their career pursuits are so important and time-consuming, any children they might have would not have the proper home environment. Furthermore, there are persons whose marriages are so unstable that they question the wisdom of having children—at least until the conditions causing the marital difficulties are alleviated. Thus the decision to remain childless can be a very proper and sensible adjustment to one's life circumstances.

[8] Grantly Dick Read, *Childbirth without Fear,* rev. ed., Harper and Brothers, New York, 1953.

[9] For an extensive discussion of psychogenic sterility and case histories, see George Simpson, *People in Families,* Thomas Y. Crowell, New York, 1960, pp. 420–426.

Table 14 Desire for Children and Marital Adjustment[a]

	Poor (%)	Fair (%)	Good (%)
No children present but children desired	9	27	64
One or more children present and desired	20	33	47
No children present and none desired[b]	55	24	21
One or more children present but none desired[b]	67	22	11

[a]Adapted from Burgess and Cottrell, *Predicting Success or Failure in Marriage,* Prentice-Hall, Englewood Cliffs, N.J., 1939, p. 414.
[b]Not desired by husband or wife or both.

Although the decision to remain childless may not be indicative of deeper emotional involvements, it should be pointed out that some research available in this area indicates that the absence of desire to have children is associated with marital unhappiness.[10] Thus marriages in which children are desired, whether they appear or not, have a greater chance of success than do those in which there is no desire for children, as noted in Table 14. The reason for this association between the desire to remain childless and unhappiness in marriage is not altogether clear. It has been suggested that the desire to remain childless may be indicative of an emotionally immature personality, which, in general, has difficulty adjusting to the demands of marriage. Thus, personal immaturities may be responsible for both the unhappiness that occurs and the lack of desire to have children. Under these conditions, such immature individuals might be the very ones who are least capable of being effective parents.[11] Indeed, Magoun [12] states that when an unwanted child appears in a marriage, not only is the emotional confusion already present in the marriage increased, but one of two additional things is likely to happen. The parent either rejects the child, by loading him with feelings of hu-

[10] Robert B. Reed, "Social and Psychological Factors Affecting Fertility. VII: The Interrelationship of Marital Adjustment, Fertility Control and Size of Family," *Milbank Memorial Fund Quarterly,* 25 (October 1947), pp. 383–425. Another finding that may reflect the importance of being able to control the size of family is that of Christensen and Philbrick, which states that marriage happiness tends to decrease with an increase in family size. Harold T. Christensen and Robert E. Philbrick, "Family Size as a Factor in the Marital Adjustment of College Couples," *Am. soc. Rev.,* 17 (June 1952), pp. 306–312. See also Ernest W. Burgess and Leonard S. Cottrell, *Predicting Success or Failure in Marriage,* Prentice-Hall, Englewood Cliffs, N. J., 1939, p. 414.
[11] Paul Wallin and Howard M. Vollmer, "Marital Happiness of Parents and Their Children's Attitudes to Them," *Am. soc. Rev.,* 18 (August 1953), pp. 424–431.
[12] F. Alexander Magoun, *op. cit.,* pp. 289–290.

miliation, inferiority, helplessness, stupidity, unattractiveness, guilt, and fear, or becomes oversolicitous, hating the child with all of his "love." The falseness of such love, says Magoun, is betrayed by a series of traumatic inconsistencies, such as exaggerated expressions of affection followed by such acts as forgetting the child's birthday. Magoun claims that children are not spoiled by too much love, but that they are spoiled by a false love. It is unfortunate that the pressures in American society to have children create a situation in which parents have children against their better judgment. Obviously, this is bad for the parents, the children, and the community.[13]

Having considered childless marriages and the motivations behind childlessness, we now turn to the motivations that often underlie the desire for parenthood.

Motivations for Parenthood

The fact that a person desires to become a parent does not in itself ensure adequacy in parenthood. Instead, parental adequacy can be achieved only when the motivation for parenthood is mature, when the marriage itself is sound, and when the prospective parents are mature and integrated people. In regard to motivations for parenthood, it is evident that some motivations are mature and others immature. Immature motives are present when the child is used to aid the parent in the resolution of a personal difficulty, such as loneliness, or as a source of fulfillment of frustrated personal wishes. The child's capacity for and the direction of growth are then greatly restricted, since the child must always fit into parental needs and requirements, irrespective of what may ultimately be in the best interests of the child himself.

Immature Motivations for Parenthood

Immature motives for parenthood may be categorized into several types.

DESIRING PARENTHOOD AS A MEANS OF HOLDING TOGETHER A POOR RELATIONSHIP. This motive for parenthood is immature, since parenthood here is viewed as a method of holding together a man-woman relation-

[13] Jessie Bernard, "Developmental Tasks of the N.C.F.R.-1963–1988," *J. Marr. Fam.*, **26**, 1 (February 1964), pp. 29–38.

ship that is in the process of deteriorating. In addition to the problems that may arise from the inability to appreciate the responsibilities of parenthood, this motive is further fraught with difficulty in that parenthood is not a cure for an unhappy marriage.[14] Not only is parenthood an unlikely solution for marital problems, but the responsibilities that it entails will more than likely add further problems to a relationship already overburdened with difficulty. Parenthood may sometimes function somewhat as a "trap," holding one or both of the partners to a poor relationship. But instead of making a poor relationship more satisfying, parenthood, as already noted, tends to create further unhappiness for the marriage partners.

There is the case of a twenty-eight-year-old woman who was married to a successful professional man. The marriage was poor from the outset. The woman's solution to the marital difficulties was to become pregnant in the hope that her husband would not then wish to abandon her. Although there was every indication that the relationship with her husband was deteriorating, the woman continued in her belief that children would preserve her marriage. By the age of thirty-three this woman had three children, all conceived with the same motive. The parents were in continual conflict, and the children experienced considerable neglect. Shortly after the third child was born, the husband became involved with another woman and left his wife.

DESIRING PARENTHOOD AS A MEANS OF AVOIDING LONELINESS. In some marriages the relationship is so poor that the wife, husband, or both feel a profound sense of loneliness and distance from each other. Although such people may feel hopeless about the relationship becoming better, they believe that they might be less lonely if a child were present. To be sure, children can and do add a great deal to the life pattern of the parents, but the attempt to use children to overcome personality deficiencies, or marital deficiencies, results in considerable harm for the child. Such a parent, or parents, may make excessive demands on children, perhaps expecting them never to leave home, to marry, or to have a life of their own in any context. We discussed this point in some detail in connection with parent and in-law involvements.

DESIRING PARENTHOOD AS A MEANS OF REALIZING UNFULFILLED GOALS. In some cases a child may be desired so that a parent may realize through the child the goals he was unable to achieve by himself. Thus the son of the frustrated baseball player might be expected to be a successful participant in the Little League. To the extent that the parent's projection of his frustrated desires does not take into account the talents,

---

[14] Paul H. Landis, *op. cit.,* p. 518.

skills, interests, and experiences of the child himself, this becomes a pattern of the parent's exploitation of the child, that is, of the use of the child for the parent's own benefit. Hence the motive for parenthood as a means of achieving exploitative ends is regarded as being immature.

DESIRING PARENTHOOD AS A MEANS OF ATTAINING SECURITY. To greater or lesser degrees, the need for security enters the motivation for parenthood in at least three kinds of cases. First, some persons derive the feeling of security from the ability to carry on the family line. These people value the child as a means of continuing the family name (in cases of a boy) and as a means of living up to, and indeed even adding to, the family's already "splendid" achievements.

Second, there are those who see parenthood primarily as a means of deriving security (financial and other) in their old age. We are not referring here to those cases in which elderly parents receive emotional and/or financial support from their children, given and accepted with the love and understanding that characterize a meaningful parent-child relationship. We are referring to those cases in which the parent initially regards the child as an investment that can be called on later to yield returns; the obligation to do so is at the parent's bidding.

Third, there are those who derive a sense of security from knowing that they, by becoming parents, have fulfilled an expectation that society makes of married couples. These people consider it to be "normal" and "right" to have children; hence to be counted among the "normal" and "right" they, too, must strive to be parents.

These three motives identified with attaining security may be present to greater or lesser extent in many couples' desires for parenthood. When, however, they become the predominant motives for parenthood, they are regarded as being essentially immature, because in these cases the child is not viewed as an end in himself, but rather as a means to an end.

Mature Motivation and Meaningful Setting for Parenthood

The motivation for parenthood is mature when the child is not viewed as a means to a parental end, but as an end in itself. Parents under these circumstances desire children because of what children intrinsically represent. In such an atmosphere the child will feel free to grow and develop in terms of his own interests, talents, and wishes.

THE SIGNIFICANCE OF THE MARITAL RELATIONSHIP FOR SUCCESSFUL PARENTHOOD. In addition to mature motivations, successful parenthood is also dependent on other factors in the marital environment. When the husband and wife share a meaningful relationship with basic satisfactions, a favorable emotional climate is present which is conducive to the growth of the child.

One author, in pointing out the reciprocal nature of the love that characterizes meaningful family life, states that when both spouses derive gratification from each other, a "psychological reservoir [is created] from which the emotional security of the child is nourished." [15] Another author sums it up in this way:

> The family atmosphere surrounding the child in early infancy and childhood is the most important single factor in personality development for he absorbs the atmosphere of the life about him. Impressions and attitudes resulting from these early experiences carry over through the individual's lifetime, affecting many other relationships.[16]

PERSONALITY FACTORS IN SUCCESSFUL PARENTHOOD. In addition to the quality of the marital relationship, the personality makeup of the prospective parents is significant in successful parenthood. There are several problems that the prospective parents have to deal with and to resolve before they are ready to assume the task of parenthood.

The Insecure Parent. Parents who are insecure in their marriage, or in their person, may view the child as a threat rather than as a pleasure. For each marital partner, parenthood may mean that affection will have to be shared with the infant. Insecure people may react with resentment toward the infant in these instances.

The Egocentric Parent. Parents who are egocentric may view the child as a disturbance to personal plans. The personally pleasurable activities of mixing and socializing and of participation in clubs may have to be curtailed, and such curtailment can be experienced as an imposition. Furthermore, the daily routine of marriage may be disturbed. These changes involve some personal reorientation, which may be trying and difficult for egocentric people.

Although most people consider themselves emotionally equipped for parenthood, few probably are. Significant evidence for this is found in the high incidence of emotional instability in our society which is marked in childhood and adult psychological disorders. Much of this reflects a failure on the part of parents to provide a healthy climate for the development of mature and emotionally stable personalities.

---

[15] Therese Benedek, *Insight and Personality Adjustment,* Ronald Press, New York, 1946, pp. 32, 123–124.
[16] Paul H. Landis, *op. cit.,* p. 527.

Parenthood in Contemporary America

The insecurity, egocentricity, and rigidity in the parents just described was perhaps less serious in the past than it is today. The shift in roles of parenthood and child rearing, emphasizing the intellectual and emotional development of children, today demand a higher level of personal and social maturity on the part of the parent than was essential in the past. The extent and nature of these demands on parents may be appreciated by examining the changes as described by Evelyn Duvall. After having studied the changes that have occurred in parental roles, as well as those that have occurred in the role of the child, she dichotomizes the changing concepts of the role of mother and child into the traditional (i.e., previously accepted ideologies concerning the roles) and the developmental (i.e., contemporary ideologies concerning the roles).[17] She finds that a good mother in the traditional conception was one who:

- kept house—washing, cooking, cleaning, mending, sewing;
- took care of child physically—keeping child healthy, guarding his safety, feeding, clothing and bathing him, and seeing that he rested;
- trained child to regularity—providing a schedule, seeing to it that regular hours were given to performing important functions;
- disciplined—correcting child, demanding obedience, rewarding good behavior, keeping promises, was firm and consistent;
- made the child good—teaching obedience, instructing in morals, building character, praying for the child and seeing to his religious instruction.

Whereas a good mother in the developmental conception is one who:

- trains for self-reliance and citizenship—trains for self-help, encourages independence, teaches child how to adjust to life and how to concentrate;
- sees to emotional well-being—keeps child happy and contented, makes a happy home in which the child feels welcome and secure, thereby overcoming his fears;
- helps child develop socially—provides toys, companions, plays with child, supervises child's play;

[17] Evelyn Millis Duvall, "Differential Concepts of Parenthood," Ph.D. dissertation, University of Chicago, 1946, pp. 40–41. See also Daniel R. Miller and Guy E. Swanson, *The Changing American Parent*, Wiley, New York, 1958.

- provides for child's mental growth—gives educational opportunities, provides stimulation to learn, reads to child, tells stories, guides reading, sends child to school;
- guides with understanding—sees child's point of view, gears life to child's level, answers questions freely and frankly, gives child freedom to grow, interprets, offers positive suggestions;
- relates self lovingly to child—shows love and affection, spends time with child, shares with child, is interested in what child does and tells;
- is calm, cheerful, growing person herself—has outside interests, is calm, gentle, humorous.

In describing the changes that have occurred in the role of the child, the same author finds that a good child in the traditional conception was one who:

- kept clean and neat, obeyed and respected adults, pleased adults, respected property, was religious, worked well, and fitted into the family program.

A good child in the developmental conception is one who:

- is healthy and well, shares and cooperates with others, is happy and contented, loves and confides in parents, is eager to learn and grows as a person by developing an ability to handle himself and to handle different situations.

It is evident that the changes that have occurred in the role of the mother are primarily the result of a movement away from an emphasis on fitting the child into the family program toward emphasizing the worth and importance of the child himself. This trend is further evident in the following description of the changing role of the American father as described by another author who, using the same dichotomy of the traditional and developmental roles, found that the traditional father was one who: [18]

- was a strong individual, always right, and regarded the child as his ward;
- knew what the child should be so he did not have to seek to understand the child as an individual;
- was interested only in activities which he determined were his responsibility for the child's good;
- placed emphasis on giving things to and doing things for the child;
- was interested in child's accepting and attaining goals set by the father;

[18] Rachel Ann Elder, "Traditional and Developmental Conceptions of Fatherhood," unpublished M.A. thesis, Iowa State College, Ames, Iowa, 1947.

- found satisfaction in child's owing father a debt which could be repaid by the child's obedience and by bringing honor to the father through achieving the goals established by the father;
- felt that parenthood was a duty which the church, family and/or society expected him to discharge, or which was forced on him as a biological function.

A good father in the developmental conception is one who:

- sees himself and the child as individuals and therefore seeks to understand the child and himself;
- concerns himself with all the activities and needs of the child;
- places emphasis on the growth of the child and of himself;
- is interested in child's determining and attaining goals which the child himself has selected;
- finds satisfaction in child's becoming a mature individual and in the child's contribution to his (the father's) growth;
- feels that parenthood is a privilege which he has chosen to assume.

Once parents assume the developmental goals instead of the traditional ones, they have assumed a burden of considerable magnitude. For it is probably more difficult to be an adequate parent in the developmental sense than it is, and was, in the traditional sense. The traditional parent was an authoritarian. Thus he operated on the basis of rules and norms that were dictated by tradition. The authoritarian role enabled the parent to cover up or obscure his personal inadequacy. He could possess all kinds of personal problems, he could be aloof and distant, rigid and inflexible, unsympathetic and inconsiderate. The presence of these parental traits, moreover, did not make the parent incompetent to fulfill his role, since the goals of parenthood were different in the past. Much greater emphasis was placed on integrating the child into the family and society without regard to the child's own wishes and values.

The modern, middle-class parent, who is concerned with developmental child-rearing goals, is confronted with a series of objectives that demand of him or her a degree of maturity and integration that is often difficult to meet. To begin with, one has to be committed to the concepts of personal development and self-realization in terms of one's emotional and intellectual potentialities. Parents who are emotionally disturbed themselves, and who have serious inhibitions about their own development, may be blocked in appreciating the need for self-realization. Furthermore, the parental commitment to developmental goals requires the parent to possess the integration to create an atmosphere in which the full potentiality of the child may be realized. In the authors' view, such a development can best occur in a home where the affectional function is adequately fulfilled.[19]

Developmental Goals in Parenthood and the Affectional Function

In the final section of this chapter we deal with the affectional function (which was introduced in Chapter 4) and discuss its significance in the achievement of the developmental goals just described. With respect to the affectional function, we emphasized earlier the significance of a family atmosphere that is conducive to the development of patterns of interaction characterized by feelings of dignity and respect for individual members, as well as the importance of an emotional climate where each partner lives with warmth, emotional acceptance, and the possibility of self-realization.[20] At this point, however, we wish to deal with the affectional function in a more detailed manner. The purpose for our doing so is to show how the achievement of the developmental goals just discussed is exceedingly dependent on the fulfillment of three characteristics of the affectional function:

1. Affective dimensions.
2. The emergence of individuality.
3. The development of interpersonal relatedness.

[19] See also Nelson N. Foote and Leonard S. Cottrell, Jr., *Identity and Interpersonal Competence*, University of Chicago Press, Chicago, 1955, which contains an excellent statement of a related framework with respect to the goals of family life. Also Orville G. Brim, Jr., *Education for Child Rearing*, Russell Sage Foundation, New York, 1959, pp. 56–75. For a discussion of the fact that middle-class family behavioral patterns tend to be the norms of the society and that lower-class children, despite their socialization, tend to be expected to live up to these norms, see George Simpson, *op. cit.*, pp. 290–292.

[20] Karen Horney, "The Neo-Freudian View: Man for Himself," in Samuel Koenig, Rex D. Hopper, and Feliks Gross, Eds., in *Sociology: A Book of Readings*, Prentice-Hall, Englewood Cliffs, N. J., 1953, pp. 65–67. See also Reuben Hill, "The American Family: Problem or Solution?" *Am. J. Sociol.*, 53 (September 1947), pp. 125–130.

Affective Dimensions—The Development of the Capacity for Positive Feelings

The first significant characteristic of the affectional function, namely affective dimensions, pertains to the development of human relationships characterized by positive feelings. From the points of view of both husband and wife, this involves an interpersonal relationship characterized by empathy, understanding, respect, and appreciation. When a marital relationship of this type is present, the emergence of positive feelings in the child toward himself and toward others (empathy, understanding, respect, and appreciation) becomes a possibility. The emergence of this affective component is intimately tied to the second characteristic of the affectional function: individuality.

The Emergence of Individuality

Individuality is the right of a person to be the active agent in his own life and to select his own values out of the array of values that are available (as was discussed in Chapter 3). Mature individuality is cognizant of, and has respect for, the rights and dignity of others, and is not to be confused with indiscriminate rebelliousness (to be discussed later in this chapter).

The realization that one is accepted for what one is, as evidenced by the emergence of satisfying affective relationships, is a significant determinant in the development of individuality. The desire and courage to be oneself emerges from a respect for what one is. Individuality, therefore, emerges out of a set of human relationships that engender in the person a fundamental respect toward himself. This self-attitude may include the courage to trust one's judgments, form opinions, express oneself without fear, and choose insofar as possible the values that are meaningful to him. From these self-attitudes emerges an inner core of strength, to which the individual can turn in adjusting to the problems inherent in living.[21] The answers to personal problems may then be sought within the individual, rather than from exclusive reliance on others or from the conflicting opinions of family and friends. The person who has no confidence in his own judgment, in our sense, lacks indi-

[21] Karen Horney, *Our Inner Conflicts,* Norton, New York, 1945, Chs. 3 and 4.

viduality, because he must compulsively rely on the judgments of others.[22]

The achievement of individuality is no simple task, however, for the capacity to appreciate individuality in oneself and others is unfortunately not a common experience. The most serious obstacles to the development of individuality are overprotection and rejection.[23] Overprotection retards individuality; it leaves the child with a pervasive feeling that personal security can only be found in giving oneself up to others and their wishes. The phenomenon of rejection, on the other hand, fosters the feeling that one is unacceptable to others; from this, fears of expressing healthy convictions emerge.[24] Of special importance is parental sensitivity to the way in which the child's differences from other children emerge in early life. Sometimes these may be referred to as nuances of the child, the special flavor of the child that makes him or her a little different from a brother or sister. For parents to be in touch with this component may be of the essence in fostering individuality, since it is the uniqueness of the child that ultimately enables him to both *become himself* and yet live in the midst of differences. It may be the manner of response, a smile, a frown, the expression of an idea. These are signs of emergent individuality, when the child can begin to trust his or her own reactions, when the child's own differences bring acceptance rather than disaster. Parental understanding of this phase of development is crucial. For, indeed, to miss it may mean to undo much positive parental guidance already accomplished.

Persons who have not had the opportunity for individuality to emerge experience hopelessness and despair, which emanate from the realization that one has little control over his personal destiny. The person who achieves individuality, however, has experienced one of the most fundamental processes in human development.[25]

The significance of individuality in human development may be more fully appreciated when compared with the phenomena of indiscriminate, "blind" conformity and indiscriminate rebelliousness.

INDISCRIMINATE, BLIND CONFORMITY. Conformity is a necessary ingredi-

[22] At the marital level individuality is nurtured when the partners possess a recognition and appreciation for the healthy differences that exist between them and when they make efforts toward integration of these differences.
[23] Herman Lantz, "Problems of Social Class," in Caldwell and Foster, Eds., *Analysis of Social Problems*, Stackpole, Harrisburg, Pa., 1954, pp. 544–596. Also Leo H. Bartemeier, "The Practical Application of Basic Mental Hygiene Principles by the Cornelian Corner," *Bulletin of the Menninger Clinic*, 12 (July 1948), pp. 113–116.
[24] Arnold W. Green, "The Middle-Class Male Child and Neurosis," *Am. soc. Rev.*, 11 (February 1946), pp. 31–41.
[25] Karen Horney, "The Neo-Freudian View: Man for Himself," *loc. cit.*

ent of group life and is present within the framework of individuality. The nature of conformity in individuality is essentially different from that of indiscriminate, blind conformity, however. The person in whom individuality has emerged has developed the capacity to rationally assess a course of action with respect to whether conformity in a particular instance should or should not be followed.[26] Thus when a person of this type conforms, he does so because he believes in what he is doing.

The blind conformist, on the other hand, has learned to view individuality and self-expression with fear. In his life history, his early efforts directed at individuality were met with ridicule, rejection, and humiliation, and one available adjustment for him was the indiscriminate taking over of all group values. Thus when this person conforms, he does so merely for the purpose of conforming, without having given his behavior any thought. Such a development may not only become a blight on the individual's integrity, but may drive him to act against his best interests.

INDISCRIMINATE REBELLIOUSNESS. Individuality must also be distinguished from indiscriminate rebelliousness. Like the blind conformist,

[26] "The sociological meaning of individuality: when we extend the meaning of individuality to man we find it essential to use the term in its sociological reference. Here we say that a social being has more individuality when his conduct is not simply imitative or the result of suggestion, when he is not entirely the slave of custom or even of habit, when his responses to the social environment are not altogether automatic and subservient, when understanding and personal purpose are factors in his life activities. Individuality in the sociological sense is that attribute which reveals the member of a group as more than merely a member. For he is a self, a center of activity and responses expressive of a nature that is his own. This conception stands behind the admonition we often give to others—or to ourselves—"be yourself." Being oneself need not mean just originality; it certainly does not mean eccentricity. A strong individuality may, in fact, express more fully the spirit or quality of his country or his time, but he does so, not because he is quickly imitative or easily suggestible, but because of his sensitivity to the age itself.

"It is true that when members of a group are more individualized they will reveal greater differences and they will express themselves in a greater variety of ways. But the criterion of individuality is not how far each is divergent from the rest. It is, rather, how far each, in his relations to others, acts autonomously, acts in his own consciousness and with his own interpretation of the claims of others upon himself. When the possessor of individuality does as others do, at least in matters he deems important, he does it not simply because others do it, but because his own self approves that particular behavior. When he follows authority, except in so far as he is compelled to, he follows it partly because of conviction, not only because it is authority. He does not superficially accept or echo the opinions of others—he has some independence of judgment, some initiative, some discrimination, as we often say, some 'strength of character.' The degree in which he exhibits these qualities is the degree in which he possesses individuality." From R. M. MacIver and Charles H. Page, *Society: An Introductory Analysis*, Rinehart, New York, 1949, pp. 50–51.

the rebellious person lacks the capacity for rational assessment of group norms and personal modes of conduct. However, instead of a compulsive need to accept group norms, he has a compulsive need to reject them. The early life of such a person may have been characterized by the enforcement of very strict standards of conduct, thus creating rebellion.

The development of true individuality represents one of the fundamental problems in democratic social organization. This problem centers on how best to achieve a system of integrated social values while providing for individual selection and interpretation of social norms.[27]

Whatever else recent student movements may suggest, they do indicate needs of long-standing origin. The cries of the universities' contribution to alienation and impersonality also suggest an alienation and impersonality created earlier in life within the family. The conformist and the rebellious person may not be as far apart as they think; they may be part of a similar problem. Thus a person who finds it impossible to be an individual, may abandon attempts at individuality and conform to the expectations of others; however, periodically, when the constraints become too great he may rebel against such inner conformity. At these times conventional authority structures may become targets—university administrations, parents, and the like. The point here is not to defend authority structures or to castigate rebellious students, but simply to suggest that the problem of alienation and rebellion has origins that go back into the history of the person.

Development of Interpersonal Relatedness

By interpersonal relatedness, the third constituent of the affectional function, we mean the ability to engage in interaction with a minimum of fear, hostility, and anxiety. Interaction based on fear and anxiety stems from needs to be envious of others, to prove oneself to others, and to use others for affirmation. Only in a family in which positive feelings, related self-acceptance, and individuality have emerged can the individual be given the stability that will enable him to interact with a minimum of anxiety. Why is this so? The need to prove oneself to others stems from a rejection of oneself and fundamentally from a need to prove oneself to oneself. The need to be envious of others and the need to use others stems from a hopelessness about one's ability to attain accomplishments with any measure of success. Thus one may feel resentful about the accomplishments of others and believe that only by using oth-

[27] R. M. MacIver, *The Ramparts We Guard,* Macmillan, New York, 1950, pp. 51–53. Also Kimball Young, *Personality and Problems of Adjustment,* F. S. Crofts, New York, 1940, Ch. 23.

ers can anything worthwhile be achieved. When, however, one's individuality has had an opportunity to emerge, a feeling for what one may be able to accomplish can occur; this realization will tend to negate the need to use and manipulate others or resent their accomplishments.[28] Under these conditions interaction is characterized by an identification with—and a feeling of happiness about—the success of others.

Parental Problems in the Fulfillment of the Affectional Function

The task of developing relationships in which husband and wife are capable of fulfilling the affectional function is no simple matter, for it usually requires that the parents come from backgrounds in which the three characteristics of the affectional function have been an important part of their personal experience. That one can more readily experience toward others what one feels toward oneself is a well-recognized psychological axiom.[29] Thus the person who has been nurtured in a social milieu that has fostered the development of positive affective dimensions, individuality, and interpersonal relatedness has had the opportunity to realize the significance of these qualities. An intellectual appreciation for these characteristics of the affectional function is by itself insufficient, however, because an intellectual understanding, although it permits one to verbalize about the significance of the affectional function, does not necessarily prepare him to effect the affectional factor. For example, when the proper familial background has not been present, parents may encounter real difficulty in their attempts to create the emotional atmosphere necessary for the unfolding of the affectional function. In view of our analysis, therefore, it becomes obvious that some parents, in terms of their socialization, have greater difficulty in fulfilling the requirements of the affectional function than do others. It is of the greatest significance that individuals appreciate their shortcomings in this regard and that they attempt to do something about them in order to be able to realize their fullest potential as wives, husbands, and parents.[30]

[28] MacIver and Page, *op. cit.,* p. 52. Also Karen Horney, "The Neo-Freudian View: Man for Himself," *loc. cit.*
[29] George Herbert Mead in *Mind, Self, and Society,* Charles W. Morris, Ed., University of Chicago Press, Chicago, 1934, p. 138.
[30] Eleanore B. Luckey, "Family Goals in a Democratic Society," *J. Marr. Fam.,* **26** (1964), pp. 271–278.

Summary

All young married couples should be prepared to face the possibility of unanticipated early pregnancy. For some couples, however, it is the inability to achieve pregnancy that will be confronted. Both of these possibilities and their effects on the marital relationship were discussed in this chapter.

In fact, the entire area of family planning was considered, including the motivations that people have both for desiring to remain childless and for desiring to become parents. In regard to the latter, it was noted that certain motivations for parenthood are regarded as immature. These include such motivations as desiring parenthood (1) as a means of holding together a poor relationship, (2) as a means of avoiding loneliness, (3) as a means of realizing unfulfilled goals, and (4) as a means of attaining security. Mature motivations for parenthood, on the other hand, are those in which the child is not viewed as a means to a parental end, but rather as an end in himself. Mature motivations for parenthood, as well as a healthy atmosphere for child rearing, tend to be based on secure and meaningful marital relationships, consisting of marital partners whose personalities are devoid of insecurity, egocentricity, and rigidity. This is particularly true in the American society, where the emphasis is not on the traditional roles of parenthood, but rather on the developmental roles of parenthood. Such a setting is conducive to the emergence of the affectional function and its three characteristics: (1) affective dimensions, (2) the emergence of individuality, and (3) the development of interpersonal relatedness.

Questions

1. Discuss the pros and cons concerning (*a*) having a baby during the first year of marriage and (*b*) postponing pregnancy until later in the marriage.

2. Discuss the reasons offered by voluntarily childless couples for wishing to remain childless.

3. List and discuss the four immature motivations for parenthood described in this chapter. Explain exactly what a mature motivation for parenthood is.

4. In what ways do insecure parents and egocentric parents affect child rearing? Give examples.

5. Describe the difference between traditional and developmental roles for the mother, the father, and the child.

6. List and describe in full the three characteristics of the affectional function.

Projects

1. Make an analysis of your own parent-child relationships, noting those aspects that you regard as having resulted in a successful relationship and those that you regard as having resulted in an unsuccessful relationship.

2. Interview a number of male and female students to learn:
   a. Whether or not, when married, they desire to become parents.
   b. Their reasons for desiring to become parents or their reasons for desiring to remain childless.
   c. How soon after marriage would those who desire parenthood prefer to begin their family.

   Analyze your results in order to determine whether you find any differences between the answers given by men and those given by women.

Suggested Readings

Bergler, Edmund, *Parents Not Guilty! Of Their Children's Neurosis,* Liveright, New York, 1964.

Bettelheim, B., *Dialogues with Mothers,* The Free Press, Glencoe, Ill., 1962.

Erikson, Erik H., *Childhood and Society,* Norton, New York, 1963.

Farmer, Robert A., *How to Adopt a Child,* Arco, New York, 1967.

Hoffman, Martin L., and Lois W. Hoffman, *Review of Child Development Research*, Russell Sage Foundation, New York; Vol. 1, 1964; Vol. 2, 1966.

Kawin, Ethel, *Parenthood in a Free Nation*, Vols. 1, 2, and 3, Macmillan, New York, 1963.

Landis, Judson T., Thomas Poffenberger, and Shirley Poffenberger, "The Effects of First Pregnancy upon the Sexual Adjustment of 212 Couples," *Am. soc. Rev.*, **15** (December 1950), pp. 766–772.

Medinnus, Gene, Ed., *Readings in the Psychology of Parent-Child Relations*, Wiley, New York, 1967.

Merrill, Francis E., *Courtship and Marriage*, Henry Holt, New York, 1959, Ch. 17, "Reproductive Roles," Ch. 18, "Prenatal Roles," and Ch. 19, "Parental Roles."

Offen, J. Allen, *Adventure to Motherhood*, Simon and Schuster, New York, 1965.

Read, Grantly Dick, *Childbirth Without Fear*, rev. ed., Harper and Brothers, New York, 1953.

Straus, Murray A., "Power and Support Structure of the Family in Relation to Socialization," *J. Marr. Fam.*, **26** (August 1964), pp. 318–326.

Stroup, Atlee, and Katherine J. Hunter, "Sibling Position in the Family and Personality of Offspring," *J. Marr. Fam.*, **27** (February 1965), pp. 65–68.

Chapter Twenty

DIVORCE AND REMARRIAGE

THROUGHOUT THE book we have discussed the man-woman relation-ship as it emerges and matures; in this chapter marital dissolution is the subject. It should be clear that in spite of all that a couple may endeavor to do to resolve their marital conflicts, they may be faced with the realization that there is no longer any basis for the continuance of the relationship; thus breaking the marriage becomes a consideration. A broken marriage may be viewed as the discontinuance of a previously existing marriage relationship, which may come about either from death or from the decision of one or both of the marital partners to end their marriage relationship. We shall be concerned with the latter—that is, the voluntary termination of a marriage relationship. With this end in view, the discussion will center on such specific topics as the means by which marriage relationships may be terminated, cross-cultural and historical aspects of divorce, the legal and causal factors associated with divorce, the social factors and implications of divorce, who the divorced are, the predivorce and postdivorce stages, those who do not divorce, and remarriage.

ILLUSTRATION: Lady, Nurse, and Child, c. 1740. Courtesy of the Victoria & Albert Museum, Crown copyright.

396

The Means by Which Marriage Relationships May Be Dissolved

Desertion

One common method of dissolving a marriage is desertion—one partner simply leaves and no longer functions in the marital role. This "poor man's divorce," as desertion is sometimes called because it appears to be more common at the lower income levels,[1] may be more traumatic than divorce itself, because it is unannounced and more often than not comes as a surprise to the unprepared party remaining in the marriage. Desertion usually presents further trauma in that it occurs more frequently in the lower social class, which has a relatively high birthrate. This means that the children must be cared for by the marital partner who remains in the marriage and who receives no help from the partner who deserted.

Annulment

A second way in which marriages are sometimes terminated is through annulment. An annulment of a marriage is a legal decree stating that no valid marriage was contracted because the legal requirements of marriage were not met. This may involve fraud or deception, present at the time of the marriage on the part of one or both of the marital partners. One or both partners may have been under legal age; one or both might not have legally dissolved a previous marriage. The annulment is frequently used as a means of terminating marriage relationships in states where it is very difficult to obtain a divorce because the grounds on which a divorce can be granted are limited. Information on grounds for annulment is included in Appendix C.

Separation

A third means of terminating a marriage relationship is legal separation. Legal separation means that the marital partners have agreed to

[1] William M. Kephart and Thomas P. Monahan, "Desertion and Divorce in Philadelphia," *Am. soc. Rev.,* **17** (December 1952), pp. 719–727.

live separately and not function together as husband and wife. Legal separation does not grant the partners the right to remarry; that is, although the marital partners are not living together, in the eyes of the law they are still regarded as being married and, consequently, are not free to remarry. In spite of the fact that legal separation does allow those persons whose religion prohibits divorce a means of severing the marriage relationship, it frequently leads to major problems, particularly in cases where one or both of the separated partners become emotionally or erotically involved with another person, whom they cannot marry because of their legal marital status.

Divorce

The fourth and most common method of terminating a marriage relationship is through a divorce. Divorce is a legal means for dissolving a legally recognized union of marriage for some cause that arose after the establishment of the marriage. Through divorce the marital partners are legally returned to their single statuses and are free to remarry if they so desire.

Cross-Cultural and Historical Aspects of Divorce

Some perspective on the subject of divorce may be useful. Provisions for divorce are found in practically all societies of the world, going back to ancient times. Primitive societies permitted divorce; in fact, some primitive societies were more liberal in this respect than many contemporary societies.[2] In some societies, such as the Navaho, Cooper Eskimos, Alorese Reindeer Chukchee, and the Hopi Indians, divorce was almost encouraged.[3] And at least one society, the Crow Indians, actually encouraged divorce.[4]

In the pre-Revolutionary United States divorce tended to be rather infrequent, although there was variation from area to area. In the New

[2] Willystine Goodsell, *A History of Marriage and the Family*, Macmillan, New York, 1934, p. 30.
[3] William N. Stephens, *The Family in Cross-Cultural Perspective*, Holt, Rinehart and Winston, New York, 1963, pp. 234–235.
[4] George P. Murdock, "Family Stability in Non-European Cultures," *Ann. Am. Acad. Polit. Soc. Sci.*, **272** (1950), pp. 195–201.

Table 15 United States Divorce Rate per 1000 Married Females, 15 Years Old and Over, 1867 to 1963[a]

Year	Divorce Rate
1867	1.5
1887	2.7
1900	4.0
1910	4.7
1920	8.0
1930	7.5
1940	8.8
1945	14.4
1946	17.9
1950	10.3
1955	9.3
1960	9.2
1961	9.6
1962	9.4
1963	9.6

[a]Abstracted from Bureau of the Census, *Marriage and Divorce Statistics, United States 1887–1937,* and Bureau of the Census, *Statistical Abstract of the United States 1966* (87th Annual Edition), p. 61, Table 72.

England colonies, for example, divorce was somewhat infrequent, in the middle colonies it was even more infrequent, and, according to Kephart, it did not occur at all in any of the Southern colonies. In fact, one Southern area, South Carolina, did not permit divorce for any reason until 1949.[5]

Table 16 Percent Distribution by Marital Status for Persons 14 Years Old and Over, by Sex, in the United States, 1890 to 1966[a]

Year	Male				Female			
	S	M	W	D	S	M	W	D
1890	31.9	61.8	6.1	0.3	23.8	58.1	17.7	0.4
1940	30.7	62.6	5.4	1.3	24.2	59.3	14.8	1.6
1950	26.2	67.4	4.7	1.7	20.0	63.9	14.0	2.1
1960	25.3	69.1	3.7	1.9	19.0	65.6	12.8	2.6
1966	23.9	70.8	3.0	2.3	18.7	66.1	12.0	3.2

[a]*Current Population Reports, Population Characteristics,* Series P20, No. 159, January 25, 1967, p. 1, Table A.

[5] William M. Kephart, *The Family, Society, and the Individual,* 2nd ed., Houghton Mifflin, New York, 1966, p. 147.

Table 17 Divorce Rate per 1000 Marriages in Selected Western Countries, 1900 to 1960[a]

Country	1900	1930	1960
United States	75.3	173.9	259.0
Germany	17.6	71.4	88.7
Belgium	11.9	34.8	70.4
Norway	12.6	46.4	88.5
Sweden	12.9	50.6	174.6
France	26.1	68.6	82.4
England and Wales	—	11.1	69.5

[a]William J. Goode, *World Revolution and Family Patterns,* The Free Press, Glencoe, Ill., 1963, p. 82.

The United States divorce rate has increased considerably since the Colonial period, peaking in 1946 and then more or less stabilizing itself at a lower level, as shown in Table 15. The percentage of divorced persons in the United States has also increased, as shown in Table 16. The United States divorce rate is higher than those in other Western societies, as can be seen in Table 17. Although it tends to be the highest in the Western societies and among the large nations of the world,[6] it was not always the highest. Japan, for example, exceeded the United States in this respect until the early 1900s and Algeria until the 1940s.

With regard to the contemporary divorce pattern in the United States, there are certain pertinent facts concerning how the law functions that should be pointed out.

WRONGED AND WRONGDOER. Theoretically, divorce is almost never granted when both marital partners agree that they have contributed to the marital difficulty. Instead, divorce can be granted only in cases where one partner proves to the state that he has been offended by the other marital partner. This means that in most divorce proceedings there is one who is identified as the "wronged" and another who is identified as the "wrongdoer." In some instances this concept has led to rehearsals in the attorney's office prior to a court hearing. The object of the rehearsal is to be certain that the person suing for divorce, the wronged, knows how to respond in court. In some instances the "wronged" has become upset during the actual court proceedings and in the confusion of the moment revealed information concerning his or her personal contribution to the marital difficulty. Such cases are frequently dismissed,

[6] However, the divorce rates in about 60 percent of all small preliterate societies are higher than those found in contemporary United States. See George P. Murdock, *op. cit.,* p. 197.

since both parties have now admitted their contribution to the marital difficulty.

GROUNDS FOR DIVORCE. With respect to the legal grounds for divorce, there are vast differences among the states concerning what constitutes a basis for divorce. In some states divorce can be granted only when it is proved that one of the marital partners has committed adultery, whereas in other states divorce can be obtained also on the grounds of cruelty, desertion, nonsupport, alcoholism, committing a felony, impotence, pregnancy at marriage, and drug addiction. A list of the grounds for divorce in each state is found in Appendix C.

DIFFICULTY IN OBTAINING OBJECTIVE STATISTICS. Because of the requirement that one marital partner must be the wrongdoer and the other the wronged and because of the differences that exist between the state laws constituting grounds for divorce, it is exceedingly difficult to study objectively the causes of divorce by means of the data obtained from court records. The concepts of the wronged and wrongdoer obscure the real causes of divorce. In a vast majority of cases the party being sued for the divorce, the wrongdoer, does not contest the divorce; [7] consequently this person appears in the court data as the partner solely responsible for the difficulties in the marriage.[8] Moreover, it is generally easier for the wife to obtain the divorce than for the husband. The court is inclined to protect the woman and more likely to be conservative in granting a divorce to a man. When the wife applies for divorce, the court often assumes that a woman has considered the social and economic consequences and is prepared to accept them. Thus the fact that a woman sues for divorce does not imply that she necessarily desires a divorce. It may only indicate that she, her husband, and the attorney decided it would be the simplest way of attaining the divorce. An objective study of divorce on the basis of court statistics is also made difficult by the need to fit marital offenses into the grounds for divorce permitted within the specific state. Hence people seeking a divorce (irrespective of their reasons for doing so) frequently permit legal counsel to couch their reasons to suit the laws of the state. Indeed, the lawyer himself, regardless of the conditions involved in the particular marriage, will probably select to use grounds that will ensure that the divorce is obtained with a minimum of difficulty.

Consequently, even though some students compile statistics in the at-

[7] Alfred Cohen, *Statistical Analysis of American Divorce*, Columbia University Press, New York, 1932, p. 43.

[8] For a discussion of the "guilt" criterion in American divorce laws, see Paul W. Alexander, "The Follies of Divorce—A Therapeutic Approach to the Problem," *Law Forum*, 1949, pp. 695–711.

tempt to show what percentages of divorces are granted on the grounds of cruelty, desertion, neglect to provide, adultery, drunkenness, and the like, it is highly questionable just how accurately these statistics depict the real causes of divorce.[9]

Domestic Relations Law—Social Implications

It is obvious to observers of the legal scene that there are many problems associated with domestic relations law. It frequently places clients in the position of having to distort the truth in order to obtain a divorce. This often results in personal and social embarrassment, if evidence of mental cruelty or adultery, for example, is "trumped up" in order to meet requirements acceptable to the court in states where the only acceptable grounds are mental cruelty or adultery. Periodically the public becomes disturbed about the inconsistency, and sometimes cruelty, of domestic relations law, but usually such concern is of short duration. The American Bar Association, on the other hand, has given considerable attention to the problems involved, in the hope of working out some of the difficulties.

In order to understand some of the current problems in facing up to the difficulties with domestic relations law, it becomes important to deal with two considerations. First, although the basic reasons for divorce have changed, the legal grounds for divorce have remained essentially the same.[10] The legal grounds for divorce in America, which go back to early English law, are concerned with whether or not the marital obligations have been adhered to. These obligations are essentially moralistic in nature, involving such things as mental cruelty, impotency, adultery, drunkenness, and neglect. These grounds for divorce may have been reasonable when the basis of marriage was more narrowly construed as centering on procreation and economic considerations. Under these circumstances the grounds for divorce listed above were the only types of violations that could become a basis for marital dissolution. Today, however, marriage is rooted in several other affectional considerations

[9] For a study that attempts to get at the real reasons for divorce and desertion, see Ernest R. Mowrer, "The Variance Between Legal and Natural Causes for Divorce," *Social Forces,* 2 (March 1924), pp. 388–392.

[10] W. Freidman, *Law in a Changing Society,* University of California Press, Berkeley and Los Angeles, 1959, pp. 207, 225.

previously discussed. Thus the real basis for divorce is often more generally found in some form of interpersonal incompatibility. Domestic relations law, for the most part, fails to take into account the change in the
basis of marriage and the resultant causes of marital failure.

A second consideration affecting revisions in domestic relations law
concerns the political ramification for those individuals who would recommend change. Members of legislative bodies, and others concerned
with such change, are invariably fearful of attacks either from those who
wish to maintain the law as it is or from those who wish to liberalize and
change the laws. Fears of antagonizing some section of the populace have
resulted by and large in a "hands-off policy" with respect to domestic relations law.[11]

Divorce—Social Implications

Although throughout history more American marriages have been
broken by death than by divorce, the divorce trend has shown an increase over the years.[12] Indeed, of all marriages taking place in 1900 only
about one in twelve resulted in termination through divorce, and in
1922 about one in eight; whereas it is believed that of all marriages taking place currently at least one in four will be terminated by divorce.[13]
Furthermore, an increase in the American divorce rate is occurring even
among couples who have children.[14]

It is believed that the increased rate of divorce is the result of the vast
social changes that have been taking place in the American society and of
the marital incompatibilities that are related to these changes. The
reader will recall that in Chapter 3 we stressed the significance of the
change from rural to urban society, the economic emancipation of
women, the increased secularization of American social life, the resulting decline in religious sanctions, the individualistic basis for mate se-

[11] Fowler V. Harper, *Problems of the Family*, Bobbs-Merrill, Indianapolis, 1952,
pp. 771–775.
[12] In 1890, 33 marriages per 1000 were terminated annually; of these 3 by divorce and
30 by death. In 1957, 27 marriages per 1000 were terminated annually; of these 10 by
divorce and 17 by death. Paul H. Landis, *Making the Most of Marriage*, 2nd ed.,
Appleton-Century-Crofts, New York, 1960, p. 25.
[13] *Ibid.*, p. 612.
[14] Paul H. Jacobson, "Differentials in Divorce by Duration of Marriage and Size of
Family," *Am. soc. Rev.*, 15 (April 1950), pp. 235–244.

lection, and the individualistic basis of marital expectations. All of these have been responsible for a new basis for family life, which has not yet had sufficient opportunity to stabilize itself. It is axiomatic that whenever social systems of any type go through change, instability will result. It is important, therefore, to view the current instability of the American family in proper perspective. There are some people who see the high divorce rate as an indication that the institution of marriage and the family are becoming individualistic and atomistic; they see a grim future for the family and predict ultimate disintegration of family life as we know it today. The vast majority of professionals, however, see the current crisis in family life as one phase in the process of social change. Thus the current crisis is viewed as stemming from the fact that the traditional basis of family has disappeared, but a new basis for family living has not yet fully emerged. When such emergence is complete, it is believed, families will be integrated around the concept of democratic-individualistic values. Under these conditions people will remain married not because society expects them to, but because they so desire, since their most cherished values are to be found in family living.[15] Until such time we can expect a continuation of instability—an instability, however, that may be avoided in some instances and stabilized in others through marriage education, marriage counseling, and the like.

Divorce—Personal Implications

Divorce is a procedure that enables those who are involved in an unhappy marriage to legally start over again in the pursuit of marital happiness. Nevertheless, for many people divorce may solve little. Those who are divorced for neurotic reasons may not be capable of benefiting from the second chance that divorce offers them; instead, divorce may merely result in a series of unsuccessful marital ventures. One authority, for example, claims that divorce is merely a temporary respite and strategic retreat in the great battle of neurosis.[16] By this he means that many neurotics seek a divorce when their neurotic way of life is questioned or disturbed.

[15] Mabel A. Elliott, "The Scope and Meaning of Divorce," in Howard Becker and Reuben Hill, Eds., *Family, Marriage, and Parenthood,* 2nd ed., D. C. Heath, Boston, 1955, p. 669.
[16] Edmund Bergler, *Divorce Won't Help,* Harper and Brothers, New York, 1948, p. 27.

There was the case of a middle-aged man with an excessive need to dominate. For years he was able to dominate his wife, much to the amazement of the immediate family and close friends. At one point in their marriage the wife decided to go to a university in order to develop whatever potential she might possess and to pursue the esthetic values that interested her. Such action on her part resulted in a prolonged series of arguments in which the husband attempted to discourage his wife by disparaging her goals. He was unsuccessful in his attempt to discourage her and discovered that she was becoming increasingly self-reliant. At this point the husband forbade his wife to continue attending school. After a series of violent disputes in which the wife refused to stop attending school, the husband threatened and finally arranged to divorce her. Two years later the husband remarried. This time he married a woman very similar to his former wife as she had been during the early part of their marriage—insecure, timid, and very self-effacing. He divorced his first wife because she no longer fitted in with his neurosis, and he sought another woman who would. If his second wife were to mature, the husband would be faced with a similar set of problems.

It should be noted that many people who are married to neurotics and emotionally immature individuals make the necessary adjustments so that life is tolerable. Nevertheless, these adjustments are usually made at a considerable sacrifice in terms of the personal happiness that can be derived from marriage; acceptance of the sacrifices entailed should only be done after serious deliberation.

From all that we have said it should be clear that individuals in marital conflict should attempt to make some effort to assess their motivations for seeking divorce. Particularly, they need to have some understanding of the variables, personal and social, that have led to the deterioration of their relationship. Only then is there hope that these individuals will have some appreciation of what has happened, and some vision regarding how to avoid similar involvements.

Who the Divorced Are

In earlier chapters we discussed certain factors that were found to be associated with successful marriage and certain other factors that were found to be associated with unsuccessful marriage. An understanding of these factors will not only give the reader a general picture of divorce, but may also provide him with an understanding of certain aspects of his own marriage. First, it should be pointed out that those factors that were discussed in Chapter 11 as being related to unsuccessful marriage tend to be found to a large extent among the divorced population. These include, among others, such factors as the marital partners' coming from markedly different cultural backgrounds, educational levels, and social classes; displaying domineering, pessimistic, or overly sensitive personality characteristics; lacking self-confidence or being overly self-sufficient; having inadequate sexual knowledge and training; having unhealthy attitudes toward sexual relations; and using inadequately the courtship stage of the man-woman relationship.

In addition to these findings derived from marriage prediction studies, there are other significant factors that have been reported, such as the findings in regard to ethnic origin, rural and urban environments, race, age at marriage, duration of marriage, economic status, educational level, childless marriage, and size of family.

Ethnic Origin

The American divorce rate is highest among persons born in this country whose parents are also native Americans. The next highest rate is found among native Americans whose parents were (or at least one parent was) foreign-born. Those who show the least rate of divorce are the foreign-born Americans. The fact that the foreign-born show the least rate of divorce probably reflects a number of factors. For example, it may be that divorce as a means of solving marital difficulty is simply not a part of the cultural heritage of these people. Or, as one sociologist notes, perhaps the expectations of the foreign-born regarding marriage are less demanding; hence these people may experience fewer of the frustrations and disappointments that might lead them to seek divorce. Also, many of them are likely to be followers of Roman Catholicism and, therefore, not likely to divorce.[17]

Rural and Urban Environments

Urban areas have a higher divorce rate than do rural areas. This might mean that marital expectations are higher and more individualistic among urban dwellers; thus more marital frustration would be experienced. Or this higher urban divorce rate could also point to a predominance of occupational frustration in the urban setting, causing some

---

[17] Jessie Bernard, *Remarriage,* Dryden Press, New York, 1956, p. 79.

people to attempt to displace their hostility in the man-woman relation-ship.[18]

Race

When the divorce rates of Negroes and whites coming from the same community background are compared, the Negro grouping reflects the higher divorce rate, although the proportion of divorced persons among all Negroes is relatively small.[19] This apparent contradiction is ex-plained by one sociologist, interested in the study of divorce, as resulting from the fact that the Negro grouping is predominately found in rural areas, which, as we have already seen, produce fewer divorces than do urban areas.[20] It should be noted, however, that the Negro divorce rate itself may be of questionable significance, since, particularly among the lower-class Southern Negroes,· many marriages tend to be informally contracted (common-law) and require no formal divorce for their termi-nation. Consequently, marital disorganization among the Negroes may be even higher than would be apparent in the divorce statistics.

Age at Marriage

One study, which is representative of other similar studies, showed that the divorced, both men and women, tended to marry at a younger age than did the nondivorced (those still married). The average age of first marriage for divorced females was 19.9 years and for nondivorced females 21.5 years; for divorced males it was 23.2 years and for nondi-vorced males 24.1 years.[21] This may imply that those who marry at an earlier age tend to be less socially and psychologically mature than are those who marry later. Or it could mean that earlier marriages are asso-ciated with lower educational and income groupings, because each of these, as we shall see presently, tends to be related to high divorce rates.

Another interesting finding concerning age and divorce is that among the divorced the difference in the age of husband and wife is greater than it is among the nondivorced.[22] In this regard, although the risk of di-vorce is present when the husband is quite a bit older than his wife, it is

[18] George Simpson, *People in Families*, Thomas Y. Crowell, New York, 1960, p. 355.
[19] See Jessie Bernard, *loc. cit.* See also William J. Goode, *After Divorce*, The Free Press, Glencoe, Ill., 1956, Ch. 4.
[20] Jessie Bernard, *loc. cit.*
[21] Harvey J. Locke, *Predicting Adjustment in Marriage*, Henry Holt, New York, 1951, pp. 101–104.
[22] *Ibid.*

even more apparent in marriages where the wife is quite a bit older than her husband.[23] The relationship between age differential and divorce is probably best explained in terms of differences between the marital partners in regard to such items as sexual adequacy and social values, since both of these tend to be affected by age.

Duration of Marriage

The first five years of marriage are the most hazardous years in that the majority of the divorces that occur do so during this period.[24] The high divorce rate during this period probably results from the fact that this is the period of marriage during which the majority of incompatibilities appear and adjustments between the spouses are made. Some couples may be able to accommodate and adjust to each other; these couples remain married. Other couples, however, may be unable to effect satisfactory adjustments; these marriages tend to become the potential divorce cases.

Economic Status

Contrary to common belief, divorce is most frequent at lower income levels.[25] This finding might imply that, although all marriages require adjustments on the part of the spouses, the added strain of financial burdens decreases the desire to work at making such adjustments for those in low-income brackets. Thus these people may have less incentive to effect marital happiness.

Educational Level

In spite of the findings above pertaining to economic status and divorce, the divorce rate tends to increase as the level of education increases up to and including graduation from high school; however, the divorce rate for college graduates is lower than the divorce rate for any other educational level.[26] This drop in the divorce rate for college graduates may be the result of the education received; or it may mean that college attendance caused marriage to occur at a later age. The significance of this latter point was discussed previously.

[23] See Mabel A. Elliott, *op. cit.,* p. 686.
[24] Paul H. Jacobson, "Differentials in Divorce," *loc. cit.*
[25] Harvey J. Locke, *op. cit.,* p. 283.
[26] This study pertains only to native white American men. William F. Ogburn, "Education, Income, and Family Unity," *Am. J. Sociol.,* **53** (1947–1948), pp. 474–476.

Children and Divorce

In a previous chapter we noted that the presence or absence of children in a marriage does not tend to be related to marital success, but that the desire to have children is found more frequently among the successfully married and the lack of desire for children is found more frequently among the unsuccessfully married. Regarding divorce and children, couples with no children tend to have a higher divorce rate than do couples with children; this is particularly true for those who have been married for five years or less.[27] After five years of marriage, however, the divorce rates between those with children and those without children tend to become more similar; and by the eighteenth year of marriage the divorce rate for both groups is very similar.[28] This could imply that the inability to have children might be an area of marital conflict during the earlier years. Or that the decision to have children reflects a satisfaction with the marriage relationship, whereas in unsatisfactory marriage relationships there may be a reluctance to have children.

In regard to the number of children and divorce, the findings suggest that the greater the number of children, the smaller the divorce rate.[29] This could reflect the presence of large families among Roman Catholics for whom divorce is prohibited; or it could imply that "the inseminatory success manifested to the father by the presence of his large brood may be a compensation to the husband and father for conditions which might otherwise lead to divorce." [30]

It is particularly interesting to note the fact that the low divorce rate for large families when coupled with the high divorce rate for low-income levels would seem to suggest that in the low-income grouping those with few or no children are extremely susceptible to divorce. It would also appear to suggest that persons in the higher income levels who have large families are extremely well protected from divorce. But, indeed, more research, with combinations of various factors included, is needed before we shall be able to understand more fully the conditions of divorce.

Finally, we wish to add that although the reasons for the association between divorce and the social variables we have discussed are not completely understood, they do provide a couple with potential indices of

[27] Paul H. Jacobson, "Differentials in Divorce," *loc. cit.*
[28] *Ibid.*
[29] *Ibid.*
[30] George Simpson, *op. cit.,* p. 352.

vulnerability, and such awareness may enable the couple to understand with more clarity some of their difficulties.

Having discussed briefly the factors that have some relationship to divorce, we now consider the psychic and social circumstances that precede and follow divorce.

Predivorce and Postdivorce

Contrary to the widespread notion that people go through a divorce with a minimum of psychic disturbance, divorce is generally an emotionally, psychologically, and socially traumatic experience, which leaves its marks and scars on the personalities involved. To begin with, many individuals experience a sense of personal rejection, which is painful. Even when there is mutual agreement that the divorce is necessary, each may feel that he was not wanted or desired by the other. Furthermore, there may be a profound feeling of having failed in a personal sense. It is as though the couple "should have made it work" in spite of any obstacles in their path. The extent to which one is disturbed by a divorce is frequently increased when one member of the former marriage decides to remarry. For the remaining individual the remarriage of his former spouse may prove to be rather traumatic. This is particularly so when one member of the relationship continued to hope, as many do, that somehow even after the divorce "they would get back together." Sometimes these people become martyrs, waiting for the mate to return. In other instances they may desperately plunge into a new relationship prematurely in order to prove that they are still lovable and desirable.

Divorce and the Middle Class

Among the middle class, especially, divorce may come as a crisis. Middle-class people are frequently insecure about their positions in the community and are usually very eager to be thought well of by others. Thus they are particularly vulnerable to the negative definitions that others in the community might have regarding divorce. These negative reactions from the community may be based on several factors. For some people divorce represents the dissolution of a unit that is the basis of orderly group life; for others it has sinful connotations that are rooted in religious conviction. For a good many others, however, divorce is upsetting because they see it as a potential solution for their own inadequate marriage; nevertheless, because of personal fear or pressure from community or church, they attempt to drown out the temptation by denying any valid basis for divorce and by condemning persons who do divorce. Often the marriages of the people who do not divorce are fundamentally far worse than many marriages that end in separation or divorce.

There is the case of a couple who had been married for twenty years; these people had never been happy in their marriage, and throughout most of it they had been involved in serious marital conflict. Whenever they interacted with each other for an extended period of time, they ended up arguing about even minor issues. Thus over a period of time their relationship deteriorated until they had almost nothing to do with each other. It is interesting to note, however, that this couple, with an exceedingly poor relationship, were the most outspoken members of their community against the divorce of others.

In spite of the personal and social complications, people do adjust to divorce, and the degree of trauma in achieving this adjustment decreases as the mutuality in desiring the divorce increases. If, for example, there has been a prolonged period of estrangement or the partners have not seen each other for an extended period of time, divorce is much less of a crisis. Although some divorces appear to be sudden and without a prior history of marital discord, there is most often a process through which the couple pass before reaching a final decision. Let us consider this process in greater detail as we discuss the predivorce and postdivorce stages.

Willard Waller was perhaps the first sociologist to make a study of the impact of divorce on the persons involved about thirty-five years ago. His effort consisted of a sample of case histories, which he analyzed. Many of Waller's observations described in *The Old Love and The New* and in *The Family* are still of relevance. Some of his comments on the predivorce and postdivorce stages are outlined below.[31]

31 Willard Waller, *The Old Love and The New*, Introduction by Bernard Farber, Southern Illinois University Press, Carbondale, Ill., 1967, a reissue. Willard Waller and Reuben Hill, *The Family*, rev. ed., Dryden Press, New York, 1951, pp. 513–515.

Some Disturbance of the Affectional-Sexual Life

This usually involves the withholding of affectional response because of some unsatisfactory marital condition; or it may involve more subtle forms of attempting to compensate for lack of rapport in other areas of marital life by an overemphasis on the demands made in the affectional-sexual area. It is not uncommon for one or both members of the relationship to become involved with someone outside the marriage during this initial stage. The outside affair may be a variable in initiating the marital disturbance, an impetus in furthering the deterioration of the marriage, or both. Although vigorously denied by some, a good many of those who become divorced have either already established a relationship outside of marriage, or at least they believe that the possibilities of doing so are promising.

The Mention of the Possibility of Divorce

Just as the declaration of love and the intent to marry initiates the courtship period, so the mention of divorce by one or both marital partners indicates the presence of rather marked difficulties in the marriage relationship.

The Appearance of Solidarity Is Broken

At this point the couple begin to openly admit to friends that their marriage is in difficulty, and increasingly they come to take the world into their confidence. This may include more emphasis on blaming the marital partner for the crisis. During this stage parents and friends in attempting to help may agree with each marital partner in turn or even set out on their own to try to "patch things up" for the couple; usually a series of homespun lectures based on cliches are offered.

The Decision to Divorce

The decision to divorce is sometimes made in haste and anger, but more frequently it tends to be the result of a continued state of extreme dissatisfaction with the marriage, which one or both partners simply decide to terminate. The fact that in most cases it is the wife who files for divorce does not necessarily mean that wives are more desirous of divorcing than are husbands. In some cases this may be so, but when there is an equal desire to divorce, it is usually the wife who files for the divorce.

Also, in certain cases where the husband may actually be the partner who first desires divorce, he may create a series of circumstances that make it ultimately necessary for the wife to desire and to file for divorce.[32]

Crisis of Separation

During this stage the marital partners live apart. This often tends to be a traumatic phase, since it involves the realization that a new way of life must be established. However, the extent of the trauma may be markedly reduced in those cases where the partners are already involved in new love relationships.

The Divorce

This is the final severance of the marriage relationship. And although both partners by now have had time to prepare emotionally for the reality of divorce, the finality of divorce at this point still tends to be difficult to accept, unless, of course, a new love affair has emerged.

The Period of Mental Conflict

The stage following the divorce is generally a difficult one. One student of divorce found that most people regretted their divorces, feeling that perhaps they had acted too hastily.[33] This finding, however, has been questioned.[34] It is at this time that the reconstruction of one's new life pattern must crystalize; this is never worked out simply. The reconstruction usually calls for establishing a new social pattern and a new circle of friends. For despite the soundness of previous friendships, the individual frequently discovers that he no longer feels comfortable with the married couples of his previous acquaintance.[35] Also, one has to break established patterns of eating, sleeping, and sexual behavior.

Women have particular problems in this regard, since the divorcée may discover that other married or engaged women consider her a threat to their own relationships. The belief is that the woman who has already

[32] William Goode, *op. cit.*, Ch. 11.
[33] Willard Waller and Reuben Hill, *The Family*, *rev. ed.*, *op. cit.*, p. 514. See also Willard Waller, *The Old Love and The New*, *op. cit.*
[34] William Goode, *loc. cit.*
[35] In one study of divorced women, however, it was found that they did not regard themselves as social outcasts but instead were able to retain their previous circle of friends. William Goode, *loc. cit.*

been divorced is less governed by conventional patterns and may seek involvement with other men. Furthermore, she has certain related difficulties in her relationships with men. Many men, married or single, look on the divorcee as one who has already participated in sexual relations, is now without sexual activity, and is therefore "a pushover" for the right individual. Thus many divorced women complain that it is exceedingly difficult for them to establish relationships in which men are not out to exploit them sexually.

One divorced woman reported that she had received numerous proposals of marriage, but all of them were contingent on sexual involvement before marriage. In each instance refusal to participate in sexual relations resulted in a decline in interest on the part of the male.

At any stage in the alienation pattern a couple may decide to attempt a reconciliation and to remain together as husband and wife.[36] For some couples reconciliation seems to work, but for many others it tends to lead to a series of reconciliations necessitated by the repeated occurrence of crises, which themselves tend to become increasingly serious in nature.

Divorce Avoided after Suit Has Been Filed

Not all people who file for divorce end up getting a divorce. Indeed, one study found that between 20 and 45 percent of all divorce cases filed were dismissed.[37] This study notes that the reason for nearly all dismissals was reconciliation, but it also notes that in a large percentage of these cases reconciliation did not last and the couples eventually divorced. Dismissal was more likely to occur if there were children, the partners claiming that their attempted reconciliation was for "the good of the children." Advice on the desirability of dismissing a divorce suit is sometimes but not generally sought from the lawyers and judges involved in the cases.[38]

[36] Indeed, some couples even attempt a reconciliation after they have been divorced, for, as one study points out, a significant proportion of the divorced persons who take mates of like marital status involves persons who had been married to each other previously; they marry each other again. Paul H. Jacobson, *American Marriage and Divorce,* Rinehart, New York, 1959, p. 67.

[37] Quentin Johnstone, "Divorce Dismissals, a Full Study," *Kansas Law Rev.,* 1, 3 (May 1953).

[38] Some authorities feel that many lawyers and judges are not capable of performing such counseling in spite of the fact that this would appear to be not only a desirable but also an important aspect of their roles. Paul W. Alexander, *loc. cit.*

In many cases of reconciliation little improvement in the marriage actually occurs. Instead the couple, although very unhappy, decide to accept their state of unhappiness. The relationship for these people has lost its meaning and is held together by other considerations. Thus some people prefer to remain together in spite of marked incompatibility because of religious considerations. Others fear being left alone. Still others remain together because of neurotic needs. For example, a vindictive person who has a need to "get back" at the mate will cling to a bad relationship in order to inflict suffering on the partner. A masochistic person will remain in an undesirable marriage in order to punish himself. An individual with a need to dominate will remain in a marriage in order to satisfy that need. Thus some people actually enjoy the unhappy state of their marriage, because it fulfills for them certain neurotic needs that they have developed.[39]

Holy Deadlock: Unhappy Marriages in Which No Divorce Suit Is Filed

Finally, as was mentioned in an earlier chapter, there are unhappy marriages in which the partners never file suit for divorce, although they may threaten to do so. These people frequently remain together because of religious considerations, fear of being left alone, the need to hurt the other, punish oneself, or dominate or be dominated in very restrictive ways. The failure to file for divorce, therefore, is no indication of marital success, because these marriages may, indeed, be very poor qualitatively.[40]

[39] We have discussed, in an earlier chapter, the immature needs on which a love relationship may be based. See also the chapter on marital conflict.

[40] One writer, LeMasters, suggests that in marital failure of this type the male tends to suffer more than the female. E. E. LeMasters, "Holy Deadlock: A Study of Unsuccessful Marriages," *Sociol. Quart.*, 21 (1959), pp. 86–91. He attributes this to the fact that women's substitutes for unhappy marriage, such as concentration on children, church, and the like, are more in line with the basic values of society than are the men's substitutes, which frequently include liquor, women, and gambling. LeMasters thinks that persons involved in unhappy marriages, but nevertheless able to minimize the degree of personal disorganization that they experience, achieve this by (1) developing an ability to tolerate frustration, or (2) displacement, or (3) creating and living in "separate worlds."

Another researcher, Landis, whose sample included almost 3000 college students, who were questioned about their parents' marriages, found that among the unhap-

Effects of Divorce on Children

The relationship between the occurrence of divorce and its consequences on the children who are involved has always interested the layman and the professional. The traditional view has been that such family
dissolution was devastating for the children, involving an uprooting
from relationships with family and friends. This view is based on the assumption that before divorce the children involved had a set of warm,
stable, and dependable relationships, which were suddenly dissolved.
Although such a situation is possible, in general this is probably an unwarranted assumption. For indeed in many cases the relationships prior
to divorce were devoid of any stability and predictability. In such cases
the actual occurrence of separation or divorce might prove to be less traumatic for children than a continued existence in a family atmosphere of
hostility and distrust.

One authority feels, for example, that divorce is frequently overestimated as the factor most harmful to children, because in reality the state
of unhappiness and family trauma that precedes divorce may play an
equally or even more damaging part than the divorce.[41] Thus it is conceivable that the continued exposure to family trauma may prove more
harmful to children than the actual severing of the family relationship
through divorce. This suggests that just as divorce offers marital partners "another chance" for marital happiness, so too may it offer children
"another chance" of being exposed to a more secure and meaningful
family atmosphere.[42]

Having pointed this out, we must also indicate that divorce under any
circumstances probably involves some trauma for the child. The exact
significance of the trauma is questioned by at least one researcher, whose

pily married those who divorce tend to (1) marry younger, (2) have more education,
(3) involve wives working outside the home, and (4) be more nonreligious; whereas
those who remained married in spite of the unhappy marital state (1) were older
when married, (2) had less education, (3) involved wives not working outside the
home, and (4) tended to be more religious. Judson Landis, "Social Correlates of Divorce or Nondivorce Among the Unhappy Married," *Marr. Fam. Living*, **25**, 2
(May 1963), pp. 178–180.

[41] J. Louise Despert, *Children of Divorce*, Doubleday, New York, 1953.

[42] F. Ivan Nye, "Child Adjustment in Broken and in Unhappy Unbroken Homes,"
Marr. Fam. Living, **19** (November 1957), pp. 356–361.

findings raise questions about whether family dissolution is as influential a factor in children's lives as many consider it to be.[43] It would appear, however, that some degree of insecurity would be likely for the child of the broken family, and in those instances where there already is marked insecurity, the final act of divorce can create, at least for the moment, even more insecurity. In this regard we must remember that particularly young children with limited understanding may interpret divorce as a sign of rejection in an intensely personal way. Thus a young child may come to feel that a father who left the family has really abandoned him and for some reason no longer loves him. The fact that young children cannot always communicate such fears raises the possibility of unintended but nevertheless undesirable personality consequences for the child. Responsible parents must always be alert to this in order that they be able to cope with these destructive interpretations that children may come to believe.

Divorce in any event is a serious step, usually affecting the lives of several people. Thus it is important to understand when divorce will constitute a solution to one's difficulties and when the the dissolution of a family will present more problems than it will solve.

Remarriage

In the final section in this chapter we would like to discuss the question of remarriage. Such a discussion may prove of general interest, since it will help orient the reader to certain pertinent facts about those who remarry. It may also be of personal interest to those who have terminated their marriages and who contemplate remarriage.

Remarriage after divorce is a common experience, and the chances for happiness in subsequent marriages are fair. Most persons who remarry after divorce do so in a relatively short period after their marriages are dissolved.[44] Women tend to remarry approximately 4.6 years after divorce and men 2.5 years after divorce.[45] In fact, it is interesting to note that divorced people tend to remarry sooner than the widowed. In one

---

[43] In the same study, the impact of family reconstitution on the child's life is also questioned; see Lee Burchinal, "Characteristics of Adolescents from Unbroken, Broken and Reconstituted Families," *J. Marr. Fam.*, **26** (February 1964), pp. 44–51.

[44] Paul H. Jacobson, *American Marriage and Divorce, op. cit.*, pp. 69–70.

[45] Jessie Bernard, *op. cit.*, p. 11.

study it was reported that three fourths of all divorced persons were re-married within five years; however, of those who had been widowed for five years, only one half of the men and one fourth of the women had remarried.[46] In regard to contemporary community attitudes toward the remarriage of divorced people, it appears that the trend is toward greater receptivity, and the attitudes at present seem to be more favor-able than unfavorable.[47]

Who Remarries [48]

THE REMARRIED WOMAN—A STATISTICAL AVERAGE. The remarried woman was at first marriage in her very early twenties. Her marriage lasted approximately 5.8 years, which means that she was in her later twenties when divorced. She remained unmarried for a period of about 4.6 years and remarried in her early thirties. She had, on an average, slightly more than one child. She retained sole custody of the child after divorce. Her child's attitude toward her remarriage ranged from that of favoring it to that of showing indifference toward it; and toward her new spouse the attitude of her child tended to be friendly. This attitude was reciprocated by the new spouse (new father) who felt affection for her child; however, the remarried woman's attitude toward her spouse's children, although affectionate, was less affectionate than was her new husband's attitude toward her child. On the latter point it should be noted that the custody of the children tends to fall to the mother; there-fore, the remarried woman does not usually live with the children of her new husband. The attitude of the parents of the remarried woman tends to be more favorable toward her second marriage than they were toward her first marriage.

THE REMARRIED MAN—A STATISTICAL AVERAGE. The remarried man at first marriage was approximately twenty-four years old, his marriage lasted for about seven years. This means that he was in his early thirties when divorced. He remained unmarried for only 2.5 years and remar-ried in his middle thirties. He did not get the custody of his child (aver-age children 1.39); the attitude of his child toward his remarriage was largely one of indifference, and the child's attitude toward his new spouse ranged from neutral to friendly. As we have noted, his wife's atti-tude toward his child ranged from affectionate to neither affectionate nor rejecting, but his attitude toward her child was more affectionate. The attitudes of the parents of the remarried man, very similar to the

[46] *Ibid.*, pp. 65–66.
[47] *Ibid.*, pp. 12, 37.
[48] *Ibid.*, pp. 11–12.

attitudes of the parents of the remarried woman, were more favorable toward his second marriage than they were toward his first marriage.

Having presented a brief sketch of the remarried woman and the remarried man, let us now examine the findings in regard to marital success or failure for these groupings. Although it is noted that the divorce rate for remarried persons is higher than it is for the first marriage—incidentally, this tends to increase with each successive remarriage [49]—most studies find that over half of the remarriages are reported to range in happiness from above average to extremely successful.[50] This would seem to uphold clearly the statements made earlier that many people are capable of utilizing the opportunity that divorce offers them to begin a new marital relationship in which they can find happiness. However, the data also suggest that for others, remarriage is associated with marital unhappiness similar to that of the first marriage. In such cases, until the personality problems and immaturities involved are dealt with, these people will be unable to participate meaningfully in any marriage relationship.

Summary

Marriages may be dissolved involuntarily by death or voluntarily by desertion, annulment, separation, or divorce. In this chapter consideration was given to marriages that are dissolved by divorce. The cross-cultural and historical aspects of divorce were considered, as well as the social and personal implications of divorce. The relationships between divorce and ethnic origin, rural-urban residence, race, age at marriage, duration of marriage, economic status, educational level, and the presence or absence of children were described. Predivorce and postdivorce stages were discussed. The predivorce and postdivorce stages include the following: (1) some disturbance of the affectional-sexual life; (2) the mention of the possibility of divorce; (3) the appearance of solidarity is broken; (4) the decision to divorce is made; (5) crisis of separation begins; (6) the divorce takes place; and (7) the period of mental conflict that follows divorce.

Also discussed were the effects that divorce has on the marital partners and on the children who are involved. In this regard it was noted that

[49] *Ibid.*, pp. 66–67.
[50] *Ibid.*, pp. 108–113.

when both marital partners are desirous of obtaining a divorce, a minimum of psychic trauma results. However, if only one of the partners desires the divorce, the trauma may be increased tremendously. With regard to children, it was noted that a parental divorce always involves some amount of psychic trauma. However, it was suggested that in some cases the harmful effects of this trauma may be less than those experienced by the child who is forced to live in a parental environment saturated with hostility and anxiety.

Remarriage was then discussed and a description was given of the remarried man and woman in the United States today.

Questions

1. List and define the four ways in which marriages may be voluntarily dissolved.
2. Compare the prevalence of divorce:
   a. In primitive societies and contemporary societies.
   b. In early United States society and present-day United States society.
   c. In contemporary United States society and other contemporary societies.
3. What are the difficulties confronted in attempting to obtain objective statistics concerning causes of divorce?
4. What is the relationship between social change in the American family and divorce rates? Explain your answer and give examples.
5. Discuss the relationships between divorce and the following factors:
   a. Ethnic origin.
   b. Rural-urban residence.
   c. Race.
   d. Age at marriage.
   e. Duration of marriage.
   f. Economic status.
   g. Educational level.
   h. Presence or absence of chilren.
6. List and describe the stages that one tends to go through prior to, and after, divorce.
7. For what reasons do some couples, although unhappily married, select to remain married? Explain your answer.

8. Among the unhappily married, describe how those who do not divorce tend to differ from those who divorce in:
   a. Their background characteristics.
   b. Their manner of minimizing disorganization.
9. Under what circumstances does remarriage tend to be successful and under what circumstances does it tend to be unsuccessful? Explain your answer.

Projects

1. Interview several clergymen to learn about the attitudes of their churches toward divorce. Check particularly on any changes in the attitude of the churches that may have occurred in the past 100 years.
2. Have a panel discussion concerning whether or not divorce is harmful to marital partners and whether or not it is harmful to the children involved.

Suggested Readings

Ackerman, Charles, "Affiliations: Structural Determinates of Differential Divorce Rates," *Am. J. Sociol.*, 69, 1 (July 1963), pp. 13–20.

Bergler, Edmund, *Divorce Won't Help*, Harper and Brothers, New York, 1948.

Bernard, Jessie, *Remarriage*, Dryden Press, New York, 1956.

Blake, Nelson Manfred, *The Road to Reno*, Macmillan, New York, 1962.

Goode, William J., *After Divorce*, The Free Press, Glencoe, Ill., 1956.

Hunt, Morton M., *The World of the Formerly Married*, McGraw-Hill, New York, 1966.

Leslie, Gerald R., *The Family in Social Context*, Oxford University Press, New York, 1967, pp. 583–624, Ch. 18.

Monahan, Thomas P., "Divorce by Occupational Level," *Marr. Fam. Living*, 17 (November 1955), pp. 322–324.

Nye, F. Ivan, "Child Adjustment in Broken and in Unhappy Unbroken Homes," *Marr. Fam. Living*, 19 (November 1957), pp. 356–361.

Perry, Joseph B., Jr., and Erdwin H. Pfuhl, Jr., "Adjustment of Children in 'Solo' and 'Remarriage' Homes," *Marr. Fam. Living,* **25,** 2 (1963), pp. 221–223.

Waller, Willard, *The Old Love and the New,* Southern Illinois University Press, Carbondale, Ill., 1967.

Chapter Twenty-One

OBTAINING PROFESSIONAL ASSISTANCE

A<small>S EXPLAINED</small> in Chapter 1, this book is problem-oriented. Hence we have focused much of our attention on the many dilemmas in the man-woman relationship. Some of these, as we have indicated, may be dealt with by the marital partners themselves. Many of the marital conflicts that we have discussed, however, are sufficiently complex to require the services of a professional. In this final chapter, therefore, we turn our attention to a discussion of such services.

Our society is very much concerned with the development of professional counseling and therapy to aid persons involved in marital conflict. One reason for this interest is society's concern for the plight of marriages as well as its concern for the plight of the individual caught in family conflicts. Society recognizes that it has a stake in what happens to families not only from a humanitarian point of view, but also because any concentration of disturbed familial relations ultimately has its broader ramifications for the total society. A second factor that has spurred the growth of professional services is society's recognition that social forces play an important part in creating marital conflicts. (In several chapters we discussed the part that social changes have played in marital and family conflict.) Thus society believes that it has a responsibility to make help available to those families and individuals in need of it. As a result of these concerns, there are now in existence numerous public social work and family agencies which offer services. For those who desire and can afford to pay for private assistance, there are numerous private practitioners who are available to help individuals and families caught in conflict.

The availability of professional services, public or private, to assist the person in marital conflict does not mean that people necessarily seek out such services. Indeed, many turn to nonprofessional sources for assistance; some, for example, go to friends and relatives. Unless the friend is professionally competent, such a procedure is not likely to be rewarding.[1] Friends can be notoriously unobjective, in a positive or a negative direction. On some occasions they may praise a person for certain actions, in other instances they may be judgmental and fix blame too readily. The danger of gossip is also something to be reckoned with. Moreover, confiding of marital problems to friends may place a burden on the continuation of the friendship—one may feel embarrassed about what was revealed under stress even to a friend, and the friend, in turn, may feel embarrassed about what was heard and may find continuation of the relationship difficult. The motivations that underlie the need to tell friends about one's marital difficulties should be examined. For indeed, quite apart from any desire for help, there may be a need to injure the spouse by distorting the nature of the difficulty.

In addition to friends, another nonprofessional source is the newspaper, where marital difficulties are aired to a public audience. It should be clear that the advice given through such media, though not altogether bad, is limited and often superficial, since it is of necessity based on insufficient knowledge, half-truths, and distortions. Furthermore, the solution of most marital difficulties is not to be found in well-meaning advice, but depends instead on the marital partners' understanding of the complexities involved.

Nevertheless, great sums of money are spent each year on non-professional sources of information, and people in trouble are much more prone to consult such sources of information than they are to go to professional counselors for help.[2] Why is this so? One reason lies in the need to avoid responsibility for the problem. The person who consults a professional counselor has usually either accepted the fact that there is a problem that must be examined or is told by the counselor to

[1] Lawrence S. Bee, *Marriage and Family Relations,* Harper and Brothers, New York, 1959, pp. 315–316.
[2] For a discussion of the use and misuse of the marriage manual, see George Simpson, *People in Families,* Thomas Y. Crowell, New York, 1960, pp. 524–525.

do so. If the counselee is evasive, he will usually be informed that the counseling relationshp can only be successful when there is a willingness to examine difficulties in an open, direct, and straightforward manner. Counselor and counselee are in face-to-face interaction, and the business at hand is out in the open. However, many people are emotionally unable to deal with their difficulties in this way; they have to be evasive and circuitous. And whereas no good counselor encourages the avoidance of responsibility for problems, other media inadvertently do, since there is no face-to-face confrontation on issues. Thus the woman who writes to the newspaper can present her version of how she has been wronged, and while she admits to having a difficulty, the can avoid responsibility for her actions. To be sure, people often are informed by the newspaper consultant that all is not well with them, but this is always done in an impersonal and rather light fashion, so that the impact may be of little consequence.

A second factor that keeps people from seeking professional assistance for their problems concerns the antiintellectual, antiscientific attitude that pervades much of our time. We noted earlier the tendency to compartmentalize science—we accept science as applied to the physical, chemical, and biological aspects of the world, but frequently reject its use in human affairs. Thus many people feel that problems in human relations are part of the unknown and the unknowable, hence are not susceptible to scientific inquiry.[3] Such people avoid professional counselors.

A third reason why people avoid professional assistance with their marital problems lies in the view that people with problems are weak people; those who do not have problems are therefore strong people.[4] These are naive views, to say the least; problems are inherent in life. Thus all of us have difficulties, although some people have more than others. Many of the so-called people of strength turn out frequently to have many problems, often well covered by arrogance and aggressiveness. Perhaps the real test of strength of character is the ability to face up to what is true about oneself; this means the recognition of problems and of the personal consequences that have emerged. Such recognition is not for weaklings, for there is much pain in self-examination and in stripping away delusions. From a professional point of view, the prognosis is

[3] One author states that many people are skeptical about the use of marriage counseling in any romantic realm. Francis E. Merrill, *Courtship and Marriage,* Henry Holt, New York, 1959, p. 380.

[4] For a discussion of a similar point, namely the reluctance to see a counselor because doing so is an admission of failure, see Norman E. Himes and Donald L. Taylor, *Your Marriage,* rev. ed., Rinehart, New York, 1955, p. 338.

always much more favorable for the person who appears for counseling because he accepts the fact that he has problems and feels that an examination and resolution is necessary than it is for the person who comes to counseling through coercion and self-deception, implying that he is not in need of help.

Selection of the Professional

The selection of a professional person for help with one's marital difficulties is not simple, however, and is complicated by at least three factors. One factor has to do with certification of qualified personnel. As the professions of counseling and therapy grow, there is a very real problem of developing standards of certification so that unqualified persons are not allowed to tamper with marriages and human personalities. The official professional societies representing the different counselors and therapists are making very strenuous efforts to ensure that persons engaged in counseling and therapy have been properly trained and understand all of the ramifications of dealing with personality and relationship difficulties. To achieve the goal of keeping unqualified persons from engaging in counseling is a difficult task, requiring perhaps legislation and an alert and well-informed public. The laws in this country regarding who may and who may not provide counseling and therapy have been exceedingly lax.

A second factor that complicates selection of a professional person for assistance has to do with where such persons are located. There has been a marked tendency for therapists and counselors to locate in relatively large urban centers, so that extensive sections of semirural and rural America are virtually without their services. Part of the reason for the neglect of such areas has to do with the greater demands that heavily populated centers make for such services. The fact that qualified counselors and therapists are not plentiful further aggravates the situation.

Perhaps another reason why few counselors and therapists are found in small communities is that these professionals are inclined to think that persons in such communities, characterized by an individualistic spirit, tend to believe that marital problems are best resolved by the individuals concerned. Hence many professionals do not consider the small community a rewarding place in which to practice.

A third factor that complicates the selection of a professional for assistance concerns the differences in training and professional maturity that exist even between professionals; there are psychiatrists, psychologists, and marriage counselors. Some of these devote full or part time to work in public and private agencies; others are engaged exclusively in private practice.

Psychiatry and Psychoanalysis

Psychiatrists are physicians who have specialized in the handling of deep-seated emotional difficulties. The most highly trained are those who have been certified by the American Board of Psychiatry and Neurology; the Board's standards are accepted as being exceedingly high. Within this group there are further subdivisions. One group practices general psychiatry, which may include psychotherapy as well as physical and chemical therapies. Another group is devoted to the practice of psychoanalysis. Although most psychoanalysts are also physicians, there are analysts who are not physicians. They are presumably well trained. These are people who have received training in nonmedical psychoanalytic institutes and have been certified by them to engage in the practice of psychoanalysis. Psychoanalysis differs generally from psychotherapy in that its goals involve attempts at a total change of personality and orientation, rather than the removal of specific symptoms or problems. Furthermore, psychoanalysts, who are physicians, will use physical or chemical therapies only in extreme emergencies. The psychoanalyst functions with certain premises, which often distinguish him from other therapists. Some of these premises may be stated as follows:

1. Strong reliance on the unconscious as the source from which personality conflicts may be revealed.[5]
2. Belief in the significance of dreams as an expressions of conflicts.[6]
3. Belief in the importance of free association as a means of assisting the patient in understanding his difficulties. Free association may be

[5] Indeed, not only is the unconscious an important source for revealing personality conflict, but it is also viewed by one analyst as the important level at which conflict is solved. "Like good intentions, self-knowledge is of little value unless it penetrates to the unconscious levels of the human spirit. On this depends the future of marriage." Lawrence S. Kubie, "Psychoanalysis and Marriage," in Victor W. Eisenstein, *Neurotic Interaction in Marriage*, Basic Books, New York, 1956, pp. 10–43, especially p. 31.

[6] For case histories involving dream analysis, see Martin H. Stein, "The Unconscious Meaning of the Marital Bond," in Victor W. Eisenstein, *Neurotic Interaction in Marriage*, Basic Books, New York, 1956, pp. 65–80.

defined as a technique in which the patient reports all of the associations that enter consciousness, irrespective of content. The analyst, with the assistance of the patient, attempts to interpret the meaning of the associations in the context of the patient's difficulties.

Psychoanalysis is both costly and long. A complete analysis runs for several years, and during this time the patient is seen three to four times a week.

Although psychoanalysts have much in common, there are psychoanalytic schools that differ from one another in several respects. One of the most basic distinctions between the analytic schools relates to how far they have deviated from the original teachings of Sigmund Freud, the founder of psychoanalysis. Freud himself, as do those who have clung to his original views, minimized the role of social and cultural factors in personality disturbances. Those analysts who have deviated from Freud have generally accorded much more significance to the role of society and culture in creating human difficulties. These deviant analytic schools of thought have been identified as Neo-Freudian and represent the followers of such persons as Karen Horney, Harry Stack Sullivan, and Franz Alexander. For readers interested in the differences between these Neo-Freudian schools as well as between orthodox Freudianism and Neo-Freudian schools in general, there is now a great deal of literature to be consulted.[7]

Now that we have briefly discussed psychiatry and psychoanalysis, we might ask about its relevance to marital conflict. When the marital conflict is primarily the result of deep-seated personality problems of long-standing nature and the individuals involved seek a basic change and reorganization of personality, they may wish to investigate the possibilities of either psychiatry or psychoanalysis. Qualified psychiatrists and psychoanalysts are listed in standard medical directories, with statements of training and experience included. Nonmedical psychologists trained in psychoanalysis are also certified by their respective associations.

Psychologists

Practicing nonanalytic psychologists have different orientations. Many of these practitioners have been markedly influenced in their

[7] Joseph Jastrow, *Freud, His Dream and Sex Theories*, Pocket Books, New York, 1954.

thinking by Freud and the Neo-Freudians, although they are not personally engaged in the practice of psychoanalysis. Their practice is concerned with enabling the individual to overcome specific personality difficulties—perhaps shyness, feelings of inferiority, or marked aggression—that interfere with his ability to get along with others. The goal of such therapy is not to bring about a reorganization of personality, but is more limited in scope. Psychological counseling is generally of much shorter duration than psychoanalysis, and usually much less expensive.

When the marital conflict is primarily the result of personality difficulties and such difficulties are few and not deep-seated, the individual may wish to seek psychological counseling. It should be noted in this regard that some psychologists experimenting with short forms of psychotherapy have reported much success.[8]

Marriage Counseling

Marriage counseling services represent another source of professional help for disturbed relationships.[9] Medical people frequently engage in marriage counseling, but most certified marriage counselors tend to be nonmedical persons who are trained in the behavioral sciences. Although all marriage counselors are vitally interested in the marital relationship, they differ in their views in regard to the role of the marriage counselor. One group of marriage counselors believes that the function of the counselor is to deal primarily with matters of value incompatibility. These persons believe that the marriage counselor should avoid dealing with deep-seated personal difficulties, including the uncon-

[8] Perhaps the best known of these persons is Albert Ellis, a practicing psychologist in New York, who has developed a theory of "Rational Psychotherapy." Albert Ellis, "Rational Psychotherapy," *J. gen. Psychol.,* **59** (1958), pp. 35–49.

Qualified psychologists and marriage counselors are sometimes hard to find. The American Psychological Association certifies marriage counselors. In addition to such certification one might look for an advanced degree in the science of human behavior, the Ph.D. or its equivalent. Universities are often in a position to recommend counselors and are usually happy to assist persons from the community in this respect. See also Rex A. Skidmore, Hulda Van Steeter Garrett, and C. Jay Skidmore, *Marriage Consulting,* Harper and Brothers, New York, 1956, pp. 233–234.

[9] For a study of professional attitudes toward marriage counseling, see Richard K. Kerckhoff, "The Profession of Marriage Counseling as Viewed by Members of Four Allied Professions: A Study in the Sociology of Occupations," *Marr. Fam. Living,* **15** (November 1953), pp. 340–344.

scious. A second substantial body of professional opinion on marriage counseling considers personality problems and immaturities to be the basis of most marital conflict.[10] Professionals who hold this view believe that marriage counseling itself is really a form of psychotherapy and that the marriage counselor, if he is to function adequately, must at times deal with the deeper personal disturbances as they relate to marital difficulties.

Although the couple may have some difficulty deciding what type of professional aid to seek, they can have confidence that any qualified psychiatrist, psychologist, or marriage counselor will be able to determine the extent to which personality difficulty is involved in marital conflicts. Hence when the therapist or counselor does not feel competent to deal with a case himself, he will usually make the necessary referral to someone else. Appendix D contains a list of agencies from which accredited persons may be sought, and any of these agencies is a reliable starting place in looking for help.[11]

Function of Therapists and Counselors

There is considerable confusion regarding the kinds of things therapists and counselors attempt to do; it would seem appropriate, therefore, to outline some of the essential functions. To begin with, probably the main difference between psychotherapy and counseling, in the ideal sense, is that the psychotherapist deals with deep-seated attitudes and the counselor works primarily only with conscious material. Both psychotherapy and counseling do have certain common elements, however, which should be pointed out. To begin with, it should be clear that therapists and counselors, if competent, are not backslappers whose primary function it is to pass on cliches to make one feel better; nor are they people who simply sit around telling a person what he ought or ought not to

[10] Robert W. Laidlaw, "The Psychiatrist as Marriage Counselor," *Am. J. Psychiat.,* **106** (April 1950), p. 736. One noted psychiatrist defines marriage counseling as a form of short-term psychotherapy dealing with interpersonal relationships in which problems relating to marriage are the central factors; quoted by Emily H. Mudd in *The Practice of Marriage Counseling,* Association Press, New York, 1951, p. 206.

[11] See also Robert K. Leik and L. K. Northwood, "The Classification of Family Interaction Problems for Treatment Process," *J. Marr. Fam.,* **26** (1964), pp. 288–294. This paper outlines a procedure for classifying certain problems and demonstrates the relationship of this classification to particular types of counseling procedures.

do. Competent counselors are not going to waste their time or that of the counselee such superficial approaches to the complexities of human behavior.

Furthermore, thereapists and counselors do not possess a preconceived view that all marriages must be saved regardless of the personal sacrifice involved. They are primarily interested in revealing the real problems in the marriage, including their ramifications and complications, in order that the patient or counselee be in a position to deal with them effectively. This may be accomplished only when the individual understands his difficulties. Thus competent therapists and counselors are persons who, through training and experience, are able to create a climate in which the counselee or patient can examine his problems. This is facilitated by permitting the counselee to talk at some length about his marriage, which enables him to unburden himself, a process that is sometimes referred to as catharsis.

A second important component in the therapeutic and counseling process is the ability of the professionally trained person to accept individuals and their problems. This does not mean that he condones all behavior; nor is he likely to blame or create guilt in the marital partners. For, indeed, he recognizes that the life experiences of the counselee have resulted in certain values or personal immaturities that have now emerged in marital conflict. The task is to see how the circumstances of life have, in a sense, created behaviors that the individual did not necessarily select himself.

Over a period of time and under favorable circumstances the counselee comes to see his problems, the attitudes associated with these problems, and the disturbances that these bring to his marriage. Only when the counselee knows what his problems are is he in a position to employ his intellect to do something about them.[12] This is an important point, since many laymen are under the erroneous impression that the solving of one's problems is simply a matter of common sense (by this they mean a matter of intelligence). The woman who continues to remain in love with an alcoholic whose chances for rehabilitation are very slim knows better, but she feels emotionally compelled to continue her love. Only when she can come to understand why she needs to love an alcoholic, when she has some appreciation of the underlying needs and emotional forces that are operating, can she make some rational choice—or use her intelligence.

Furthermore, it should be noted that newer forms of marriage counseling are increasingly coming into vogue, each offering interesting pos-

[12] Marie W. Kargman, "The Clinical Use of Social System Theory in Marriage Counseling," *Marr. Fam. Living,* **19** (August 1957), pp. 263–269, especially p. 263.

sibilities. For example, Leslie, an experienced marriage counselor and family sociologist, reports that *conjoint therapy* (spouses counseled together rather than separately) can be rewarding. Such counseling may enable the counselor to observe the couple more directly, to bring differences out into the open more readily, and to arrive at basic problems in a minimum of time. The authors are inclined to endorse these observations.[13]

Speck describes a procedure in which the counselor goes to the home of clients in order to engage in counseling. He suggests certain advantages—there is less chance of absenteeism on the part of counselees, the setting is natural, and the family is in interaction.[14]

With an even-increasing number of marital and family difficulties, it is inevitable that professionals will seek shorter and more effective means of reaching as many who need help as possible. Some techniques will prove fruitful; others, like all efforts for human betterment, will prove unfruitful.[15]

Importance of Counseling and Therapy

There is much benefit that may be derived from competent counseling and therapy. For it is not only the total marriage that is involved, but also the lives of the marital partners, which are perhaps even more important than the relationship. Successful professional assistance enables the partners to clarify the values and goals they seek in marriage, the incompatibilities that may have had their origin in those pursuits, and the personal contribution each partner has made to the marital conflicts that have emerged. After that, they may be in a position to choose whether they desire to dissolve the present relationship or whether it is feasible and possible to attempt to rehabilitate it. In any event, competent professional assistance will enable the couple to clarify these issues and minimize future problems whether they arise in the relationship they now have or in some future involvement.

[13] Gerald R. Leslie, "Conjoint Therapy in Marriage Counseling," *J. Marr. Fam.*, **26**, 1 (1964), pp. 65–71.
[14] Ross V. Speck, "Family Therapy in the Home," *J. Marr. Fam.*, **26**, 1 (1964), pp. 72–76.
[15] See also the following: Aaron L. Rutledge, "Husband-Wife Conferences in the Home as an Aid to Marriage Counseling," *Marr. Fam. Living*, **24**, 2 (1962), pp. 151–154; Alan Klein, "Exploring Family Group Counseling," *Social Work*, **8**, 1 (January 1963), pp. 23–29; Ruby Neuhaus, "Family Treatment in Focus," *Marr. Fam. Living*, **24**, 1 (1962), pp. 62–65; Richard H. Klemer, "The Marriage Counselor in the Physicians' Office," *J. Marr. Fam.*, **28**, 3 (1966), pp. 287–292; and Gerald Albert, "Advanced Psychological Training for Marriage Counselors, Luxury or Necessity," *Marr. Fam. Living*, **25**, 2 (1963), pp. 181–183.

Professional counselors and therapists certainly cannot solve all marital complications. There are still gaps in knowledge and techniques that must be overcome and understood. Gradually, however, more and more of the complexities of the human relationship are better understood. What was once part of the mysterious is now part of the knowable. And, as we continue to study and engage in research, many of the areas of the human relationship that were inaccessible to understanding will be understood. Such accomplishments will be the result of human efforts; for human beings possess not only the ability to complicate their lives, but also the capacity to understand and build their lives.

Finally, it should be mentioned that counseling and therapy aim at removal of marital conflict and cannot provide individuals with aims, goals, and values. Nor can therapists lead the individuals through life by the hand. Therapy can liberate and create the ingredients out of which a meaningful and productive life may be generated. But it is ultimately the persons themselves who must continue to deal with life in the future, its conflicts and purpose. It is their ultimate willingness to become engaged in this process that may determine what lies ahead for them in their relationships, marital and other.

Summary

The simple solutions to marital problems that tend to be found in soap operas and fairy tales unfortunately are rarely found in the realities of living. For, indeed, the complex nature of marital conflict frequently makes it necessary for individuals not only to expend much time and energy in solving their problems, but also to seek professional assistance in resolving their conflicts. Some people, however, although in need of professional assistance, turn to nonprofessionals (friends, relatives, newspaper colums, etc.) for help with their problems. They do this for a number of reasons: (1) they may wish to avoid assuming any responsibility for their problems, and, consequently, they may fear that the direct face-to-face confrontation with a professional person will make such avoidance impossible; (2) they may feel that problems in human relationships are part of the unknowable, hence are not susceptible to the scientific inquiry of the professional realm; or (3) they may feel that to admit that they have problems and to seek professional help in solving them implies that they are very weak people. Needless to say, the authors cannot accept these views. But what is more important, particularly since these views keep people who are in need of professional assistance from receiving it, the authors regard the existence of these views as being extremely unfortunate.

In this chapter various types of professional assistance available to couples to help them in resolving marital conflict were discussed; these are psychiatry, psychology, and marriage counseling. Also discussed were the similarities and differences that exist between the functions of therapists and counselors, each of whom is trained to assist people in resolving marriage problems.

Questions

1. For what reasons is the United States society very much concerned with the development of professional marriage counseling and therapy? Discuss.
2. Why do some people try to avoid a face-to-face confrontation with a professional counselor and instead seek other sources of advice concerning their marital problems?
3. List and discuss the three factors that complicate the selection of a professional counselor.
4. When couples are receiving marriage counseling, who actually solves the marital conflict—the counselor or the counselee? Discuss this in full.

Projects

1. Check all agencies in your community that might be doing marriage counseling and report to the class what facilities are available in your community.
2. Invite someone who is trained in the area of marriage counseling to speak to your class about counseling as a career.

Suggested Readings

Bowman, Henry A., "A Critical Evaluation of Marriage and Family Education," *Marr. Fam. Living*, 15 (November 1953), pp. 304–308.

Buhler, Charlotte, *Values in Psychotherapy*, The Free Press of Glencoe, a Division of Collier-Macmillan, New York, 1962.

Foster, Robert G., "How a Marriage Counselor Handles a Case," *Marr. Fam. Living*, 16 (May 1954), pp. 139–142.

Greene, Bernard L., Ed., *Psychotherapies of Marital Disharmony*, The Free Press, Glencoe, Ill., 1965.

Mowrer, O. Hobart, *The New Group Therapy*, Van Nostrand, Princeton, N.J., 1964.

Mudd, Emily H., et al., Eds., *Marriage Counseling: A Casebook*, Association Press, New York, 1958.

Rutledge, Aaron L., "Marriage Counseling Today and Tomorrow," *Marr. Fam. Living*, 19 (November 1957), pp. 386–390.

Satir, Virginia M., *Conjoint Family Therapy: A Guide to Therapy and Technique*, Science and Behavior Books, Palo Alto, Calif., 1964.

Nash, Ethel M., Lucie Jessner, and D. Wilfred Abse, Eds., *Marriage Counseling in Medical Practice*, University of North Carolina Press, Chapel Hill, N.C., 1964.

Vincent, Clark E., Ed., *Readings in Marriage Counseling*, Thomas Y. Crowell, New York, 1957.

Appendices

In this book our concern has been with the man-woman relationship and its essential features. However, two important areas of information that have bearing on the man-woman relationship in marriage were not formally discussed in this book—sex and reproduction and consumer problems. The discussions that follow are designed to supplement the several areas of the marital relationship with information on medical and economic aspects to enable the reader to understand more clearly some of the problems in these areas. In this revised edition the authors have tried to bring their respective sections up to date.

APPENDIX A

Medical Guidelines for Married Couples

HANS LEHFELDT, M.D.

Dr. Hans Lehfeldt, who contributed this section, is a physician of wide professional experience, both in Europe and in the United States. His major medical interests are in gynecology and obstetrics. Dr. Lehfeldt's approach to his specialty in medicine suggests an appreciation and sensitivity for the psychological and sociological factors that may be implicated in obstetric and gynecologic problems. Furthermore, his many years of teaching experience have put him in close touch with the kinds of medical information that those about to be married need. A brief statement of Dr. Lehfeldt's experience and interest follows. Cofounder and codirector of Birth Control and Marriage Counseling Clinic of Society for Sexual Reform (GESEX); member of Arbeitszentrale für Geburtenregelung, Berlin, 1928–1935. Private practice, Berlin 1928–1935, New York 1936 to date. Clinical assistant, department of Obstetrics and Gynecology, New York University, lecturer on Contraception, 1937–1945. Clinical assistant, OPD, Lenox Hill Hospital, 1936–1964. Chief of Contraceptive Clinic, New York University Bellevue Medical Center, 1958 to date. Clinical Professor of Obstetrics and Gynecology, New York University College of Medicine, 1959 to date. Member of Medical Committee, Planned Parenthood Federation of America, 1958 to date. Past officer of the Rudolf Virchow Medical Society. Cofounder, member of executive committee, and past president of the Society for the Scientific Study of Sex. Author of *Buch der Ehe,* Berlin, 1930; translator of *Gynecologic Radiography* by Dalsace and Garcia-Calderon, Hoeber-Harper, New York, 1958; contributor to The *Encyclopedia of Sexual Behavior,* Hawthorne, New York, 1961 (new revised edition in print), and to *Man-*

438

ual of Contraceptive Practice, Williams & Wilkins, Baltimore, 1964.

Dr. Lehfeldt's material is organized into several parts; each is designed to deal with one major medical aspect of the man-woman relationship in marriage. Part 1 discusses the anatomy and physiology of sex organs and includes details of structure and descriptions of functions. Dr. Lehfeldt deals with the phenomena of menstruation, puberty, and menopause. Masturbation is also discussed.

Part 1 Anatomy and Physiology of Sex Organs

Anatomy of the Female Sex Organs

The female generative or reproductive system (Figures 1 and 2) can be divided into the external and the internal genitalia. Whereas the external organs are in general outside of the body, the interior organs are situated within the pelvic cavity.

The external organs are the vulva and the vagina. The *vulva* consists of the labia, the clitoris, the openings of the urethra, and the vagina and the hymen. The labia or lips consist of two symmetrical pairs of skinfolds, of which the outer lips (labia majora) are larger, and the inner lips (labia minora), smaller. The skinfolds start below the pubic hair and extend toward the region of the anus. The clitoris is located in the center of the upper part of the labia minora and is usually the shape and size of a

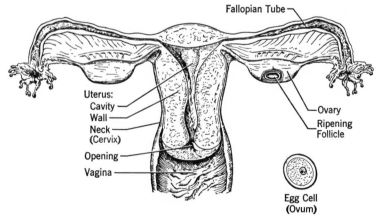

Figure 1   Female sex organs—front view.

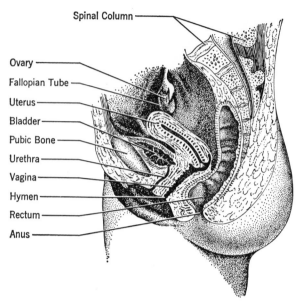

Figure 2   Female sex organs—side view.

pea. A little below the clitoris is the urethral opening. Still further down is the vaginal opening or the introitus (Latin for entrance). Each of the labia majora contains a gland, called Bartholin's gland, whose secretion lubricates the introitus. In a virgin, a thin bandlike membrane, called the hymen, narrows the introitus. The hymen is usually ruptured during the first cohabitation. At their posterior or lower part the labial folds unite again, forming the "fourchette." The anatomical structure situated between vulva and anus is called the perineum.

The *vagina,* although invisible without an instrument (speculum), is nevertheless considered part of the external female genitalia. It is situated between the bladder and the rectum. In the nulliparous woman (one who has never borne a child), the vagina is a tubular structure with a closed end. At its upper or proximal terminus lies the uterus or womb, the lowermost part of which forms the cervix. The cervix is a fingerlike structure which dips into the vagina, causing it to form pouches, called fornices, one in front of the cervix (anterior fornix) and one behind (posterior fornix). The posterior fornix is deeper than the anterior one. The vagina is remarkably elastic, and during the birth process, stretches sufficiently to become a part of the birth canal. During menstruation, the vagina also serves as the passageway for the blood that flows from the uterus. (For the coital function of the vagina, see Part 2 of this appendix —"Marital Relations.")

The internal organs consist of the uterus, two fallopian tubes, and two ovaries. In shape and size the *uterus* resembles a pear. The small, lower end of this pear-shaped organ has already been described as the cervix; the upper part of the uterus is called the body, corpus, or fundus. The uterus is a hollow organ. Its inside cavity is shaped like an inverted triangle. At the cervical end of the uterus is a small opening, the external os (mouth), which connects with the vagina. Two still smaller openings link the upper part of the uterine cavity with the *fallopian tubes,* which curve from the upper end of the uterus toward the ovary on each side extending in a funnellike shape called the fimbrial end. Thus a system of canals connects the ovaries via the tubes, the uterine cavity, and the cervical canal, with the vagina. The *ovaries* are the female sex glands, the size and shape of an almond.

Physiology of Female Sex Organs

The function of the female sex organs (as well as of those of the male) is governed by the *pituitary gland,* a small structure situated at the base of the brain. In the woman, hormones secreted by its anterior lobe (follicle-stimulating hormone, FSH, and luteinizing hormone, LH) bring about a ripening of the eggs in the ovary. Furthermore, these hormones induce the ovary to secrete two hormones of its own, estrogen and progesterone, which are responsible for ovulation and menstruation. No function of the sex organs is possible without the pituitary; this gland has therefore been described as the "motor of sexual function."

In the mature woman the *ovary* has two functions: production of eggs (ova) and secretion of estrogen and progesterone. In the newborn female baby, the ovaries contain about a quarter of a million egg cells. In the mature woman the monthly ovarian cycle begins with the growth of "follicles," groups of cells arranged circularly around the ovum. These follicles grow and mature by multiplication of their cells, by enlargement of the ovum itself, and by accumulation of fluid inside the follicle. Every month one of the many follicles ripens in this manner, and the enlarged ovum assumes an eccentric position in the follicle. This so-called *graafian follicle* rises to the periphery of the ovary; the fluid inside the follicle increases until finally the follicle bursts, and the ovum is expelled into the lateral or fimbrial end of the fallopian tube. This process, called ovulation, takes place in midcycle, that is halfway between two menstrual periods. A few days after ovulation, the ruptured follicle is transformed into a yellow body, the "corpus luteum." If the ovum is not fertilized, the corpus luteum degenerates into a pale scar, the corpus albicans; if the ovum is fertilized, the corpus luteum continues to grow until about the seventh month of pregnancy when it is finally absorbed.

The growing follicles secrete estrogen, while the corpus luteum produces progesterone in addition to some estrogen.

Estrogen is produced mainly during the first three weeks; progesterone, during the fourth week of the menstrual cycle. These hormones, secreted into the bloodstream, affect the lining of the uterus, the endometrium. During the first three weeks of the cycle, the endometrium enters the so-called proliferative phase by gradually growing thicker under the influence of estrogen. In the fourth and last week of the cycle, the endometrium, now under the influence of progesterone, enters the so-called secretory phase, preparatory to either menstruation or implantation (nidation) of the fertilized ovum. If the egg is not fertilized, the superficial layers of the endometrium are pushed off, thereby reducing the thickness of the uterine lining to one-fourth. This process opens blood vessels, and menstrual bleeding ensues. A few days later the loss of layers in the endometrium is compensated by the cells of its basic layer which grow at the beginning of the next cycle, again forming first another proliferative, and later, a secretory endometrium.

These cyclic changes in the uterus are subject to cyclic changes in the ovary, which in turn are dependent on the hormones produced by the anterior pituitary. As the pituitary is dependent on normal functioning of the thyroid and of the adrenal glands, it becomes obvious that only women with a normal general endocrine system will have a physiological and regular menstrual cycle.

Menstruation, or the periodic flow of blood from the uterus, occurs at fairly regular intervals of 28 days. Individual variations of the cycle, however, are not necessarily abnormal. The length of the cycle, that is, the interval between the first day of the last and the first day of the following menstruation, may range from 21 to 35 days. A normal menstruation lasts three to five days. Some pain during menstruation is not unusual. Severe and incapacitating pain, however, indicates dysmenorrhea. Medical treatment with hormones or pain-relieving drugs is usually beneficial. Some instances of dysmenorrhea are psychogenic and require psychotherapy. Many women are moody, tense, or depressed during the week preceding the period. This "premenstrual tension syndrome" can also be alleviated by medical treatment or psychotherapy. For protection during the menstrual flow many women wear tampons, such as Tampax, instead of sanitary napkins, a practical and harmless convenience. Much is said in advertisements about "female hygiene," involving douching with disinfectants, particularly after sexual intercourse or after menstruation. Most modern gynecologists consider douching completely unnecessary for a healthy woman, as the normal vagina has a self-cleansing faculty far superior to any chemical preparations.

PUBERTY. Puberty, the transition period between childhood and adult life, usually extends over several years. Its first physical signs are appearance of secondary sex characteristics, which, in the female, are growth of pubic hair and development of the breasts. The first menstruation (menarche) usually occurs between the ages of twelve and fourteen, but its onset may vary widely. Menarche before the age of nine, or after the age of seventeen, is considered abnormal.

In the past hundred years, there appears to be a tendency toward an earlier onset of puberty, which has been attributed to improved hygienic and nutritional conditions. For one to two years after menarche, the quality of flow, as well as the intervals between periods, may vary widely. Often menstruation is regularly established, but no ovulation takes place; in other words, many adolescent girls produce the phenomenon of anovulatory menstruation, that is, menstruation without a preceding ovulation. This explains the *relative* infertility of adolescent girls. Gradually, there are fewer anovulatory menstruations, until finally every menstrual period is preceded by ovulation.

Psychic phenomena accompany these physical changes. Adjustment to adolescence entails a variety of moods, which require understanding by parents, teachers, and adult friends.

MENOPAUSE. Menstruation ceases between the ages of forty-two and fifty-two (average, forty-seven). As a rule, the earlier the menarche, the later the menopause. Concurrent with the "change of life" are retrogressive changes in the breasts and the generative organs. As in puberty, a number of anovulatory menstruations occur, lowering the fertility. However, conception may take place, even after a period of several months of amenorrhea. Menopause is caused by the cessation of the ovarian function. During this period, the ovary gradually loses its follicles and is transformed into nonfunctioning tissue, while the anterior pituitary gland shows signs of hyperactivity. In the aging male, however, this gland exhibits signs of decreasing function. The overactivity of the anterior pituitary gland in women during change of life causes endocrine disturbances, affecting several other glands—the thyroid and the adrenals. This pluriglandular disturbance probably accounts for some of the vasomotor disorders occurring during this period. Although three fourths of all women experience some disturbances during menopause, 90 percent of them pursue their usual activities. In general, the *symptoms* are mild, consisting of flushes, or a prickling sensation in the fingers or toes. They respond well to hormonal therapy, which is harmless and does not produce cancer. Psychological alterations in menopause are sometimes pronounced, such as anxiety syndromes and depressions; they may be ascribed partly to the fear of aging or to the fallacious assumption that menopause signifies loss of sexuality. Actually, libido and sex enjoyment often increase during and after menopause with the elimination of the fear of pregnancy.

Anatomy of Male Sex Organs

The male sex organs (Figure 3) consist of external structures: the penis and scrotum; and of internal structures: the vas deferens, the seminal vesicles, and the prostatic gland. The penis has the double function of serving as an implement for urination and for coitus. The *penis* consists of head (glans), rim (corona), and shaft. The shaft lies below the symphysis to which it is firmly attached. A cross section of the penis shaft reveals three structures: a single structure surrounding the urethra, called corpus cavernosum urethrae, and two symmetrical structures, the right and left corpus cavernosum of the penis.

Underneath and behind the penis is the *scrotum,* a sac containing the two *testicles* and the two *epididymides.* From each side of each epididymis, a small tube, the vas deferens, runs through the inguinal canal and into the pelvic cavity behind the endopelvic segment of the urethra. At the point where the bladder continues into the urethra and attached to the posterior surface of the bladder lie two symmetrical sacs, the *seminal vesicles.* The *vas deferens* conducts the secretion of the testicles, the spermatozoa, from the epididymis, through the inguinal canal into the

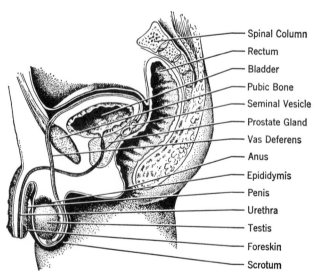

Spinal Column
Rectum
Bladder
Pubic Bone
Seminal Vesicle
Prostate Gland
Vas Deferens
Anus
Epididymis
Penis
Urethra
Testis
Foreskin
Scrotum

Figure 3   Male sex organs—side view.

seminal vesicles. Behind the two seminal vesicles, the bladder, and the pelvic portion of the urethra, is a large structure, the *prostatic gland,* which encircles the uppermost part of the urethra.

Physiology of Male Sex Organs

The main mass of the semen derives from the seminal vesicles where it is stored. The prostatic gland produces a part of the seminal fluid, which activates the spermatozoa. During erection they continue into the urethra where, mixing with the prostatic secretions, they form into the final ejaculate. The anatomical pathway of the mature sperm is a complex one (Figure 3).

The testicles are about 4 to 5 cm long and about 2½ cm thick. They have a double function: in addition to producing spermatozoa, they are endocrine organs which control secondary sex characteristics, such as male type of hair growth and voice, and the virile structure of the body. The typical eunuch characteristics of high voice and beardlessness, produced by castration before puberty, illustrate the endocrine function of the testicles.

Spermatogenesis, that is, the formation of spermatozoa, starts around the age of 16 and continues to old age. This means that man produces spermatozoa and is fertile throughout his adult life. The development of the spermatozoon is a long and complicated process. In its first stage, there is an undifferentiated male germ cell called spermatogonium; after having passed through several stages of transformation, it assumes its final form. The process of spermatogenesis is controlled by the pituitary gland as well as by the endocrine secretion of the mature testicle.

The mature spermatozoon has a total of 46 chromosomes, which are in fact 23 pairs; one of these pairs, the **XX** (female) or **XY** (male) chromosomes, are dissimilar in length and shape. Called the sex chromosomes, they are determinative for sex.

Examination under an ordinary microscope shows the normal spermatozoon divided into four sections: head, neck, middle section, and tail. The head is oval in shape and the tail is approximately 10 to 12 times the length of the head. The quantity of an ejaculate is subject to great variations; 3 to 5 cc of seminal fluid may be considered an average amount. Each cubic centimeter of seminal fluid contains about 60 to 120 million sperm cells, of which 60 to 80 percent are motile. Low motility, or a high percentage of abnormal cells, or a sperm count below 20 million per cubic centimeter, are indicative of impaired fertility. However, men with even lower sperm counts may be able to impregnate.

Erection originates in the central nervous system. Under sexual stimulation, the reflux of blood from the corpora cavernosa in the penis is blocked, and the penis distends and becomes rigid. If the stimulation continues, erection is eventually followed by ejaculation.

The endocrine as well as the sperm-producing testicular functions depend on other endocrine glands, particularly the anterior pituitary. Good testicular function is also dependent on a well-functioning thyroid.

PUBERTY. Puberty in the male usually starts a couple of years later than in the female. Its most significant signs are hair growth and change of voice. While erections may and frequently do occur during early childhood, ejaculation generally begins in puberty. Nocturnal erections during dreams followed by ejaculation, called pollution, or nocturnal emission are not infrequent during this epoch. Such physiological phenomena may have a frightening effect on a child or an adolescent boy, unless explained. Early sex education is therefore of great importance.

Masturbation is a frequent practice in adolescents, as well as in people of all ages and both sexes. It is not dangerous—contrary to the beliefs still held by some adults.

IS THERE A MALE MENOPAUSE? This question is raised again and again by physicians and laymen. Some psychological and somatic phenomena occurring in middle age have been attributed to a "male climacteric." Actually, there is no anatomical or physiological basis for this assumption. Male potency and fertility continue into old age, although potency diminishes somewhat in older men.

Part 2   Marital Relations

> *In Part 2 Dr. Lehfeldt turns his attention to marital relations. The purpose is to provide the married couple with a knowledge of physiological and psychological facts necessary for successful performance of the sex act; and of pathologies when the sex act is not consummated successfully. Dr. Lehfeldt gives particular attention to the nature of orgasm and its psychological manifestations. In addition, he deals briefly with the physiology of coitus, coital behavior, and the technique of defloration.*

Physiology

Coitus, also called cohabitation, copulation, or sexual intercourse, consists of insertion of the erect penis into the vagina, followed by more or less vigorous thrusts of the penis in the direction of the cervix. The cohabitation ends with ejaculation; most of the seminal fluid is deposited around the cervix and into the posterior fornix of the vagina. Spermatozoa reach the cervical canal a few minutes after unprotected intercourse.

The pioneer work of Masters and Johnson has provided new insights into the physiology of sexual intercourse. In eleven years of research, these scientists developed revolutionary new methods for the investigation of the coital act. During coitus, length and width of the vagina increase considerably, the latter in the proximal third. Other changes occurring during cohabitation affect the circulation, the heart, and the brain. Consequently, electrocardiograms and electroencephalograms taken at the time of cohabitation show considerable changes.

The frequency at which individual couples have intercourse is subject to great variations. Two or three times a week is considered average. In the later years of marriage, and with advancing age, the coital frequency decreases gradually.

The duration of the coital act also varies; 2 to 5 minutes is an average length of time. Healthy men of normal potency can extend the act to about 20 or 30 minutes. There are many different techniques of cohabitation; the choice depends on experience and individual preference, as well as on the somatic and psychologic condition of the partners. Sex play, which frequently precedes cohabitation, includes lip kissing and stimulation of the sex organs.

Various Coital Positions

In the most commonly known coital position, the male lies above the female who faces him. In other frequently used positions, the female lies above the male or the male and female lie on their sides facing each other. A wide variety of positions are described in the extensive literature on the subject, for instance, in the famous *Kama Sutra* by Vatsyayana, published in India more than 1600 years ago, and in the Roman literature by such authors as Apulaeus, Ovid, and Lucian. One of the best-known modern writers on sex techniques is Van de Velde, whose books were first published some forty years ago.

TECHNIQUE OF DEFLORATION. In the female's first sexual intercourse, the hymen must be penetrated. If the hymen is thin and elastic, it will break or dilate with little or no discomfort; if it is rigid, entry may cause pain. Understanding and gentleness on the part of the male will greatly help to relax the female and thus to overcome, or at least soften, the pain. The breaking of the hymen usually causes a slight bleeding, which may recur during a few subsequent cohabitations. In the rare instances where full penetration is not possible, or where coitus continues to be painful for the female as late as two weeks after the first cohabitation, medical advice should be sought. Usually a simple procedure, such as stretching a rigid hymen, or dissection, will straighten out the difficulty.

Tactful behavior during a couple's first coital experience is of the greatest importance for marital sex adjustment. If the first cohabitation precipitates an inexperienced young woman into a state of anxiety, serious marital difficulties may result. A honeymoon, therefore, should be regarded not solely as a time for lighthearted pleasure and happiness, but also as a decisive period leading to greater understanding and happiness.

ORGASM. The peak of sexual activity is called orgasm. The partners suddenly become tense, experience muscular spasm for a number of seconds, and then return to a normal, or sometimes subnormal, physiological state.

Orgasm is the prototype of a psychosomatic reaction. Physical changes during the orgasm include an increased heart rate, elevated blood pressure and respiration, and an increased flow of blood into the genital organs. These symptoms are followed by spastic contractions of the muscles surrounding the genital area. At the time of orgasm, the male ejaculates seminal fluid, while in the female orgasm no discharge of gametes occurs. The long-established belief that the secretion produced by the woman during intercourse originates in the Bartholin and cervical glands was disproved by Masters and Johnson, who found definite evidence that it derives directly from the vagina. This finding is of great importance: hysterectomy (removal of the uterus), or excision of the Bartholin glands, does not impair the woman's sex enjoyment.

Orgasm, in both the male and the female, is usually coupled with a short loss of consciousness, preceded by a feeling of elation, and followed by a sensation of complete relaxation. This peaceful sensation after orgasm is one of its notable aspects.

With the exception of ejaculation, the phenomenon of orgasm is precisely the same in both sexes. The studies of Kinsey and his group seem to indicate that the length of time needed to achieve orgasm is also approximately the same for both sexes. Up to that time, the assumption had been that women were slower in reaching orgasm and, in general, had a different orgastic curve. In the male, relaxation after orgasm was believed to set in almost immediately, while the female was supposed to return to normal after some delay (Kehrer, Van de Velde).

The psychoanalytic school of thought emphasizes the importance of vaginal versus clitoral orgasm. According to the Freudians, only vaginal orgasm can provide full sexual satisfaction. Physiologically there is no difference between the two forms of orgasm; individual couples may alternate clitoral and vaginal orgasm in various cohabitations. The studies of Masters and Johnson quoted above have proved through direct observation in the laboratory that clitoral and vaginal orgasm are identical.

The preceding paragraphs have dealt mainly with the technique of sexual relations. Technique can be learned by inexperienced couples, either from books or through expert advice, but technique is not all. Satisfactory sexual union for both husband and wife can be achieved only if the two have an intimate psychologic relationship, dominated by love, devotion, and deep understanding. All too often frigid women or impotent men consult their physician, in the vain hope that reading a few chapters on sex technique in the right book will cure their ills. Although the doctor can successfully advise couples whose failure to adjust sexually is based solely on inexperience, he cannot always cure other, more deeply rooted inadequacies.

Pathology

The foregoing remarks about orgasm clearly indicate that no woman capable of clitoral orgasm, or of any orgasm, should be considered frigid. Frigidity can be described as the inability to achieve orgasm; in its absolute form it is rare, while relative frigidity, that is, occasional inability to achieve orgasm, is not infrequent. This condition may be due to a difference in the sexual "appetites" of the partners.

Males seem to have a more frequent desire for intercourse than females. When the drive for cohabitation is absent in the woman, she will frequently not achieve orgasm. If there is mutual understanding, this situation need not endanger the marital relationship.

Generally, frigidity has no organic or endocrine cause, although it may be produced temporarily by a severe disease. In most cases, frigidity is a psychological disorder caused by deep-seated conflicts. The logical treatment is therefore some form of psychotherapy, including psychoanalysis. Pseudofrigidity—not to be confused with frigidity—is generally due to sexual inexperience of one or both partners and can often be cured by marriage counseling. It may also originate in an aversion of the woman for her partner, in which case neither psychotherapy nor marriage counseling is likely to help.

The counterpart to female frigidity is impotence in the male. In mild cases, the erection time is shortened and ejaculation occurs early, at times before insertion of the penis (premature ejaculation). In more severe forms of impotence, the erection is impaired and intercourse becomes impossible. In another form of impotence there is failure of the male to achieve ejaculation.

Impotence is rarely caused by a physical disorder; consequently hormonal therapy is of little value. The treatment for impotence is psychotherapy. Frequently men are impotent with one woman, but highly potent with another, a fact that clearly points to the psychologial origin of this condition. There is a physiological lowering of potency with increasing age, but even octogenarians do not entirely lose their capacity for sexual intercourse.

Part 3   Family Planning

Part 3 deals with the important problem of family planning and should be of considerable interest to the reader irrespective of religious persuasion. Some of the significant problems dealt with in this section include those associated with planning of pregnancy for different age groupings, child-spacing methods, infertility, and sterility. Medical methods for dealing with these problems are described.

Planning a successful marriage and planning pregnancies are much more important than planning the wedding. Two different personalities must adapt their ways of life—always a difficult change, even if one or both partners have had previous marital experience.

Family planning is not synonymous with limiting pregnancies. Most couples have definite ideas about the number of children they want, even though they may modify their plans later. All pregnancies should be desired and planned. No couple should have their children before being ready for them and unless the marital relationship is sound and solid. The expectation that a child will solve marital problems is a dangerous fallacy. If two people cannot adjust to each other, it is irrational to burden the marital relationship by the new and more complex adjustment to parenthood, which involves not two but three people. Thanks to modern methods of contraception, it is unnecessary to bring children into the world haphazardly. In some cases, for instance after a severe illness, the physician may advise postponement of pregnancy; or he may favor early pregnancy, or a rapid succession of pregnancies, as in the case of endometriosis, the presence of endometrial tissue in abnormal locations, or in the presence of uterine fibroids. Elderly couples also should have their children early in marriage, for several reasons: (1) pregnancy complications are more frequent in elderly mothers, as will be discussed later, (2) the incidence of fetal deformity is higher in older parents, particularly the incidence of mongoloid children, and (3) fertility in women definitely decreases with age. Of twenty-year-old females, only 3 percent are sterile, while by the age of thirty the percentage reaches 12, and by age forty, it is 32.

Medical experience has emphasized the merits of child spacing, particularly in the case of young parents, where an interval of about two years between deliveries is often desirable for physical and psychological reasons. In making a decision, each family must of course consider its individual situation. The situation might be discussed with a physician, a marriage counselor, or a spiritual ádviser. The Catholic Church, while prohibiting all mechanical methods of contraception, permits the rhythm method, by which intercourse is avoided during the fertile days of the cycle. Today, however, this method, which can be used only by women who have a regular cycle, is under criticism even by Catholics. Thus, John Rock, the prominent Catholic scientist who was instrumental in developing oral contraception, has urged the Vatican (1963) to permit use of the pill as a preventive method. The majority report of the Papal Study Commission on Birth Control (*New York Times*, April 17, 1967) labeled the rhythm method as "very deficient"; it stated that "only 60 percent of women have a regular cycle" and that "intervention ought to be done in a way more conformed to the expression of love and to the respect for the dignity of the partner." The Pope, however, has rejected the recommendations of his own Commission. In his encyclical "Of Human Life," issued in July, 1968, he has banned all mechanical and chemical contraceptives. According to the GAF (Growth of American Families) study (Ryder and Westoff), 53 percent of Catholic contraceptors in America use a method other than the rhythm method.

The entire field of contraception has undergone drastic changes in the last 10 years. Two new techniques, oral and intrauterine contraception, have revolutionized sex and marital life. Large groups, who previously had not used any birth control techniques, have become regular contraceptors. Their changed attitude may be explained by several reasons. In contrast to the conventional older methods (with the exception of the cervical cap), the new techniques dispense with special preparation for each individual sex act and thus permit strict separation between contraception and cohabitation. This makes the new methods more acceptable. Based on the data collected in a survey of reproductive behavior of married American women under the age of 45, Ryder and Westoff (GAF study, quoted above) predicted that the oral contraceptive might become the principal method of fertility regulation in America, "if no developments in contraceptive technology were to be expected." These authors observed that oral contraception was especially popular with young women and those who attended college.

ORAL CONTRACEPTION. The pill poses a moral problem relating to the unmarried: does this method, by its convenience, promote promiscuity? We have no evidence that it does, but it is a fact that it has reduced the number of unplanned pregnancies.

The basic research that led to the development of the pill was done by John Rock (1956) and Gregory Pincus (1958). Contraceptive pills consist of a combination of two synthetic hormones, progesterone and estrogen. They prevent pregnancy by suppressing ovulation. If ovulation is prevented—as it is during pregnancy—no conception can occur. At present, eight such oral contraceptives are commercially available in the United States, all obtainable by prescription only. Most physicians prescribe one tablet per day for 20 days, from cycle day 5 to cycle day 24.

The effectiveness of oral contraception is 100 percent, if medication is taken as prescribed. In virtually every case of pregnancy it was found that the woman had omitted one or several pills. They sometimes produce weight gain, nausea, tenderness of the breasts, and breakthrough bleeding, but these side effects are mostly minor and usually disappear within a few months.

In addition to these combination pills, there are the "sequentials," a variety that may produce slightly fewer side effects but, in contrast to the combination pill, is not 100 percent effective. A woman on sequentials, beginning also with cycle day 5, takes 15 pills containing estrogen alone, followed by pills containing estrogen plus progesterone for five more days.

INTRAUTERINE CONTRACEPTIVE DEVICES (IUD). The second new technique, the IUD, dates back to Ernest Gräfenberg, a Berlin gynecologist who later practiced in New York City. His devices were first made of silkworm gut, later of silver, gold, or platinum. Grafenberg's method enjoyed only brief popularity in the 1920s. The reasons for the renascence of intrauterine contraception are twofold: (1) today's IUDs are made of nonreactive material, stainless steel or plastic, and (2) while infections occurring in wearers of such devices (not caused by the device) were a serious complication before the advent of antibiotics, such infections are easily controlled today, even without necessitating removal of the IUD.

The IUD method is highly effective, even though its mode of action in the human is still unexplained. Its great advantage is that once the woman has selected this method and has had the device inserted, she does not have to think about contraception any more and can be protected for years, or up to the moment when she desires pregnancy.

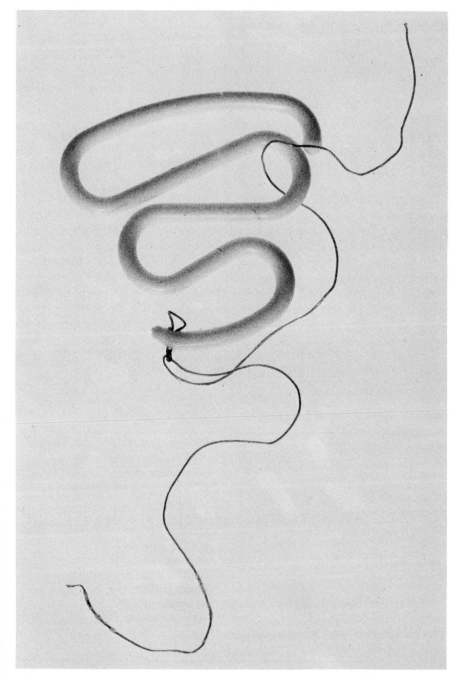

Figure 4   The Lippes loop, the most commonly used intrauterine contraceptive device.

Unfortunately, the method still has a number of shortcomings. It is generally unsuitable for nulliparous women (women who have not given birth), because in these women the insertion can be extremely difficult and painful and, furthermore, the degree of effectiveness is lower than in general. Another disadvantage is that a minority of women expel the device and some others have to have it removed because of bleeding or menstrual pain. The method is suitable for 80 percent of the women who have had children.

The most extensive IUD study (Tietze), a statistical evaluation of more than 22,000 insertions performed by 33 investigators, indicates that the large plastic loop invented by Lippes is the IUD of choice (Figure 4).

THE "CONVENTIONAL" METHODS. The *diaphragm* combined with jelly or cream is still widely used by middle-class women; in the lower-income groups, it has by now been largely replaced by the pill. Thus, in 1963, roughly one fourth of the contraceptive clinic patients at Bellevue were still using the diaphragm (Lehfeldt, 1965), while today less than 10 percent of the new patients coming to the clinic select the diaphragm.

A less frequently used method is the *cervical cap.* If made of plastic material, the cap can be worn throughout the entire cycle, thus providing prolonged protection. However, it is unsuitable for women who have any pathology of the cervix.

Special *creams* and *jellies* have been developed for use *alone,* that is, without diaphragm. This method is only fairly effective.

Table 18   Contraceptive Techniques

Most effective	Oral contraception (combination pills)
Highly effective	Diaphragm with jelly or cream
	Cervical cap with jelly or cream
	Condom
	Intrauterine devices (IUD)
	Oral contraception (sequentials)
	Coitus interruptus
Very effective	Aerosol vaginal foams
Fairly effective	Creams and jellies alone
	Foam tablets
	Suppositories
	Rhythm method
Very little effective	Breast feeding
	Vaginal douche

Aerosol foams have a greater degree of effectiveness, but are inferior to the diaphragm-jelly and cervical cap methods.

Table 18 shows a reclassification of available contraceptive techniques according to effectiveness.

It is good advice to a young couple not to attempt to cope with the complex problem of family planning unassisted, but to obtain expert counsel. The physician should not limit himself to one single method of family planning, for if this method proves unacceptable to a particular couple, they will discard it after a short while. The physician who is successful in prescribing a technique suited to individual needs will obtain the highest rate of acceptance and thus will be most helpful to his patients.

Infertility and Sterility

Two types of impaired fertility exist: infertility and sterility. Infertility can be defined as the inability to produce living children; in this condition conception occurs but the pregnancy is terminated before the baby is viable, ending either in spontaneous abortion or in premature delivery. In sterility, no conception takes place. The expressions sterility and infertility are frequently erroneously used as synonyms.

In antiquity, and in some primitive civilizations even today, barrenness is blamed exclusively on reproductive failure in the female. Actually, we should not think in terms of infertile or sterile men and women, but of barren couples. In general, it may be said that males are the cause of sterility and infertility as often as are females. In many instances, both partners are responsible for the failure to conceive.

Infertility and sterility present delicate problems of diagnosis and treatment because the process of reproduction, as shown in the foregoing sections, is a very complicated one. Usually, any dysfunction in the male is much easier to diagnose. An examination of the semen will reveal deficiencies in motility, abnormal forms, or a low sperm count; or in cases of male sterility, absence of motility or no sperm at all. Any investigation of a barren couple should therefore start with the examination of the male.

For the examination of the female, a number of procedures are necessary. First, we need to determine whether ovulation takes place. A few physicians have been able to observe the process of ovulation in the living woman by means of a culdoscope, an instrument similar to the cystoscope, inserted into the peritoneum through a vaginal incision while the patient was under anesthesia.

In the majority of cases, however, physicians have to rely on indirect signs of ovulation, that is, the effects produced in connection with ovulation. Menstruation, as has been stated previously, is not in itself proof of ovulation. Cyclic changes in the endometrium, which occur in the ovulating woman, can, however, be used to determine indirectly whether ovulation has occurred. Through endometrial biopsy (an office procedure) small parts of the endometrium can be removed and examined after the presumed ovulation time; they will show, or fail to show, secretory changes which are indicative of ovulation. A simpler method is taking the basal temperature every morning. A typical basal temperature chart shows the so-called dip, the temperature reaching its lowest point on the 12th day of the cycle, followed by a sustained, elevated temperature curve from the 14th to the 27th day of the cycle. Among laboratory tests to determine ovulation are vaginal smears, examination of the cervical mucus, and special urine tests.

Another important method used in the investigation of female sterility is the uterotubal insufflation, the Rubin test, also an office procedure. Carbon dioxide gas is inflated under pressure by means of a canula through the cervical canal into the fallopian tubes. The escape of the gas through the tubes can be heard by the physician. When the patient assumes the erect position after the test, she will experience shoulder pain, if the tubes are open. Another technique to determine tubal patency is hysterosalpingography: a contrasting material is injected through the cervical canal in order to obtain a radiological picture of uterus and fallopian tubes. This method, usually employed after uterotubal insufflation has failed to demonstrate tubal patency, frequently helps to localize the site of tubal obstruction. Both the Rubin test and hysterosalpingography are not only diagnostic but therapeutic procedures as well, and often help to restore tubal patency and to cure sterility.

The technique of operations to restore tubal patency has been improved in recent years. According to the latest large survey, the percentage of live births following such operations was 20 to 35 (Kleegman and Kaufman).

Part 4   Pregnancy

In Part 4 the phenomenon of pregnancy is presented in detail. Dr. Lehfeldt's purpose here is to provide the reader with an understanding

*of pregnancy in its many aspects. Thus the signs of pregnancy are dis-
cussed, including laboratory tests for pregnancy. The physiology of
pregnancy is fully described. Finally Dr. Lehfeldt addresses himself to
the subject of proper prenatal care and pathology of pregnancy.*

Physiology

Pregnancy begins at the moment when a mature ovum, expelled from
the ovary and having entered the fallopian tube, is fertilized by a spermatozoon. As mentioned before, a single ejaculate contains several hundred million spermatozoa. Most spermatozoa perish in the hostile secretion of the vagina, but some reach the cervical canal and ascend from
there into the uterine cavity and into the lumen of the fallopian tubes.
Here they encounter the ovum, but only a single spermatozoon will pe-
netrate the membrane of the ovum and fertilize it. After the head of the
spermatozoon has entered the ovum, the tail disappears; head and neck
migrate toward the center of the ovum and unite with its nucleus into
one cell. This cell divides into two cells, which again subdivide to form
more and more cells, arranged in circular fashion. Some of these, the so-
called auxiliary cells, multiply faster than the center cells and form a
layer around them. The center cells, the so-called formative cells, are the
ones from which the embryo later develops. A fluid, probably secreted
by the auxiliary cells, soon appears in the center of the cell accumulation, so that the entire structure looks like a small balloon filled with
water. At the same time that the cell divisions and modifications take
place, the fertilized ovum moves toward the uterine cavity, taking from
six to seven days to complete its migration. The endometrium then enters the so-called secretory phase, characterized by wide and tortuous
glands and a thickened mucus membrane full of blood vessels. In this
condition the endometrium constitutes an ideal medium for the nesting
(nidation) of the fertilized ovum. After nidation, the fertilized ovum develops into the embryo. Its nutrition is effected through the affiliation of
maternal endometrial cells and of some of the auxiliary cells of the fertilized ovum. The cells at the periphery of the ovum form into villous
structures (wormlike processes) which facilitate the alimentation of the
growing embryo. The entire mass of villi is called the chorion. The cell
membrane covering the inside of the embryonic sac is called the amnion.
The fluid in which the embryo is suspended is called the amniotic fluid,
or baby water, and is contained in the amniotic sac. From the chorionic
villi, the afterbirth (placenta) develops.

In this space we cannot discuss in detail the full development of embryonic life, but will have to limit ourselves to a few basic facts. There

exists a beautiful set of photographs of the developing embryo, assembled by Geraldine Flux Flanagan, who has also written an explanatory text. "Mrs. Flanagan makes the story of life's beginning *in utero* not only understandable but fascinating and beautiful," writes the distinguished embryologist George Washington Corner. In the fourth week the embryo is about 1 cm long and already shows rudiments of eyes, ears, and nose. In the second month of pregnancy, the embryo is about 2½ cm long, and the external genitalia start to develop. In the third month, the fetal length is about 8 cm; fingers and toes are visible. In the fourth month, the fetus measures about 16 cm; in the fifth month 25 cm. Already in the third month the fetus starts to move, but its movements are not noticeable yet. Usually, fetal movements, called "quickening," are noticed by the expectant mother in the fifth or sixth month of her first pregnancy, and earlier in subsequent pregnancies.

Usually the first indication of pregnancy noticed by the woman is the discontinuation of menstruation. Other subjective signs are a tendency to urinate more frequently, swelling of the breasts, nausea, or a slight feeling of faintness. A woman who observes any of these symptoms usually consults her physician. It is advisable to have such a consultation about a week or ten days after the first missed period. Even in the early phase, the physician may be able to diagnose pregnancy: the uterus is slightly enlarged, somewhat softer, and more congested; the breasts are fuller, and frequently a fluid, the so-called colostrum, can be expressed from the breasts. These diagnostic indications differ only slightly from findings in the nonpregnant uterus shortly before the onset of the next period. If reexamination one or two weeks later shows more pronounced changes, the diagnosis is more certain.

A number of biological tests have been developed that help the physician diagnose pregnancy at an early stage. The best known is the so-called A-Z test, developed by Aschheim and Zondek. For this test, urine from the expectant mother is injected into immature female mice. In case of pregnancy, the mice react with swelling, congestion, and hemorrhages into their ovaries. In modifications of the A-Z test, rabbits, rats, and frogs are used. All of these tests show a high degree of accuracy, but it must be emphasized that no test is 100 percent reliable. An accurate diagnosis at an early stage can be made only through physical examination combined with observation of the woman. Another important point is that any result of such a pregnancy test, be it positive or negative, must be regarded as unreliable if the test is made earlier than 10 days after the first missed period. A simple test for determination of early pregnancy is the fern test, which is based on examination of the cervical mucus, for the so-called crystallization phenomenon. This test, which is done in the doctor's office and can be interpreted immediately, is accurate only in a negative way, that is, as a method of ruling out pregnancy. Its advantage is that it can be performed as early as a few days after the missed period, at which time the A-Z test or its modifications fail to give adequate information.

While clinical as well as biological tests usually enable the physician to arrive at a comparatively early diagnosis, they are not 100 percent reliable. A definitive diagnosis is possible only by observation of the clinical symptoms produced by the fetus. By the third month, the fetal bone formation is advanced enough to be detected by X ray, but today such an examination is considered harmful. In the fourth or fifth month the fetal heart can be heard in a soundproof room by means of sound amplification; at this time the mother herself will begin to feel fetal movements or "quickening." Special acoustic instruments enable the physician to hear fetal heart sounds as early as 10 to 12 weeks after the first day of the pregnant woman's last menstrual period.

The question whether the sex of the baby can be determined before birth has preoccupied people from time immemorial. Theoretically, it can be done today by puncturing the amniotic sac and by aspirating some amniotic fluid; this fluid contains cells from the fetus that will reveal its sex under microscopic examination. As puncture of the amniotic sac is dangerous, it is in most cases advisable to abstain from sex determination before birth.

Prenatal Care

Prenatal care, which today is a routine procedure in the United States, has been instrumental in lowering maternal and infant mortality. Early in pregnancy the woman is given a complete physical examination, including blood count, urinalysis, and blood serology (Wassermann). In addition, the patient's—and, if necessary, her husband's—blood type and Rh factor are determined. The bony pelvis is measured, a fairly reliable method to determine whether the pelvis is wide enough to allow smooth passage of the baby at birth. Until a few years ago, many obstetricians took pelvic X-rays of every patient expecting her first baby. In the light of modern knowledge concerning possible harmful effects of radiation on the baby, X-ray studies during pregnancy are now done only if there is a compelling reason, and then only very late in pregnancy.

Pregnancy lasts roughly 40 weeks. During the first 20 weeks the expectant mother should not gain weight; the physician, who sees the patient about once a month during this period, will prescribe caloric restrictions, if necessary, and will see her more frequently if she tends to gain weight. During the second 20 weeks, an average gain of one pound per week is normal; but many women gain more, even on an apparently normal diet. Stricter medical supervision during the second half of pregnancy is necessary; the patient is seen every two to three weeks, and usually once a week during the last month. The prevention of abnormal weight increase is one of the most important prophylactic methods in the fight against late toxemia. Besides weight, blood pressure and urine are checked at each visit—another safeguard against late toxemia.

During the second half of pregnancy, supplementary vitamins and minerals, among them iron, are usually prescribed. Occasional blood counts are taken to check possible development of pregnancy anemia.

The obstetrician is frequently asked about the advisability of traveling and of physical and sexual activity during pregnancy. Even extensive traveling—as documented by experience during World War II—does not in any way endanger a normal pregnancy. Exhausting long motor trips—any overexhaustion, at that—should be avoided. Physical activity should be encouraged. Any sport, including horseback riding, can be safely continued during pregnancy if the woman has practiced such sport before. In a normal pregnancy, sexual intercourse does not constitute any danger. The baby is so well protected in the uterus that it is virtually immune to injury. Abstention is advisable only for the last two weeks before the expected date of confinement.

The prenatal visits are important not only from the medical, but also from a psychological point of view. They help physician and patient to get thoroughly acquainted and to establish confidence, so that the expectant mother will face childbirth optimistically and fearlessly.

Pathology of Pregnancy

Nausea and vomiting in early pregnancy are rather common disturbances; they are more frequent during the first pregnancy. This condition, called *early toxemia,* has also been described as morning sickness, since the patient often suffers from it in the morning, even on an empty stomach. Nausea may also occur in the later hours of the day, and may continue until late in pregnancy. In most instances, this condition is alleviated by a number of available medications. Only rarely, in cases of severe nausea and vomiting, suppositories or injections are required. Dietary measures are helpful; they must be adapted to individual needs. Some patients fare better on a liquid, others, on a solid diet. Cold food is often tolerated better than hot meals. Some pregnant women have a definite aversion against, others a craving for, particular foods.

A far more serious condition is *late toxemia,* characterized by extreme weight increase and by swelling of ankles and legs. In severe cases, the patient has an elevated blood pressure, and sometimes kidney and liver damage. The best method to fight this condition is prophylaxis. Regular visits to the doctor's office facilitate early detection and treatment.

Ankle or leg swelling is not always caused by toxemia, but may be due to varicose veins, which sometimes form during pregnancy. Another cause of ankle and leg swelling is water retention, which is easily checked by restriction of liquid intake and by proper medication. However, when ankle swelling is associated with elevated blood pressure and albumin in the urine, the condition must be considered serious. A strict diet must be maintained, including not only liquid but also salt restriction; often bed rest may be necessary. If no quick improvement results from such treatment, hospitalization becomes necessary. The mortality from late toxemia has greatly decreased in the United States because of these precautions.

Bleeding during pregnancy is always an ominous sign. Early in pregnancy it may be the first indication of a threatening miscarriage. It is therefore important in case of bleeding that the pregnant woman notify her doctor immediately. Bleeding occurring late in pregnancy may be indicative of an even more dangerous situation: while slight staining is not infrequently an early sign of impending childbirth, any stronger bleeding should be considered a danger sign, and the doctor must be notified immediately.

Often such bleeding is due to abnormal implantation of the placenta, called *placenta previa*. If there is the slightest suspicion of placenta previa, the woman must be hospitalized immediately and kept under strict observation. If bleeding caused by placenta previa occurs around the 34th or 36th week of pregnancy, or later, the baby is usually viable and can be saved by cesarean section. Maternal death as a consequence of placenta previa has become a rare occurrence, due to modern precautionary measures, such as the availability of blood for transfusion, and to generally improved obstetrics.

Erythroblastosis

Erythroblastosis is sometimes confused, by lay people, with "blue baby." A blue baby is one who is suffering from a congenital heart condition which produces the blue discoloration of the skin and mucus membrane. In erythroblastosis the baby is not blue but turns yellow. Erythroblastosis of the newborn is caused by the incompatibility of maternal and paternal blood groups. Besides the four main blood types (O, A, B, AB) there are blood factors which also exist in the Macacus and Rhesus monkey and which are called **Rhesus** or **Rh** factor for short. Eighty-five percent of the entire population are "Rh-positive," which means that their blood contains this rhesus factor. Erythroblastosis can occur only in that 15 percent of women who are both Rh-negative and married to Rh-positive men. Even for these couples the risk of having an erythroblastotic baby is practically nil for the first-born child and only 5 percent for subsequent children. It has become established practice to test Rh-negative women for Rh antibodies repeatedly during pregnancy. An increase in these antibodies may be a sign that the expected baby may be erythroblastotic. A recently developed method aims at prevention of fetal erythroblastosis: the Rh-negative mother is injected with a special gamma globulin, with the purpose of desensitizing her and thereby preventing the increase in antibodies, which are responsible for the development of fetal erythroblastosis. It is important to be prepared for such a possibility, as many erythroblastotic babies can be saved by exchange transfusion, by which their own blood is replaced by blood from a donor, soon after birth, sometimes within hours after delivery.

Part 5   Childbirth

In Part 5, the final section of this appendix, Dr. Lehfeldt introduces the subject of childbirth. Here he deals with several pertinent issues that are of concern to prospective parents. The author is much interested in ways of orienting the expectant mother so that she may enter childbirth with confidence and a minimum of anxiety. As part of such orientation he provides a careful description of the signs of impending childbirth, the birth process, cesarean section, the puerperium, and postpartum care.

Childbirth, like pregnancy, is a physiological process. In the great majority of cases, childbirth produces no complications; in a very small fraction, however, mothers as well as babies are faced with a potentially dangerous situation. The danger can be minimized by hospitalization. The generally accepted practice in the United States of hospitalization during childbirth has greatly contributed to the lowering of the rate of maternal mortality. Hospitalization has also caused some decrease in neonatal mortality, even though the loss of newborn babies is still considerable.[1]

Although the advantages of hospital delivery are obvious, it must be conceded that hospitalization at this time and during the puerperium creates a number of psychological difficulties for some mothers, occasionally even for the entire family. The expectant mother is removed from her own environment into an unfamiliar atmosphere; she is often exposed to cries of pain from women in active labor; the bare hospital room and the unknown faces of nurses, interns, or residents—all these circumstances may produce a feeling of isolation and even anxiety. The newborn baby usually is not allowed to stay with the mother but is transferred to the hospital nursery; only during feeding time does the mother have a chance to see and enjoy her baby. In most hospitals she can see her husband only during visiting hours. A few progressive hospitals have initiated the so-called rooming-in procedure to overcome the effects of separation of mother and child during the puerperium. Unfortunately, rooming-in requires additional medical personnel and is therefore the exception rather than the rule. The modern practice of shortening the hospital stay after childbirth to between three or five days (formerly ten to fourteen days) has somewhat mitigated this problem.

If the expectant mother can be relieved of her fears, she will be more relaxed and more cooperative during labor. In former years, many deliveries were performed in twilight sleep, induced by injections or oral or rectal medication. Women who are delivered in twilight sleep experience a retrograde amnesia, so that they do not remember either labor or delivery. They may wake up without even knowing that they had their baby. This method of delivery deprives the mother of a wonderful experience. In addition, instances have occurred where the drugs given for induction of twilight sleep have affected the baby's respiratory center. For this reason, physicians have become more cautious in using these drugs. Today we have new drug combinations to relieve labor pains which have little or no influence on the baby. Nevertheless, many physicians prefer to use the "natural childbirth" method, where no drugs are administered, whenever possible.

Preparations for natural childbirth start during pregnancy. The expectant mother must thoroughly understand the mechanism of the birth

[1] In 1935, more than 60 mothers in 10,000 lost their lives in giving birth; in 1958, fewer than 4 mothers in 10,000 failed to survive childbirth. There has also been a marked reduction in the hazard of birth for the baby. In 1935, more than 60 babies in every 1000 deliveries failed to survive; during 1957 to 1960, this figure had been reduced to 26.4 per 1000 live births (Reid).

process; it is then that she learns the different breathing techniques, aimed at relaxation, which she has to use in the various phases of the delivery. An important part of the natural childbirth method is the presence of the husband during labor and, possibly, during delivery. This point is stressed by the British as well as the French advocates of this technique (Read, Lamaze, Vellay). If adequately prepared, a woman will be able to help actively the progress of labor; if, however, in spite of such preparation, she experiences intolerable pain, she most certainly should get analgesics or anesthesia. In normal deliveries, the necessity for using drugs seldom arises, provided patient and physician have confidence in the method of natural childbirth.

Signs of Impending Childbirth

While there are variations in the length of time, childbirth is expected to occur in nine months plus seven days after the first day of the last menstrual period. Around this time, the expectant mother will know that delivery is impending, from one of three signs, or from a combination of the three: (1) the start of regular uterine contractions, (2) the breaking of the bag of waters (the amniotic sac), and (3) some staining. Irregular contractions usually occur during the last weeks of pregnancy; contractions signifying the beginning of labor are regular, occurring at intervals of 15 to 20 minutes, and each lasting for 30 to 60 seconds. If contractions of this type recur for one hour, it is necessary to notify the physician. The patient should also get in touch with her doctor if she notices staining, or if she feels the loss of baby water, even if she has no regular contractions. The loss of baby water is not always easily detected, as the patient may confuse it with profuse discharge or the escape of urine. In case of doubt it is always advisable to discuss the question with the obstetrician.

The Birth Process

The birth process is divided into three stages. In the first stage, the lowermost part of the uterus, consisting of cervix and lower third of the uterine body, dilates to form part of the birth canal. When this dilation is accomplished, the second stage starts, during which the baby is expelled by contractions of the uterus, assisted by the abdominal muscles. In the third stage, the afterbirth or placenta follows, 10 to 15 minutes after the birth of the baby, or is expressed by the obstetrician.

Ninety-five percent of all deliveries are vertex presentations, which means that the presenting part—that is, the part first appearing at the mother's perineum—is the vertex or head. In slightly over 3 percent of the cases, the buttock or breech is the presenting part. Very shortly after the presenting part has passed the perineum, the rest of the baby's body is expressed through the birth canal, formed not only by the cervix and the lower uterine segment, but also by the vagina. The obstetrician now cuts and double-ties the umbilical cord. The baby usually cries immediately under the influence of the atmospheric air, and will thereafter breathe normally and regularly.

Cesarean Section

Approximately 5 percent of the deliveries in the United States are done by cesarean section, for which there are various medical indications. One, placenta previa, has already been mentioned; in extreme cases, the location of the placenta actually blocks the baby's passage through the birth canal (*placenta previa centralis*); toward the end of the first stage of labor, with increasing dilation, the placenta separates from the uterus and bleeding occurs, endangering the baby's and even the mother's life. The situation is less dangerous when the placenta is not centrally located and when only part of it reaches into the lower segment of the uterus; then the bleeding is generally less profuse. After rupture of the membranes, the baby's head may compress the placenta during the descent and stop the bleeding, thereby eliminating the need for cesarean section.

Another indication is cephalo-pelvic disproportion, which exists when the baby's head is too big to pass through the bony pelvis of the mother. Severe cases of late toxemia and fetal distress may also require section.

The decision to perform this operation should not be made lightly; while it is nowadays a very safe procedure, its mortality rate, although very low, is slightly higher than that of vaginal deliveries. Another point to be considered is that, according to the opinion prevailing among obstetricians, women who have had one abdominal delivery should also be sectioned in subsequent deliveries. Most obstetricians recommend tubal sterilization at the time of the third cesarean section. For a woman with many preceding abdominal deliveries, each pregnancy becomes more hazardous. For this reason, this procedure must be considered as one lowering the woman's fertility.

The pregnant woman's age may yet be another indication for section: in the elderly primigravida—women thirty-five years of age or older who give birth for the first time—conditions that complicate delivery, such as hypertension, uterine fibroids, or uterine inertia (failure to produce strong contractions), are more frequent than in the younger woman. The above-described risk of repeated abdominal deliveries is greatly reduced for older women, as their fertility is lowered and their chances of successful future pregnancies are smaller.

It has become common practice in this country for obstetricians, contemplating delivery by cesarean section, not to make this important decision alone but only after consultation with another specialist.

The Puerperium

The German expression for puerperium, "Wochenbett" (week-in-bed), translates the age-honored habit of letting the newly delivered woman stay in bed for at least one week. Modern obstetricians make young mothers get up 12 to 24 hours after delivery. Due to this new regimen, vascular complications, such as thrombophlebitis and embolism, have been reduced to a minimum. Physical activity early after childbirth must therefore be considered as desirable. Nevertheless, a period of rest of several weeks after delivery is still as important as ever.

Until recently, bottle feeding, a safe and easy method, was used by United States city populations as an almost exclusive method. Today, nursing has again become somewhat more popular. There is a new awareness in women that breast feeding is a more natural method than bottle feeding. It also has definite advantages. The sucking action of the baby, through a reflex mechanism, produces uterine contractions which help the uterus resume its normal size much faster. More important still is the psychological advantage that both mother and baby derive from nursing. Nursing actually provides sexual enjoyment of which nonnursing women deprive themselves; they also deprive their baby, for the bottle is a poor substitute for the intimate contact established between mother and child through nursing.

For young mothers who resume professional life soon after childbirth, nursing is, of course, impossible. Breast feeding is contraindicated in a few rare situations, such as anemia after cesarean section, erythroblastosis of the baby, and acute infectious disease of the mother. It is a myth that nursing impairs the mother's figure; no excessive eating is necessary for the nursing mother, and the shape of her breasts is not affected by nursing.

Postpartum Care

Modern obstetrical care includes supervision during the first few months after the delivery. Usually, the patient is reexamined in the doctor's office two weeks after childbirth. About six weeks postpartum, during the second visit, the cervix is also examined for possible lacerations or minor infections, which are rather common. If attended in time, they are completely harmless.

Intercourse can be resumed six to eight weeks after childbirth; at the second postpartum consultation, the planning of further pregnancies should also be discussed.

Suggested Readings

Part 1

Dickinson, Robert L., *Human Sex Anatomy*, Williams and Wilkins, Baltimore, 1933.

Eastman, Nicholson, J., *Williams Obstetrics*, Appleton-Century-Crofts, New York, 1950.

Reid, Duncan E., *A Textbook of Obstetrics*, Saunders, Philadelphia and London, 1962.

Part 2

Ellis, Albert, *The Art and Science of Love*, Lyle Stuart, New York, 1960.

Kinsey, Alfred C., et al., *Sexual Behavior in the Human Male*, Saunders, Philadelphia and London, 1948.

Kinsey, Alfred C., et al., *Sexual Behavior in the Human Female*, Saunders, Philadelphia and London, 1953.

Masters, William H., and Virginia E. Johnson, *Human Sex Response*, Little, Brown, Boston, 1966.

Oliven, John F., *Sexual Hygiene and Pathology*, Lippincott, Philadelphia, 1955.

Stekel, Wilhelm, *Frigidity in Woman*, Liveright, New York, 1926.

Stekel, Wilhelm, *Impotence in the Male*, Liveright, New York, 1927.

Van de Velde, T. H., *Ideal Marriage*, Covici, Friede, New York, 1930.

Part 3

Calderone, Mary S., Ed., *Manual of Contraceptive Practice*, Williams and Wilkins, Baltimore, 1964.

Dickinson, Robert L., and Louise S. Bryant, *Control of Conception*, Williams and Wilkins, Baltimore, 1932.

Freedman, Ronald, et al., *Family Planning, Sterility and Population Growth*, McGraw-Hill, New York, 1959.

Guttmacher, Alan F., et al., *The Complete Book of Birth Control*, Ballantine Books, New York, 1961.

Kleegman, Sophia J., and Sherwin A. Kaufman, *Infertility in Women*, F. A. Davis, Philadelphia, 1966.

Knaus, Hermann, *Woman's Fertile and Infertile Days and How to Compare Them*, Ivan Obolensky, New York, 1962.

Lehfeldt, Hans, "Willful Exposure to Unwanted Pregnancy (WEUP)," *Am. J. Obst. Gynec.*, **78** (1959), pp. 661–665.

Lehfeldt, Hans, "The First Five Years of Contraceptive Service in a Municipal Hospital," *Am. J. Obst. Gynec.*, **93** (1965), pp. 727–733.

Ogino, Kyusaku, *Conception Period in Women*, Medical Arts Publishing Company, Harrisburg, 1934.

Portnoy, Louis, and Jules Saltman, *Fertility in Marriage*, Signet Books, New York, 1951.

Rock, John, *The Time Has Come, A Catholic Doctor's Proposals to End the Battle over Birth Control*, Knopf, New York, 1963.

Ryder, Norman B., and Charles F. Westoff, "Use of Oral Contraception in the United States, 1965," *Science*, **153** (1966), pp. 1199–1205.

Sanger, Margaret, and Hannah M. Stone, Eds., *The Practice of Contraception*, Williams and Wilkins, Baltimore, 1931.

Stone, Hannah M., and Abraham Stone, *A Marriage Manual*, Simon and Schuster, New York, 1953.

Tietze, Christopher, "Contraception with Intrauterine Devices," *Am. J. Obst. Gynec.*, **96** (1966), pp. 1043–1054.

Parts 4 and 5

Calderone, Mary S., Ed., *Abortion in the United States*, Hoeber-Harper, New York, 1958.

Eastman, Nicholson J., *Expectant Motherhood*, Little, Brown, Boston, 1947.

Flannagan, Geraldine L., *The First Months of Life*, Simon and Schuster, New York, 1962.

Gebhard, Paul H., et al., *Pregnancy, Birth and Abortion*, Hoeber-Harper, New York, 1958.

Guttmacher, Alan F., *Having a Baby*, Signet Books, New York, 1950.

Hall, Robert E., *Nine Months' Reading*, Doubleday, Garden City, N.Y., 1960.

Levine, Milton I., and Jean H. Seligman, *A Baby Is Born*, Simon and Schuster, New York, 1949.

Read, Grantly D., *Childbirth without Fear,* 3rd ed., William Heinemann, London, 1956.

Spock, Benjamin, *The Pocketbook of Baby and Childcare,* Pocket Books, New York, 1950.

Vellay, Pierre, *Childbirth without Pain,* Dutton, New York, 1960.

APPENDIX B

Consumer Problems
of Married People

DONALD S. LONGWORTH, PH.D.

Professor Longworth is a sociologist by profession, and has for many years been keenly interested in consumer problems as they relate to family living. As a teacher of family sociology and a marriage counselor for many years, he has been close to the kinds of adjustments that persons starting out in marriage are called on to make. Professor Longworth has accumulated a vast range of knowledge in the area of consumer problems; some of this knowledge is offered in the presentation that follows. Professor Longworth's background and experience include the following. B.S. and M.A. from Bowling Green State University in Bowling Green, Ohio, and Ph.D. from Ohio State University in 1952. He was a member of the Sociology Department at Bowling Green State University from 1949 to 1955 and Chairman of that department from 1958 to 1965. Professor Longworth has also served as Visiting Professor at Western Michigan University. Since 1966 he has been Professor of Home and Family at Texas Technological College.

In this appendix Professor Longworth discusses the consumer problems of married people in all phases of the family cycle. Special attention is given to the newly married couple with college training. The discussion covers the cost of maintaining a home and the general problems of family finance, methods of coping with financial shortages, and family security needs.

Spending the Family Income

Most young people want and need a realistic picture of what their future financial situation is likely to be. Ignorance or wishful thinking often leads to plans and hopes that reality can never fulfill. In a study dealing with several areas in which marital couples had to make adjustments, the financial area was one of the areas found to be of major importance.[1] Balancing available income against the needs of the family is frequently a difficult adjustment. The couple who have a realistic conception of the cost involved in maintaining a family and the probable income that will be available have a decided advantage. In planning for the future, one way to approach the problem is to estimate what the family will need.[2] A minimum requirement for launching a marriage is that the couple be free of extensive debts at the time of marriage; it is helpful if some cash savings are available. Generally speaking, the larger the sum saved the better, because during the early years of marriage many families discover that there is a shortage of money. The cost of furniture, a car, and the expense of maintaining a home all add up to a large amount of money. In many instances the situation is further complicated by the arrival of a baby. The actual cost, however, is partially determined by the values of the couple and the cultural pattern to which they have grown accustomed. If a family lives in a so-called two-car neighborhood, they may be under considerable social pressure to own two cars even though they have little need for a second car for transportation purposes.

Because of the differences involved in specific cultural patterns, it is difficult to predict the actual expense of supporting a family; but a sufficiently realistic estimate can be made to expedite successful planning. In this regard the construction of a plan of specific anticipated expenses is helpful. However, in constructing such a financial plan it must be noted that newlyweds frequently tend to exaggerate probable income and underestimate the cost of maintaining a family. The findings shown in Figure 1 are very interesting on this point.

The earnings of most American males are comparatively small while they are in the twenties; this is true even for college-trained men. However, as we have already pointed out, this is the time when most families are expanding, and in comparison to income expenses are very high. The adjustment is further complicated by the fact that some people are motivated to marry in the hope of improving their economic position. These people apparently do not recognize that it has taken approximately 25 years for their parents to establish their present level of living. Thus it is reasonable to expect a somewhat lower level of living during the early years of marriage than that to which one has been accustomed in the parental home.

[1] Judson Landis, "Length of Time Required to Achieve Adjustment in Marriage," *Am. soc. Rev.*, 11, 6 (December 1946), pp. 666–667.
[2] Howard F. Bigelow, *Family Finance*, rev. ed., Lippincott, New York, 1953, p. 322.

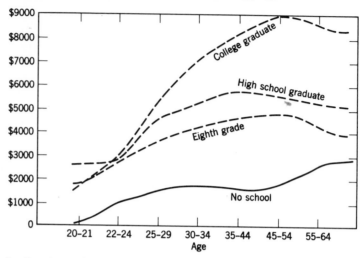

Figure 1   Earnings of American men, 1960. Fron "Educational Attainment," Spe- cial Reports, Vol. 2, U. S. Bureau of Census, 1960.

In some instances the bride and groom have been reared in homes where the general level of living is markedly different. This condition adds to the complexities of marriage adjustment. When the income is $6200 in a family with three children, a pattern of purchasing and con- sumption gradually emerges. It is taken for granted, for example, that dresses and suits will be worn for several seasons. Also, the purchase of such items is limited to the type of store that stresses maximum quality at a medium price. Style and the type of store are of secondary importance. On the other hand, in a family with three children where the income is in excess of $15,000 a year, the style of the item purchased and the exclu- siveness of the store in which it is purchased become important consid- erations.

It is interesting to note that in two families of the same size with the same income, it is possible that one family will maintain a considerably higher level of living than the other. This difference in the level of living may be due to the types of financial management employed. Proper management of funds can greatly raise the level of living for a family. The elasticity in terms of stretching available funds is not unlimited. In all probability, the elasticity is greater in those families where the in- come is above the minimum level.

About the time that the children reach high school or college age the expense of maintaining a family reaches its highest level. At this time the resources of most families are seriously taxed. Fortunately, this is also the time when earnings reach their maximum level in many instances. Savings accumulated in earlier years can reduce some of the strain.

In the "empty nest" phase of the family cycle—that is, the phase when all of the children are grown and have left the home, leaving only the father and mother—income usually declines. Sometimes health needs and service functions performed for the family produce a financial burden. The numerous private and public retirement benefit programs have materially reduced the strain at this phase in the family cycle. However, some people do not reserve sufficient savings for their later years. The current emphasis on the improvement of retirement programs and provision for part-time employment after retirement portend better prospects for retired persons in future years.

Methods of Coping with the Financial Shortage

When a family discovers that its wants exceed its available funds, what are the possibilities? First, there are several things the members of the family can do to increase the benefits from funds available and, secondly, in some instances it is possible to increase the available funds. The more common and practical methods of realizing these two possibilities will be discussed.

When a family is confronted with financial difficulty, someone invariably suggests that the way to cope with the problem of inadequate funds is to live by a budget. A popular misconception relative to a budget, however, is that it will increase the funds available. A budget will enable a family to spend existing funds in such a manner that they will get more of the goods they really want, but it will obviously not increase the number of dollars available to the family.

Some families are capable of managing their affairs much more successfully when they employ a budget, while others become "budget slaves." The proper use of a budget is essential if it is going to contribute to the welfare of the family. In its most elementary form a budget is nothing more than a written record of the income and expenses of a family. There are several budgetary techniques that can be employed by a family.

One approach is to start at the beginning of the month and allocate available funds to the various areas of anticipated expense. For example, $80 would be reserved for food. Purchases are made as long as funds are available. If funds are exhausted by the 28th of the month, no more purchases are made even though there might be a need for additional food. This approach has several overtly impractical features, but for some families it seems to work better than any other plan.

Another approach is to utilize one of the prepared budget books. Space is provided for entries relative to income and expenses in the more common areas. Usually two columns are provided under the general heading of expense, one entitled "estimated expense" and the other "actual expense." Some books provide suggestions as to the proportion of a family's income that should be spent for housing, food, and the like.

Table 19 shows a long list of items that might be included as budget headings and subheadings.[3] No family will need to use all these headings. The list is intended to suggest a great variety of possible items that a family may wish to include in working out its own set of budget headings.

The use of a budget enables a couple to live within its income. Generally, a family should plan to operate with a balanced budget. A family can experience a deficit for brief periods without jeopardizing marital happiness. An extended period of deficit spending, however, can lead to marked difficulty, for in addition to the personal trauma it entails (al-

Table 19   Suggestions for Budget Headings

Food	Special assessments
Groceries	Insurance
Meats	Repairs
Baked goods	Depreciation allowance
Fresh fruits and vegetables	House operation
Butter	Public utilities
Eggs	Water
Milk	Gas
Meals purchased outside home	Electricity
Clothing	Fuel
For husband	Telephone
For wife	Garbage removal
For each child	Services
Housing	Resident maid service
Charges on rented home	Nonresident service
Rent	Supplies
Repairs paid by tenant	Home cleaning supplies
Other expenses paid by tenant	Stationery and postage
Rent for garage	Furniture, furnishing and equipment
or	Repairs
Charges on owned home	Payments
Payments on principal	Laundry service and dry cleaning
Interest charges	Automobile maintenance
Taxes	Initial purchase

[3] *Ibid.,* p. 502.

Upkeep and operating expense
Insurance
Allowance for depreciation
Monthly payments
Transportation expenses
Car rental
Bus
Taxi
Railroad
Personal expenditures
Personal supplies
Allowances
Health
Medical doctor
Hospital
Drugs
Dentist
Eyeglasses
Nursing
Education
School expenses
Reading matter
Private lessons

Recreation
Amusements for the family
Entertainment of others
Children's toys and play equipment
Vacation expense
Organization memberships
Church
Professional organizations
Labor unions
Fraternal orders
Social clubs
Savings and security
Real estate
Savings account
Life insurance
Property insurance
Expenditures for others
Charity
Gifts
Taxes
Income tax
Property tax
Sales tax

though some people are much less annoyed by bill collectors than others), repeated inability to meet financial obligations will ultimately impair the credit rating of the family.

Much has been written relative to the proportion of the income that should be spent for each of the items in the budget. It is difficult to make specific suggestions that have practical value when applied to the individual family. Table 20 is an abbreviated budget for a newly married couple with one five-months-old child. The wife is not employed. You will note that actual expenses generally exceed estimates. This table may also suggest the proportion of the income that should be spent in each area.

Few people have economic means that they consider entirely adequate for taking care of all the monthly expenses associated with a home. The amount of $418 per month seems more than ample, and the estimated expense for the couple whose budget was presented in Table 19 totaled $418. It is obvious that when expenses exceed available income ($566 − $418 = $148), the family has a problem.

The largest discrepancy occurs in connection with the expenditure for transportation. A new car may be much more expensive than the

Table 20 Thirty-Day Budget for a Newly Married Couple with One Child on an Income of $418 per Month

Item	Estimate	Actual Expenditures
Food	$ 65	$ 80
Clothing		
Husband	22	26
Wife	15	12
Child	6	9
Housing		
Rent	80	95
House operation	35	48
Furniture	25	34
Transportation		
(New Ford—plan to trade cars every 2½ years)	45	112
Personal expenditures		
Husband's	5	5
Wife's	5	5
Health	12	13
Education	6	9
Recreation	20	32
Organization memberships		
Church, clubs, union, etc.	13	19
Savings and security	10	0
Other expenditures	12	14
Taxes	42	53
Total	$418	$566

couple had anticipated. A car is thought to be a necessity by most families in the United States, although it really is not required in every location. Public transportation, when available, is usually more economical than private transportation. Many people reason that it is more economical to buy a new car every two or three years and avoid the high cost of repairs on an aging vehicle. This kind of reasoning was more applicable in times past, when repair costs were very important in the operation of a car. Today, however, although repair costs are still high, they have not advanced so rapidly as other costs in the operation of an automobile: two of the largest costs for the modern car owner are depreciation and finance costs. A family wishing to reduce transportation costs should (1) pay cash for the family car, thus eliminating finance charges, and (2) buy a good used car. If a new car is purchased, it should be kept at least five or six years in order to reduce the depreciation loss.

The family budget is a spending plan. It is a tentative estimate of the family's income and the family's expenditure for a realistic list of items. It is a guide to intelligent spending. In the final analysis it is a tool that provides a service for the family. If the use of a budget seems to create more problems than it solves, the plan should be altered or abandoned altogether.

One approach that sometimes works in instances where the usual budget seems to produce added tension is for the couple to keep an accurate record of all expenditures during the course of the month. This at least enables a family to know how its money is being spent. At the end of the month, family members can review the spending pattern for the previous month and possibly alter their behavior in the following months. This plan seems to work better, at times, than a more formal budget.

The budget should never be thought of as a means to force the marriage partner "into line" on the matter of spending money. If this attitude exists, something more fundamental is wrong in the relationship of the couple, and the budget keeping will not correct the difficulty.

Few people have economic means that they consider entirely adequate. The family with an income of $6000 may think their problems would be solved if they could double the income. Additional income, although it has advantages, frequently brings with it additional problems in adjustment. There are many families of limited means that are happy and well adjusted. Whatever the actual dollar income, careful management and agreement with regard to purchases produce their rewards. A couple can learn much about buying and borrowing that will help in family financial management.

Buying on a cash basis has some advantages. The chief advantage is that the policy of paying cash tends to prevent overbuying. Buying for cash makes it possible to shop around and buy where quality and prices are most satisfactory.

One disadvantage of operating entirely on a cash basis is that no credit ratings are kept on cash customers; then if it does become desirable or necessary for these people to use credit, it takes them a little longer to establish a credit rating. This is probably a more important disadvantage in urban centers than in rural areas. Cash buyers often complain that in many stores they are not treated with the consideration that is accorded to the charge customers. Sometimes they have more difficulty in returning merchandise or securing repairs.

The chief advantage of charge accounts is their convenience. The charge account offers a further advantage in that it represents a complete record of expenditures. All the conveniences offered by the charge account, however, are reflected in the prices paid for goods. To operate a charge account system, delivery service, and the many other conveniences provided by the modern store costs money. Thus when you trade at a store that provides these services, you usually pay higher prices for comparable merchandise, because the cost of these services must be added to the purchase price.

Borrowing is sometimes necessary in order to purchase the required goods for a family. Unexpected expenses may arise because of illness or accident before there has been an opportunity to accumulate savings. In other situations, people may decide they want the immediate use of a new refrigerator, car, or furniture, and they mortgage their future income to obtain these goods.

Several sources of credit are open to people who want to borrow. The interest rates that are charged vary greatly from one agency to another. The rates are charged according to the risks involved in the lending. College-trained people generally fall in the low-risk group. Many schoolteachers, however, are notorious for their inability to take advantage of the lowest interest rates available. Credit is a commodity, the same as any other goods that might be purchased. Thus the intelligent course of action is to shop for the lowest interest rate available. Because of a lack of information, many people with a good credit rating borrow money from agencies that specialize in lending to people who have a poor credit rating. In so doing these people pay unnecessarily high interest rates.

The small loan company, for example, charges a very high rate of interest because very little collateral is required. In some instances the interest rate is as high as 36 percent per year. It is a mistake to be misled by the 3 percent per month appeal. This type of loan company has its place in the economy, but the point we are making here is that many people who employ its services could borrow more advantageously at another type of lending service.

Let us consider a hypothetical case, which will enable us to review much of what we have said this far. Let us assume that a couple lacks the cash to purchase a desired item—what might they do? The first step they might take is to "muster up" all of the buyer resistance possible. In so doing the following questions might be raised. Is the item really needed? Is it possible to manage without the item until a future time when it is easier for the couple to make the purchase? If it is decided that the item is not needed immediately and that its purchase can be postponed, the problem is solved. If, on the other hand, the purchase of the item is deemed necessary in spite of the lack of immediate funds, the next step that the couple might take is to go to a commercial bank or credit union and attempt to borrow the necessary money. If this is not possible, the couple might attempt to purchase the item on a charge basis. Some stores do not make an additional charge if the item is paid for within a limited period of time. If your credit rating is favorable (and this is determined by whether or not you have paid your previous bills when you said you would), it is fairly simple to open a charge account. We might point out that in regard to maintaining a favorable credit rating you should be prompt in paying your bills; and if at any time you cannot make a payment when it falls due, you should call or go to the credit office and explain your circumstances.

As we have already noted, purchasing goods on an installment basis involves the paying of somewhat higher costs. In spite of this, you will be urged in advertisements to purchase on a time basis at a small additional charge. The purpose of these advertisements is to attract more customers for the business of selling credit. Credit is one of the largest businesses in the United States, and when properly understood and properly used it plays a very functional part in the economy. It must be recognized that the people who sell credit, just as the people who sell anything else, except to earn a profit.

In determining the amount to be paid under the installment sales contract, a regular service charge is added to the unpaid balance. This charge, which is too often confused and compared with pure interest rates, must cover interest on the money lent, credit and collection expense of the lending agency, a reasonable allowance for bad debt losses, allowance for expenses involved in repossession and reconditioning, and certain types of insurance as specified. This charge is quoted in terms of nominal simple interest percentages (the amount of service charge expressed as a percentage of the total amount borrowed on a per annum basis, on the total initial unpaid balance). The actual effective rate of interest is generally about twice the nominal rate, because the borrower is constantly decreasing the outstanding balance by monthly payments made throughout the loan period.

To further illustrate the difference between nominal and actual interest rates, an example is in order. Assume that you contract to buy a $3000 car for 25 percent down, or $750 and assume that the balance is to be paid in 24 monthly payments at a nominal interest rate of 8 percent. The dealer would grant you credit of $2250 with an interest cost of $180 per year, or a total cost of $360 for interest (0.08 × $2250 ×′2). Therefore, you will pay monthly payments of $108.75 for a period of 24 months. This appears to be an interest rate of 8 percent, but the real rate of interest you pay each month will be substantially more than 8 percent: you pay $15 interest per month ($1/12 \times 0.08 \times \$2250$) throughout the two-year period, but you owe the seller or lender the full amount of interest for the first month only. For the rest of the period you have borrowed less than $2250, the amount decreasing to $93.75 in the last month.

To further illustrate installment buying costs, let us assume that a couple with an income of $550 per month wishes to make many of their purchases on a cash basis, although we recognize that this might entail some inconvenience. The items listed in Table 21 are not normally pur-

Table 21   Items for Which the Majority of Families Pay Cash

Food	$ 80.00
Rent and operation of home	143.00
Personal	11.00
Health	14.00
Education	9.00
Recreation	32.00
Organizations	19.00
Savings	10.00
Taxes	53.00
Total	369.00

chased on an installment basis. The amount of income available for installment purchases is $550 − $369 = $181 per month. The amount available for installment purchases on a yearly basis would be $2172 (12 × $181 = $2172). If the average rate of interest paid on installment purchases were 20 percent per year, this would reduce the purchasing power of the $2172 to $1737.60. The $434.40 (20 percent × $2172 = $434.40) might be regarded as a cash gain to the family which is tax-free, if no installment purchases were made.

Getting the most for each dollar spent should be the goal of every family; and to achieve this goal, the cultivation of buyer resistance on the part of each member of the family is extremely helpful. Other suggestions that will help to achieve the stretching of available funds are the following:

1. The purchasing of goods in quantity, where the family's needs are such that this is a practical procedure.
2. Trading at stores that sell strictly on a cash basis.
3. The purchasing of goods on an off-season basis.

4. Buying used items when they will adequately serve the needs of the family.

5. The proper care and repair of clothing, tools, and equipment.

6. Home processing of food.

7. Wearing the proper clothing for activities.

8. "Do it yourself" where the necessary skills and tools are available.

9. Having a garden, if you have gardening "know-how" and can use the fruits and vegetables produced.

10. Eating at home as much as possible.

11. Devising recreational activities that require a minimum cash outlay.

12. Trying to purchase items that will have multiple usage and selecting things that can be used by more than one member of the family.

Several consumer guides are available to assist families in securing the maximum value for cash spent. These guides are of the greatest value to the family that is contemplating purchasing an item with which they have had no previous experience. For example, if a family wishes to purchase an automatic washer, but have never owned or operated one, they can obtain information relative to capacity, efficiency, and price of the various washers from consumers' guides.

The best known of the consumer guides are *Consumers' Research, Inc.,* in Washington, New Jersey, and *Consumers Union,* 17 Union Square West, New York, New York. These two organizations work similarly. They are independent of all business organizations; secure their income from sales of books, reports, and reprints; do not accept money or articles to be tested from manufacturers; and put the items they test on the open market. No one can pay in money, goods, or services to have any product recommended, or any unfavorable comment made, modified, or omitted from the reports. These guides give a rating of many types of articles and explain the basis of the rating. One of the chief values of this type of service is that it will stimulate the buyer to study values and to buy intelligently.

The most important limitation of the consumer guides is that sometimes an item given the highest rating is not available in the area where the buyer wishes to make a purchase. Aware of this problem, the consumer guides try to concentrate their ratings on items that are distributed nationally. It is not desirable to follow blindly the recommendations made by these organizations, but their discussions of the various considerations that determine the quality of specific items are helpful.

Sometimes a couple who wants to marry but feels that there is an insufficient income to maintain a home decides to share a home with in-laws. There are several reasons, as indicated in the text, why it is difficult to work out a satisfactory adjustment when a home is shared with in-laws. These reasons may be summarized in the following way. (1) Most homes do not provide the necessary privacy when two families occupy the same dwelling. This is especially true in the area of the sexual and affectional adjustment. (2) A part of the satisfaction in marriage comes from being confronted with problems, and then solving these problems. The in-laws frequently volunteer suggestions as to how the problems of the newly-weds can be resolved. As a result the newlyweds miss the thrill and satis-faction of solving their problems. To the in-laws, the newly married couple appear to be dangerously idealistic about coping with marriage adjustment. (3) A third source of tension is misunderstanding on the part of the two families with regard to their respective roles and respon-sibilities. In the United States the social roles of two families in this type of situation are not clearly prescribed. The result is a considerable amount of confusion and tension on the part of the two families.

Although it is possible to reduce the cost when two families share a home, and in some instances a pleasant adjustment is attained, it is gen-erally true that the two families will find it advisable to establish separate dwellings even though the income available is very limited.

Every additional member in a family increases the pressure on the family income. If both husband and wife want a baby and they are ready to assume the responsibilities of parenthood, the arrival of a child can add considerably to the hapiness of the home. Some authorities estimate the cost of rearing one child to adulthood—in situations where the par-ents are college-trained—to be approximately $20,000. In all probabil-ity, many families, especially middle-class families, spend more cash than is necessary to promote the welfare of the child. To postpone having children for a brief period in order to stabilize the family's economy is feasible; but for the couple to intentionally avoid for years the arrival and responsibility of children may ultimately impair the welfare of the home.

When a wife is employed outside the home, there is usually some in-crease in the cash income of the family. However, in order for the wife to be employed, there are certain additional necessary expenses (and the amount of income tax a family will have to pay is increased when the wife is employed). There are more expenditures for transportation, food, dues, clothing, laundry, and other items when a wife is employed. These items may total over $100 a month, and they are seldom less than $50 per month. Whatever this amount happens to be, it should be subtracted from the gross income of the wife to obtain the net increase. If there are children that must be cared for while the mother is working, there may be an additional cash outlay. If the earnings of the wife are modest, it is possible that her employment could result in a financial loss for the family. If the members of the family as a whole are happier, however, when the wife is employed outside the home, then the net income increase may be a secondary consideration. Of course, it is also possible that whatever additional income is available as a result of the wife's working may relieve some of the financial pressure on the family.

Providing for Family Security

Economic security is a very important factor in the happiness of a family. As has already been discussed, in most families expenses will exceed income for some periods, and emergencies may occur that will severely tax the resources of the family.

A family economic plan is not complete until some provision has been made for savings. It is important to establish the principle that something will be saved from each pay check. Some families decide that they will save whatever is left when the bills have been paid. This approach is not usually very productive. The months and years pass and the family tends to have nothing to show for its efforts. A very definite savings plan should be effected, and this plan should be reviewed periodically, with the amount put into savings increased whenever practical.

Another very important part of a family's security is making provision for adequate housing. The newly married couple will be faced with the decision of whether to rent or to buy a home. Before a couple makes a final decision, they should seriously consider their needs and the advantages and disadvantages of renting and buying a home.

When renting a house, you should be certain just what is to be included in the rental price. In furnished apartments, water, electricity, and sometimes gas are supplied. Whether garbage and rubbish collection is included or not may be a point about which to make inquiry. In most houses that are rented unfurnished you pay all the utilities on a metered basis to the city. It may be more economical for a couple to rent a furnished apartment than to own their furniture if it is necessary to move frequently from one location to another.

In those instances where a family decides that it is desirable to purchase a home, a program of finance will have to be worked out. In the majority of instances, a down payment is made, which may range from a few hundred dollars to several thousand dollars. The balance or remainder of the indebtedness is paid out of income over a period of years.

Selecting a house, old or new, requires considerable skill and good judgment. The location of a house is a matter of great importance. Many hours of time can be wasted in getting to jobs, school, and church if the family makes an unwise choice of location. The social status of the family is also in part determined by the area of residence.

It is no longer practical to think of a home purchase as a one-time only expense. The mobility of our society and the needs of a family contribute to change with regard to housing, so that lifetime residence in one location is not usually the pattern. For the most part, it is probably unwise to purchase a home if the family does not expect to live in the same area for at least three years. The couple should always ask their real estate agent these questions: "If we found it necessary to sell the house next month, who would be interested? Who could buy? What would be the probable selling price?"

When a house is found that meets the needs of the family, is generally of sound construction, and is available below the prevailing price for similar construction in the neighborhood, it represents the best buy for the family. Good value and reasonable purchasing price are always assets; then if it becomes necessary to dispose of the house, the seller will be protected against a loss.

A real estate agent can be helpful in locating a suitable home and in arranging the financing of the home. Generally a real estate agent can provide more assistance if he knows the family's needs and preferences, the amount of available funds, and probable income.

It is sometimes possible to buy directly from the owner without buying through a real estate agent. The agent receives a commission of several hundred dollars for selling a house. It is obvious that the price of the home must be somewhat higher if an agent is involved. However, many times the agent will provide helpful information that is worth the fee he is paid. A real estate agent can be especially helpful in providing assistance for arranging the financing of the home—which is the next step once you have found a home for sale that appeals to you and meets your needs. The family must decide what they can pay as a down payment. Remember, there will be expense in connection with moving previous belongings and furnishing the home. The down payment may be very small or it may be as much as 40 percent of the purchase price. Never pay anything, or sign anything, until you are absolutely certain you want to purchase the home.

The interest rate that you will have to pay will vary depending on general economic conditions and the lending agency. Credit is a commodity and the borrower should attempt to get the lowest possible interest rate. The difference in an interest rate between 5 percent or 6 percent is very important when the loan is large and extends over a number of years.

You might consider mortgage payments on a house very much as you do installment payments on a car, a television set, or the like. The larger the down payment, the smaller will be the monthly installments, and the less the actual cost of the item. It may be something of a shock to see in black and white how much it costs to pay the interest on the principal borrowed for a number of years. The total number of dollars needed to pay for a home will greatly exceed the stated purchase price. The data in Table 22 illustrate the desirability of paying for a home as quickly as possible.

Table 22 The Cost of Borrowing $8000 at 5 Percent Interest for Various Numbers of Years

Number of Years to Pay	Monthly Payments	Amount Paid for Interest
15	$63.27	$3388
20	52.80	4672
25	46.77	6031
30	42.95	7462

You will note that if the loan runs for thirty years, the amount you have to pay for interest is nearly equal to the stated purchase price. In some instances it will be to the financial advantage of a couple to buy a very modest home initially. When an equity has been established in this home, it can be sold and a better home purchased. This pattern can be repeated several times in a twenty-year period. The advantage of this plan is that the interest cost for home financing is kept to the minimum. At about the time the children reach high school a family can own a home, and the monthly payments of the family will have been within their means. The family will experience less inconvenience in moving if they purchase the so-called lifetime home initially. It will, however, require from eight to twelve years longer to pay for a home using this plan.

A family may decide that available housing is unsuitable or that it is too costly. The "do-it-yourself" pattern has been extended to include housing. It should be recognized that many hours of labor are needed to construct a home and that it is necessary to possess many professional skills. The modern home represents engineering refinements that were not available at any cost a few decades ago. A major cost in building a home is the labor. This can be saved if a family has lots of time and multiple skills. Financing the home becomes somewhat more complicated when the family does most of the work in building its home.

Since World War II, an increasing proportion of the population has elected to live in mobile homes. Modern trailers are well constructed and possess many of the features of modern homes. A trailer has the advantage of providing furniture and shelter for a family. The rental charge for parking a trailer should be included with the purchase price in the housing cost.

Family security is not complete without provisions for meeting fire loss, automobile accidents, and possible death. The purpose of an insurance plan is to enable a family to cope with those emergencies that they would otherwise lack the necessary financial means to handle. The primary purpose of insurance is to provide protection.

One of the first items a couple usually purchases is a car. Should the car be damaged in an accident or stolen, the loss to the family might cause considerable inconvenience. There is also the possibility that the driver of the car might contribute to the damage of another car or the injury of its passengers. This is known as liability damage. In some states all drivers are required to carry liability insurance. Even though you never expect to cause an accident, you should never drive a car without carrying liability insurance. A comprehensive automobile policy will cover all possible accidents. The drivers who are less likely to be involved in accidents are able to get their insurance at lower rates.

If any property is owned, the family should consider carrying protection against loss by fire, theft, or natural causes. This type of protection is not very expensive. It is important that the policy provide comprehensive coverage.

During the last decade, so-called health insurance has become very popular. Some plans pay only a part of the hospital expenses and others pay the doctors' bills. Sometimes a couple will purchase this type of insurance in the hope that they will be able to reduce at least their medical costs. If a family should have unusually heavy medical expenses, it is advantageous to have medical insurance. The main advantage of medical insurance for a typical family is that they can pay their medical bills on an installment basis. In fact, families who do not have cash savings that can be used in meeting medical emergencies probably cannot afford to be without medical insurance.

There is always the possibility that some member of a family will die or be physically incapacitated. In the event of death, there will be expense in connection with the burial and the last medical bills. If the individual is a "breadwinner" in the family, the future welfare of his dependents may be impaired. An insurance program that provides protection against economic loss can be of great value in assisting the family to make adjustments.

Much of the confusion relative to insurance can be avoided if it is recognized that the primary purpose of insurance is protection. If a family has the necessary economic means to meet all emergencies, there is little need for an insurance program. In an insurance program you buy protection to cover the financial losses that you could not handle with resources available.

The first step in establishing an insurance program for a family is to determine its needs. Usually a minimum of $1500 worth of protection is needed for each marital partner; the $1500 would be necessary to pay last medical expenses and burial debts in the event of death. The expense might be much larger. The bulk of the insurance should be carried by the primary "breadwinner" of the family; for purposes of illustration, we are assuming that this is the husband and that $1500 is the only insurance carried on the life of the wife. On the life of the husband, however, over and above the $1500, an additional minimum of $1000 protection should be provided. This additional protection is designed as an adjustment fund for the wife in the event of the death of her husband who was her sole support. The approximate figure of $1000 is based on the assumption that the wife is employable and that she will be employed within a 90-day period following the death of her husband. A much larger sum may be necessary in other instances.

In all probability, the family will have some indebtedness for a car, furniture, or installment purchases. This indebtedness should be covered by insurance. A representative newly married couple might need $2000 worth of protection in this area. If there is indebtedness on a home, the mortgage should be covered by either mortgage insurance or additional life insurance. If there are children, at least $3000 protection should be carried on the life of the father for each child in the family. Most newly married couples will need at least $5000 worth of protection. In some instances the necessary protection will exceed $20,000. The next step is to select the proper type of insurance.

There are several types of policies to choose from and many different companies. All of the major companies charge essentially the same rate, so that the choice of a company is largely a matter of individual preference for a particular plan or agent. Three basic types of life insurance are available. The first type is term insurance, which provides the maximum protection for the smallest premium. The insurance policy is written for a stated period of time, such as one year. The protection provided is stated in the policy; as an example here, we shall assume that it is for $5000. The rate or premium is determined by the age of the person insured. A man needing $5000 protection for one year who is twenty-two years of age could buy $5000 of term insurance for approximately $50 a year. Often, when the family income is low, this is all that the family can spend for insurance. Term insurance does not have loan value or cash surrender value, and the rate becomes progressively higher as the insured grows older. These are, of course, the distinct disadvantages of this type of insurance. A family with a very low income in the early years of the marriage, however, might find it desirable to use term insurance for a few years to provide the necessary protection and then gradually convert to other types. In these cases it is important that the person buying term insurance buy the type of contract that can be converted to another type policy at any time without a physical examination.

For the family that is interested in protection and some other additional insurance benefits, a second type of life insurance, namely a limited or ordinary life policy, may be the most desirable. On this type of insurance the rate or premium remains constant throughout the years the policy is in force, and the insured pays premiums for a stated period of years, such as 20 or 30 years. If the insured dies at any time after the policy is in force, his estate will receive the amount stated on the face of the policy plus any dividends that might have accumulated. It is desirable, in the majority of instances, to have an insurance plan paid up at the time the "main breadwinner" reaches age sixty-five. And it is most desirable to begin such an insurance plan at an early age. A man wanting $5000 protection who is twenty-two years of age, for example, could purchase a limited payment life plan that would cost approximately $110 a year. The same man desirous of the same amount of coverage would have to pay more per year if he initiated the policy at a later age.

Besides a constant premium rate, ordinary life insurance has some other advantages. The policy has loan value and cash surrender value. The loan value of a policy is the amount of money the insured can borrow from an insurance company. This amount is usually somewhat lower than the total premiums that have been paid to date. The interest rate charged is generally lower than that charged by banks. The cash surrender value is the amount paid by the insurance company to the insured if it becomes necessary to drop the policy prior to its normal termination date. Many companies have a plan whereby, if it becomes necessary to drop a policy, the premiums that have been paid are not lost. The insurance company permits the policyholder to take paid-up insurance. The amount stated on the face of the policy is reduced proportionally to the premiums that have been paid. No further payments are made.

The third type of life insurance is the endowment policy. An endowment policy enables a person to accumulate a fund of money, which will become available to him on a future date named in the policy. Because the policy includes a savings program, the premium rate is higher than that of a comparable term of an ordinary life insurance policy.

The endowment policy is designed for those who need not only life insurance protection for dependents, but also a definite sum of money or income at some future date to supplement or replace their earnings. An endowment policy might be used to provide funds to send a child to college. If the insured dies prior to the maturity date of the policy, his estate receives the full amount stated on the face of the policy. The loan value of endowment insurance is very high.

Endowment insurance can usually be converted to paid-up insurance if it is necessary to drop the policy prior to maturity. A man twenty-two years of age needing $5000 could purchase an endowment policy at an approximate cost of $250 a year for a 20-year period. An annual expenditure of this amount, however, might be prohibitive in some families.

The core of most family insurance programs should be built around ordinary life or limited payment life policies. The various plans available may incorporate more than one type of policy. There are so many policies issued by the various companies that a family should be able to find a plan that fits its needs. Most insurance agents are professional people who have a sincere interest in serving the needs of the client. An insurance plan for a family should be reviewed periodically to determine if the necessary protection is provided.

In recent years group insurance has become increasingly popular. The hazard to the company and the administrative cost are reduced in this type of plan. Generally the premium rate will be lower, especially for older people. In some instances a part or all of the cost of this type of insurance is paid by the employer. When available, group insurance is usually a good buy.

It is the privilege of each policyholder to designate a beneficiary. In the majority of instances a husband would designate his wife and children as beneficiaries. Where the option is available it is generally best to arrange for the payment of life insurance benefits on a monthly basis over a period of years, because many people lack the necessary financial skill to manage a large sum of money.

If you are eligible for Social Security survivorship and old age insurance benefits, these will help provide the protection that you and your family need. The local office of the Federal Security Agency of the United States Government nearest to you will be glad to give you information about Social Security.

What has been presented in this appendix is an analysis of the consumer problems that are likely to be encountered in marriage. A careful consideration of these potential difficulties and their solutions will enable a couple to get the most out of their financial resources and perhaps minimize relationship disturbances that emanate from consumer problems.

Suggested Readings

Bergler, Edmund, *Money and Emotional Conflicts*, Pageant Books, Paterson, N.J., 1959.

Bigelow, Howard F., *Family Finance*, Lippincott, Chicago, 1953.

Cavan, Ruth S., Ed., *Marriage and Family in the Modern World*, 2nd ed., Thomas Y. Crowell, New York, 1965, especially Chs. 2, 12, and 13.

Consumer Reports, published monthly by Consumers' Union of the United States, Inc., 256 Washington Street, Mount Vernon, N.Y.

Feldman, Races Loman, *The Family in a Money World*, Family Service Association of America, New York, 1957.

Follmann, Joseph F., Jr., *Medical Care and Health Insurance*, Richard D. Irwin, Homewood, Ill., 1963.

Gordon, Leland J., *Economics for Consumers*, American Book, New York, 1953. Institute of Life Insurance, *Life Insurance Fact Book*, 488 Madison Avenue, New York, annual publication.

Kyrk, Hazel, *The Family in the American Economy*, University of Chicago Press, Chicago, 1963.

Lasser, J. K., and Sylvia F. Porter, *Managing Your Money*, Henry Holt, New York, 1956.

Locke, Harvey J., *Predicting Adjustment in Marriage: A Comparison of a Divorced and a Happily Married Group*, Henry Holt, New York, Ch. 13.

National Manpower Council, *Work in the Lives of Married Women*, Columbia University Press, New York, 1958.

Rapaport, Robert, and Rhona Rapaport, "Work and Family in Contemporary Society," *Am. soc. Rev.*, **30** (1965), pp. 381–394.

Troelstrup, Arch E., *Consumer Problems,* McGraw-Hill, New York, 1952, Chs. 1, 2, 3, and 4.

U.S. News and World Report, "New Ways to Use Insurance," March 1958, pp. 80–91.

Tables on Marriage Laws and Divorce Grounds

ERNEST K. ALIX, Ph.D.

The tables on marriage and divorce were revised by Ernest K. Alix, Ph.D. Dr. Alix, who is a sociologist, studied law for several years and has a long-standing interest in the relationship between sociology and law. His presentation gives an updated version of the legal aspects of marriage and divorce.

The following tables are from *Boardman's New York Family Law,* Clark-Boardman, New York, 1966.

State or other jurisdiction	Age at which marriage can be contracted with parental consent		Age below which parental consent is required		Common-law marriage recognized	Physical examination and blood test for male and female		Waiting period	
						Time limit between examination and issuance of marriage license	Scope of medical examination	Before issuance of license	After issuance of license
	Male	Female	Male	Female					
Alabama	17	14	21	18	Y	30 da.	(a)	....	....
Alaska	18	16	21	18	N	30 da.	(a)	3 da.	....
Arizona	18	16	21	18	N	30 da.	(a)	....	....
Arkansas	18	16	21	18	N	30 da.	(a)	3 da.	....
California	20(b)	17(b)	21	18	N	30 da.	(a)	....	....
Colorado	16	16	21	18	Y	30 da.	(a)	....	....
Connecticut	16	16	21	21	N	40 da.	(a)	4 da.	....
Delaware	18	16	21	18	N	30 da.	(a)	....	1 da.
Florida	18(c)	16(c)	21	21	Y	30 da.	(a)	3 da.	....
Georgia	18(c)	16(c)	19	19	Y	30 da.	(a)	....	3 da.(d)
Hawaii	18	16	20	20	N	30 da.	(a)	3 da.	3 da.
Idaho	15	15(e)	18	18	Y	30 da.	(a)	....	....
Illinois	18	16	21	18	N	15 da.	(a)	....	....
Indiana	18	16	21	18	N	30 da.	(a)	3 da.	3 da.
Iowa	18	16	21	18	Y	20 da.	(a)	3 da.	....
Kansas	18(f)	16(f)	21	18	Y	30 da.	(a, i)	3 da.	....
Kentucky	18(g)	16(g)	21	18	N(h)	15 da.	(a)	3 da.	....
Louisiana	18	16	21	21	N	10 da.	(a)	....	3 da.
Maine	16(j)	16(j)	21	21	N	30 da.	(a)	5 da.	....
Maryland	18(k)	16(k)	21	18	N	..	N	2 da.	....
Massachusetts	18(l)	16(l)	21	18	N	..	..	3 da.	....
Michigan	18	16(m)	18	18	N	30 da.	(a)	3 da.	....
Minnesota	18	16	21	18	N	..	N	5 da.	....
Mississippi	17(n)	15(n)	21	18	N	30 da.	(a)	3 da.	....
Missouri	20	17	21	18	N	15 da.	(a)	3 da.	....
Montana	18(f)	16(f)	21	18	Y	20 da.	(a)	5 da.	....
Nebraska	18	16(o)	21	21	N	30 da.	(a, p)	....	....
Nevada	18(f)	16(f)	21	18	N	..	N	....	....
New Hampshire	14(g)	13(g)	20	18	N(r)	30 da.	(a)	5 da.	....
New Jersey	18(f)	16(f)	21	18	N	30 da.	(a)	3 da.	....
New Mexico	18	16	21	18	N	30 da.	(a)	....	....
New York	16	14(s)	21	18	N	30 da.	(a)	....	1 da.
North Carolina	16	16(t)	18	18	N	30 da.	(a, u)	(v)	....
North Dakota	18(w)	15(w)	21(w)	18(w)	N	30 da.	(x)	....	....
Ohio	18	16	21	21	Y	30 da.	(a)	5 da.	....
Oklahoma	18(k)	15(k)	21	18	Y	30 da.	(a)	3 da.(y)	....
Oregon	18(z)	15(z)	21	18	N	30 da.	(aa)	7 da.	....
Pennsylvania	14(a,b)	12(a,b)	21	21	Y	30 da.	(a)	3 da.	....
Rhode Island	14(f)	12(f)	21	21	Y	40 da.	(ac)	(ad)	....
South Carolina	16	14	18	18	Y	..	N	1 da.	....
South Dakota	18	16	21	21	N	..	(a)	....	....
Tennessee	16(ae)	16(ae)	21	21	N	30 da.	(a)	3 da.(af)	....
Texas	14	14	21	18	Y	15 da.	(a)	....	....
Utah	14	14	21	18	N	30 da.	(a)	....	....
Vermont	16(ag)	16(ag)	21(ag)	18(ag)	N	30 da.	(a)	....	5 da.
Virginia	18(k)	16(k)	21	18	N	30 da.	(a)	....	....
Washington	17	17	21	18	N	..	N	3 da.	....
West Virginia	18	16	21	18	N	30 da.	(a)	3 da.	....
Wisconsin	18	16	21	18	N	15 da.	(a)	5 da.	....
Wyoming	18	16	21	21	N	30 da.	(a)	....	....
District of Columbia	18(g)	16(g)	21	18	Y	..	N	4 da.	....

(a) Venereal diseases.

(b) Parental and court approval necessary where male under 18 or female under 16.

(c) Under these ages license may be granted at discretion of court if parties are parents or expectant parents.

(d) Unless both 21 or female pregnant regardless of age.

(e) Female under 15 may marry if consent of probate court is obtained.

(f) If male under 18 or female under 16, parties may marry with parental consent but subject to approval of court.

(g) No parental consent required for party previously married.

(h) Recognized only for purpose of recovery under state's Workmen's Compensation Act.

(i) Feeblemindedness.

(j) If parties under 16 they may marry with parental consent but subject to approval of court.

(k) Only if female pregnant may parents consent to marriage of male under 18 and female under 16. License may issue only on physician's certificate.

(l) Court may permit marriage of persons under 18 or 16 with parental consent.

(m) Consent of one parent or guardian required for marriage of female under 18.

(n) There is no statutory, categorical prohibition against marriage of a person under the minimum age and the age requirement may be waived by the court.

(o) If female under 16 and pregnant, parental consent and court approval required.

(p) Test may be waived by court if female pregnant or death of either party imminent.

(q) Court approval also required when male under 20 or female under 18.

(r) Persons cohabiting openly as husband and wife for 3 years are presumed to have been legally married, but common law marriages are not recognized.

(s) If female under 16 but not over 14, approval and consent of judge of Family Court required.

(t) Female between 12 and 16 may marry with consent of parties and court, if pregnant or has given birth.

(u) Epilepsy, idiocy, imbecility, mental defectiveness, unsound mindedness, tuberculosis, and venereal diseases.

(v) 2 days in certain counties for nonresidents.

(w) If both parties nonresidents they may not marry unless parents of either party reside in state, except that court must issue license to nonresidents if they produce license from their own state issued within preceding 60 days.

(x) Feeblemindedness, imbecility, insanity, chronic alcoholism, and venereal diseases.

(y) 3 days waiting period only when parties under 21 and 18.

(z) If female under 17 or male under 19, parental consent and court approval required.

(aa) Venereal diseases, epilepsy, feeblemindedness, mental illness, drug addiction and chronic alcoholism.

(ab) If either party under 16, Orphan's Court approval also required.

(ac) Tuberculosis and venereal diseases.

(ad) 5 day waiting period for female nonresident.

(ae) No statutory requirement for parental consent but if female fails to swear to being over 18, notice of application for license sent to her parents unless parent, guardian or next of kin joins in application.

(af) No waiting period if both parties over 21.

(ag) A nonresident applicant having license must present affidavit that proposed marriage is not contrary to law of his or her home state.

DIVORCE LAWS *
As of January 1, 1966

State or other jurisdiction	Residence required before filing suit for divorce	Adultery	Mental and/or physical cruelty	Desertion	Habitual drunkenness and/or alcoholism	Impotency	Nonsupport	Insanity	Pregnancy at marriage	Bigamy
				Grounds for absolute divorce						
Alabama	1 yr.(a)	•	•	1 yr.	•	•	•	5 yrs.	•	..
Alaska	1 yr.(b)	•	•	1 yr.	•	•	•	....		..
Arizona	1 yr.	•	•	1 yr.	•	..	•	•		..
Arkansas	2 mos.	•	•	1 yr.	•	..	•	3 yrs.	..	•
California	1 yr.	•	•	1 yr.	•	..	..	3 yrs.	..	..
Colorado	1 yr.(c)	•	•	1 yr.	•	..	•	3 yrs.	..	..
Connecticut	3 yrs.(d)	•	•	3 yrs.	•	..	..	5 yrs.	..	..
Delaware	2 yrs.(d)	•	•	2 yrs.	•	..	•	5 yrs.	..	..
Florida	6 mos.	•	•	1 yr.	•	•	..	....		•
Georgia	6 mos.	•	•	1 yr.	•	•	..	2 yrs.	•	..
Hawaii	1 yr.		•	6 mos.		..	..	3 yrs.	..	..
Idaho	6 wks.	•	•	1 yr.	•	..	•	3 yrs.	..	..
Illinois	1 yr.(d)	•	•	1 yr.	•	•	..	....		•
Indiana	1 yr.(e)	•	•	2 yrs.	•	..	..	5 yrs.	..	..
Iowa	1 yr.(f)	•	•	2 yrs.	•	..	..	....	•(r)	..
Kansas	1 yr.(g)	•	•	1 yr.	•	..	..	5 yrs.	..	..
Kentucky	1 yr.	•	•	1 yr.	•	•	..	5 yrs.	..	..
Louisiana	(h)	•	..	....	..	..	..	....	..	..
Maine	6 mos.(d)	•	•	3 yrs.	•	•	•	....	..	..
Maryland	1 yr.(f, i)	•		18 mos.	..	•	..	3 yrs.	..	..
Massachusetts	5 yrs.(d)	•	•	3 yrs.	•	•	•	....		..
Michigan	1 yr.(d)	•	•	2 yrs.	•	•	•	....	..	..
Minnesota	1 yr.(d)	•	•	1 yr.	•	..	..	5 yrs.	..	..
Mississippi	1 yr.(j)	•	•	1 yr.	•	•	..	3 yrs.	•	•
Missouri	1 yr.(d)	•	•	1 yr.	•	..	..	....		..
Montana	1 yr.	•	•	1 yr.	•	..	•	5 yrs.	..	..
Nebraska	1 yr.(k)	•	•	2 yrs.	•	..	•	5 yrs.	..	..
Nevada	6 wks.(d)	•	•	1 yr.	•	•	•	2 yrs.	..	..
New Hampshire	1 yr.(l)	•	•	2 yrs.	•	•	•	....	..	..
New Jersey	2 yrs.(d)	•	•	2 yrs.	..	..	..	....	..	..
New Mexico	1 yr.	•	•	•	•	..	•	5 yrs.	..	..
New York	(m)	•	..	..	..	..	..	....	..	..
North Carolina	6 mos.	•	..	1 yr.	..	•	..	5 yrs.	•	..
North Dakota	..	•	•	1 yr.	•	•	..	5 yrs.	..	..
Ohio	1 yr.	•	•	1 yr.	•	•	•	....	..	..
Oklahoma	6 mos.	•	•	1 yr.	•	..	..	5 yrs.	•	..
Oregon	1 yr.	•	•	1 yr.	•	•	..	2 yrs.	..	..
Pennsylvania	1 yr.	•	•	2 yrs.	..	•	..	....	..	..
Rhode Island	2 yrs.	•	•	5 yrs.	•	•	•	....	..	..
South Carolina	1 yr.	•	•	1 yr.	•	..	..	....		..
South Dakota	1 yr.	•	•	1 yr.	•	..	•	5 yrs.	..	..
Tennessee	1 yr.	•	•	1 yr.	•	•	..	....	•	•
Texas	1 yr.	•	•	3 yrs.	..	..	..	5 yrs.	..	..
Utah	3 mos.	•	•	1 yr.	..	..	•	....	..	..
Vermont	6 mos.(n)	•	•	3 yrs.	..	..	•	5 yrs.	..	..
Virginia	1 yr.	•	..	1 yr.	..	..	..	....	•	..
Washington	1 yr.	•	•	1 yr.	•	•	..	2 yrs.	•	..
West Virginia	1 yr.(o)	•	•	1 yr.	•	..	..	....	..	..
Wisconsin	2 yrs.	•	•	1 yr.	•	..	•	....	..	..
Wyoming	60 days(p)	•	•	1 yr.	•	..	•	2 yrs.	..	..
District of Columbia	1 yr.(q)	•	..	1 yr.	..	..	..	....	..	..

* Unable to revise because of lack of necessary legal sources.

(a) 1 year residence by plaintiff if defendant is a nonresident but where both parties appear and one is domiciled in Alabama, no time period of residence is necessary.

(b) When marriage is solemnized in state and plaintiff a resident, no time period of residence is necessary.

(c) No residence required where ground is adultery or extreme cruelty and offense was committed within the state.

(d) Under certain circumstances a lesser period of time may be required.

(e) Either party, but 5 year residence required for divorce based upon incurable insanity.

(f) Except where defendant is a resident and was served by personal service.

(g) Anyone who has resided in or been stationed at a U.S. post or military reservation within the state for 1 year may file a divorce action in any county.

(h) When either party domiciled in state immediately prior to marriage, even though marriage contracted elsewhere or if husband abandons wife or commits any other act giving her right to separation or divorce under Louisiana law, wife may es-

tablish domicile and obtain separation or divorce.

(i) Only where the cause of action occurred out of state. 2 year residence required for either party when ground is insanity.

(j) Either party.

(k) Under certain circumstances a longer period of time may be required.

(l) None, but both parties must be domiciled in state when action commenced or plaintiff was so domiciled and defendant personally served, or if plaintiff domiciled in state for 1 year and presumably defendant cannot be personally served.

(m) No specific time period required; a married woman dwelling within the state at time of commencement of action is deemed a resident, although her husband resides elsewhere.

(n) 6 months before commencement of action and 1 year before final hearing. For a divorce based upon insanity, 1 year residence required.

(o) 2 year residence required if residence was acquired after cause of action arose.

(p) Except for adultery.

(q) 2 years for any cause occurring out of the district and prior to residence.

494

DIVORCE LAWS *
As of January 1, 1966

Felony conviction or imprisonment	Drug Addiction	Fraudulent contract	Relationship within prohibited degrees	Other	Period before parties may remarry after final decree — Plaintiff	Defendant	State or other jurisdiction
•	•	..	..	(s)	60 days	60 days	Alabama
•	•	..	..	(t)	.....	.....	Alaska
•	..	..	..	(u)	1 yr.	1 yr.	Arizona
•	..	..	..	(af, u)	.....	.....	Arkansas
•	•	..	..	(v)	(A)	(A)	California
•	•	..	..	(w)	(B)	(B)	Colorado
•	..	..	..	(x)	.....	.....	Connecticut
•	..	..	..	(y,w)	3 mos.(C)	3 mos.(C)	Delaware
..	..	..	•	(z)	.....	.....	Florida
..	..	..	..	(aa)	.....	(C)	Georgia
•	•	..	..	(w)	.....	.....	Hawaii
•	•	..	..	(v)	.....	.....	Idaho
•	..	..	..	..	.....	.....	Illinois
•	..	..	..	..	(D)	.....	Indiana
•	..	..	..	..	1 yr.(C)	1 yr.	Iowa
•	..	..	..	(v)	6 mos.	6 mos.	Kansas
•	..	..	..	(u,v,w)(ab,ac,ah)	.....	.....	Kentucky
•	..	..	..	(w)	wife, 10 mos.	wife, 10 mos.(E)	Louisiana
..	•	..	..	..	.....	.....	Maine
•	..	..	..	(w)	.....	.....	Maryland
•	•	..	..	(v)	6 mos.	2½ yrs.	Massachusetts
•	..	..	..	(z)	.....	(F)	Michigan
•	..	..	..	..	6 mos.	6 mos.	Minnesota
..	•	..	•	..	.....	(G)	Mississippi
•	..	..	..	(ad)	.....	.....	Missouri
•	..	..	..	(v)	.....	.....	Montana
•	..	..	..	(v)	6 mos.	6 mos.	Nebraska
•	..	..	..	(v,w)	.....	.....	Nevada
•	..	..	..	(u,v)	.....	.....	New Hampshire
..	..	..	..	..	3 mos.(C)	3 mos.(C)	New Jersey
..	..	..	..	(t)	.....	.....	New Mexico
..	..	..	..	..	.....	(H)	New York
..	..	..	..	(s)	.....	.....	North Carolina
•	..	..	..	(v)	(C)	(C)	North Dakota
•	..	•	..	(v,x)	.....	(M)	Ohio
•	..	..	..	(v,t,z)	6 mos.	6 mos.	Oklahoma
•	..	..	..	..	6 mos.	6 mos.	Oregon
•	..	..	..	(s,y)(ab,ac,ae,ah,ag,af)	.....	(E)	Pennsylvania
•	•	..	..	(v,s)	6 mos.	6 mos.	Rhode Island
..	•	..	..	..	.....	.....	South Carolina
•	..	..	..	(v)	.....	(I)	South Dakota
•	..	..	..	(s)	.....	(E)	Tennessee
•	..	..	..	(s,w)	(J)	(J)	Texas
•	..	..	..	(v)	3 mos.(C)	3 mos.(C)	Utah
•	..	..	..	(x)	6 mos.(C)	2 yrs.(C)	Vermont
•	..	..	..	(s,w,ag)	4 mos.	4 mos.(K)	Virginia
•	..	•	..	(w,v,y,ab,ac,ag,ah,af)	(B)	(B)	Washington
•	•	..	..	..	60 days	60 days(L)	West Virginia
•	..	..	..	(w)	1 yr.	1 yr.	Wisconsin
•	..	..	..	(a,ad)	.....	.....	Wyoming
•	..	..	..	(w)	6 mos.	6 mos.	District of Columbia

(r) Unless husband had an illegitimate child and this fact was unknown by spouse.
(s) Sexual perversion.
(t) Incompatibility.
(u) No cohabitation.
(v) Gross neglect of duty.
(w) Voluntary separation and no cohabitation.
(x) Unexplained absence.
(y) Non-age.
(z) Obtaining foreign divorce.
(aa) Mental incompetence while married.
(ab) Force or duress.
(ac) Hansen's disease.
(ad) Vagrancy of husband.
(ae) Color or race.
(af) No intent to cohabit.
(ag) Prior unchastity.
(ah) Venereal disease.
(A) Final decree is not entered until one year after interlocutory decree.
(B) Interlocutory decree is issued providing that parties shall be divorced 6 months after date of decree.
(C) In the discretion of the court.
(D) Two years where service on defendant is by no other notice than publication.

(E) When divorce is granted on ground of adultery, guilty party cannot marry the accomplice in adultery.
(F) Not more than two years in court's discretion.
(G) When divorce is granted on ground of adultery, court may prohibit remarriage. After one year court may remove disability upon satisfactory evidence of reformation.
(H) Defendant is prohibited from remarrying unless after 3 years court removes disability upon satisfactory evidence of reformation.
(I) When divorce is granted on ground of adultery, guilty party cannot remarry.
(J) When divorce is granted on ground of cruelty, neither party may remarry for 12 months.
(K) When divorce is granted on ground of adultery, the guilty party cannot remarry. After 6 months the court may remove disability for good cause.
(L) In court's discretion, guilty party may be prohibited from remarrying for a period not to exceed one year.
(M) In cases where alimony or child support is granted, the decree is delayed until payment is made.

APPENDIX D

Marriage and Family Counseling Resources

The resources listed below are only a few of the many responsible agencies from which professional assistance for marital problems may be obtained. Interested persons might also consult the council of social agencies in their local community for additional resources.

American Association of Marriage Counselors, Inc., 27 Woodcliff Drive, Madison, New Jersey 07940.

American Institute of Family Relations, 5287 Sunset Boulevard, Los Angeles, California 90012.

American Social Health Association, 1790 Broadway, New York, New York 10019.

Council of Jewish Federations and Welfare Funds, 729 Seventh Avenue, New York, New York 10019.

Family Life Commission, Lutheran Church, Missouri Synod, 210 North Broadway, St. Louis, Missouri 63102.

Family Service Association of America, 215 Fourth Avenue, New York, New York 10013.

National Association for Mental Health, Inc., 10 Columbus Circle, New York, New York 10019.

National Catholic Welfare Conference, Family Life Bureau, 1312 Massachusetts Avenue N.W., Washington, D. C. 20205

National Council of Churches of Christ in the U.S.A., Department of Family Life, 475 Riverside Drive, New York, New York 10027.

Planned Parenthood Federation of America, Inc., 501 Madison Avenue, New York, New York 10002.

Rabbinical Assembly of America, 3080 Broadway, New York, New York 10027.

Marriage Council of Philadelphia, 1422 Chestnut Street, Philadelphia, Pennsylvania 19102.

Merrill-Palmer School, Institute of Human Development and Family Life, 71 Ferry Street, East Detroit, Michigan 48202.

Name Index

Aberle, David, 22
Abse, D. Wilfred, 436
Ackerman, Charles, 421
Ackerman, Nathan W., 13
Adams, Bert N., 332, 336
Adams, James Truslow, 39
Adams, John B., 265
Albert, Gerald, 433
Alexander, Paul W., 401, 414
Allport, Gordon W., 13
Anshen, Ruth Nanda, 79
Aschheim, Selmar, 458
Axelson, Leland J., 309, 315

Babchuk, Nickolas, 224
Baber, Ray E., 45, 236, 244
Bain, Read, 82
Barnett, Larry D., 234, 243
Bartemeier, Leo H., 388
Bates, Alan P., 224, 326
Becker, Howard, 48, 404
Bee, Lawrence S., 112, 147, 195, 197, 198, 240, 241, 259, 425
Belknap, Ivan, 61
Bell, Robert R., 96, 141, 151, 161
Benedek, Therese, 382
Benson, Purnell, 370
Berger, Bennett, M., 2
Berger, Morroe, 40
Bergler, Edmund, 393, 404, 421, 490
Bernard, Jessie, 65, 223, 235, 285, 286, 379, 406, 407, 417, 421
Berne, Eric, 302, 310
Bettelheim, Bruno, 76, 393
Bierstedt, Robert, 40
Bigelow, Howard F., 471, 490
Blake, Nelson Manfred, 421
Blanton, Smiley, 99, 123, 124, 127
Blazer, John A., 219, 277
Blitsten, Dorothy R., 75, 79
Blood, Robert O., Jr., 58, 69, 96, 155, 182, 183, 265, 290, 315, 319, 354
Blumberg, Leonard, 141
Boalt, Gunnar, 31, 214
Boll, Eleanor Stoker, 239, 244, 255, 338
Bossard, James H. S., 91, 237, 239, 244, 255, 338
Boszormenyi-Nagy, Ivan, 138, 370
Bowman, Claude C., 61

Bowman, Henry A., 282, 339, 350, 365, 370, 436
Breed, Warren, 188
Brenton, Myron, 282
Bridenbaugh, Carl, 37
Briffault, Robert, 19
Brim, Orville G., Jr., 386
Britton, Margaret, 55, 61
Brown, Lawrence Guy, 287
Bryant, Louise S., 467
Buck, Pearl, 312
Buhler, Charlotte, 436
Burchinal, Lee, 332, 417
Burgess, Ernest W., 24, 48, 58, 79, 106, 137, 154, 155, 161, 182, 196, 199, 202, 204, 210, 215, 220, 221, 222, 230, 231, 236, 277, 290, 293, 302, 378
Burkle, Jack V., 151
Burma, John H., 235

Cahnman, Werner J., 255
Calderone, Mary S., 467, 468
Calhoun, Arthur W., 35, 36, 39, 40, 41, 42, 44, 45, 46, 49, 51, 61
Cannon, Anthon S., 344
Caplow, Theodore, 188, 198, 202, 205
Carpenter, Niles, 164
Catton, William, 214
Cavan, Ruth Shonle, 13, 58, 96, 157, 168, 188, 198, 202, 235, 354, 355, 490
Chilman, Catherine S., 74, 347
Christensen, Harold T., 31, 83, 151, 152, 157, 161, 183, 193, 197, 347, 375, 378
Christie, Richard, 43
Christopherson, Victor A., 350
Clark, Alexander L., 265, 276
Clay, Mary, 307
Clothier, Florence, 161
Cohen, Alfred, 401
Cohen, Nathan E., 79
Cole, Arthur Charles, 46
Coleman, James C., 285
Coleman, Richard P., 2
Connery, Maurice, 79
Cooley, Charles H., 124
Coombs, Lolagene, 376
Coombs, Robert H., 217
Cotton, John, 223

Subject Index